The publisher and the University of California Press Foundation gratefully acknowledge the generous support of the Richard and Harriett Gold Endowment Fund in Arts and Humanities.

In the Studio

In the Studio

*Visual Creation and
Its Material Environments*

———

Edited by Brian R. Jacobson

UNIVERSITY OF CALIFORNIA PRESS

University of California Press
Oakland, California

© 2020 by Regents of the University of California

Library of Congress Cataloging-in-Publication Data

Names: Jacobson, Brian R., editor.
Title: In the studio : visual creation and its material environments / edited
 by Brian R. Jacobson.
Description: Oakland, California : University of California Press, [2020] |
 Includes bibliographical references and index.
Identifiers: LCCN 2019058278 (print) | LCCN 2019058279 (ebook) |
 ISBN 9780520297593 (cloth) | ISBN 9780520297609 (paperback) |
 ISBN 9780520969896 (ebook) LCSH: Motion picture studios—History—
 20th century.
Classification: LCC PN1993.5.A1 I49 2020 (print) | LCC PN1993.5.A1 (ebook) |
 DDC 384/.85—dc23
LC record available at https://lccn.loc.gov/2019058278
LC ebook record available at https://lccn.loc.gov/2019058279

Manufactured in the United States of America

27   26   25   24   23   22   21   20
10   9   8   7   6   5   4   3   2   1

CONTENTS

ACKNOWLEDGMENTS

Every book, as acknowledgments so often acknowledge, represents an accumulation of debts; this is perhaps even more true with edited books. First and foremost, I thank the twelve authors who gave their time, energy, labor, and patience to this project. I also thank those would-be contributors whose work, for various reasons, did not end up in the final version but has nonetheless helped shape it.

I am grateful for the institutional support that gave me the time and resources to prepare this volume, the majority of which was completed at the University of Toronto. I thank Cinema Studies Institute directors Corinn Columpar and James Leo Cahill, Innis College principal Charlie Keil, and my other CSI colleagues. Important parts of the project coalesced during a fellowship year at the University of Rochester Humanities Center. My sincere thanks go to Joan Rubin, Jennie Gilardoni, Elana Shever, and the colleagues who made the year both intellectually stimulating and enjoyable, especially Joel Burges, Peter Christensen, Rachel Haidu, Jacob Lewis, and Jason Middleton.

Because this volume grew out of ideas first developed in my graduate work, its debts run particularly deep. I remain grateful to the mentors at USC who helped shape my thinking in the early stages: Priya Jaikumar, Akira Mizuta Lippit, and especially the dearly missed Anne Friedberg. For her enduring guidance, I am ever grateful to Vanessa Schwartz.

The editorial team at the University of California Press has made the publication process smooth and enjoyable. I thank Raina Polivka for taking an interest in the project, and for her valuable guidance throughout, and Madison Wetzell for keeping me on track at every turn. Thanks also to Joe Abbott for patient and rigorous copyediting, and to Cynthia Savage for the index.

Richard Abel and the anonymous reviewer provided valuable support and insightful suggestions. I thank them for their devotion to the review process.

Portions of chapter 8 were previously published in "Happy Furniture: On the Media Environments of the Eames Chair," in *Happiness by Design: Modernism and Media in the Eames Era*, by Justus Nieland (Minneapolis: University of Minnesota Press, 2020). Copyright 2020 by the Regents of the University of Minnesota. Reprinted by permission of the University of Minnesota Press. The figures that appear in the introduction were provided by the Cinémathèque française. I thank these institutions for making these materials available.

My work has been bolstered by the support and community provided by friends and colleagues too numerous to name, especially, in recent years: Nadya Bair, Elisheva Baumgarten, Robert Burgoyne, James Leo Cahill, Yaacov Deutsch, William Diebold, Sarah Easterby-Smith, Jennifer Fay, William Hedberg, Jason Hill, Cecily Hilsdale, Tim Holland, Martin Johnson, Laura Kalba, Jeff Menne, Joshua Neves, Justus Nieland, Brian Price, Tom Rice, Andrew Ross, Jonathan Sachs, Nicholas Sammond, Eric Smoodin, Meghan Sutherland, and Jennifer Wild.

To my family: thank you, as always, for your patience and encouragement. Thank you to the C-Team for keeping things light. My greatest thanks go to Catherine Clark.

Introduction

Studio Perspectives

Brian R. Jacobson

If you're reading this book, you're probably at work. Be that a specific place (your office, say), or someplace else, wherever you are has become, in the predicative sense *(to be working)*, a workplace. Consider, for a moment, that place, with its chair and surface; its screen or screens; the shelves and piles of papers and books; a mug, perhaps, or a thermos or paper cup; those pictures that remind you of somewhere else, or other windows to the world outside—the non-, or after-, work. If you're a professor, your workplace may be the stereotypical image of order in chaos, or maybe you like it *just so.* If you're a student, an adjunct professor, or just someone who avoids offices, you may be at home on the sofa or surrounded by library patrons or coffee and tea drinkers. Wherever you are, this is the world of your work; the world you make to work; the world your work—the act of working—makes. If all goes well, you probably don't think too much about this place while you're working; it just *is.* It is the condition of your labor, and your labor is its condition. As such, this place has no doubt left an indelible mark on your work. But can you define it in any precise way? Has it left a legible, knowable trace?

Try now to forget about that place again (you are *working,* after all). Writers have always had such places, however different, ephemeral, or tentative they may have been. Think of Hemingway's Paris morning routine in his *chambre de bonne,* or Emily Dickinson, who wrote everything in the Homestead, or Walter Benjamin, famously holed up in the Bibliothèque nationale or, more provisionally, seeking peace and quiet in the woods of Ibiza.[1] These places, whether given or made, are one condition of writing and the written worlds we create. Our work is always, in this sense, doubly constituted: we create these worlds—these conditions of creation—for the purpose of creation. They are everywhere in our work and also nowhere.

This book is no exception. Behind its words lie specific places and all of the material, economic, and political realities that more quietly—at a distance—define its pages. Though we don't often foreground them, those spaces, with all of their hidden costs, need to be thought.

This volume applies such thinking to a place—the studio—that has often been subjected to this kind of reflexivity by the artists and filmmakers who use them. Take, for example, René Clair's 1947 film *Le silence est d'or.* Set in the early days of French cinema, the film appealed to France's silent-studio past in a moment of tremendous uncertainty about its studio future. Clair, having spent the war in the United States, no doubt chose this reflexive narrative as an appealing way to announce his return—and, he surely hoped, his home industry's return to prominence. One of the great challenges French filmmakers faced when Clair landed in Paris was precisely how to redevelop an aging studio infrastructure that, even where it hadn't been damaged during the war, trailed far behind the newer studios found in places like Clair's recent filmmaking home, Hollywood. As set designer Lucien Aguettand lamented in an undated memo written, most likely, in late 1945: "There is something incomprehensible about the fact that our films, which are highly appreciated on the foreign market, come out of old studios, most of them 30 years old, with few or no technical advantages. If no effort is made, we may soon find ourselves with these installations worthy of film antiquity, unable to continue our productions."[2]

The end of the war had left Aguettand, like his counterparts in other French industries, charged with imagining a new future for French infrastructure. For cinema that meant studios. In addition to listing more technical concerns about what it would take to compete with the facilities at Pinewood or Cinecittà, Aguettand insisted that in reimagining their studios, French industry leaders must not neglect the human element, for, indeed, studios were workplaces like any other. Early studio designers had, Aguettand insisted, created almost "inhuman," "monstrous" working environments "and surrounded these demonic places with so-called 'workers' cities,' too often hopeless, sad and pitiful, making even more painful and discouraging the lives of those who work in the factories."[3] Now was the time to avoid the mistakes of their predecessors.

It was particularly fitting, then, that Clair would make those earlier places his film's subject. The project could hardly have been more reflexive. Shooting took place on the foundations of a key site of what Aguettand could now dismiss as "film antiquity" but that had once been the height of French studio glory: the former Pathé studios at Joinville.[4] In his preparatory images for the film's sets, Léon Barsacq, like Aguettand, one of France's most significant set designers from the interwar years, conjured this studio past for the present, reproducing in fine detail a studio interior that readily reprises Georges Méliès's first studio at Montreuil-sous-Bois and the similar glass-enclosed studios built by Pathé in the decade that followed (fig. 0.1).[5]

FIGURE 0.1. Léon Barsacq, Maquette de décor, *Le silence est d'or* (ca. 1956). Dessin sur carton; 18.8 × 24.6 in. Cinémathèque française, Bibliothèque du film. © 2019 Artists Rights Society (ARS): New York / ADAGP: Paris.

The film's plot—with a love triangle featuring an aging director (Maurice Chevalier), his younger assistant (François Périer), and a young woman (Marcelle Derien) newly arrived from the countryside—sounds like something from the Nouvelle Vague. More significant, the industry's deep concern with the studio infrastructure necessary to make such films highlights the importance studios retained in France in the leadup to, and the aftermath of, the movement so lauded for its preference for shooting on location. In Aguettand's desperate desire to develop an "ideal," socially conscious studio environment in the midst of Reconstruction-era impoverishment, as in Clair's reflexive studio (re)turn, and in Barsacq's faithful reprisal of France's glorious studio past, we find the blend of material concerns, profilmic needs, labor practices, textual products, and symbolic values that make studios rich objects of historical analysis.[6]

With attention to all of these facets of studio history, this volume emphasizes the critical role studio spaces and their creation have played in the history of visual culture. Together, its chapters examine how studio worlds have been made and how such worlds, in turn, have made the worlds of the moving image. The book's collective argument, stated most broadly, is that when we foreground these worlds and the processes through which they are created, inhabited, and used, we gain new insights into moving-image culture and the material, ecological, social, political, and economic determinants that prefigure and mark, if not always in readily legible ways, the worlds that appear on our screens. These chapters focus on studios from specific, if widely diverse, geographic locations and historical periods. But together they offer approaches, as I will argue in this introduction, with much broader application for historians and theorists of the (moving) image who may not be interested in studios per se but who may seek methods, be they spatial, material, ecological, or political-economic, for understanding the conditions that shape images and image culture.

. . .

The studio has long held a central role in the practices and discourses of art and global media. On the one hand, studios have, for centuries, been at the very heart of visual cultural production and the language used to describe it. For all of the changes to moving-image culture in the age of "new" media, studios continue to define the daily work of artists and film and television crews in physical locations around the world, as well as the virtual spaces—software suites, apps, and other digital creation platforms—that increasingly allow forms of "studio" production to take place in any location with electricity and a network connection. Despite the dispersal of production across such sites, real and virtual alike, cinema remains marked by its studio past. We continue to use the term *studio* to designate Hollywood's classical industry ("the studio system"), to deploy the buildings as metonymic substitutes for the companies they house ("the studios"), and, more recently, to refer to the virtual spaces—Final Cut Studio, DaVinci Resolve Studio, Corel VideoStudio, Microsoft Visual Studio, etc.—in which virtual image worlds are increasingly made.

On the other hand, the studio—as a physical place—has consistently been overlooked in film and media studies, even despite the "spatial turn" that has generated such a substantial literature about cinema's relationship to urban environments, its treatment of space and place, and its representations of architecture and infrastructure. This paradox, as I have argued previously, has partly to do with the nature of studios themselves.[7] From their origins studios were designed to generate technological visibility by remaining unseen. As a hidden necessity for illusionary forms of cinematic and televisual production, they were often present but rarely noticed by film and television viewers or acknowledged by critics. Hiding in plain sight, these critical sites readily faded into the background of text- or exhibition-focused critical discourse.

Or, one might say, studios were *made* to recede from critical view as part of the disciplinary formation through which film studies, not altogether unlike art history (especially in its modernist strain), has focused on visual form, textual analysis, and aesthetic lineages—the formations of style—more than the conditions from which texts arise. To wit, film and media students tend to learn film language and textual analysis first. The "film analysis" paper or "scene analysis" test (or, in art history, the identification exam and visual analysis paper) embody disciplinary emphases on form, style, and text. Such norms of instruction emphasize the capacity to recognize form and to analyze representations, not to ask whence and how those forms come to be. As Lee Grieveson has argued, this emphasis, at least in the American context, has roots in efforts by the Hollywood film industry, dating to the silent period, to make the study of film a form of connoisseurship, or "appreciation," thereby discouraging studies of the political economy of media or its potential ideological effects on audiences.[8] One might posit a less insidious intention behind this move, but the field's roots in English departments has nonetheless helped encourage a focus that, although it shifted with the New Historicist tradition and related New Film History, remains rooted in analyses of textual forms. The merging of film studies and art history around analyses of film and/as art has reinforced this emphasis on form and its textual histories, even if it has also encouraged greater attention to sites of exhibition as film and media scholars and art historians converge at the sites and histories of "expanded" cinema, the "black box" in the "white cube," and other forms of (new) media installation.

Meanwhile, work like the latter, which has challenged this focus on texts, often by calling attention to their contingent meanings and ideological effects, has at times shifted attention further away from the conditions of production. Led by feminist film theorists and, more recently, by scholars working in queer and critical race history and theory, such work has highlighted the important processes through which visual forms come to have different meanings according to variations in exhibition setting and, especially, spectator experience. This mode of analysis can often, and for good reason, temporarily bracket off the messy details of how film texts, at least in the dominant mode of industries like Hollywood, arrive on our screens loaded with all of the ideological weight of heteronormative, patriarchal production norms, the product of which—the text—may nonetheless be productively subjected to deconstruction, reading against the grain, or analyses of fans' capacity to (re)use the content for their own ends. When it does not take this for granted, for example by tracing inequalities in Hollywood production practices, such work demonstrates one value of analyzing the working conditions behind the screen.[9]

Three recent research initiatives have created fertile ground for yet more attention to such conditions. In film and media studies, the subfield devoted to media industry studies, or "production studies," has put renewed focus on the practices of media making. Working at the intersection of political economy, cultural studies, and varying iterations of anthropology, sociology, and media ethnography, its scholars have taken up what Vicki Mayer, Miranda Banks, and John Caldwell describe as "the crisis of representing producers, their locations, industries, and products."[10] Part of this "crisis" is precisely the spatioepistemological gap separating sites of exhibition (and the media texts displayed in them) from the harder-to-access places and social conditions from which those texts emerge. The work of overcoming this gap by getting behind the scenes has not, however, tended to mean greater attention to the studios themselves. In fact, production studies scholars have often explicitly bypassed the studio on the assumption that studio knowledge is old news. As Mayer, Banks, and Caldwell put it, "It was not so long ago that studies of film and television production limited their geographic considerations to the space of a studio set," a limitation that leads their contributors to seek production stories elsewhere.[11]

At work here is a broader assumption, dating at least to canonical accounts of the "studio system," that even the most detailed analyses of studio working practices need not consider the studio itself in great depth. Take, for instance, the descriptions in *The Classical Hollywood Cinema* (1985). In her essential sections about Hollywood's mode of production, Janet Staiger acknowledges that "it is not unimportant that this system of production centralized its work processes in the studio/factory . . . the focal site of the manufacturing of fictional narrative films." The system itself—hence the "studio" moniker—was, Staiger argues, "particularly manifest in the physical plant of a Hollywood studio," with its buildings numbered according to the ordered division of tasks that defined filmmaking as a form of factorylike assembly.[12] Staiger's account includes early attention to what scholars have only recently come to recognize as the critical material and environmental costs of creating the studio world, which, in the case of the Lasky studio built in 1918, to cite just one example, reportedly required "a tract of timberland in Oregon and a private sawmill and steamers to transport the wood to Southern California."[13] There, however, largely ends the account of studios, at least as sites and material forms. The emergence of production studies, with its primary focus on the working practices of the present, has—with few important exceptions, including sections of Ben Goldsmith and Tom O'Regan's useful study, *The Film Studio: Film Production in the Global Economy* (2005)—not seen fit to extend that view in either historical or materialist ways.[14]

The emergence of media infrastructure studies has offered perhaps greater potential to reconsider sites of media production, at least those of the recent past. Recognizing that media technologies, as Brian Larkin has argued, "are more than transmitters of content" and that "they represent cultural ambitions, political machineries, modes of leisure, relations between technology and the body, and . . . the economy and spirit of an age," such work has highlighted the significance of the many materials, objects, and systems that define the media world behind, around, and beyond moving-image texts.[15] Attention to these media infrastructures, defined by Lisa Parks and Nicole Starosielski as "situated sociotechnical systems that are designed and configured to support the *distribution* of audiovisual signal traffic," has helped to flag the significance of the long-overlooked networks and objects of media distribution: satellites, antennae, cables, waystations, and so forth.[16]

Once again, however, this emphasis on distribution and exhibition has tended to imply that production infrastructures are already sufficiently understood. As Parks and Starosielski put it, part of the power of "adopting an infrastructural disposition" is precisely to counter the tendency "to prioritize processes of production and consumption, encoding and decoding, and textual interpretation."[17] In adopting this otherwise significant approach, however, work about media infrastructure has too readily collapsed, as this description does, "processes of production" (itself an overly tidy category) into the work of "encoding" and "textual interpretation." Production processes and their infrastructures are *not*, as it turns out, something media scholars already know (more than) enough about. The sheer quantity of new insights found in this volume should make that point amply clear.

The related emergence, in film and media studies and in art history, of significant subfields devoted to artistic materials and media ecologies has offered newly productive routes into such knowledge. Parks and Starosielski, for example, emphasize the heuristic utility of tracing the relationship between infrastructure and materials, noting that "exploring material forms and practices . . . bring[s] new settings, objects, and stakeholders into the arena of media and communication research."[18] So, too, with a reconsideration of studios. In both their physical forms and as nodes in networks of modern life, studios embody and facilitate broader interactions between cinema and the worlds of science, technology, architecture, and ecology. The focus on materials, particularly as it intersects with ecology, has done perhaps the most to encourage reconsideration of studios as material, resource-dependent environments. Nadia Bozak and, more recently, Hunter Vaughn, both citing a key 2006 UCLA study about the relative "sustainability" of the motion picture industry in Los Angeles, have foregrounded the environmental costs of making culture. As Bozak put it first, and most succinctly, "cinema is intricately woven into industrial culture and the energy economy that sustains it."[19] As I have argued, and as Jennifer Fay has taken up more recently, the film studio embodies not just this resource dependence but also cinema's broader worldmaking ambitions—an anthropocentric desire to control and simulate the nonhuman world.[20]

As these growing subfields—with their respective concerns about production, infrastructure, and materials/environments—should suggest, the studio's relative absence from critical discourse represents a significant blind spot in film and media historiography. The failure by historians to consider the studio as an architectural space and material form speaks to the broader tendency to overlook material histories that are now being urgently recovered. This reconsideration of the material is especially important at a moment when, as Giuliana Bruno recently highlighted in *Surface: Matters of Aesthetics, Materiality, and Media*, the virtual has so come to define media experience and discourse.[21] One of this volume's goals, then, is to contribute to the widespread reconsideration of immaterialist accounts of today's "new" media by foregrounding just how much film and media studies has to gain from the materialist turn in infrastructure studies and media archaeology, as well as from the broader emphasis on "new materialism" across humanities disciplines. At the same time, this book is not an indictment or dismissal of any existing approach. On the contrary, it seeks to open new analytic possibilities that can readily build on and be joined with the fruitful work being undertaken elsewhere, whether by scholars attentive to industry formations, those concerned with sites and spaces of exhibition, or those focused on texts and the work they do.

The essays that follow perform this epistemological opening through a cross-national and transhistorical examination of studio design and use. They take the studio as a common point of comparison for understanding the heterogeneous contributions that materials and architectural forms have made to cinematic space and film form. Although filmmakers have long shared the need for controlled environments with regulated illumination and freedom from the contingencies of location shooting, architects have responded to those needs in a variety of place- and period-specific ways. Numerous historical, cultural, and regional contingencies have shaped studio forms, including architectural vernaculars, municipal building codes, available materials, infrastructural technologies, film production practices, the requirements of genres and subjects, and the limitations imposed by politics and economics. By turning our attention to such contextual factors, these chapters seek to open film and media history to new questions about the conditions that shape the construction of profilmic spaces and their products, as well as the kinds of archival materials needed to address them.

In turning to materials and questions more commonly associated with architectural history, the history of technology, and art history, the contributors offer both histories and approaches with intellectual purchase well beyond their specific studio subjects. By either bypassing film/media texts altogether or situating their formal features in broader discussions of the forms of physical spaces, some essays contribute to the displacement of the moving-image text from its onetime centrality as the discipline's privileged subject. While images were the ultimate product of studio production, these essays foreground the nontextual goals that drove studio design and use, goals such as controlled and comfortable architectural interiors, corporate prestige, efficient labor practices, patterns of workplace sociability, and control of employee behavior. Other essays highlight the value of applying textual analysis beyond the moving-image text to the studios themselves in order to examine media companies' various nonfilm forms of aesthetic production. Other essays use historical knowledge about media spaces and studio forms to rethink theoretical questions about the nature of cinematic space and the work of the apparatus. Finally, several essays contribute to work about cinema's contemporary transnational character by examining studios as physical nodes in the networks through which circulate the workers, materials, and commodities that make and define global cinema.

Existing studies of studio space, especially in art history and more rarely in film and media studies, suggest the historical and methodological contributions that such work offers.[22] In *The Soundscape of Modernity: Architectural Acoustics and the Culture of Listening in America, 1900–1933*, architectural historian Emily Thompson demonstrates the value of situating the emergence of synchronized film sound within broader changes to the meaning of noise, the culture of listening, and the new architectural materials and building forms that defined the modern soundscape in early twentieth-century America. By putting film history in dialogue with the history of architectural materials, building practices, and the discourses they defined, Thompson offers new ways of understanding not simply the early forms that film sound took but also why film's artificial studio-produced sound was so desirable in the first place. In *Hollywood Cinema and the Real Los Angeles*, Mark Shiel highlights the importance that film studios had in the material and urban development of a city literally shaped by film production.[23] And in *TV by Design: Modern Art and the Rise of Network Television*, Lynn Spigel uses the history of NBC's and CBS's respective "television cities"—a category on which she expands in this volume—to explore how televisual space and movement emerged not simply out of existing film aesthetics but within new modern architectural practices that TV executives employed with the aim of both enhancing their corporate prestige and establishing new production practices and aesthetic styles. Television studio architecture, Spigel shows, offers a multilayered form of product differentiation that cannot be understood by focusing only on the TV text.

Finally, in editing this collection, I have endeavored to push forward, expand, and challenge the arguments of my own work about early studios in the United States and France. In that work I situated the studio's formal character and its role in shaping the content and form of studio films in the architectural traditions that had defined theatrical stages, photography studios, factories and mills, greenhouses, and international exposition structures and in the development of building materials, including diverse forms of glass, iron, steel, Portland cement, and reinforced concrete. By positioning cinema in the developments of the Second Industrial Revolution that historians of technology have termed the "human-built world," I sought to define cinema as a technological system for the production of environments—or in more recently prominent terms, to use the studio to consider cinema's "anthropocentric" ontology. Studio cinema epitomized the broader worldbuilding ambitions that made cinema, from its earliest Western foundations, both a product of and critical contributor to the processes now associated with the so-called "Anthropocene."[24] This included the extrastudio logics whereby filmmakers looked on "natural" landscapes with studio eyes, reimagining what would come to be termed "locations" as potential sets that could be mined and extracted to generate cinema's human-built virtual worlds and with them a humancentric conception of nonhuman nature.[25]

How, this collection asks, did such processes work elsewhere, both in other Western contexts and non-Western ones, and in later historical periods? How did different architectural and technological traditions define studios in places like Japan and Brazil? How did the differing patterns of industrial development condition studios from Mexico to the Middle East? How have cultural specificities and aesthetic norms, both of film and architecture, shaped studio designs and vice versa? How did world-renowned studios such as Cinecittà and Pinewood develop and become models in their own right? Are there aspects of studio design that transcend national and cultural lines? How do film, television, and new media production spaces compare? And what is the studio's likely future in the digital age and beyond? While no volume could address all of these questions with complete satisfaction, one of my hopes in editing this book is that it will encourage further work along these lines. This is especially the case for analyses of studios in geographic locations that could not be included here, often owing to institutional pressures—one set of working practices that have shaped this work—that discourage scholars from publishing in edited volumes.

STUDIO APPROACHES:
ENVIRONMENT-NODE-SYMBOL

Three general approaches to studios appear consistently in this volume's twelve chapters, suggesting both their utility and portability across geographic space and historical time. Without intending to suggest that these frameworks can be applied to or encompass any and all studios, in the remainder of this introduction I outline them with a view to creating a working methodological schematic that can be used to frame future analysis. Rather than writing standard chapter summaries, here I "introduce" each chapter in a patchwork of examples that illustrate methodological and thematic overlaps across the volume's wide-ranging contexts. If this book is successful, it will be in part because its chapters have so productively modeled these approaches in forms to which future studies can aspire.

Studios as Environments (Virtual + Material)

Reduced to the most essential definition, studios are spaces for the creation of spaces, worlds for worldmaking, and environments designed to generate other environments. As such, studios uniquely embody powerfully complex relationships of visual representation. From the modernity-defining blurring of reality and its image, or the framing of the world, to use Heidegger's lasting phrase, as a picture, to postmodernism's untethering of signifier from signified, the simulating work of the studio offers an unusually rich analytic opportunity to trace the precise means through which the real becomes virtual, the material becomes immaterial, the profilmic becomes diegetic. Studio environments have long structured and thereby exposed these strange, estranging transitions, as well as key theoretical discourses that emerged to explain them. Walter Benjamin famously used the studio's artificially generated "equipment-free aspect of reality"—in which reality itself has become the unattainable "'blue flower' in the land of technology"—to diagnose modernity's broader conditions of technological simulation and domination.[26] Siegfried Kracauer, writing about the sets at Ufa in 1927, similarly saw in the studio a profound encapsulation of human worldmaking ambitions and the process through which all of the world, as revealed in the studio's explicitly artificial one, was being manufactured in human-built form.[27]

This volume's essays explore these conditions and the discourses about them beyond interwar and Western contexts, demonstrating, on the one hand, that such arguments were not unique and, on the other, that worldmaking ambitions—studio and nonstudio alike—were often as much aspiration as reality. As Diane Wei Lewis shows, for example, early Japanese studios contributed to a broader "ecological modernity" in which entertainment culture structured similar experiences of environmental simulation and control, from world's fair exhibits to popular aquariums and reconstructions of Mt. Fuji. Writing about studio rhetoric in 1920s Brazil, Rielle Navitski demonstrates that the desire for studio control also extended powerful political ideologies. There, the capacity to recreate reality in the studio represented modernity itself, both in the aspiration to reproduce Hollywood's industrialized production practices and in the erasure of indigenous populations whose image did not fit racist national imaginaries. As each of these chapters makes clear, however, such controls could not be guaranteed, whether, in the Japanese case, because flooding or typhoons disrupted the studio world, or, in the Brazilian case, again because of weather, in this case heat, or because of economic conditions that made ephemeral studio infrastructure more common than permanent, purpose-built constructions.

As Benjamin and Kracauer intuited, the changing conditions through which architects and designers fulfilled studios' worldmaking ambitions reveal a great deal about the underlying ideals that drove what the (film) world should be. For Brazil's white urban critics, as Navitski argues, both Brazil and, by extension, its cinema should be defined by a technologized, resource-fueled extractive economy, an ambition that could be only partially fulfilled in studio spaces. In midcentury Mexico, as Laura Serna shows, similar ambitions drove powerful stakeholders to invest new studio infrastructure with their aspirations for a national film industry, even if, in its ultimate form, that industry (and its studios) would bear the traces of Hollywood influence and transnational compromise. Meanwhile, across the ocean at Britain's iconic Pinewood Studios, economic determinations directed, in very different ways, British efforts to maintain studio production against Hollywood incursion. As Sarah Street describes in her analysis of the implementation of a midcentury technology known as the "Independent Frame" (IF), novel forms of studio world-creation made visible the complex entanglement of business imperatives, studio design and labor practices, and the changing forms of the textual worlds these conditions produced. A new technology and technique designed to streamline studio set design, the IF aimed, as Street puts it, for the "creation of a total, immersive world," one that would put more of the onus on preproduction, thereby eliminating the contingencies of location shooting and allowing for a mode of "continuous production" that better fit a political economy of quotas.

By the late 1930s, the language of efficiency had become a staple of studio systems the world over, though the intended outcomes were by no means uniform. As

Robert Bird describes in his chapter about Aleksandr Medvedkin, in 1938 the Soviet studio Mosfilm implemented reforms designed to increase efficiency and reduce costs through IF-like practices of backdrop-heavy, modular set design. At stake in this shift, especially for Medvedkin, Bird argues, was the future of socialism and its competing "models of possible worlds." Returning to a fixed studio after his short-lived experience leading a mobile studio on rails, Medvedkin faced the task of refining cinema's power to create a metaphorical discursive environment for socialism in a new literal environment. In this sense studio practice was, for Medvedkin and others, a theoretical praxis through which film's material worlds might create first virtual but eventually concrete political realities.

In his chapter about Charles and Ray Eames's studio, Justus Nieland tracks a similar form of ideological dispersal as it radiated out from an unassuming low-rise at 901 West Washington Boulevard in Venice, California, across the circuits of midcentury American design thinking that linked the technology industry to the Hollywood studios, other sites of art practice, and the university. As Nieland argues, this ideology of "happy, creative living" both arose from and reinforced a studio form and practice of postindustrial flexibility for which 901 was the "heuristic environment." As with the IF at Pinewood and socialist models of efficiency at Mosfilm, 901 was driven by modularity but in the cybernetic form and language of iteration, recombination, and feedback.

Across these contexts the question of how studio worlds could and *should* generate screen worlds reveals remarkable continuity but also distinct differences that richly illuminate differing conceptions of cinema as a medium—and more, too. In (re)conceptualizing their studio worlds, filmmakers and critics have consistently sought to enact broader visions for the social and political environments that films and their spaces, real and virtual alike, might be used to model. In short, the material studio environment has long encapsulated, reproduced, and thereby indexed discursive projects with stakes that go beyond the also important, sometimes related, question of how film's material worlds become textual ones.

Studios as Nodes (Methodological, Material, Sociopolitical)

Just as they open onto broader discursive and political projects that have framed cinema, so analyses of studios offer methodological opportunities to look beyond cinema and film and media studies to broader historical relations that can enrich film and media histories. As new kinds of material environments, studios have roots in the broader transformations of nineteenth-century Western science, technology, and architecture. Across the twentieth and now twenty-first century, studios have continually been shaped by—and shaped—materials and working practices across these networks. Part of the studio's heuristic value is to encourage film and media scholars to attend to such histories by investigating how studios, and cinema and television by extension, fit into historical systems that have not always been part of film and media's historical narratives. For those strictly concerned with film or media themselves, studios allow these more broadly conceived analyses to remain centered, helping avoid simply, as Charles Musser has described in the context of studies of "pre-cinema," expanding and diluting into more general cultural history.[28] More important, when approached as network nodes, studios illuminate the convergence of forms of scientific and technical knowledge; technologies, resources, and raw materials; and groups of people as diverse in their expertise as their social backgrounds. To account for such convergence, studio histories encourage us to reach beyond traditional methods, often using nontraditional archives, and thereby to open new epistemological routes for media analysis.

This volume's chapters explore studios' shifting positions in networks of technologies, aesthetic styles, cultural influences, financial flows, politics, and laboring peoples. In some cases these histories track new historical connections across familiar sites. In her chapter about early interwar television, for instance, Anne-Katrin Weber examines model television studios built at exhibitions and trade fairs, signaling the still-new medium's place in the celebratory narratives of novelty, technological spectacle, and virtual experience that world's fairs consolidated in the nineteenth century. Weber traces this influence to the first permanent TV studios, including the 1851 Crystal Palace itself, which after being relocated to South London became home to John Logie Baird's television company. As Lewis notes in her chapter, Japan's first glass studio took its name from the same Crystal Palace, just one example of the importance the fairs had for Japan's (and its cinema's) relationship to Western modernity.

Other chapters demonstrate the important links between studio technologies and the infrastructural networks that supported the emergence and industrialization of cinema and television. As Navitski notes, Brazilian studio development was in part a question of infrastructural development, with telling links such as the use of trolley-car tracks as an intermittent source of power for ephemeral studio lighting. In both practical and more conceptual ways, Medvedkin's film train, as Bird describes, drew on rail, telephone, and electrical networks while also being imagined as a force akin to electricity itself, flowing across Soviet infrastructure to connect and power, like the resources being filmed, Soviet ideology.

In political economic terms studio histories illuminate critical forms through which economic policies and cultural practices have shaped the movements of resources, commodities, and workers across an expanding and shifting network of production sites. As Serna argues, the history of Churubusco illustrates broader tensions within Mexican and American film histories over how much involvement American companies and investors would have in an industry that risked becoming a Hollywood vassal but also benefited from its financial inputs. Noa Steimatsky's chapter about the fate of Cinecittà during the 1940s—a newly expanded version of the story she has told previously about its use as a refugee camp during

World War II—examines the darkest version both of this kind of subordination and of just what studios' controlled environments could, in all of their modularity, become.[29] As a site both for containing prisoners and producing fascist cinema, Cinecittà, Steimatsky shows, played host to "the interlacing of the spaces and circumstances of film production with those of war" in ways that put unique pressure on "our conception of these histories and how they might be told."

Steimatsky's analysis of the forced movement of Cinecittà's unlikely labor force may represent a limit case, but it speaks no less to the kind of social history that studios, as network nodes, make visible in their more banal typicality. The Independent Frame, for example, was designed precisely to marshal studio infrastructure to reduce working hours, threatening workers with the mechanization of their art and labor. Today, such efficiency involves a complex ebb and flow of production teams moving through a global network of competing production sites defined by infrastructure, legal frameworks, and local labor forces. In their respective chapters about Lucasfilm and Dubai's Studio City, J. D. Connor and Kay Dickinson illuminate the complex movements of workers—following resources and capital—through these systems, which become particularly visible from studio nodes. As Dickinson argues, tracing such networks outward and "grappling with how [the film studio] instrumentalizes the current vicissitudes of both the global supply chain and the international property market [allows us] to get closer to the impact of capital's harmfully mercurial character." As Connor demonstrates, that character also surfaces in the work of planning and publicity through which media firms implement their studio infrastructures and thereby define their corporate identities.

The post–World War II American university's important place in these networks comes into focus in Jeff Menne's chapter about the Digital Arts Laboratory (DAL) at SUNY Buffalo, site of what might be considered the first "new media" studio. As Menne shows, the DAL, created in the late 1970s by Gerald O'Grady and Hollis Frampton, emerged from the rich convergence of aesthetic influences, technological developments, and capital flows that linked New York City's art world and experimental film scene with the State of New York's public funding for education and the arts with upstate technology hubs and rural culture. O'Grady and Frampton leveraged university and federal government wagers on the value of educational technology infrastructure to fuse such networks into a physical location for education and creation. Like the Eames studio at 901, the DAL combined and consolidated the intermedial artistic visions and worldviews that have shaped visual culture since the mid-twentieth century.

Such views become visible, as Menne states most explicitly, when we consider the studio, in its straightforward economic sense, as a cost, whether of art making or doing business. In justifying and implementing that cost, whether in the university, at Lucasfilm, in Venice Beach, or in the Dubai free zone, artists and institutions reveal both their approaches to film practice and their broader understandings of economic and legal policies and cultural and social politics. As Nieland demonstrates particularly well in his analysis of the Eames practice at 901, reading centrifugally from studio nodes out across networks of aesthetic influence and economic and political relations has tremendous intellectual purchase for scholars interested in how visual cultural practice intersects with broader social, cultural, and political histories. These chapters are all, to varying degrees, examples of this method applied to distinctive contexts.

Studios as Symbols

Finally, for all of their value as indexes into broader histories and methods that encourage us to read out from their nodal fixity, studios themselves have long functioned as powerful symbols that may offer as much, as objects of visual analysis, as the texts they produce. In early Hollywood, for example, studio architecture offered the new film industry one way to project visual messages about what it would mean for the city, whether by insisting on its continuity with local traditions, typically by appropriating the Spanish Colonial style, or by using neoclassical motifs as symbolic markers of strength and stability.[30] The image of Alice Guy Blaché (fig. 0.2), posing in front of her first Solax studio in Flushing, New York, captures further dimensions of the symbolic power studios have long held. Positioned, like the studio itself, in profile, Guy aligns herself and her power with her new infrastructure, the world created for her increasingly independent creations. Distanced from Gaumont's Paris headquarters, Guy, the only person in the photo, stands as the powerful controlling center of a new world whose productive chaos rests blurrily just beyond her knowing gaze, emerging along a diagonal that expands as if directly from her creative mind.

Though studios require no such visual splendor for their basic functionality, and thus might just as well—and at times do—disappear into the anonymous sameness of industrial warehouse design, film companies continue to use studio style to cultivate corporate identity. Highlighting the power of studio visibility, the chapters in this volume offer numerous examples of active identity-making, as well as efforts to keep the studio and its practices out of view. As Lewis describes, the image of Japan's "Crystal Palace" studio, imbued with the aura of its namesake, became a powerful symbol of the film industry and modernity more generally. The BBC's first studio in Alexandra Palace, as Weber explains, served similar symbolic purposes for early British television broadcasting at a time when programs themselves may not have been enough. Even Studio City Dubai, which otherwise, as Dickinson describes, blends into its local warehouse surroundings, employs overt cinematic symbolism—a kitschy filmstrip bridge (see fig. 12.3)—to evoke the site's ideals of creative connectivity and fluid circulation. In contrast, Lucasfilm, as Connor explains, has worked hard to limit its visibility, not only by distancing itself from Hollywood but also by actively concealing infrastructure at the Skywalker Ranch.

FIGURE 0.2. Alice Guy Blaché at the Solax Studio (ca. 1909). Cinémathèque française.

This visual symbolic work has often supported the more metaphorical symbolism that studios—here also in the familiar naming convention—also serve. For Lucasfilm, studio location again served practical and symbolic purposes in both enacting and signaling a different relationship to Hollywood's business-as-usual. From mid-century Mexico back to silent-era Brazil, from Medvedkin's film train to Mosfilm, and from Pinewood to Cinecittà, studios, even only imagined ones, have served powerful, if contradictory, symbolic functions. Such symbolism at times circulates with studios' textual products, as was the case with the Eames studio. As Nieland argues, 901, appearing in reflexive films that took the studio itself as one of their subjects, helped propagate "powerful normative horizons for orienting consumers at home and abroad toward designed objects and 'ways of life'" that ensured viewers that the whole world could, in a sense, become a "studio" for optimized living.

The symbolic power of studios appears perhaps most forcefully in this volume in the chapters about television. As Weber's chapter makes clear, for would-be audiences in the 1930s television existed, first and foremost, not as a textual form but as a set of technologies on display at trade fairs and exhibitions. There, the TV itself, but more importantly the TV studio, became a new symbol of modern communication. Before broadcasting could achieve the ubiquity that might allow audiences to forget their programs' sources, institutions such as the BBC sold the studio image, which, in Weber's words, "participated in a network of signifiers that symbolically shaped the image of British television." Tracing this symbolic value across a longer historical time frame, Lynn Spigel demonstrates that radio and television "cities" used both architectural style and publicity events to call attention to themselves and thereby to orient viewers to their material and symbolic function as figures of modernity. In terms that could be applied widely to studio networks past and present, Spigel argues that such media architectures became "material spaces for the flow of commerce and communication while offering audiences new mental maps through which to navigate an increasingly mediatized nation."

THE STUDIO DESIGN

With these broad framing approaches in mind, the reader may proceed through the following chapters, as with most volumes of this kind, in piecemeal fashion. The book proceeds in roughly chronological order from early cinema to the present, in subgroups that readers interested in specific historical eras might think of in periodizing terms: early–classical–modern–contemporary. Though such traditional categories do largely hold, I have opted instead to name these sections somewhat differently in an effort both to acknowledge the unevenness of media chronologies across geography and to indicate other ways of imagining studio histories. Part 1, "Formations," thus does focus on silent-era studios but within a more conceptually open consideration of the lengthy time frame in which studio infrastructures took form, especially beyond the West. While the inauguration of Universal City in 1915 or the development of "dark" studio warehouses in 1920s Hollywood might signal the modern foundations of a stable studio cinema in the United States, for much of the world the process of formation happened otherwise, especially if we attend to the intersecting development of television.

Part 2, "Foundations," which roughly spans the "classical" period of Western studio systems, considers "foundational" studios that became icons, the significance of which—both as symbols and ongoing sites of production—continue today. Alongside Churubusco, Pinewood, and Cinecittà, this section might well have included any of the major Hollywood or Western European studios, as well as the powerful and lasting studio infrastructures established in Japan, India, and elsewhere during the middle part of the twentieth century. These studios may, at least for their largest local industries, have proved foundational, but of course that which is foundational will eventually become outmoded. Moreover, what is for some foundational will be for others simply hegemonic. We still need studio histories of the alternative infrastructures that challenged, or more quietly existed alongside, these studio icons.

Part 3, "Alternative Routes," points to such histories, first by upending the chronology, moving back to Medvedkin's film train (and later film truck) while also comparing the train-studio with another iconic formation, Mosfilm. During the silent era many filmmakers had sought flexible, modular systems that might allow studios to be constructed ephemerally in any location. Directors such as Medvedkin, on his studio train, or Jacques Yves Cousteau on his *Calypso* studio ship, extended this ideal of the movable studio world, as did the colonial and industrial filmmakers who, by necessity, sought to reproduce studio-like conditions far beyond studio walls. But "Alternative Routes" also, in the chapters about the Eameses at 901 and Hollis Frampton at the SUNY Buffalo campus, points to the convergence of film and broader artistic and intellectual worlds in spaces reconceived for different moving-image forms. Here the volume most explicitly crosses over into art historical studio lineages, and readers might well consider (and follow the bibliographic references to important studies about) the related studio work of figures such as Andy Warhol and Claes Oldenburg, the cultural work of architectural studios such as Diller Scofidio + Renfro, or, following the university-artist links highlighted by Menne, to Moholy-Nagy or György Kepes, to name only some well-known examples.[31]

Finally, "Studio Futures" again tracks back to the past, using Lynn Spigel's century-spanning survey of the "broadcast city" to position contemporary media conglomerates in long institutional and infrastructural lineages—and their visions of futures past—before turning to two other more recent studio developments: Skywalker Ranch (and Lucasfilm's related studio sites) and Studio City Dubai. As I described earlier, today's media infrastructure has increasingly gone online, as "studio"-named software and cloud storage—materially based, of course, in the real infrastructure of server farms—make it possible to imagine a future in which studios have become a thing of the past. Yet from Dubai to Cinecittà to Paramount to Churubusco to the Cité du cinema outside Paris to Pinewood and its global offshoots, physical studios remain critical sites of moving-image production culture with no end in sight. This book about the studio's past thus ends by turning toward its future, with an eye to just how many things—aesthetic, material, conceptual, economic, social, and political—these not-so-simple, not-so-already-understood structures create and contain.

NOTES

1. On Dickinson see Fuss, *Sense of an Interior*, 9–30; on Benjamin's forest workspace in Ibiza see Eiland and Jennings, *Walter Benjamin*, 397.

2. Lucien Aguettand, "Etude générale sur l'état actuel et la possibilité de production des plateau français," undated manuscript, Aguettand171-B10, Fonds Lucien Aguettand, Bibliothèque du film, Cinémathèque française.

3. Aguettand, "Bases pour une étude sérieuse d'un centre cinématographique," Feb. 6, 1945, Aguettand101-B7, Fonds Lucien Aguettand.

4. For more on the Joinville studios see Jacobson, *Studios Before the System.*

5. Barsacq later published an important history of set design. See Barsacq, *Le décor de film*; Barsacq, *Caligari's Cabinet and Other Grand Illusions.*

6. Aguettand, "Vers le studio idéal!" (1946), Aguettand104-B7, Fonds Lucien Aguettand.

7. Jacobson, *Studios Before the System.*

8. Grieveson, *Cinema and the Wealth of Nations*, 240–46.

9. See, e.g., Cooper, *Universal Women*; Hill, *Never Done*; and Field, Horak, and Stewart, *L.A. Rebellion.*

10. Describing their method, Mayer, Banks, and Caldwell write that "we have integrated historical and materialist accounts of cultural industries, work practices, and organizational formations as the columns upon which we construct well-rounded investigations of production cultures." Mayer, Banks, and Caldwell, "Introduction," in *Production Studies*, 4–5.

11. Mayer, Banks, and Caldwell, 8.

12. Bordwell, Staiger, and Thompson, *Classical Hollywood Cinema*, 119, 142.

13. Bordwell, Staiger, and Thompson, 142; Staiger cites "From Forest to Film," *Photoplay*, April 1918, 94.

14. Goldsmith and O'Regan, *The Film Studio.*

15. Larkin, *Signal and Noise*, 2.

16. Parks and Starosielski, introduction to *Signal Traffic*, 4 (emphasis added).

17. Parks and Starosielski, 5.

18. Parks and Starosielski, 6.

19. Bozak, *The Cinematic Footprint*, 1; see also Vaughan, *Hollywood's Dirtiest Secret.*

20. Jacobson, *Studios Before the System;* Fay, *Inhospitable World;* see also Jacobson, "Fire and Failure."

21. Bruno, *Surface.*

22. Art historical work addressing studio spaces includes Jones, *Machine in the Studio;* Alpers, "The Studio, the Laboratory, and the Vexations of Art"; Alpers, *Rembrandt's Enterprise;* Galison and Jones, "Factory, Laboratory, Studio"; and O'Doherty, *Studio and Cube.*

23. See also Scott, *On Hollywood.*

24. See Jennifer Fay's terrific analysis of the weather-simulating set designs by Buster Keaton, through which Fay explores the world-controlling potential that filmmakers found in their controlled studio worlds. Fay, "Buster Keaton's Climate Change," 25–49.

25. Jacobson, *Studios Before the System*, 185–92.

26. Benjamin, "The Work of Art in the Age of Its Technological Reproducibility"; see also Jacobson, *Studios Before the System*, 19.

27. Kracauer, "Calico World"; see also the insightful reading of this essay in Fay, *Inhospitable World*, 5–8.

28. Musser, *The Emergence of Cinema*, 17.

29. Steimatsky, "The Cinecittà Refugee Camp (1944–1950)."

30. See Jacobson, "Fantastic Functionality."

31. See Jones, *Machine in the Studio;* and Dimendberg, *Diller Scofidio + Renfro.*

PART ONE

Formations

1

"The Longed-For Crystal Palace"

Empire, Modernity, and Nikkatsu Mukōjima's Glass Studio, 1913–1923

Diane Wei Lewis

The past is now not a land to return to in a simple politics of memory.
—ARJUN APPADURAI, "DISJUNCTURE AND DIFFERENCE
IN THE GLOBAL CULTURAL ECONOMY"

In the earliest years of cinema, cameras and projectors were novelties, and location shoots drew crowds of gawkers. Film production and exhibition technology were of as much interest to the public as the films on the screen. Taking advantage of this fascination, many early Japanese filmmakers used location shoots to generate publicity for their films, but these shoots were too irregular and informal to be truly effective for developing public relations.[1] In the 1910s, Nikkatsu film company's glass studio in Mukōjima, Tokyo (1913–23), gave Japanese film production greater visibility—especially, and most significantly, to moviegoers in Asakusa, a nearby entertainment district from which the studio could be seen. The studio's brilliant edifice itself was an attraction, its glass a symbol of modern visuality. As "akogare no suishōkyū," a popular catchphrase suggests, Mukōjima's "longed-for Crystal Palace" invited an admiring and even desirous gaze.[2] Interest in film studios soon became widespread after the 1923 Great Kanto Earthquake forced Tokyo filmmakers to relocate west to Kyoto, which became known as the "Hollywood of Japan." By the late 1920s, studio tours, star-centered journalism, films about filmmaking, and professionalizing practices (training schools, labor specialization, job qualifications, and study groups) conferred legitimacy on cinema by strengthening associations among its production cultures, emergent social practices, and affluent lifestyles. Public fascination with the Nikkatsu Mukōjima studio foreshadows these film industrial developments while drawing attention to how the film studio as a site and architectural form was connected to new forms of modern display and reflected desire for but also ambivalence toward modernization in Japan.

This essay examines how Mukōjima's nickname invites us to consider it as one of Tokyo's architectural attractions and explore the film studio's relationship to the visual and spatial idioms typified by the international world's fairs. It is no accident that Mukōjima was compared to the Crystal Palace, the marvelous iron and glass structure that was erected to house London's 1851 Great Exhibition of the Works of Industry of All Nations. The glass studio's artificial environments exemplified the new kinds of virtual spaces made for visual consumption that originated at industrial expositions and proliferated with the rise of entertainments such as the aquarium, the amusement park, the diorama, the zoo, and the circular panorama. These new genres of display, their associated architectural forms, and their corresponding strategies of crowd control were freighted with cultural and political significance in modernizing Japan, a country that had begun dismantling its feudal system in 1868 and was developing new institutions, laws, and practices to create a modern, spectating public.

Descriptions of Mukōjima studio as the "Crystal Palace on the Sumida River" pepper the memoirs of early Japanese film workers, including those of director Tanaka Eizō (1886–1968) and actress Urabe Kumeko (1902–89). As a young girl who dreamed of coming to Tokyo, Urabe read about Nikkatsu's "Crystal Palace" (suishō no kyūden) in the regional newspapers.[3] When she finally stood on the Azuma Bridge in Asakusa, her heart leapt at her first glimpse of the studio on the far-off shore: there it was, the "longed-for Crystal Palace" (akogare no suishōkyū), a "proud glass studio" that "glittered dazzlingly like a big enchanted mirror."[4]

From a film-historical perspective the obvious importance of the large, bright glass stage (garasu sutēji, as glass studios were called in Japan) is that it allowed Nikkatsu's set designers to construct detailed, life-size, one-room interiors within a fixed and controlled environment. Glass stages represented an important technical advancement over earlier film sets, which were rudimentary temporary constructions shielded from the elements by cloth tents. The first glass stage was built in Meguro, Tokyo, in 1908 by Mukōjima's later designer, Kawaura Ken'ichi (1868–1957), for his firm Yoshizawa Shōten. According to Nikkatsu director Tanaka Eizō, Mukōjima's studio sets were not only superior to those of other Japanese film companies but even rivaled the constructions used on the modern Japanese stage. Tanaka was invited to join Mukōjima studio by his former drama school instructor, Masumoto Kiyoshi (1883–1932), with whom Tanaka discussed his frustrations with the shingeki (modern drama) theater world. Before accepting work at Nikkatsu, Tanaka decided to visit Mukōjima to see a film shoot for himself. The cast and crew were out location shooting, so Tanaka was given a tour of empty studio grounds. It was the glass stage, says Tanaka, that ultimately persuaded him to become a filmmaker. A set for a hardware shop had been constructed in the middle of the building. It looked exactly like the real thing, down to the set dressings, and Tanaka was floored.[5]

Yet by the time Mukōjima was completed, glass studios were already becoming defunct in industrialized filmmaking countries as filmmakers moved away from natural lighting and began to use darkened studios with electricity for illumination.[6] Mukōjima's glass studio design was already quaint by Hollywood standards. Moreover, Nikkatsu Mukōjima's staple product—formulaic *shinpa* melodramas based on "new school" plays from the 1880s—already had an antiquated quality and were savaged by the Japanese film reformers who hoped to "liberate" film from theatrical influences.[7] This is why, despite its incorporation of important innovations in studio design, construction, and layout, Nikkatsu Mukōjima studio is mostly invoked by film historians as having been a target for film reformers' derision toward "old-fashioned" melodrama films. Considering Mukōjima studio solely in terms of film-historical developments, it is easy to miss the full connotations of its architectural form and difficult to explain the allure of its construction materials.

Only by considering the cultural politics of the glass studio can we make sense of the apparent contradiction between Mukōjima's inferior studio design and its glamorous image as "the longed-for Crystal Palace" on the Sumida River. Why this curious epithet, with its dreamlike reference to the past? The studio's old technology and hoary productions consigned it as "backward" in relation to Europe and the US. At the same time, in its visibility and scale, the Nikkatsu Mukōjima studio complex was unlike any Japanese film studio that had ever existed. Its glass was a symbol of Japan's rapid industrialization. Its phantasmagoric appearance—compared to a glittering mirage on Tokyo's horizon—yoked it to Japan's modernization project and the utopian dimensions of modernization. Simultaneously marvelous and outdated, then, Japan's "Crystal Palace" carried myriad and contradictory associations. "Crystal Palace on the Sumida River" captures this very tension: it is an equivocal image of Japanese modernization that presents the studio as a vision of the future from the past of the West.

World's fairs shaped Meiji-era visual culture, Japanese imperial modernity, and their spatial imagination. Much has been written about industrial expositions and their relationship to Japanese urbanism, museum practices, and commercial display cultures, but far less attention has been paid to the influence of expositions on Japanese filmmaking, film studios, and theater architecture. Here I examine that influence and, in the process, consider the relationship of cinema to modernity in Japan. The visual and spatial tropes that developed at the world's fairs cannot be separated from the function that they served for visitors and exhibitors from industrialized countries. The fairs celebrated conquest and technology as means of bringing the world "closer" while shoring up national identities and reinforcing geopolitical hierarchies. What, then, should we make of descriptions of Nikkatsu Mukōjima studio as a miniature, nostalgic, and "longed-for" replica of the iconic

Crystal Palace built for London's 1851 world's fair? What role did exposition architecture, cinema, and other entertainments play in bringing the imperial imagination to Japan, a country that was never colonized but had an anxious relationship with the West?

NIKKATSU MUKŌJIMA STUDIO AND THE MEIJI EXHIBITIONARY COMPLEX

Nikkatsu Mukōjima studio succeeded several smaller Tokyo-area studios that were operated by the firms M. Pathe, Yoshizawa Shōten, and Fukuhōdō, which in 1912 merged with the Kyoto-based company Yokota Shōkai to create Nikkatsu, the first joint-stock film company in Japan. At the time of the 1912 merger Nikkatsu's production facilities included Yoshizawa Shōten's Meguro studio in southwest-central Tokyo, established in 1908 by Kawaura Ken'ichi and the first movie studio in Japan; M. Pathe's Ōkubo Hyakuninchō studio (1909–12) in central-west Tokyo; and Fukuhōdō's Nippori studio in north-central Tokyo (1910–12). All three facilities were built on rented land. It was decided that rather than pay rent for these three Tokyo studios, it would be better to open a new site owned and operated by Nikkatsu. After an attempt to buy land in Shiba Park in south-central Tokyo fell through, land for Mukōjima was purchased from Sugiyama Shigemaru (1864–1935), the powerful politician and member of the ultranationalist group Genyōsha.[8] The glass studio was designed by Kawaura and cameraman Yoshimoto Keizō.[9] Construction began in January of 1913 and was completed in October of the same year.

Before Mukōjima, studios were modest, stand-alone structures that sometimes consisted simply of a wooden platform and a tent. Mukōjima was the first Japanese studio to feature a campus-style layout. The studio grounds were located north and east of Asakusa and were surrounded on three sides by water, bordered on the west by the Sumida River and to the east by a canal that ran parallel to the river for the full length of the complex before turning west into the river, creating the studio ground's southern boundary. The glass studio was perched on the Sumida River shoreline, allowing unobstructed views of two of its sides from long distances across the water. The shorter side of the studio (about seventy-five feet long) came right to the Sumida River's edge with a veranda on the river. The longer side of the glass studio (approximately 131 feet) was what most onlookers would have seen approaching the studio from the southwest, from central Tokyo.

In addition to the glass studio, the studio complex included several other buildings. A Western-style building housed main offices, spaces for reception and security, a projection room, a break room, a darkroom for still photography, and rooms for all the work involved in developing negatives and making prints—a negative and positive film developing room, a printing room, two drying rooms, space for washing and tinting films, a perforation room, and a room for filming intertitles. Housed separately, the actors' dressing rooms and bath were in a large traditional Japanese house known as the *omoya* (main building). Here actors and staff also gathered to read through scripts. The famous *onnagata* (female impersonator) Tachibana Teinosuke's family lived on studio property, in another old Japanese-style house just north of the glass studio. On the opposite, southern end of the studio grounds screenwriters wrote and sometimes spent the night at an attractive teahouse dubbed "the planning department" *(kōanbu)*. Smaller structures on the grounds included an outhouse, a guardhouse, a pond, and, on the southeast corner of the grounds, an *inari* shrine.[10]

Mukōjima studio's glass stage appeared just as demand for window glass began to rise exponentially in response to falling prices and increased supply with the onset of domestic plate glass manufacturing (fig. 1.1, 1.2).[11] In the Meiji period, glass architecture symbolized power, enlightenment, and industry. A material with valuable scientific and military applications, glass was a symbol of knowledge and might. Before the 1868 Meiji Restoration, only a handful of lords *(daimyō)* supported artisanal glassmaking, and there was no feudal precedent for industrial glass production. There was no coordination among *han* (domains), and patronage was easily disrupted by shifts in clan leadership. Thus, as Kazunobu Nakanodō points out, glassmaking provided revenue for the fiefs, but without the active personal patronage of individual *daimyō*, it could not flourish.[12] At the very end of the Tokugawa period (1603–1868), when the shogunate began to end its policy of seclusion and reopened trade and diplomatic relations with the West, glass began to replace the window materials used in Japanese architecture. In traditional Japanese buildings, instead of glass windows, latticed wooden shutters called *shitomido* opened to let in light and air, and *shōji* screens with panels of translucent paper created illumination while providing some protection from the elements. Japan continued to rely heavily on imported glass for windows, watch faces, lamps, and lightbulbs, as well as imported lenses for weapons and scientific instruments. Until plate glass manufacturing was established in Japan, extensive use of glass as a building material was limited to small specialized structures such as greenhouses and aquaria. Most Meiji glassmaking was dedicated to the manufacture of housewares and decorative objects.[13] Attempts to develop domestic commercial plate glass failed repeatedly until 1902, when the Shimada Glass Factory in Osaka successfully achieved the process.[14] In 1909 the Asahi Glass Company, which was funded by the industrial-financial conglomerate Mitsubishi, employed the Belgian technique of manufacturing plate glass using handblown cylinders. The Asahi Glass Company was the only Japanese company manufacturing commercially viable glass in the 1910s, and when WWI disrupted European production and raised the price of Belgian glass, Asahi was able to export its inferior product to England, Australia, and South and Southeast Asia.[15]

FIGURE 1.1. Interior views of the glass studio, including a film shoot in progress (upper right). Originally published in *Nikkatsu shashi to gensei* (Nikkatsu company history and current state of affairs, 1930).

The first glass studios were built in France by Georges Méliès in 1897 and in the UK by Robert W. Paul in 1898.[16] In Japan the first glass studios were built by the entertainment entrepreneur Kawaura Ken'ichi. Kawaura's commercial real estate development projects mobilized the symbolic associations of modern architectural forms, bringing the sights and experiences of modernity to Tokyo. As head of Yoshizawa Shōten, a trading company specializing in magic lantern projectors and slides, Kawaura obtained one of the Lumière brothers' Cinématographes in 1897 and became one of the most successful importers and exhibitors of cinema in Japan. In 1902 Kawaura established a London exchange to ensure a steady supply of new films. In 1903 he opened the first permanent movie theater in Japan, the Denkikan (Electric Hall), in Asakusa by remodeling a former *misemono* (attractions) hall. After opening the Denkikan, Kawaura departed for St. Louis, Missouri, for the 1904 Louisiana Purchase Exposition, carrying with him a small selection of Yoshizawa Shōten films, including films of the Russo-Japanese War (1904–5) and exotic scenes of Mt. Fuji and geisha.[17] While in the US, Kawaura toured several eastern studios. After returning home, he built Japan's first permanent film studio in 1908, the Yoshizawa Shōten glass studio in Meguro, Tokyo. It is commonly said that this studio was based on Kawaura's inspection of the Lubin Company studio

FIGURE 1.2. Interior of the glass studio. Originally published in *Kakushinseru Mukōjima satsueijo* (Reforming Mukōjima Studio, 1923).

in Philadelphia and Edison's studio in the Bronx, but it is also likely that Kawaura drew inspiration, as well, from the "Palaces" or glass sheds used in the Louisiana Purchase Exposition to house exhibits. In 1910 he opened Asakusa's Luna Park (1910–11), the first American-style amusement park in Japan.

Kawaura's trip to St. Louis is not remarkable in itself—Japan had been an official participant in world's fairs since 1867—but it suggests the genetic connections among the world's fairs, Japanese exhibition practices, and Japanese cinema. As scholars have argued, the emergence of institutions such as the public museum, the zoo, and the imperial procession was shaped by the Meiji modernization project, which stressed industrialization, nation-building, and military expansionism. These forms can be said to have constituted the Meiji "exhibitionary complex"—Tony Bennett's term for exhibition practices that inscribe the relations of knowledge and power that obtain between the state and its subjects.[18] Noriko Aso points out that "many of the figures that played important roles in establishing the Meiji exhibitionary complex were participants at the [1867 Paris Exposition universelle], where they gathered formative impressions and gained practical experience" related to the expression of state authority and national values through collection, curation, display, and crowd control.[19] On returning to Japan, the dignitaries, researchers, and exhibitors who visited the fairs introduced forms of display such as the museum and the circular panorama—novel spatiovisual technologies that spectacularized power relations and reflected prevailing social and global hierarchies. For instance, industrialist Shibusawa Eiichi, one of the investors behind Japan's first panorama, the Nippon Panoramakan in Asakusa, was a member of the official Japanese delegation to Paris in 1867. The Nippon Panoramakan was the first Asakusa entertainment to be operated as a joint-stock company and was backed by such eminent figures as Shibusawa, Ōkura Kihachirō, and Yasuda Zenjirō. Shibusawa was also the creator of the Tokyo Stock Exchange and the first Japanese bank based on joint-stock ownership, although he is perhaps best known as an urban developer and major proponent of the garden city. One of Shibusawa's most visionary projects was the Tokyo suburb of Denenchōfu, which was planned and constructed in the late 1910s and early 1920s according to Ebenezer Howard's ideals.[20]

The Louisiana Purchase Exposition (April 30 to December 1, 1904) overlapped with an important juncture in the histories of Japanese militarism and cinema: the Russo-Japanese War (February 8, 1904, to September 5, 1905) and the motion picture boom it inspired. With the breakout of hostilities between Russia and Japan in Manchuria, enthusiasm for cinema reached unprecedented heights. The conflict, which was fought for dominance over southern Manchuria and the Korean peninsula, created overwhelming demand for patriotic films. Russo-Japanese War films included actualities, reenactments, and films that combined newsreel footage and dramatization. The popularity of cinema in Japan continued to grow even after the war ended, contributing to movie-theater building booms in Japan's major metropolitan areas. This period of fevered construction beginning around 1907 gave rise to Asakusa's "movie town."

The Russo-Japanese War threatened Japan's participation in the St. Louis world's fair, but as a fledgling imperial power engaged in its own territorial struggles, Japan was determined to make a good showing. The Louisiana Purchase Exposition marked the centennial of US Manifest Destiny and celebrated colonial expansionism. Its commemoration of military conquest drew clear distinctions between imperialism's winners and losers. Scattered across the twelve-hundred-acre fairground site, more than one thousand sculptures by more than one hundred artists celebrated the Louisiana Purchase by depicting "the larger and grander phases in the adventurous lives of those explorers and pioneers who won the wilderness from its brute and barbarian inhabitants as well as those achievements of later civilization, wrought by the genius of the American intellect."[21] At the main entrance to the fair, on the Plaza of St. Louis, a one-hundred-foot-tall Louisiana Monument "was erected to commemorate the American genius which subdued the forces of nature and savagery in the new world inland empire."[22] The fair's largest exhibit was a

"Philippine Exposition" that housed approximately eleven hundred villagers from more than ten different ethnic groups on a plot of forty-seven acres and was designed to introduce fairgoers to the native inhabitants of America's first colonial territory. The United States acquired the Philippines as part of the 1898 Treaty of Paris, which ended the Spanish-American War, broke up the Spanish Empire, and brought Guam and Puerto Rico under US administration. A smaller "Apache Village" featured Apache chief Geronimo and Nez Perce leader Chief Joseph as part of a "living display," while Japan and other nations displayed examples of their own colonized populations at the "Department of Anthropology" pavilion.[23]

It is unclear what impression these spectacles made on Kawaura. Like many early filmmakers, he was an intrepid entrepreneur with diverse business interests, as indicated by the fact that Yoshizawa Shōten was the first company to manufacture film equipment in Japan, the first Japanese company to own a permanent film theater, the first Japanese film company to operate an overseas exchange, and the first whose owner also managed an amusement park. Kawaura even opened a hot springs resort.[24] Given these diverse entrepreneurial activities, it makes sense to frame Kawaura's activities in the US very broadly—not simply as background research for building modern film studios but as a more general investigation into the various, interconnected forms of entertaining and edifying simulation that were increasingly in demand in Meiji Japan. Most notably, Kawaura's participation in the fair shows how the nationalist-imperialist aspects of the Meiji exhibitionary complex always existed together and in tension with the role such institutions played in the creation of modern commercial enterprise and spectator publics.[25] Cinema was one part of an imperial display culture that included panoramas, "living exhibits," and zoos, which mobilized an acquisitive gaze and celebrated the forward march of civilization and its conquests.

The image of Mukōjima studio as the "Crystal Palace on the Sumida River" reminds us that early cinema was only a small part of a rich global cultural field in which new visual and spatial idioms were used to celebrate industrialization, stimulate consumption, structure national identity, and shape attitudes toward racial and ethnic "others," reproducing (and extending) the regulatory mechanisms of the modern nation-state while justifying imperialist expansion. In the nineteenth century the rise of industrial capitalism hastened the movement of people, technology, images, and information across national borders. Capitalist development not only involved the rapid growth of manufacturing and urbanization but also required new supplies of resources and labor, as well as external markets to ensure steady economic growth. This fueled the creation of global trade networks and colonial expansion throughout the nineteenth century, culminating in what Eric Hobsbawm has called "the Age of Empire" (1875–1914).[26] By the beginning of the twentieth century, extensive connections among industrial capitalism, tourism, colonialism, the transportation industry, and travel media reflected the expansionist impulse to conquer new territory. As Tom Gunning has observed, their conjunction produced a "truly modern perception" of time and space that was shaped by technology, speed, and "a belief that images can somehow deliver what they portray."[27] This acquisitive gaze, which went on to powerfully shape the visual and display cultures of modernity, found its apogee in the nineteenth- and early twentieth-century world's fairs and their unabashed celebrations of industry and empire.

Global trade, technology transfer and internationalization, the development of military and industrial power in pursuit of colonial ambitions, as well as national defense—all played a crucial role in Japan's modernization following the Meiji Restoration of 1868, which was precipitated in large part by British and American gunboat diplomacy to force Japan to trade with Europe and America. During the Meiji period Japan sent emissaries abroad on study missions to learn about Western industry, technology, education, military development, and government. The world's fairs provided important opportunities for Japanese to learn about Western science, society, culture, and commerce, and their exhibition practices played a role in shaping Japanese national identity and imperial culture.[28] As Aso notes, the Japanese state adopted the linked forms of collection, curation, and public display that flourished in Europe and America in the 1870s, which it used to "raise Japan's international profile to gain a share in global markets and to harness for its own ends the symbolic tools of Euro-American imperial power."[29] Aso traces how the visual, spatial, and rhetorical strategies developed by the Japanese state for use in government museums, national expositions, and delegations to international world's fairs soon spread to private sector museums, as well as commercial entities such as department stores. First conceived as a tool for mass education, the museum evolved into "a mechanism to mobilize the populace for industrialization."[30] Later on, commercial department stores adopted museum-like tactics, teaching the public how to be ideal consumers.

Japan's modern culture (including its cinema) was permeated with foreign influences; at the same time, Japan's position within an uneven global power structure necessarily tempered the utopian imagination that posited modernity as limitless mobility, fluidity, and potency. Japan's uncertain yet ambitious position within the world order suggests that the equivocal image of Mukōjima's glass studio as the "longed-for Crystal Palace" is what Walter Benjamin would call a "dialectical image." Benjamin argues that the anxieties of modernization are sometimes negotiated through the return of "primal" images of futurity, which reframe the unsettlingly new as kitsch. Writing of industrializing Europe, he suggests that such dialectical images provided a means of enjoying modernity in a form that offered respite from the pressures of unbridled development and fears of failure:

Corresponding to the form of the new means of production, which in the beginning is still ruled by the form of the old (Marx), are images in the collective consciousness in which the new is permeated with the old. These images are wish images; in them the collective seeks both to overcome and to transfigure the immaturity of the social product and the inadequacies in the social organization of production. . . .
 . . . Ambiguity is the appearance of dialectic in images, the law of dialectics at a standstill. This standstill is utopia and the dialectical image, therefore, dream image.[31]

In Japan, "nostalgic" Western buildings such as Nikkatsu Mukōjima studio, the likes of which never actually existed in Japan's own past, created accessible, dream-like images of modernity for popular consumption. These images enabled the public to encounter modernity and imagine its forward-looking utopian possibilities without a sense of constraint or compulsion. The importation of historical European architectural forms allowed the West to be represented as the past rather than as Japan's future, deferring the problem of "Westernization" and allowing Japanese to enjoy the subversive pleasure of "looking back" at Europe and America. I would argue this was especially the case with Nikkatsu Mukōjima studio's glass architecture, given Japan's late adoption of glass under the conditions of rapid top-down modernization in a race to prove its mettle to the imperialist West.

Cinema, with its "virtual voyages" to other times and places, played an important role in shaping fantasies of modernization.[32] A technological medium that made modernity accessible as sensuous representations, even before modern lifestyles and conveniences were a reality in Japan, cinema made it possible for audiences to adopt a reflexive attitude toward modernization and attendant transformations in the built environment.[33] The importance of the studio in this regard and the history of the studio as an architectural form, site of industrial production, and locus of cultural meaning is often overlooked. Yet as Brian Jacobson has persuasively argued, new, modern film studios existed within a "circuit of production and reproduction" through which newly built spaces refashioned the city while, in parallel fashion, "cinematic technology offered a means both to reimagine the built environment and to re-create artificial worlds on the screen."[34]

Mukōjima's vexed image can be used to examine Japan's fascination with Western modernity. Japan's internalization of imperialist ideology was troubled by its semicolonial relation to the West, but dialectical images such as the "Crystal Palace on the Sumida River" pleasurably circumvented linear temporal narratives of development and progress according to which Japan would always be "behind" the West. The studio—its design and its proximity to Asakusa's innovative spaces of play—allows us to trace relationships among Japanese cinema, urban architecture, and industrial modernity, drawing our attention to the role of cinema and cinematic architecture in disseminating (and mediating) fantasies of mobility, progress, mastery, and mutability.

PHANTASMAGORIC ASAKUSA

Kawaura's travels provide a concrete link between Nikkatsu Mukōjima studio and the world's fairs, but a more likely explanation for the fantastical image of Nikkatsu Mukōjima studio as Tokyo's own Crystal Palace is the studio's visibility from the entertainment district of Asakusa. Asakusa epitomized the confluence of stimulating display, play, and simulation found at world's fairs and their concessions. Located in northeast-central Tokyo, near the industrial wards of Honjo and Fukagawa, Asakusa was a magnet for Tokyo's burgeoning urban masses. Here miscellaneous entertainments were presented in a mixture of architectural formats, which included spectacular Occidental-style buildings, smaller makeshift stalls, and back-alley tents that were eventually cleared out to eliminate fire hazards.[35] Most of these entertainments were run by small entrepreneurs, but some of Asakusa's bigger ventures were backed by prominent statesmen and industrialists, and a number of attractions were modeled on entertainments introduced at the world's fairs. In Japan the panorama, the bazaar (*kankōba,* a precursor to the modern department store), and pavilion architecture first appeared at domestic National Industrial Exhibitions inspired by the world's fairs before going on to become popular attractions in Asakusa.[36] World's fairs featured signature works of architecture that represented the latest achievements in design and engineering. These structures ushered in a new gaze desirous of modern commodities and introduced the spatial, architectural, and visual forms that would become synonymous with modernity and modernism. They included, in Paris, the Trocadéro (an important site for the 1867, 1878, and 1937 fairs), the Galerie des machines (used in 1889 and 1910), and the Grand Palais (1900). Yoshimi Shun'ya argues that even Asakusa's "pavilion-style movie theaters" were inspired by exposition architecture and transformed Asakusa's streets into a standing exhibition space (fig. 1.3).[37]

Asakusa's reputation as a place for diversion long predates the Meiji era. The district grew up around Sensōji temple (est. AD 645), an important Buddhist pilgrimage site. It developed into a lively amusement quarter during the Edo period (1603–1868) after the shogunate transferred the pleasure quarters and theaters of Edo (present-day Tokyo) to the outskirts of the capital city. Asakusa became a popular stop for travelers en route to the red-light district of Yoshiwara. In contrast to much larger, grander temple precincts in other parts of the capital that enjoyed the sponsorship of wealthy patrons, Sensōji thrived on commercialism. The temple made money by leasing its lands to merchants and entertainers, and it is known for having one of Japan's oldest *nakamise,* a shopping street lined with teahouses, souvenir shops, and other businesses catering to travelers—a precursor to the modern enclosed shopping arcade (*shōtengai).* Asakusa was a zone for "prayer and play"—and consumption.[38]

In 1873 Sensōji temple's green space was requisitioned by the Tokyo city government and designated as one of Tokyo's first public parks. In the prewar and

FIGURE 1.3. *View of the Twelve-Storied Pagoda at Asakusa Park, Tokyo,* by Tamamura Kōzaburō, ca. 1895. Photograph showing the Asakusa Jūnikai, which was inspired by the Eiffel Tower, viewed from Hyōtan Pond. Gift of Jean S. and Frederic A. Sharf, collection of Museum of Fine Arts, Boston.

wartime periods the most famous view of Asakusa's "movie town" was the approach from Asakusa Park and Hyōtan Pond. Postcard photographs of Asakusa's movie theaters were usually taken from this vantage point. Jinnai Hidenobu, an architectural historian, argues that wide-open spaces and novel views of the city were engineered to stimulate a curious and acquisitive public gaze that reinforced the values of modernization. Urban views from towers and observation decks communicated a sense of mastery and symbolic power to the beholder. Such majestic vistas were an important spatiovisual trope in Tokyo during the Meiji period.[39] They offered a spectatorial position comparable to what Albert Boime has called the "magisterial gaze," referring to the commanding views found in American landscape painting circa 1830 to 1865 that gave expression to Manifest Destiny.[40] It is no coincidence that the masterful views provided by Asakusa entertainments were based on attractions at the world fairs, for Asakusa's architectural wonders likewise catered to the public's desire to consume other times and places. These entertainments—which showcased an increasingly mobile, far-reaching, technologically augmented gaze—coincided with Japan's emergence as a modern nation-state and imperial power.

Asakusa had two centers: Sensōji and its *nakamise,* and the entertainment district Rokku (Sixth District), where cinemas and popular commercial *misemono* could be found. These areas were frequently packed with visitors, and Asakusa became famous as a lively *sakariba,* or "bustling space," an urban area that draws large crowds. In Rokku unique building structures were developed to manage large groups of people, allowing exhibitors to usher long lines of patrons through displays and around viewing platforms. Around the beginning of the nineteenth century its novel architectural attractions included a faux Mt. Fuji with a viewing deck at its summit (1887–89); the circular panorama Nippon Panoramakan (1890–1909), which took its place when "Mt. Fuji" closed; the Suizokukan (1899–ca. 1933), Japan's first continuously operating aquarium to be built at a distance from the seashore, where Casino Follies stage shows (1929–33) took place on the second floor; and the Ryōunkaku or "Cloud-Scraper" tower (1890–1923), a brick minaret known by its popular nickname, the Asakusa "Twelve-Stories" or Jūnikai.

This bizarre panoply of structures shared a common attraction: each offered some stunning artificial environment or novel vantage point, such as an underwater view or a commanding panorama. Wooden, painted "Mt. Fuji" was more than 100 feet tall and measured approximately 886 feet around the base. Visitors climbed a winding, twelve-hundred foot path to a viewing platform at the pinnacle of the structure. From here, notices proclaimed, Tokyo could be viewed in every direction, with sightlines to Shinagawa Bay, as well as to the mountains and hills of Akasaka, Nikkō, Tsukuba, Hakone, Ōyama, and the real Mt. Fuji, which was located approximately sixty miles southwest of its imitation.[41] The Nippon Panoramakan occupied a sixteen-corner building approximately 66 feet high and 476 feet in circumference. It opened with a panorama of the 1861 Battle of Vicksburg by the French artists Joseph Bertrand and Lucien Sergent. Visitors climbed to an elevated platform to view the 360-degree landscape. This architecture, painterly elements, lighting effects, and set dressing worked together to create a vivid sense of actually being at the scene.[42] The exhibit was changed multiple times, including a popular installation of the 1894 Battle of Pyongyang in the First Sino-Japanese War, before the building was demolished in 1910.[43]

Another key example of the influence of exposition architecture is the Asakusa Jūnikai, which similarly offered visitors a commanding 360-degree view. The inspiration for the Jūnikai was the Eiffel Tower, which was constructed for the 1889 Exposition universelle.[44] Like "Mt. Fuji" before it, the Asakusa Jūnikai afforded a sweeping panorama of the city. Rather than climb stairs, however, customers ascended the tower via the first electric elevator in Japan. At 225 feet tall with a brick-and-wooden frame, Jūnikai may seem insignificant compared to the 984-foot, open-lattice, wrought-iron Eiffel Tower, but in 1890 brick was a relatively new building material in Japan. This was the construction material of choice for Tokyo's "bricktown," Ginza, a government-designated urban renovation project that was designed to help modernize the city, carried out between 1872 and 1877.

Last but not least, Asakusa's displays brought nature and culture together while introducing new distinctions between civilization and savagery that exculpated the violent expansion of imperialist countries. In modernizing Japan, Ian Jared Miller writes, zoological and anthropological displays "had weighty implications at a time when notions of biological race and the 'struggle for survival' (seizon kyōsō) were beginning to politicize, in an explicitly global context, the distinction between people and other animals."[45] Asakusa's entertainments participated in the exploitation, taming, and framing of nature that Miller terms "ecological modernity" to distinguish this use of nature from "disenchantment" or denaturing. Rather, Miller argues, ecological modernity encompassed novel forms of interpenetration between the natural and artificial that created a new understanding of nature as distinct from human civilization.[46]

Like the zoos that Miller examines, which gathered and showcased animals as "totems of conquered lands or foreign peoples,"[47] simulations like the faux Mt. Fuji and Nippon Panoramakan exhibits promoted nationalism and popularized an avaricious gaze. Their shared mode of viewing the world was the product of modern transit and communications, new building technologies and materials, and a restless imperial imagination.[48] The Asakusa Suizokukan (Asakusa Aquarium) exemplifies the link between such displays and the imperial project of expanding into and dominating the world's natural resources and markets. Like the film studio, the zoo, and the panorama, Japan's aquariums were introduced during the Meiji period and were deeply intertwined with the modernizing state's military, economic, social, cultural, and scientific policies. Aquariums, fisheries, marine laboratories, observation posts, and experimental stations direct our attention to "the environmental dimensions of empire," which entailed new ways of appropriating, displaying, classifying, and imagining nature.[49] Like the zoo or aquarium, the film studio was a technology that subjected nature to simplification, control, and management. As Jacobson notes, "both early cinema and modern architecture shared a place in the more general creation of an artificial built environment—a rationally constructed world that approximated nature using cinematic and building technologies."[50] The Jūnikai, the fake Mt. Fuji, the Nippon Panoramakan, and the Suizokukan—much like all these forms, Mukōjima's glass studio allowed for the capture, rationalization, and display of the natural through its use of modern building technology and carefully designed space. Recognition of this fact allows for fuller consideration of Japan's ecological modernity and its relationship to imperialism.

Ironically, although Mukōjima's materials and design allowed filmmakers to create controlled artificial environments, the studio's striking riverside location made it highly vulnerable to inclement weather. The studio was built before the Arakawa River drainage canal was completed in 1924. As a result, every autumn typhoon season, Mukōjima flooded. To prevent water damage, the glass studio had an elevated floor that was built to the same height as the dike east of the canal. Nikkatsu employees had to walk up seven or eight stone steps before entering the studio, which created enough space beneath the studio for a full-grown man to walk upright under the floor. Mukōjima's administrative offices and film labs were built in a similar fashion, with the floor raised above the ground.[51] In 1917 the glass stage was blown over in a typhoon on September 30, bringing the building crashing down on a grove of paulownia trees to the north. Luckily, these trees prevented the glass stage from damaging the studio offices. During the month it took to rebuild, Mukōjima films were shot in a tent that was taken out of storage, a relic from the days of Yoshizawa Shōten.[52] Six years later, Mukōjima narrowly survived destruction in the September 1923 Great Kanto Earthquake and fires. In this instance the studio's position on the east bank of the Sumida River seems to have protected it from the worst of the firestorms.[53] Reports of earthquake damage to the studio vary, but devastation and unrest in Tokyo caused Mukōjima staff to be transferred to Kyoto by November 14, 1923, and the studio was closed.[54]

AFTERIMAGES

In Japanese film history Nikkatsu Mukōjima studio is primarily remembered for its *shinpa* melodramas and resistance toward the Hollywoodization of Japanese film.[55] Examination of the studio design, its building materials, and its location allows for broader consideration of Nikkatsu Mukōjima in the context of Tokyo's built environment and in relation to the role that architecture, city planning, display cultures, and visual media played in the Meiji-era imperial imagination. The fact that many Asakusa entertainments used new technology and novel structures for the purposes of simulation, or to otherwise harness and frame nature, suggests fresh directions for studying Japanese empire—especially in its cultural and ecological dimensions. Finally, Asakusa's kitsch underscores modernizing Japan's equivocal position within the fin de siècle global hierarchy, pushing us to seek out more complex models for understanding processes of acculturation and "development" and to account for the affective and experiential dimensions of modernity.

The description of Kawaura's studio as the "Crystal Palace" evokes the splendor of nineteenth-century Europe, the fantastical qualities of glass materials, and the pomp of the industrial exhibitions. It conjures up a visionary image of modernity: a futuristic image of pure potentiality derived from one of the world's most famous celebrations of empire and industry. The seemingly anachronistic image, which gestures simultaneously toward the future and the past, has much to tell us about the political and economic contexts for the emergence of Japan's film industry. It denotes the utopian, phantasmagoric dimensions of modernization in a rapidly industrializing country in which modernization was usually framed as a strenuous effort to "catch up" with the West. Images such as Mukōjima's Crystal Palace propose alternative narratives of how we understand modern life and visual culture in urban Japan.

The attitude expressed by "longed-for Crystal Palace" corresponds to what Arjun Appadurai has termed "nostalgia without memory" in the global cultural economy, a seemingly anachronistic nostalgia that arises from the paradoxical temporal juxtapositions produced by global cultural flows. In his examination of a variety of "imaginary landscapes" produced by the forces of globalization, Appadurai argues that the uneven circulation of images, people, ideas, technology, capital, and commodities across national borders has resulted in the erosion of place-based and historically situated forms of identity and contributed to "certain fundamental disjunctures between economy, culture and politics" that reflect the deterritorializing forces of global capitalism.[56] In the global cultural economy, consumers in the developing world avidly consume the old cultural products of advanced capitalist countries and savor the contradictions produced by decontextualization and localization as a special form of temporality. This is what Appadurai terms "nostalgia without memory": nostalgia for another culture's old products, which do not belong to one's own historical past yet seem nostalgic when consumed for the first time. Linear modernization theories and center-periphery models would attribute nostalgia without memory to the "lag" that characterizes the "belatedness" of modernizing countries (thus the affect of sadness and longing), but Appadurai (like Benjamin) sees this nostalgia as kitsch, which suggests a more savvy, critical, entrepreneurial twist on anachronism. As Appadurai observes, deterritorialization upsets linear models of development that imagine industrializing countries as following in the footsteps of more developed countries. The mixed temporality that Appadurai analyzes is not new; it can also be found in earlier moments of global connectedness—for instance, in Meiji-era Japan, when the newly opened country voraciously consumed the entire history of Western images and ideas, sometimes without regard to "proper" historical sequence.

Viewed from Asakusa, a carnivalesque space where multiple times and places were juxtaposed, Nikkatsu Mukōjima studio was a phantasmagoric Crystal Palace. Enjoying the glass studio in this fashion, spectators could savor the fantasy of modernity without the anxieties of modernization and indulge in the pleasure of looking "back" at the West. The epithet "longed-for Crystal Palace" conveys nostalgia without memory for a vision of the future from the past.

NOTES

My research for this essay was made possible by an AAS Northeast Asia Council (NEAC) Japan Studies Grant.

1. See, e.g., Tomita Mika's discussion of *rensa geki* (chain drama) shooting and publicity practices in "Eiga toshi Kyōto" (Film city Kyoto), 41–44. Nikkatsu Mukōjima studio director Tanaka Eizō

discusses public film shoots and creative crowd-control techniques, such as using free movie tickets to get spectators to move on, in "Nikkatsu Mukōjima jidai (ni kai)" (The age of Nikkatsu Mukōjima [Part 2]), *Shinario* (Scenario) 11, no. 3 (March 1955): 28.

2. Urabe Kumeko, "Eiga koso waga inochi" (Film is my life), 26.

3. Urabe, "Eiga koso waga inochi," 25.

4. Urabe, 31–32.

5. Tanaka, "Nikkatsu Mukōjima jidai" (The age of Nikkatsu Mukōjima), *Shinario* (Scenario) 11, no. 1 (Jan. 1955): 32–33.

6. See Baxter, "On the History and Ideology of Film Lighting," 83–106.

7. For more on pure film discourse and Nikkatsu Mukōjima studio see Bernardi, *Writing in Light;* Gerow, *Visions of Japanese Modernity;* and Lewis, "*Blood and Soul* (1923)."

8. Tanaka, "Nikkatsu Mukōjima jidai" (Jan. 1955): 31. See also Baba, "Sugiyama Shigemaru Mukōjima tei" (Sugiyama Shigemaru's Mukōjima residence), 61–73.

9. *Nikkatsu shijūnenshi* (Nikkatsu's forty-year history), 41.

10. For more information on the layout of Mukōjima studio see Tanaka, "Nikkatsu Mukōjima jidai" (Jan. 1955): 30–31; and Shimazaki Kiyohiko's diagrams of the studio, printed in *Mukōjima satsueijo* (Mukōjima studio), 11.

11. Yonemura, "Meiji kōki kara Taishō shoki" (From late Meiji to early Taishō), 123.

12. See Nakanodō, "Modern Japanese Glass," n.p.

13. Oka, "Bīdoro kara garasu e" (From *bīdoro* to glass).

14. Nakanodō, "Modern Japanese Glass," n.p.

15. Chaiklin, "Miracle of Industry," 174–75.

16. For more on glass-and-iron architecture and Méliès's studio see Jacobson, *Studios Before the System,* chap. 5.

17. Anderson and Richie, *The Japanese Film,* 27.

18. Bennett, "The Exhibitionary Complex."

19. Aso, *Public Properties,* 26.

20. See Oshima, "Denenchōfu."

21. *Official Guide to the Louisiana Purchase Exposition,* 27.

22. *Official Guide to the Louisiana Purchase Exposition,* 29.

23. For a thorough account of the curation and reception of the exhibit see Parezo and Fowler, *Anthropology Goes to the Fair.*

24. Irie, "Yoshizawa Shōten shū Kawaura Ken'ichi" (Head of Yoshizawa Shōten Kawaura Ken'ichi), 34.

25. Peter High writes of the Russo-Japanese War films: "One of the most remarkable elements about these documentary 'news' features was the deep reverberation they managed to set up within the Japanese viewer. We see here the beginning of a two-faceted process; a process which similar footage of first world war Europe would go far to complete. First, there was the awakening of the Japanese people to a sense of 'world citizenship' stretching beyond the confines of their island nation. The second was the creation of a true Japanese 'public' in the modern sense of the word" (High, "Dawn of Cinema in Japan," 36–37).

26. Hobsbawn, *The Age of Empire.*

27. Gunning, "'Whole World within Reach,'" 37, 30.

28. Yoshimi, *Toshi no doramaturgī* (Dramaturgy of the city); Aso, *Public Properties.*

29. Aso, *Public Properties,* 4.

30. Aso, 4.

31. Benjamin, "Paris, the Capital of the Nineteenth Century," 33, 40.

32. See Ruoff, *Virtual Voyages.*

33. See Miriam Hansen's argument that "cinema was not only part and promoter of technological, industrial-capitalist modernity; it was also the single most inclusive, *public* horizon in which both the liberating impulses and the pathologies of modernity were reflected, rejected, or disavowed, transmuted or negotiated, and it made this new mass public visible to itself and to society" ("Fallen Women, Rising Stars," 12).

34. Jacobson, "'Imponderable Fluidity' of Modernity," 203; Jacobson, *Studios Before the System,* 77.

35. On April 10, 1896, a fire broke out at the Daikokukan, a *misemono* (attractions) hall displaying "living dolls" *(iki ningyō),* and consumed 183 buildings, burning down 90 percent of Asakusa Rokku (the "sixth district," or main drag). Subsequent to the fire, fireproofing regulations were introduced, and lean-tos were prohibited. *Enko kōgyōshi* (History of Asakusa Rokku entertainment), 48.

36. For more on the influence of expositions and their role in engendering the "new gaze," see Yoshimi, *Toshi no doramaturgī.*

37. Yoshimi, *Media jidai no bunka shakaigaku* (Cultural sociology of the media age), 190.

38. Hur, *Prayer and Play in Late Tokugawa Japan.*

39. See Jinnai, *Tokyo,* 119–70; see also Liotta and Miyawaki, "Study on the History of 'Cinema-City.'"

40. Boime, *The Magisterial Gaze.*

41. See, e.g., "Asakusa Koen ni kanseishita 'mokuzō Fuji-san'" ("Wooden Mt. Fuji" completed in Asakusa), *Yomiuri shinbun,* Nov. 9, 1887, morning ed., 3.

42. *Enko kōgyōshi,* 46.

43. For more on the Nippon Panorama and panoramas in Japan see Kusahara, "Panorama Craze in Meiji Japan."

44. Maeda, "Asakusa as Theater," 150.

45. Miller, *Nature of the Beasts,* 5.

46. Miller, 3.

47. Miller, 63.

48. See, e.g., Schivelbusch, *The Railway Journey,* 52–69; and Uricchio, "'Proper Point of View,'" 225–38. As Boime argues in *Magisterial Gaze,* "this peculiar gaze represents not only a visual line of sight but an ideological one as well" (2).

49. Tsutsui, "The Pelagic Empire," 32.

50. Jacobson, *Studios Before the System,* 110.

51. Tanaka, "Nikkatsu Mukōjima jidai" (Jan. 1955): 30–31.

52. Tanaka, "Nikkatsu Mukōjima jidai (yon)" (The age of Nikkatsu Mukōjima [Four]), *Shinario* (Scenario) 11, no. 5 (May 1955): 36.

53. For more on damage sustained by Tokyo-area studios, see Lewis, *Powers of the Real.*

54. *Nikkatsu shijūnenshi,* 47.

55. See, e.g., Lewis, "*Blood and Soul* (1923)."

56. Appadurai, "Disjuncture and Difference in the Global Cultural Economy," 6.

2

Regulating Light, Interiors, and the National Image

Electrification and Studio Space in Silent-Era Brazil

Rielle Navitski

The genesis of Brazil's best-known contribution to world cinema—the Cinema Novo movement of the 1960s and beyond—can be traced to a rejection of the carefully modulated cinematic illusions offered by the film studio. Cultivating an "aesthetic of hunger," in Glauber Rocha's famous phrase, Cinema Novo foregrounded the populace's poverty of resources and the filmmaker's poverty of means by stripping away the apparatus of industrial production and discarding classical codes of filmmaking in favor of disorienting montage, jarring handheld camera, and searingly bright images.[1] The practice of shooting with available light and without filters—a technique sometimes referred to as "naked lens" or *lente nua*—was held to display the unique intensity of Brazil's tropical sunlight, forging a visual style truly autonomous from dominant international standards.[2] According to standard accounts of Cinema Novo's emergence, these practices embodied a radical difference from the Hollywoodized aesthetics and mode of production represented by São Paulo's Companhia Cinematográfica Vera Cruz. In operation between 1949 and 1954, Vera Cruz constituted an ambitious attempt to establish studio filmmaking in Brazil—complete with glossy production values, sizable budgets, and actors on contract—executed with largely European technicians under the leadership of globe-trotting Brazilian cineaste Alberto Cavalcanti.[3] Whereas some critics perceived a tension between cinematography that hewed to international standards and sensitivity to Brazil's particularities—one opined in 1954 that Vera Cruz's cinematographers, "while competent technicians, have not yet assimilated the light and features of the land"—in Cinema Novo the visual quality of the image was itself conceived as a function of environmental conditions, particularly in the drought-stricken territories of the country's Northeast.[4]

The conventional antimony between Cinema Novo and Vera Cruz offers little critical traction for understanding the transnational coproductions and transmedia ventures that have shaped Brazil's audiovisual sphere from the *retomada* of the 1990s—a resurgence of film production following the dismantling of Brazil's state production and distribution infrastructure through President Fernando Collor de Mello's neoliberal reforms and the subsequent passage of the 1993 Audiovisual Law, which established tax incentives for film production—to the present. Yet the stark opposition between location shooting with natural light and filming within a carefully controlled studio environment—the latter viewed as embodying a mastery of imported architectural, technical, and economic models that long remained elusive in Brazil—is deeply embedded in the nation's cinematic history, structuring debates around ideals and practices of film production that date back to the silent era.

These debates gathered momentum in the mid-1920s in the pages of Rio de Janeiro film magazines *Selecta, Para Todos . . .* , and *Cinearte,* which waged a press campaign in support of Brazilian cinema that resonated on a national scale.[5] The magazines linked ambitions for the creation of a national film industry with a rhetoric of abundant natural resources—picturesque scenery and powerful if excessive natural light—that could be exploited through location shooting. Such discourses dovetailed with a national economy rooted in the export of raw materials and agricultural commodities, especially coffee. Somewhat paradoxically, given this emphasis on landscape as a resource ripe for extraction via the camera, the campaign's leaders, Pedro Lima and Adhemar Gonzaga, vehemently condemned the production of *films naturaes* (nonfiction works such as travelogues and promotional films), which they viewed as lacking audience appeal and thus as counterproductive for the incipient national industry.[6] Even more troublingly for these early film critics, the contingent character of nonfiction filmmaking threatened to "blacken" cinematic visions of the nation, both by making Afro-Brazilian, indigenous, and mixed-race populations visible onscreen and through technical lapses in the exposure and developing of footage. Anxieties about Brazil's demographic makeup—fueled by racist perceptions of nonwhite populations as ill-equipped for industrial modernity—became intertwined with fears of a lack of technical mastery.[7] The carefully controlled mise-en-scène of studio-made fiction films was thus closely linked to the projection of an image of Brazil as an industrialized and predominantly white nation. The imagined space of the studio promised the effective management of electric light—a powerful signifier of modernization—and carefully rendered interior settings, viewed by journalists as key preconditions for the establishment of a viable industry.

In practice, the strategies of semiprofessional film enthusiasts in the rapidly growing cities of Rio de Janeiro and São Paulo and the states of Minas Gerais, Pernambuco, and Rio Grande do Sul, among others, inevitably deviated from ideals of modern studio production shaped by practices dominant in the United States and Western Europe. Few film producers had the means to construct purpose-built studio spaces or acquire up-to-date equipment. Many shot with cameras considered obsolete or designed for amateur use and used precarious homegrown facilities for developing and editing. Most filmed in repurposed structures or temporary settings, ranging from modified buildings and sets erected outdoors to exterior and interior locations. As I detail below, filmmakers made creative use of available materials to build and illuminate sets, but they rarely managed to render interiors—held up as the litmus test of a film's visual quality—to the satisfaction of Rio de Janeiro critics. Instead, building on tendencies established in the early cinema period, film enthusiasts often capitalized on the appeal of location shooting, incorporating visual strategies akin to the early "local film" or "local view" that offered spectators an experience of "place recognition," linked with notions of filmmaking as a source of civic pride and a means of showcasing local modernity.[8]

The choice of locations for improvised film studios and temporary shooting locations demonstrates this impulse. For example, in Porto Alegre film producers set up shop in a repurposed pavilion built for public expositions that attested to the state's economic prosperity and technological modernity. In a parallel development several Brazilian feature films of the period made pointed references to local industry (framed as a testament to economic development), while young industrialists spearheaded the construction and repurposing of São Paulo studios. This appeal to the local in 1920s Brazilian cinema was often disparaged by critics, who called for the consolidation of scattered and precarious regional filmmaking efforts into a unified national industry.[9] Even as they reported enthusiastically on production activities dispersed across Brazil as evidence of progress toward this aim, journalists called for the centralization of filmmaking activities, querying, "Where will the Los Angeles of Brazil Be?" and eagerly reporting on ambitious, albeit never-realized, plans for studio complexes.[10]

Drawing on press coverage of silent-era studios, production stills, and surviving footage from the period, this essay traces how rhetorical and physical constructions of studio space—particularly those centered on the regulation of light and the rendering of interiors—map a divide between dominant, Hollywood-inflected ideals and locally situated architectures and practices of film production in 1920s Brazil. Implicit in this divide is a tension between technically masterful fictions that could offer a cosmetic version of Brazilian modernity and films whose appeal was rooted in the contingent, the topical, and the locally specific. Tracing the role of such appeals—mobilized in the face of technical precarity—from Brazil's earliest narrative films, I show how the elusive ideal of the electrified studio helps illuminate local uses of the "industrial thought" shaped by Hollywood's global presence, highlighting how this imaginary intersected with hierarchies of race, region, and nation as US films entered their second decade of dominance on Brazilian screens.[11]

STUDIO ARCHITECTURE FROM THE "BELA ÉPOCA"
OF BRAZILIAN CINEMA TO THE 1920S

Brazil's earliest film studios emerged shortly after the opening of the country's first permanent movie theaters in late 1907 and the production of its earliest feature-length films in late 1908.[12] These developments overlapped closely: the filmmaking activities of enterprising producer-exhibitors in Rio de Janeiro (which at that time was Brazil's capital) and the rapidly industrializing city of São Paulo led to a short-lived production boom. Marked by the presence of hugely popular *filmes falados e cantantes* ("talking and singing films" based on operettas and musical revues and accompanied by vocal performances from behind the screen), as well as actualities, comedies, and dramas (often based on topical events), the period between 1908 and 1911 is sometimes described as a "Bela Época" of Brazilian cinema, a prelapsarian moment prior to the invasion of European (and, later, US) films.[13] In the 1990s, scholars began to critique the idealization of a Bela Época.[14] José Inácio de Melo Souza, for instance, argues convincingly that locally produced films were ultimately peripheral to the development of robust exhibition markets in Rio de Janeiro and São Paulo; an abundant supply of Pathé Frères and other French films played a much more significant role.[15] This moment does, however, mark the initial development of a short-lived studio infrastructure. Exhibitors invested in locally oriented films screened in their own establishments as a means of product differentiation, a strategy with lasting impact on film style and production throughout the silent era.

In a 1916 interview, pioneering camera operator Antônio Leal offered a retrospective account of these efforts: "The best stimulants to spectators' abundant attendance at the cinema are films of their own social life, live reportage. . . . We have already verified this here: films produced in 1908 and 1909 about more or less interesting occurrences, some of them taking advantage of the popular excitement left in the wake of great crimes, achieved in Rio and the states a success never equaled by great works of art, made with expense and care, executed in the great European studios."[16] Here, Leal references how a cycle of adaptations of real-life crimes shot in Rio and São Paulo from mid-1908 to early 1909—including Leal's *Os estranguladores* (The stranglers), a reconstruction of a 1906 jewelry store robbery and murder that is considered Brazil's first feature film, and three adaptations of a São Paulo case dubbed "The Crime of the Trunk" because the victim's body was concealed in a piece of luggage—competed successfully with imported films despite their comparative lack of technical polish.

Indeed, the sense of topicality and visual authenticity prized by local audiences—the reconstructions of real-life crimes took their cue from abundantly illustrated, sensationalistic press reports, with camera operators sometimes shooting at the "scene of the crime"—entered into tension with an incipient mode of studio filmmaking.[17] This tension is highlighted by the negative reception of *O crime da mala* (The crime of the trunk, 1908), the first narrative film shot in a studio constructed by Spanish impresario Francisco Serrador, who would consolidate the powerful exhibition-distribution conglomerate Companhia Cinematographica Brasileira a few years later.[18] Drawing on a suggestive press account of a prescreening of the film for journalists and censors, Melo Souza speculates that *O crime da mala* was rejected by viewers because of its uneasy positioning between reconstituted actuality and incipient fiction, since it failed to construct a convincingly coherent diegesis or to conform to audiences' foreknowledge of the participants and locations (mediated by the illustrated press).[19] In particular, viewers noted a jarring disconnect between the location where businessman Elias Farhat was murdered by his secretary Michel Traad and its appearance in the film. *O crime da mala,* now lost, was never exhibited publicly after this ill-fated showing.

Leal seems to have realized a better return on his investment in studio facilities (referred to in the press as "ateliers de 'pose'") constructed in early 1909 in a structure that apparently functioned as a boardinghouse, located in central Rio de Janeiro.[20] Little is known about this early studio; some retrospective accounts describe it as a glass-and-iron construction reminiscent of early French studios like Pathé and Gaumont (which Leal reported visiting during a 1906–7 trip to France).[21] But these commentators may be confusing it with a later glass-and-iron studio built by Leal in the 1910s.[22] Building on previous collaborations with personnel from the local theater scene, Leal used the facilities for the production of *Noivado de sangue* (Bloody engagement), a reconstruction of a young teacher's real-life shooting of her former lover, as well as the fictional *Um drama na Tijuca* (A drama in Tijuca), a tale of a an upper-class woman who poisons herself in the wake of an unhappy love affair that featured interiors crafted by theatrical set designer Emilio Silva, among other films.[23] But the illicit dealings of Leal's business partner Giuseppe Labanca, who was running an illegal gambling operation, apparently prompted the dissolution of Leal's production company, the Photo-Cinematographia Brasileira, shortly thereafter.[24]

Beginning in 1911, the limited form of vertical integration offered by the exhibitor-producer model waned as exhibition was increasingly centralized through Serrador's creation of a unified circuit of theaters supplied with imported productions. As the export of European films dwindled during World War I, Hollywood studios expanded aggressively into international markets, opening local distribution offices as a first step in conquering global screens.[25] Despite these challenging conditions for domestically produced films, Leal—who returned from a second sojourn in Europe in 1915—and a handful of other enthusiasts participated in a second wave of narrative film production, focusing on adaptations of Brazilian literary classics and films that capitalized on a local craze for French and US serial films.

As in the previous decade, filmmakers of the period capitalized on location shooting even as they moved to develop studio infrastructure. Leal's 1916 literary adaptation *A moreninha* (The little brunette) was shot in a mansion owned by the president of the Banco do Brasil, and Leal's competitor Luiz de Barros also filmed scenes in elegant Rio de Janeiro homes for his romantic drama *Vivo ou morto* (Dead or alive, 1916).[26] Encouraged by the favorable reception of *A moreninha,* Leal convinced a group of investors—including newspaper magnate Irineu Marinho, whose business ventures gave rise to the Globo media empire—to fund the production of *Lucíola* (an adaptation of a novel by José de Alencar) and the construction of a glass-walled studio in the neighborhood of Tijuca. The characteristics of such buildings, which let in abundant light but trapped heat, proved especially problematic in Rio de Janeiro's tropical climate, to the point that the actors had difficulty performing.[27] Furthermore, domestically produced films proved unable to quickly recoup the costs of studio infrastructure. Despite the relative success of *Lucíola,* Leal's investors suffered a significant loss that led them to abandon their partnership, though portions of the crime drama *A quadrilha do esqueleto* (The skeleton gang), financed in part by Marinho, were likely shot in Leal's studio before the two parted ways.[28]

Given economic and practical obstacles to the construction of studio facilities, it is unsurprising that press and publicity discourses stressed the appeal of real locations, used both in high-society dramas shot in wealthy locals' residences and in serial-influenced films that offered "the affective sensation of realistic thrills and [were] grounded in the practice of on-location shooting."[29] One suggestive press notice for *Os mistérios do Rio de Janeiro* (1917), a tale of military espionage planned as a serial but left uncompleted, suggests the idiosyncratic mixture of literary antecedents, upper-class cachet, and sensational action characteristic of films shot in Rio de Janeiro in the 1910s. *Os mistérios* is described as "a romance of adventures . . . of the most convoluted sort, which, because it takes place in well-known locations, will arouse great interest, always maintaining the spectator's attention, one moment in tragic romantic situations, the next in the splendor of our dwellings which are as lavish and tasteful as the most opulent in Europe, or in the marvelous exuberance of our incomparable landscapes."[30] These comments recall the fascination with urban space evident during the "Bela Época" while prefiguring fan magazines' rhetoric of landscape as a cinematic resource to be marshaled in staging Brazilian modernity in the following decade.

RACE, LIGHT, AND TECHNIQUE IN THE CAMPAIGN FOR BRAZILIAN CINEMA

In the mid-1920s, renewed enthusiasm among aspiring filmmakers in Rio, São Paulo, and beyond fed into growing public interest in national production fostered by the press campaign for Brazilian cinema. The statement accompanying the launch of the column "O cinema no Brasil" in April of 1924 is telling: "We want to attend a bit to cinema in Brazil. Who knows if we might wrest it from its stagnation?"[31] This perception of a dispiriting lull in Brazilian film production was due in part to film journalists' restricted definition of cinema, which explicitly discounted the range of nonfiction works—including newsreels, promotional films, and travelogues—that acted as the main source of income for the handful of professional camera operators working in Brazil in the period.[32] Lima, Gonzaga, and like-minded critics and readers condemned films commissioned by government bodies, wealthy landowners, and industrial magnates as *cavação* (literally, digging; figuratively, hustling), contending that only narrative features could attract popular audiences and allow producers to realize their export ambitions.[33] Equally if not more seductive was the prospect of projecting visions of a modern Brazil in fiction film.[34] In one typical statement, journalist J. C. Mendes de Almeida declared, "We need narrative film [*film de enredo*], film that shows a Brazil that is modern, strong, advanced, beautiful, and civilized!"[35] In a similar vein, Pedro Lima stressed the need for "a serious cinema, with criteria, with a story and acting, on a par with our environment, our possibilities, our natural beauties . . . not only to create a most profitable industry, but to bring civilization to the most recondite region of our territory, conquering all distances with a single sentiment of nationality, fortifying national unity in a single conviction, and making us known, admired, and respected abroad."[36]

Conversely, nonfiction films—particularly travelogues depicting remote and less industrialized areas of Brazil such as the Northeast, the Amazon, and Mato Grosso—were viewed as damaging to the national image, not least because indigenous and Afro-Brazilian populations had a particularly strong presence in these regions, whereas the Southeast was populated by a larger number of European immigrants and their descendants. The rejection of nonfiction films is quite frequently expressed in racialized terms. In a representative statement published in *Cinearte*, a reader from São Paulo lambasted the travelogue *O Brasil pittoresco* (Picturesque Brazil, Cornélio Pires, 1924), asking, "When will we end . . . this obsession with showing Indians, *caboclos*, blacks, beasts, and other 'rara avis' of this unfortunate land, to the eyes of the cinematic spectator? What if, by chance, one of these films ends up overseas? In addition to lacking art, lacking technique, this will leave the foreigner more convinced of what he thinks we are: a country the same or worse than Angola, the Congo or what have you."[37] The perceived need to project a favorable image for foreign observers evident here is deeply entwined with Brazil's historical status as a slave society. The common idiomatic expression *para inglês ver* (for the English to see) refers to Brazilian government's move to limit the slave trade under British pressure while permitting it in practice in the 1820s and 1830s. Here, colonized African territories and indigenous populations are invoked—in terms typical of the scientific racism of the period—as an index of the retrograde, and racially "undesirable" portrayals are framed in terms of a lack of cinematic "technique."

A troubling 1925 editorial in *Selecta* is particularly revealing of the imbrication of race, technique, and contingency in fan magazine discourse.[38] Describing footage of military exercises, the commentator writes, "A foreigner who sees this film would presume that all our people are black [*negra*]. Dark [*pretos*], the generals present; black [*negros*], the officials gathered in groups; black [*negras*] or *mulatas,* the ladies present at the ceremony; and darkness [*pretidão*] reigns over the rank and file taking part in the athletic exercises. There is a polo game, but we guarantee that those who took part could not distinguish themselves from their companions."[39] Here, the failure to obtain a "proper" exposure—to the extent of compromising the image's legibility—provokes racial anxiety. "Blackness" is described not only as dominating the mass of soldiers but also as ostensibly distorting the racial identities of officers and elite women. Alluding to the imperative to render white skin tones in a flattering manner, an imperative that, as Richard Dyer has shown, historically shaped cinematic technologies and production practices, the editorial also signals how the element of unpredictability inherent in nonfiction filmmaking—from inadequate or shifting natural light to difficulties managing the profilmic—threatened the desired image of Brazil as a white nation.[40] Discussions of cinematic technique in *Selecta,* *Para Todos* . . . , and *Cinearte* became bound up in a broader push to manage the national image through the production of fiction films in controlled studio environments explicitly modeled on Hollywood facilities.

Paradoxically, the racialized anxieties surrounding failures of technique in nonfiction filming in 1920s fan magazines coexisted with rhetoric highlighting Brazil's unique filming conditions and the effectiveness of homegrown camera operators. *Cinearte* commented in 1926, "Our light, the extra luminosity of our atmosphere, disorients all the foreign professionals who come to work here."[41] Perhaps in response to frequent attacks on the technical quality of Brazilian productions, filmmaker Luiz de Barros, in a 1924 article, praised locals' superior ability to manage the intensity of the nation's sunlight. Recalling the production of the Anglo-Brazilian Cinematographic Co.'s *Entre o amor e arte* (Between love and art, 1916), Barros observed the failure of a foreign camera operator who used "light meters, frosted glass, etc." to precisely measure and diffuse available light during shooting, only to respond in broken Portuguese after seeing the results: "Mi non comprende sol do Brasil" (Me no understand sun of Brazil).[42] By contrast, native-born João Stamato was supposedly able to shoot the same scene without exposure problems. Barros stressed the ingenuity of Brazilian camera operators who doubled as directors, lab technicians, and editors, all while coping with substandard film stock and outdated cameras.

Acknowledging the precarity of film enthusiasts' equipment, facilities, and resources, journalists nevertheless remained highly critical of Brazilian film's cinematography, measured in terms of the clarity and evenness of lighting in interior scenes with lavish sets, characteristics that were underlined as giving American films a competitive advantage over European productions.[43] One representative article in *Selecta* endeavored to explain "Why Our Films Are Not Perfect," citing "interior sets, which have been the greatest difficulty for those who wish to film, due to the lack of lighting, and even a studio to facilitate the construction of interior settings."[44] In the face of these uneven results, *Selecta, Cinearte,* and *Para Todos* . . . continually stressed the desirability of using artificial lighting in enclosed studio spaces. Indeed, the use of electric light was conceived as dividing professionals from amateurs—a distinction that held little practical meaning in the absence of self-sustaining production companies.[45] The section "Um pouco de technica" (A little technique), which targeted hobbyists, stressed that "the amateur operator rarely works with artificial illumination. This is for technicians, for professionals."[46]

Ironically, however, both film enthusiasts and professional camera operators continued to rely wholly or partially on natural light throughout the 1920s. Furthermore, even as *Cinearte* continually stressed a move toward artificial light as an ideal of technical modernity linked with Hollywood (which had begun the transition to windowless studios lit entirely by artificial means in the early 1920s), the magazine showcased hybrid natural-artificial lighting strategies in use in Europe.[47] Such hybrid forms were, in fact, closer to the reality of Brazilian film practice, revealing the disconnect between the idealized studio spaces and electric lighting practices advocated by fan magazines and their real-life counterparts. Rather than the wholesale transfer of imported studio models envisioned by illustrated magazines, film production spaces more often derived from existing infrastructures of manufacturing, transportation, and leisure, even while an investment in artificial lighting (by critics and practitioners alike) drove ongoing modifications to studio spaces.

IMPROVISING STUDIO ARCHITECTURE AND ELECTRIC INFRASTRUCTURE

As I have noted, many interior spaces used for filming in 1920s Brazil were mounted in the interstices of existing structures dedicated to entertainment, manufacturing, and even public expositions. Film enthusiasts' reliance on this infrastructure was deemphasized in press coverage; instead, these accounts highlighted spaces' similarities to their well-equipped international counterparts. In their eagerness to hail studio infrastructure as a tangible sign of Brazil's modernization, journalists glossed over how filmmakers' efforts often relied on the repurposing of spaces linked to the forms of local civic pride on display both in fiction and nonfiction films. Indeed, both retrofitted spaces and purpose-built studios were shaped by existing spatial and electrical infrastructure and often worked to perpetuate the investment in the topical and the local embedded in practices of location shooting. This was particularly true for filmmaking initiatives in the cities of Porto Alegre (capital of Brazil's southernmost state Rio Grande do Sul), São Paulo, Campinas (a secondary city in the state of São Paulo), and Cataguases, a town in the state of Minas Gerais.[48]

Logically enough, a number of film enthusiasts in the period developed makeshift studios within existing spaces for theatrical and cinematic entertainment that possessed stages and ample room. For example, the shooting of *Entre o amor e a arte* referenced above took place in "a small studio in the Club Recreio," a Rio de Janeiro theater.[49] Almeida Fleming, an exhibitor and filmmaker working in the town of Pouso Alegre in the state of Minas Gerais, constructed interior sets for his feature *Paulo e Virginia* (1924) in the backrooms of the movie theater he operated, the Cine Iris.[50] Similarly, the São Paulo film enthusiast Jayme Redondo shot a scene of his film *Fogo de palha* (Flash in the pan, 1927), set in an elegant restaurant, in the lobby of the Cine-Theatro Republica. In a description of the shoot, *Cinearte* stressed "the perfect distribution of powerful light, which flowed from the modern equipment." The magazine also noted a peculiarly modern ailment acquired by Redondo during production: "'Studio' conjunctivitis, caused by a battery of modern lamps, received directly from Germany."[51] (Redness, swelling, and watering of the eyes were common side effects of exposure to carbon arc lamps known as Klieg lights, a condition often called "Klieg eyes" in the United States.)

Other 1920s studio spaces overlapped with existing leisure infrastructures in less obvious ways. In Porto Alegre the expansive metal pavilion constructed for the city's second Exposição Agropecuária (agricultural fair) in 1912 housed two short-lived production companies in the 1920s. ITA-Film's *Amor que redime* (Redeeming love, E. C. Kerrigan, 1928) and Uni-Film's *Revelação* (Revelation, E. C. Kerrigan, 1929) were shot in the structure on Avenida 13 de Maio (now Avenida Getúlio Vargas) in Menino Deus, a residential neighborhood south of the city center. As was the case elsewhere, large-scale public expositions were closely intertwined with cinema in early twentieth-century Brazil; the 1908 Exposição Nacional in Rio de Janeiro boasted an on-site movie theater, and the exposition commemorating the centennial of Brazil's independence in 1922 gave rise to the Brazilian state's first venture into the production of sponsored films.[52]

Though the connections between cinema and the agricultural fair specifically are perhaps less obvious, both participated in civic displays of material prosperity. The 1912 Exposição Agropecuária was hailed as "attesting once again to the notable progress of our economic life"; indeed, cattle-raising and other agricultural activities had made Rio Grande do Sul one of Brazil's most prosperous states.[53] In addition to becoming a subject for promotional films, the agricultural exposition figured prominently in the narrative feature *Entre as montanhas de Minas* (Between the mountains of Minas Gerais, Manoel Talon, 1928) shot in Belo Horizonte in the state of Minas Gerais.[54] Beyond functioning as a "testament to development" (according to a published plot summary), the agricultural fair facilitates a chance encounter between the protagonist and the young woman who becomes his love interest.[55] In a move common in the period, the producers of *Entre as montanhas de Minas* sidestepped the need for studio facilities by focusing on physical action in exterior settings; a journalist commented, "The genre chosen for this first production was the adventure drama, because it [allows one] to dispense with the installation of costly studios."[56] Later, in 1927, the Porto Alegre pavilion hosted an automobile exposition sponsored by the Associação de Estradas de Rodagem, a local group that promoted automobile racing and the construction of motor vehicle infrastructure.[57] Following on these displays of agricultural prosperity and modern transportation technology, the repurposing of the space as studio—mediated through press reports—functioned as another means of placing local progress on display.[58]

The improvised nature of the pavilion-turned-studio, not surprisingly, was minimized in an unsigned newspaper account of a studio tour during the production of *Amor que redime*, given the revealing title "Hollywood in Miniature."[59] Dramatizing the moment of entry into the structure, the journalist writes, "We came unawares on the 'studio' hard at work. Powerful bulbs, lamps of various types, gushed light, in a brilliant flood. Despite the gloomy afternoon, there within was a dazzling artificial day, fed by electric energy." Even before introducing the creative personnel and actors—staples of the well-established fan magazine genre of the studio visit—this account emphasizes the abundance of electric light and the independence it offered from environmental conditions. Belying this account of nature-defying electric potency, the structure's power source was quite precarious: during the shooting of *Amor que redime*, and *Revelação* the following year, the crew was obliged to run a cable directly from a nearby trolley line to supply the arc lamps used on set with the necessary voltage, and filming was interrupted each time a vehicle passed.[60] *Revelação's* critical reception, however, highlighted what one reviewer described as "good, spacious interiors."[61]

Like a number of Brazilian fiction films of the 1920s, *Revelação* showcased the nation's growing industrialization by taking the factory as setting (in this case, a textile manufacturing plant the heroine inherits after her father's mysterious murder). Other examples include *Mocidade louca* (Mad youth, Felipe Ricci, 1927), and *Braza dormida* (Sleeping ember, Humberto Mauro, 1928), shot in Campinas and in Cataguases, respectively. In both films the factory—another textile factory in *Mocidade louca* and a sugar refinery in *Braza dormida*—becomes the site of an urbane young wastrel's regeneration through hard work and a romance with its owner's daughter.[62]

Suggesting the cross-pollination of film production and the expanding industrial sector, São Paulo film enthusiasts from wealthy backgrounds enjoyed unique

FIGURE 2.1. Two interior views of the Visual-Film Studio in São Paulo, built in a former sawmill that offered limited natural light. *Para Todos* . . . , May 16, 1925. Hemeroteca Digital Brasileira.

opportunities to mount film studios. Adalberto de Almada Fagundes, scion of a porcelain-manufacturing family, equipped the most ambitious São Paulo studio of the period, a repurposed sawmill located in the industrial neighborhood of Barra Funda.[63] An article in the *Estado de São Paulo* described the facility in terms that underscored the structure's size and means of illumination: "Visual-Film possesses, in the center of a large lot, an ample hangar, surrounded by high walls that end in windowpanes, receiving in this way all the brightness of day. There one finds, in separate compartments, offices, laboratories, workshops, a script library for the artists, and lastly, an enormous stage. . . . It is illuminated by powerful bulbs, reinforced by lamps of varying tonalities."[64] Photographs of the studio display the building's rectangular expanse, pitched roof, and high windows (fig. 2.1). While the building's size would have allowed for the construction of expansive sets, the structure was clearly not optimized to provide abundant natural light, necessitating the use of electric illumination.[65] Although Fagundes's ambitious studio infrastructure attracted significant attention from the press, the facility was used to shoot only a single film, *Quando elas querem* (When women love, E. C. Kerrigan, 1925). The film centers on the travails of Clarinda, who—like the heroines of *Revelação, Braza dormida,* and *Mocidade louca*—is an industrialist's daughter and finds herself obliged to marry a man she does not love in order to save her father's business.

Five years later, affluent film enthusiast Joaquim Garnier—who, like Fagundes, was the son of a manufacturer—repurposed a warehouse as a studio, attracting several São Paulo camera operators and would-be filmmakers who hoped to take advantage of the owner's resources (Garnier himself directed only one film in the studio, *Às armas* [To arms, 1930]).[66] For the urban drama *Fragmentos da vida* (Fragments of life, José Medina, 1929), a tale of two hapless drifters adapted from a story by O. Henry, the filmmaker rented Garnier's studio for scenes set in a church and a restaurant. *Fragmentos da vida* survives, and Medina's use of the

FIGURE 2.2. Natural and artificial sources illuminate the set during a scene from *Fragmentos da vida* (Fragments of life, 1929) in a relatively rare instance of studio shooting in 1920s São Paulo. Acervo da Cinemateca Brasileira/Sav/MinC. Reference number FB_1535_009.

studio appears to have facilitated relatively complex camera movement and continuity editing patterns rare for Brazilian films of the period. Surviving production stills for the restaurant scene show a two-walled set housed in a large wooden structure, lit both by spotlights and a skylight (fig. 2.2).

Medina later recalled that these scenes in *Fragmentos da vida* were the only ones that his frequent collaborator, cameraman Gilberto Rossi, shot in a studio during the period.[67] Medina and Rossi's first film, *Exemplo regenerador* (*Returning Point,* 1919), was shot on outdoor sets constructed in the backyard of Rossi's home.[68] *Exemplo regenerador,* which also survives, offers a convincing, evenly lit recreation of a bourgeois living room. This illusion is disrupted only by a gust of wind that disturbs a tablecloth, a brief lapse that highlights the limitations of outdoor shooting methods that provided ample light but left filming vulnerable to environmental disruptions. Perhaps ironically, Fagundes and Garnier's forays into studio construction were ultimately short-lived in comparison to the technically

FIGURE 2.3. Hanging fabric diffuses sunlight on the two-story set of *Soffrer para gozar* (Suffer to enjoy, 1923), located in Campinas. Acervo da Cinemateca Brasileira/Sav/MinC. Reference number FB_0119_023.

precarious but inexpensive filmmaking activities of more established professionals like Rossi and Medina.

The case of studio architecture and lighting practices in Campinas between 1923 and 1927—one of the best-documented cases of the period—suggests both the discursive weight placed on studio infrastructure and illumination as evidence of Brazilian cinema's industrial potential and the manner in which these ideals reshaped studio spaces, if not to the degree advocated by film critics. The first film produced in the city in the period, *João da mata* (John of the bush), was apparently shot without a dedicated studio space and largely (though not exclusively) with natural illumination. Carlos Roberto de Souza surmises that shooting took place in modified buildings, whose roofs were removed to allow sunlight to enter.[69] The filmmakers purchased metal bounce cards to direct sunlight and cloth draping to diffuse it; they also rented electric lamps.[70] The next film to be made in Campinas, *Soffrer para gozar* (Suffer to enjoy, E. C. Kerrigan, 1923), was shot in a purpose-built wooden structure located on the city's outskirts, near the railway station.[71] Large enough to accommodate a two-story set, the building was lit with a combination of diffused sunlight and incandescent lamps (fig. 2.3).[72]

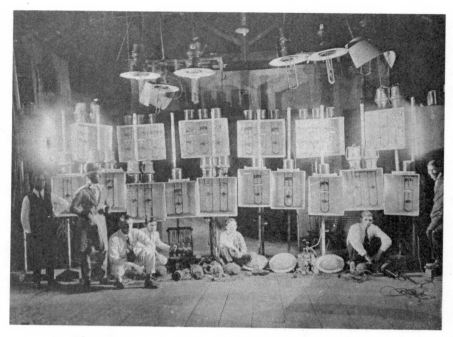

FIGURE 2.4. Film enthusiasts working with Campinas's APA-Film pose in front of an array of lamps attesting to the production company's technical resources. *Selecta*, Jan. 12, 1927. Acervo da Cinemateca Brasileira/Sav/MinC.

Campinas film enthusiasts and journalists alike continually cited the use of artificial light as material evidence of progression toward production values that would meet international standards. In a letter from director Felipe Ricci published in *Selecta*, the filmmaker stressed that for the filming of *Soffrer para gozar*, the company "used artificial light, although deficient; however, the lamps, with the insignificant output of 30,000 candles, were constructed in the [company's] own facilities! In its second production *A Carne* [The flesh, an adaptation of a naturalist novel by Brazilian author Júlio Ribeiro], APA-Film will make every effort so that it will be of a level to be compared with any good American film. Powerful reflectors will be used, with a total of 500,000 candles. This output will be used, because the filming will be done without the aid of sunlight."[73] This lighting equipment, acquired through the filmmakers' resourcefulness, was carefully arranged in a visually impressive display for a photograph published in *Selecta*, suggesting the weight given to technical resources by Rio de Janeiro journalists (fig. 2.4). The array of artificial lights is marshaled as evidence of APA-Film's seriousness and professionalism—qualities critics often found lacking in their fellow film enthusiasts—and the company's potential role in the consolidation of a Brazilian industry. During filming, Tullio made use of carbon arc lamps previously employed as streetlights in a nearby town and spotlights crafted using headlamps for locomotives owned by a local railway company.[74] This lighting equipment was arranged in a second purpose-built studio "inspired by Warner [Bros.]'s studios, naturally on a smaller scale," whose construction appears to have absorbed the profits from the exhibition of *A carne*, bankrupting the company.[75]

Ironically, as we have seen in the case of Antônio Leal's second studio, investment in studio infrastructure tended to truncate self-sustaining film production in early twentieth-century Brazil rather than guaranteeing it. Tullio, however, regrouped to make a final film in partnership with employees of the Mogyana Railway company, the aforementioned *Mocidade louca*, which was praised by critics not only for its well-lit and elaborate interiors but also for visual effects that included the use of miniatures and double exposures.[76] The case of filmmaking in Campinas in the 1920s—and its national repercussions in Rio de Janeiro fan magazines—exemplifies the discursive significance of cinematic technique and the potent imaginary of the film studio in the period, which intersected in the fascination with electric illumination and infrastructure manifested by journalists and film enthusiasts alike.

A similar trajectory in terms of the continual improvement of studio spaces and lighting equipment is evident in the filmmaking activities of Humberto Mauro in Cataguases, Minas Gerais. To an even greater extent than other film enthusiasts of the period, Mauro corresponded closely with the leaders of the campaign for Brazilian cinema, particularly Adhemar Gonzaga, and letters between the two register the impact of the ideals manifest in the campaign for Brazilian cinema on Mauro's production practices. After the completion of *Thesouro perdido* (Lost treasure, Humberto Mauro, 1927), Mauro and his business partners bankrolled the conversion of a warehouse belonging to businessman Agenor Cortes de Barros into a studio facility, equipped with a darkroom and offices, for the production of *Braza dormida*, completed in mid-1929.[77] Signaling Mauro's attempts to conform to the Americanized ideals of mise-en-scène espoused by his correspondents, the cineaste wrote to Pedro Lima, "I'm going in circles with the *interiors*. They're my *nightmare*. I must get ahold of furniture, as Gon [Gonzaga] says. The secret of American interiors is: A few *large* pieces of furniture in good taste."[78] But the lack of electric illumination in the facility limited the shooting schedule and led to interior scenes whose lighting failed to impress critics.[79]

By the time of *Braza dormida*'s premiere in March of 1930, synchronized sound—which debuted in São Paulo in April of 1929 and in Rio de Janeiro two months later—had begun to profoundly transform exhibition and production in Brazil, ushering in the nation's first self-sustaining studios. Gonzaga, fresh from his directorial debut with the high-society romantic drama *Barro humano* (Human filth, 1929), invited Mauro to Rio de Janeiro to participate in his production company and invested in the construction of two large glass-walled studio spaces (a form of studio construction increasingly considered obsolete in major film-producing countries) in the neighborhood of São Cristovão.[80] The emergence of Cinédia—which achieved the initial consolidation of a Brazilian film industry in the overtly popular mode that Vera Cruz later sought to supersede—provides a fitting coda to this account of Brazil's silent-era studio infrastructure, marked by improvisation, discontinuity, and remarkable ingenuity.

The ephemeral studios of early twentieth-century Brazil exemplify the technical and economic precarity of the nation's silent cinema, factors that ironically fueled industrial aspirations and fantasies of technological mastery. Film enthusiasts' creative utilization of existing buildings, electrical infrastructure, and available equipment deviated from Hollywoodized ideals of studio space, while showcasing more localized forms of modernity embodied by the presence of industry and acts of civic display. The discursive and physical forms taken by studio space in 1920s Brazil manifest a tension between the tight environmental and aesthetic control offered by enclosed production facilities and electrical illumination and the appeal of the local and the contingent—ranging from a fascination with topical events to an understanding of landscape as a filmic resource—that runs through Brazilian cinema's twentieth-century history. From Rio de Janeiro critics of the 1920s to the founders of Vera Cruz, champions of the Hollywood-style studio presented this idealized space as material evidence of, and as a means of cinematically staging, an exclusionary version of Brazilian modernity. As we have seen, film enthusiasts of the 1920s rhetorically embraced this position on studio space. Yet their actual practices prefigure Cinema Novo in their grounding in the local and their deviations from dominant cinematic technique, deviations that signal the profound disconnect between Brazil's economic and social realities and the modernizing project championed by film critics.[81] With the classical Hollywood studio system long dismantled in the wake of New Wave movements like Cinema Novo, deviations from classical style and production have been decoupled from social critique, becoming cost-effective strategies for mainstream commercial film. Rocha's "aesthetic of hunger" was reimagined as a "cosmetics of hunger" in hard-hitting, visually dynamic films like City of God (Cidade de Deus, Fernando Meirelles and Kátia Lund, 2002), which achieved broad global popularity.[82] At a moment when twenty-first-century media industry infrastructure, labor, and financing are becoming increasingly modular, flexible, and precarious, excavating the political and discursive economy of the 1920s Brazilian film studio helps illuminate an elusive and now-vanished ideal of technological modernity.

NOTES

1. Rocha, "An Esthetic of Hunger."

2. Shaw and Dennison, *Brazilian National Cinema*, 83. This distinctive visual style can be credited in part to cinematographer Luiz Carlos Barreto.

3. See Galvão, "Vera Cruz"; Galvão, *Burguesia e cinema;* and Rocha, *Revisão crítica do cinema brasileiro,* 69–83. Nuancing the standard reading of Vera Cruz as an irrecuperably foreign model of production that, despite its technical achievements, contributed little to an "authentically" Brazilian cinema, Ana M. López points out similarities between the Vera Cruz model and the "padrão de qualidade" (standard of quality) developed by the dominant Globo TV network. See López, "The São Paulo Connection."

4. Benedito J. Duarte, *Elite,* Feb. 1954, quoted and translated in López, "The São Paulo Connection," 130.

5. On the campaign see Xavier, *Sétima arte,* 167–97; Salles Gomes, *Humberto Mauro, Cataguases, Cinearte,* 295–366; Corrêa de Araújo, "O cinema silencioso pernambucano segundo as revistas cariocas"; and Autran, "Pedro Lima em *Selecta.*"

6. This essay preserves the spelling conventions of the historical period being discussed in direct quotations and proper names. These conventions often differ from present-day usage in Brazilian Portuguese. At times, this leads to inconsistencies (for example, *cinematographica* was the spelling used in the 1910s and 1920s and *cinematográfica* in the 1950s).

7. dos Santos, "Historical Roots of the 'Whitening' of Brazil."

8. On the local film see Jung, "Local Views"; Toulmin and Loiperdinger, "Is It You?"; and Johnson, "The Places You'll Know."

9. See, e.g., "Façamos uma convenção dos Nossos Productores," *Cinearte,* Sept. 14, 1927, 4; Pedro Lima, "Eva Nil Está no Rio," *Cinearte,* Oct. 5, 1927, 4; and "Não deve haver bairrismo," *Cinearte,* Nov. 2, 1927, 4.

10. Pedro Lima, "Onde será a Los Angeles do Brasil?" *Selecta,* July 19, 1924, n.p. *Selecta* reported on an actuality entitled *A futura cidade do film do Brasil* (Brazil's future film city), which advertised the Companhia Brasil Cinematographica's plans to build facilities "in the mold of Goldwyn, Metro, etc." near the city of Petrópolis in the state of Rio de Janeiro. "Cinematographicas," *Selecta,* August 30, 1924, n.p.

11. See Autran, *O pensamento industrial cinematográfico brasileiro.*

12. On the development of film exhibition in Rio de Janeiro see Gonzaga, *Palácios e poeiras;* and Melo Souza, *Imagens do passado,* 105–61.

13. See Salles Gomes's influential essay "Cinema: A Trajectory within Underdevelopment," esp. 245–47; Araújo, *A bela época do cinema brasileiro;* and Johnson, *Film Industry in Brazil,* 19–40.

14. Bernardet, *Historiografia clássica do cinema brasileiro,* 34–48.

15. Melo Souza, *Imagens do passado,* 67–104.

16. "O Rio vae ter uma fabrica de 'fitas' cinematographicas," *A Noite* (Rio de Janeiro), Jan. 19, 1916, 1.

17. Leal stressed the use of on-location shooting for his version of *A mala sinistra* (The sinister trunk) as a factor that distinguished his film from the competing film of the same title produced by Júlio Ferrez of the Cinema Pathé. Advertisement, *Gazeta de Notícias* (Rio de Janeiro), Oct. 10, 1908, 6. See also Leal's reminisces in a manuscript document held by journalist Pedro Lima. Unpublished manuscript, Cinemateca Brasileira, Arquivo Pedro Lima, APL-PT/1.

18. The studio, equipped with laboratory facilities, was located at Serrador's business office at Rua Brigadeiro Tobias, 31. Melo Souza, "As imperfeições do crime da mala," 110.

19. Melo Souza, "As imperfeições do crime da mala," 110–12.

20. Construction of the facilities was under way in late January, according to a notice in *O Paiz* (Rio de Janeiro), Jan. 30, 1909, 5. The first films produced in the facility were released in early March,

according to the *Gazeta de Notícias*, March 9, 1909, 1. The building was listed as the address of a boardinghouse, the Grande Pensão Alba, in *Almanak Laemmert*, 871.

21. L. B., "Cinema: Comentário do Dia," *Diário Trabalhista* (Rio de Janeiro), May 8, 1946, unpaginated press clipping, Cinemateca Brasileira, Arquivo Pedro Lima, APL-G25/270; Antônio Leal, unpublished manuscript, Cinemateca Brasileira, Arquivo Pedro Lima, APL-PT/1. On the early Pathé and Gaumont studios see Jacobson, *Studios Before the System*, 125–67.

22. Barros, *Minhas memórias de cineasta*, 75.

23. *Gazeta de Notícias*, March 29, 1909, 6.

24. Melo Souza, *Imagens do passado*, 286.

25. Thompson, *Exporting Entertainment*, 72; Melo Souza, *Imagens do passado*, 328.

26. Luna Freire, "O Cinema no Rio de Janeiro (1914 a 1929)."

27. Pedro Lima, unpublished manuscript, Cinemateca Brasileira, Arquivo Pedro Lima, APL-PI/1779.

28. Luna Freire, "O cinema no Rio de Janeiro"; Luna Freire, "Carnaval, mistério e gangsters," 159–60.

29. Bean, "Technologies of Early Stardom and the Extraordinary Body," 12. A particularly striking example is a chase scene in *A quadrilha do esqueleto*, set on a gondola used to transport sightseers to the top of Sugarloaf Mountain.

30. "Os mistérios do Rio de Janeiro," *O Imparcial* (Rio de Janeiro), March 4, 1917, 3.

31. Pedro Lima, "O cinema no Brasil," *Selecta*, April 26, 1924, n.p.

32. *Para Todos* . . . commented, "Simply, we are against films naturaes, because this is not cinema." "Filmagem Brasileira," *Para Todos* . . . , June 2, 1926.

33. See, e.g., Pedro Lima, "Cavações," *Selecta*, Nov. 14, 1925, 20; Pedro Lima, "Prevenindo contra os cavadores," *Selecta*, Jan. 6, 1926, 16; and "Filmagem Brasileira," *Cinearte*, June 23, 1926, 4–5.

34. On this point see Xavier, *Sétima arte*, 176; Schvarzman, *Humberto Mauro e as imagens do Brasil*, 34–35.

35. J. C. Mendes de Almeida, *Correio da Manhã* (Rio de Janeiro), quoted in "Filmagem Brasileira," *Cinearte*, June 23, 1926, 4.

36. Pedro Lima, "Um film sobre o Brasil," *Cinearte*, August 22, 1928, 7.

37. Letter from Jack Birck [pseud.], "Cartas para o operador," *Cinearte*, April 28, 1926, 2. *Caboclos* are multiracial Brazilians with European and indigenous ancestry.

38. See "Cinematographicas," *Selecta*, Sept. 19, 1926, n.p.

39. "Cinematographicas," *Selecta*, March 21, 1925, n.p.

40. Dyer, *White*, 82–144.

41. "Um pouco de technica," *Cinearte*, March 17, 1926, 7.

42. Luiz de Barros, "O valor dos nossos technicos," *Selecta*, June 21, 1924, n.p.

43. See, e.g., *Selecta*, Oct. 20, 1923, quoted in Salles Gomes, *Humberto Mauro, Cataguases, Cinearte*, 335.

44. "Porque os nossos films não são perfeitos," *Selecta*, August 22, 1924, n.p. See also Salles Gomes, *Humberto Mauro, Cataguases, Cinearte*, 335–36.

45. On the misplaced insistence on professionalism in 1920s fan magazines see Corrêa de Araújo, "O cinema silencioso pernambucano segundo as revistas cariocas," 239.

46. "Um pouco de technica," *Cinearte*, March 31, 1927, 7.

47. See Jacobson, *Studios Before the System*, 208. For example, an image of Germany's Ufa studios in Neubabelsberg showed the use of fabric to diffuse light in glass-roofed, glass-walled studio spaces equipped with scaffolding for electric lights. See "Um pouco de technica," *Cinearte*, Sept. 1, 1926, 26. Another displayed the combination of spotlights with targeted beams of light from plate-glass windows in the filming of *Metropolis* (Fritz Lang, Ufa, 1927). See "Um pouco de technica," *Cinearte*, Oct. 27, 1926, 30. An image of the glass-walled Invicta Film studio located in Porto, Portugal, also appeared in "Um pouco de technica," *Cinearte*, Dec. 1, 1926, 26.

48. A common thread in these ventures is director and con man "E. C. Kerrigan," an alias of the Italian immigrant Eugênio Centaro, who falsely claimed to have worked for Paramount and traveled throughout Brazil in the 1920s attaching himself to various filmmaking initiatives.

49. Pedro Lima, "Os nossos productores: Na Botelho Film," *Selecta*, August 2, 1924, n.p.

50. Annotated photograph, Cinemateca Brasileira, reference number FB_1223_012. Banco de Conteúdos Culturais, www.bcc.org.br. For more on Fleming's filmmaking activities see Gomes, *Pioneiros do cinema em Minas Gerais*, 69–84.

51. "Filmagem Brasileira," *Cinearte*, July 21, 1926, 4–5.

52. "Cinematographo Brasileiro," *Revista de Semana* (Rio de Janeiro), July 26, 1908, 685; Morettin, "Cinema e Estado no Brasil."

53. *O Brazil* (Caxias), May 4, 1912, 1.

54. See, e.g., *Exposição de galinhas e cavalos* (Exposition of hens and horses), shot by Igino Bonfioli in Minas Gerais in 1920.

55. "Entre as Montanhas de Minas," *Cinearte*, Oct. 3, 1928, 6.

56. "'Entre as Montanhas de Minas' será a Primeira Pelicula da Bellorizonte Film," *O Jornal* (Rio de Janeiro), August 10, 1928. Unpaginated press clipping, Arquivo Geral da Cidade do Rio de Janeiro, Coleção Pedro Lima, E Cx 2/6. For more on this point see Navitski, *Public Spectacles of Violence*, 202–3.

57. "A 1ª Exposição de Automóveis," *A Federação* (Porto Alegre), April 28, 1927, 2.

58. "Hollywood em miniatura: Uma tentativa seria de cinematographia em Porto Alegre," *Diário de Notícias* (Porto Alegre), Feb. 19, 1928, 16; "Cinematographia riograndense," *Correio do Povo* (Porto Alegre), Feb. 20, 1929. Unpaginated press clipping, Cinemateca Brasileira, Arquivo Pedro Lima, APL-G32/280.

59. "Hollywood em miniatura," 16.

60. "*Revelação*: Um filme riograndense produzido em 1929." Pedro Lima, unpublished manuscript, Cinemateca Brasileira, Arquivo Pedro Lima, APL-PI/1922; Stigger, "*Amor que redime*," 46.

61. Ben-Hur [pseud.], "Cinema brasileiro—*Revelação*," *O Libertador*, undated press clipping, Coleção Pedro Lima, Arquivo Geral da Cidade do Rio de Janeiro.

62. For more on this see Navitski, *Public Spectacles of Violence*, 237–42.

63. Galvão, *Crônica do cinema paulistano*, 103. See also Noronha, *No tempo da manivela*, 132–33.

64. "A novella é uma espiral," *Estado de São Paulo* (São Paulo), Nov. 19, 1925, 2.

65. *Para Todos . . .* , March 7, 1925, n.p.; *Para Todos . . .* , May 16, 1925, n.p.

66. Galvão, *Crônica do cinema paulistano*, 152.

67. Galvão, *Crônica do cinema paulistano*, 232–33.

68. The film's title literally translates as "Regenerating Example"; the title given here was used for a version of the film with English intertitles slated for a US release (it is unclear if this ever materialized). Galvão, *Crônica do cinema paulistano*, 213–14, 225.

69. Shooting in roofless buildings was relatively common in the period, as, for example, in the case of the film *Aitaré da praia* (Aitaré of the beach [Gentil Roiz, Aurora Film, 1927]) in Pernambuco. Stangerson [pseud.] to Pedro Lima, Jan. 9, 1926, Arquivo Geral da Cidade do Rio de Janeiro, Coleção Pedro Lima, A: Cx 3/11.

70. Souza, "O Cinema em Campinas nos Anos 20," 37.

71. Souza, 81.

72. Souza, 81.

73. Quoted in "A Arte do Silencio no Brasil: Preenchendo lacunas," *Selecta*, Sept. 27, 1924, n.p.

74. Pedro Lima, "Impressões de Campinas," *Selecta*, Jan. 5, 1927, 33; Souza, "O Cinema em Campinas nos Anos 1920," 187–88.

75. Souza, "O Cinema em Campinas nos Anos 1920," 189.

76. "Assistimos Mocidade Louca," *Cinearte*, Sept. 7, 1927, 4; "Cinema campineiro: um novo film," unidentified press clipping, Coleção Pedro Lima, Arquivo Geral da Cidade do Rio de Janeiro, C: Cx 1/15.

77. Salles Gomes, *Humberto Mauro, Cataguases, Cinearte*, 202, 384; Humberto Mauro to Pedro Lima, June 2, 1929, Cinemateca Brasileira, Arquivo Pedro Lima, APL-C/273.

78. Humberto Mauro to Pedro Lima, Dec. 29, 1927. Arquivo Pedro Lima, Cinemateca Brasileira, APL-C/191 (emphasis in original).

79. Ernani Serpião Nunes, "A proposito da exhibição de 'Braza Dormida,'" *O Estado de Minas* (Belo Horizonte), April 23, 1929, unpaginated press clipping, Coleção Pedro Lima, Arquivo Geral da Cidade do Rio de Janeiro; "Braza Dormida—Da Phoebus Film," *Selecta*, March 13, 1929, 43.

80. Noronha, *No tempo da manivela*, 216–17.

81. Glauber Rocha describes Humberto Mauro's films shot in Cataguases as precursors to Cinema Novo—somewhat misleadingly, one could argue, given Mauro's close alignment with the Rio de Janeiro critics' hegemonic view of Brazilian cinema—in *Revisão crítica do cinema brasileiro*, 43–55.

82. Bentes, "The *Sertão* and the *Favela* in Contemporary Brazilian Cinema," 121–38.

3
_____

Ephemeral Studios

Exhibiting Televisual Spaces during the Interwar Years

Anne-Katrin Weber

Studio productions are central to television's history in the early postwar period. As William Boddy has shown for the United States, the live teleplay in anthology format, made almost entirely in studio settings, was the centerpiece of critical attention until the mid-1950s. The shift to Hollywood-sponsored film series shot on location included a shift from a theater-based to an entertainment-based model for television prime-time programming, which constituted a "repudiation of the aesthetic values" critics had endorsed so far .[1] Similarly, Gilles Delavaud has argued that the French studio *dramatiques* represented a major genre for early TV insofar as they offered a platform for creative experimentations. The drama promised to materialize television's specificity as immediate and intimate communication while simultaneously uplifting the new medium to a new art form.[2]

While production spaces are thus understood to be part and parcel of the negotiations of cultural values and media identities during television's postwar years, the history of interwar studios remains largely unknown. More broadly, television's development in the interwar years has received comparatively little attention.[3] This observation contrasts with the medium's visibility in public space during the 1930s, when television was discussed in the general press and professional journals and regularly shown at exhibitions and industrial fairs. Although interwar television was not yet commercialized as a mass medium for broadcasting to a national public, it encountered a mass audience by offering itself as a media object on display.[4] From the late 1920s on, various televisual devices, including large-screen television and visiophones, were regularly shown in larger cities at events such as annual radio trade fairs, national exhibitions, and world's fairs. Similar to the descriptions published in journals and the press, these "television exhibitions" constituted a mediating link between the scientific laboratory and the living room. They offered a space for the first encounter between the medium and its audience and familiarized the latter with the former's potentialities.[5]

A crucial feature of television exhibits during the period was the "studio," a more or less sophisticated space dedicated to televising a live performance. Already the first television exhibitions in the late 1920s included a studio room, integrated into broader television displays and constituting one—often the major—attraction at the exhibition booth. Contrary to permanent studios, exhibition studios were built to be disassembled: their ephemerality corresponded to the exhibition's own temporality as a fleeting event for the celebration of consumer culture and new technology.

Drawing on exhibitions held in Great Britain and the United States, this essay analyzes studio displays to propose new insights into the history of a largely unknown medium and explain how ephemeral studios helped shape the identity of interwar TV. As I will argue, television's materiality, more than its content, introduced television into public space, and the studio production site, as a physical structure, constituted an essential component for the making of television in the 1930s. Importantly, the accessibility of exhibition studios allowed institutions from the mid-1930s on—here, the British Broadcasting Corporation (BBC) and the National Broadcasting Corporation (NBC)—to play the card of transparency and to invite their potential audience to peek behind television's scenes. The ephemeral studio nourished the "corporate identity" of the new medium and contributed to its smooth integration into preexisting broadcasting institutions. Familiarizing the audience with television's infrastructure, it constituted the heart of the televisual experience for fairgoers and thus represented a central space for television's encounter with its first audiences.

DEMONSTRATING TELEVISION'S SPACE-BINDING CAPACITIES

Speculating about the medium's potential in 1935, Rudolf Arnheim described television as a "pure means of transmission" that lacked "the elements of an original artistic elaboration of reality" but "modified our relations with reality itself":

> We see the people gathered together in the central square of a near-by city, we see the head of the government of a neighboring state, we see boxers fighting for the world's title on the other side of the ocean, we see an English jazz band, an Italian soprano, a German professor, the burning members of a train that has collided, the masked figures of carnival. . . . We can admire the sun setting behind Vesuvius and a second later the illuminated night-signs of New York. The need for the descriptive word disappears as the barrier of foreign language vanishes. The world in all its vastness comes to our room.[6]

According to Arnheim, television's space-binding qualities produced a map of events and sites that appeared simultaneously on the screen. Abolishing the need for linear textual description, television's new visuality recreated the world in the intimacy of domestic environments and generated a new topography in which private and public space merged.

These properties, presented as fundamental to television, echo the discursive construction of the medium as a "window on the world" that emerged with the first televisual utopias from the 1870s on. Privileging remote visuality associated with the capacity of instantaneous vision, nineteenth-century imaginaries helped shape the televisual paradigm of immediacy, presence, intimacy, simultaneity, and ubiquity. Albert Robida's "Telephonoscope," described in his science fiction novel *Le vingtième siècle* (1883), or George du Maurier's *Edison's Telephonoscope (Transmits Light as well as Sound)* (1878), translated the early conception of the televisual medium as capable of annihilating space by time. Like the telephone, to which it remains closely associated, but improving its solely audio function, the televisual device transports its user instantaneously—and *audiovisually*—to faraway places. In *Le vingtième siècle* the telephonoscope broadcasts the latest news, but also opera performances, directly into the living room; in du Maurier's caricature the parents are able to hear and see their offspring in the British colonies.[7]

This dematerialized idea of television as a means of almost ethereal communication clashes with the technological constraints—and the simple heaviness—of televisual infrastructures, for sending images "through the air" requires an important setup involving production spaces, transmitter, and receiving equipment. Throughout the interwar period the development and maintenance of this infrastructure represented a major challenge, even for established players in the telecommunications field. The first mechanical—low-tech—devices were comparatively cheap to develop and simple to handle but also had all the disadvantages of an unreliable device of inadequate quality and limited program value. They required bright light and makeup, for instance, making outdoor broadcasting nearly impossible. While the development of electronic cameras based on cathode-ray tubes promised to solve many of the quality-related problems, the research costs increased drastically, pushing most of the independent engineers and inventors out of the race.[8] In addition, the production of television programs remained an infrastructural challenge that required the instantaneous coordination of men and machines. As one NBC engineer explained in 1939, the most important aspect in television production was "timing," and more precisely, the "accurate timing" not only of "devices and split-second movements of cameras" but also of "personnel."[9] Contrary to the popular imagination that projected uses of dematerialized communication, "seeing at a distance" depended on technical systems and human resources working together in precise coordination.

By organizing television displays from the late 1920s on, inventors and corporations demonstrated their capacity to master the complexity of televisual communication and to overcome technical problems and economic restraints at least for the duration of an exhibition. By making television work in these settings, they promoted their own status in the field of telecommunications. The public display of television therefore primarily celebrated the technological feat materialized by a televisual transmission: the demonstration served as proof of technological progress and innovative strength.

To stress the technological accomplishment represented by a televisual transmission, the entire apparatus had to be shown. Only a mise-en-scène that placed the studio and the TV receivers in vicinity would allow audiences to observe the particularities of a televisual transmission. At the New York radio fair in 1929, for instance, the Radio Corporation of America (RCA) organized a display that invited an immediate comparison between the live performance and its televised image. The one-square-foot-large screen and the actors' stage "were so arranged that the spectators could compare the original scene and the received image."[10] Similarly, Ulises A. Sanabria, a key figure for the public showing of large-screen television in the United States, staged a reflexive setup in which the televisual demonstration relentlessly pointed toward itself.[11] The demonstration, organized in 1931 at the New York Moss Theater, was announced by the New York Times in some detail: "the entire television apparatus, including sending and receiving equipment will be in operation during each variety program at the Moss theatre. The television transmitting booth will be wheeled out on the stage. Suspended above the stage will be the ten-foot translucent screen on which the images will be shown. Thus, the actors will be seen by the audience both as microphone and television eye pickup their voices and images, and as they appear on the television screen suspended above."[12] Highlighted in the press, the key aspect of the demonstration was allowing the audience to visualize at one glance the apparatus, the performance, and its televised image, all aligned in the same field of vision. The screen itself, "translucent" and hanging from the ceiling above the equipment, revealed nothing more than the immediate surroundings of its own location. The performers' live act and its mediation on the screen created the spectacle of a technological doppelgänger compared immediately to its "original": production and reception space together produced a mirror effect in which television looked at itself.

In other words, early television demonstrations gave prominence to the televisual infrastructure: the new medium's material "stuff," rather than its content, was brought to the fore. Instead of pushing production spaces backstage, these spaces—and their technologies—were enthusiastically shown. To use the terms of Jay D. Bolter and Richard Grusin, the displays depended on "hypermediacy," which, instead of staging an older medium (as in Bolder and Grusin's model), staged itself. By "mak[ing] us aware of the medium," they stressed their own materiality and self-referentiality.[13]

In doing so, televisual settings at the fairs pointed back toward the televisual system and its bulky materiality: instead of providing a "window to the world" that transgressed the spatial borders of the display, they accentuated the opaqueness of a televisual loop. Raising awareness of the medium, this reflexive strategy emphasized the spatiotemporal configuration of *simultaneous* transmission *at a distance* while remaining limited to the microspaces of the exhibition halls. Within these spaces, production and reception were intrinsically linked and, *together,* constituted the main attraction. To demonstrate "seeing at a distance," the distance was made graspable for visitors: as an exhibit, television called for a reduction of its scale from (imaginary) global broadcast to literal narrowcast.

GLASS STUDIOS

Sanabria's 1931 exhibition emblematized early television demonstrations by creating a spectacle that unveiled—and thereby celebrated—the entire televisual infrastructure. Here, the "studio" space did not exist independently from transmission and receiver equipment. Pursuing comparable strategies of mise-en-scène with more elaborate means, other displays emphasized the presence of an ephemeral studio by installing glass-windowed production spaces. Creating a distinct architectural space within the exhibition halls, these studios drew attention to the television equipment while also protecting cameras, lighting grids, and other equipment, as well as technicians and performers, from curious crowds. Similar to balustrades and cordons regularly used to shield the objects on display, the transparent surface offered visual—but not tactile—access to delicate materials and its exhibitors.

In 1929, for instance, television inventor and entrepreneur John Logie Baird organized a show in London to run in parallel with the national radio fair Radiolympia.[14] Baird's transformed garage included a demonstration space hosting receivers, the studio, and the control room, the latter two shown behind windows. An exhibition map published in the journal *Television: The World's First Television Journal* highlighted the "glass windows" separating the visitors' space from the studio and the control room (fig. 3.1), and the journalist's written account insisted on the "wide expanse of plate-glass," which opened onto a "sound-proof-room."

While the "televisual" space was thus clearly separated from the space of reception, the glass also allowed "for one to watch the engineers at work."[15] To the right of the modestly equipped glass studio, two television sets were positioned (fig. 3.2). Given the small screen size, only one person at a time could see the image: "public gangways" installed in front of the receivers canalized the visitors into a disciplined line. Separated from the crowd filling the space, the visitor was prepared to view the display and simultaneously made part of the spectacle for other visitors in the room. In addition, one gangway was elevated "in order that everyone might

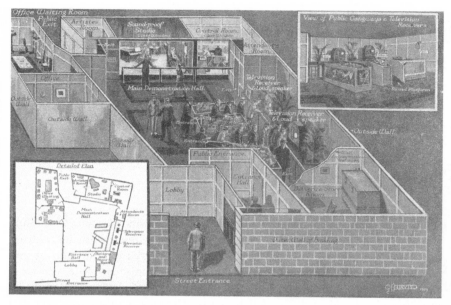

FIGURE 3.1. Map of Baird Company's 1929 exhibition adjacent to the London radio fair Radiolympia. *Television* 2 (Dec. 1929): 474.

have a perfectly clear view of the artists at work in the studio and in turn compare them with the televised image."[16] Standing a little higher than one's television-watching neighbor, one could compare the studio performance "with the television image as seen in the Baird Televisor receivers."[17]

This juxtaposition of a live performance with its televisual reproduction recalls earlier public performances of sound technologies demonstrating the fidelity of audio recording. As Emily Thompson has described, from 1915 to 1925 the Edison Company conducted similar "tone tests" throughout the United States.[18] Aiming to convince the audience that live music and phonograph recordings were comparable, these tests paralleled singers and recordings by switching between the live performance and the phonograph.[19] In highly standardized demonstrations sometimes introduced by Edison himself, the singer would stop singing while his or her voice continued to resonate on the phonograph, or the lights would be turned off and the audience left guessing who was playing: the human voice or the machine.[20] While earlier public demonstrations of phonographs had emphasized the functioning of the machine to prove that "it worked," the tone tests shifted the attention to the equivalence between original and imitation and sought, as Jonathan Sterne writes, "to erase the medium (ironically, by highlighting the technology)."[21]

FIGURE 3.2. A 1929 display by the Baird Company with a glass-enclosed television studio and television sets (on the right). Leslie Trenton, "Now! Where Do We Go from Here?" *Television* 2 (Nov. 1929): 452.

According to the journalist quoted above, the exhibition design of Baird's display sought to establish an analogous equivalence between performers in the studio and their images onscreen. Given the size of the television screen, however, the comparison "at one glance" between the show and its transmitted image, as well as the possible confounding of the two, seem an impossibility. Rather than creating a visual equivalence by erasing the medium, then, television's "fidelity" depended on the possibility of authenticating the medium's space-binding potential made possible by the infrastructure's microscale within the exhibition hall. As in Sanabria's display, the exhibition of technology—including television receivers, a control room, and a small studio—constituted the core of Baird's demonstration and created a reflexive scenario in which television endlessly pointed to itself.

In the case of Baird's exhibition, and thanks, as well, to the extensive reporting in the journal *Television*, the glass studio gained an additional meaning. Anticipating, as the journalist wrote, "*the B.B.C studio of the future*,"[22] the large glass panes that offered a view of the studio and the control room promised a surplus of visibility: they made accessible production spaces that had not even been built. The architecturally created transparency was enhanced by the publication of maps describing those rooms that were closed to fairgoers (see fig. 3.1). Suggesting openness and clarity, the window and the maps revealed production processes that would remain hidden or even nonexist-ent outside the exhibition halls. In a way, then, the settings at the fairs and on paper produced the visibility and visuality lacking in the medium on display, which merely demonstrated its own capacity for transmissions at a distance.

TRANSPARENT INSTITUTIONS

The exhibitionary *and* exhibitionist gesture of celebrating television and revealing the workings of usually invisible apparatuses and their engineers became particu-larly important with the introduction of public broadcasting in the mid-1930s, when television institutions began to advertise their regular broadcasting service on the exhibition grounds. The windowed space that revealed transmitters and studios exposed the machineries of a new medium and invited fairgoers to famil-iarize themselves with the production processes of institutional television, provid-ing a space in which education and entertainment overlapped.

In Great Britain the Selsdon Committee, appointed to discuss the future of Brit-ish television, published in January of 1935 its final report, which treated every aspect of television's development.[23] Among other things, it recommended that the BBC be responsible for the programs and for starting service with two competing TV sys-tems provided by Baird Television and Marconi-EMI. Subsequently, the better scheme would be chosen as the definite standard for Britain's public service. In this regard the committee ruled that the future public service should transmit its pro-grams over a "high-definition system" consisting of an image composed of at least 240 lines and 25 frames per second, a decision that would eventually help the firm Marconi-EMI (working with all-electronic technology) to win the competition.

The official opening of the television service, scheduled for November 2, 1936, was preceded by a test run at the national radio fair, Radiolympia, held in Septem-ber, where the public could for the first time see the television programs transmit-ted from the Baird and Marconi-EMI studios located in Alexandra Palace. Pro-duced outside the exhibition halls, the television program was not shown in the making, since BBC's exhibition design comprised only demonstration booths with television sets but no studio space. Through this exhibition format the BBC posi-tioned itself as the responsible program institution even before launching its regu-lar broadcast. But the sole staging of television as a program supplier had its draw-backs: the fairgoers' constant movement did not match the format of presentation, which accentuated television's content. As one BBC staff member wrote after the radio fair: "It was impossible to design a programme satisfactory for conditions at Radiolympia where the audience was continually being pestered and herded through the booths, and unable to observe for more than about a minute, at best about three minutes. Any performance with a theme and continuity was meaning-less."[24] Given the small booths and high number of visitors, the demonstrations had

FIGURE 3.3. BBC's exhibition studio at Radiolympia, 1938. Alexandra Palace Television Society.

to be very short: because viewers had only a few minutes to appreciate the media content, programs with narrative coherence were not convenient. For the BBC staff the decision to focus solely on television's content was, in retrospect, a mistake. In 1937 the exhibition architecture was changed slightly to allow visitors to witness the entirety of a "small programme," comprising talks and other studio productions, as well as a *Television Demonstration Film.* The film featured around thirty performances, interviews, and outdoor broadcasts, covering, according to the fair catalogue, "the most successful items televised during the first six months of the service."[25]

The following year, however, BBC revised the exhibition format entirely, shifting its focus from programs to production. For this edition the radio broadcasting theater, "hitherto almost an institution," was replaced by a television studio "with glass observation windows three feet high"[26] encircling the studio on two sides (fig. 3.3).[27] A similar studio had already been erected in the spring of 1938 on the occasion of the *Ideal Home Exhibition,* a consumer fair for the modern housewife.[28] Its reintroduction at Radiolympia confirmed the studio's effectiveness for communicating with the public. While the BBC's television signal radiated from its studios in central London toward the Greater London area, the slow distribution of receivers hindered the broadcast from effectively reaching its audience. The exhibition studio and its on-site productions, however, were seen by throngs of visitors, despite an additional admission fee to the BBC stand.

Each corner of the studio was equipped with one set, comprising a small décor for fashion shows, a ship-like structure for the variety show *Cabaret Cruise,* and a stage for *Queue for Song.* These shows were not only transmitted via a closed-circuit broadcast within the exhibition halls but broadcast as part of the regular BBC schedule, confirming the institution's will to give "a replica of actual working conditions" at Radiolympia.[29] The arrangement placing all studio sets in a corner was partly to accommodate the constraints imposed by an exhibition space whose goal was visibility: by pushing the decor to the wall, the studio made its interiors visible to visitors behind the glass windows. But it also reflected a more general practice in studio design. As Jason Jacobs has discussed, the "*centrifugal* organization" of production spaces was typical for early television studio architecture.[30] By erecting the sets on the sides, space was left for the cameras, cables, floor lighting, microphone beam, and movement of the entire crew.

Television's display at the fair was accompanied by several new features underlining the medium's growing importance for the BBC and the radio industry alike. In 1938 the cover of the fair catalogue referred for the first time not only to radio and its entertainment value but also to television by showing a "solid and substantial-looking eye, but the mere filmy ghost of an ear."[31] Furthermore, concurrent with the opening of the exhibition, the BBC put on sale a "pictorial booklet" titled *And Now: The BBC Presents Television to the World.* On thirty-two pages the pamphlet, "almost entirely devoted to pictures," presented past and current television development and programs.[32] Its publication translated intensified efforts to promote the medium to a broad audience, also visible at the radio fair. The status of television as a consumer good, however, brought forward several problems, most urgently the issue of high costs. Television sets were expensive, and receiver sales were accordingly slow.[33] The set prices were a frequent topic in the press, which reported about price reductions *and* complained about the sets' inaccessibility. As one article underlined, for the listener to become a viewer was first and foremost a financial issue.[34]

For the BBC, leading its audience toward televisual consumption required renewed efforts on several fronts, including the extension of programing hours, the education of spectators, and more affordable access to its programs. While the public corporation had no direct influence on the consumer electronics market and did not determine the price of television sets, it carried the whole responsibility for the attractiveness of televisual content. At the 1938 exhibition the institution chose to follow Baird's and others' example and to stage the production of such content.

OPENING STUDIO DOORS

While the glass studios celebrated transparency literally and symbolically by creating visual access to infrastructure and production processes, it excluded the audience physically from the production space. Toward the end of the 1930s, a new televisual attraction was introduced at fairs that suspended this exclusion. The new format invited the audience to perform live before the camera and thus allowed a transgression of the former division between production and reception spaces. In this exhibition design fairgoers experienced television's materiality as *participants*.

At the 1939 New York World's Fair, for instance, Westinghouse and General Electric installed small television studios in their pavilions, giving "fair guests not only an opportunity to see television in action but to take part in its programs."[35] In both settings the picture was transmitted to an adjacent viewing room, where several small television receivers were situated. The exceptional character of participating in a television transmission was emphasized by the distribution of attendance cards "certifying" that the particular person "has been televised" at one of the pavilions. The cards, one of many souvenirs the visitors would take home, brought a bit of television into the living room—and invariably linked the medium to a particular brand.

The Westinghouse TV exhibit was featured in an in-house film production, *The Middleton Family at the World's Fair*.[36] Shot on the premises of the corporation's pavilion, the movie glorified the contributions of free enterprise to progress and affluence by recording an "average" American family's visit to the fair.[37] Early in the film the *pater familias* and his son inspect the television studio. Reduced to only the essential elements, it comprises a stage, a microphone, and a television camera. Adjacent to the production space, and separated from it by a glass window, a receiving room with several television sets is located. On entering the space, the boy is invited to stand in front of the camera onstage. While he starts conversing with the attendant, his father walks to the viewing room to observe him on the screen. After a brief moment the boy asks through the camera, "How am I doing, father?" Without the possibility of replying verbally, the latter forms an "ok" sign with his fingers to the son through the glass window. For the son—and the movie audience alike—this gesture verifies the liveness of the transmission and thus confirms the "veracity" of the televisual experience.

In Great Britain the BBC similarly introduced a sophisticated feature at the 1938 exhibition discussed above. Called "Come and Be Televised," the one-hour program invited "celebrities and members of the general public" to be "televised in the studio at Radiolympia,"[38] passing from behind the glass windows into the studio space. According to a BBC memo, among the participants "of interest" were an American journalist who had survived an encounter with "American gangsters," an English businessman building his own house, a lady "whose hobby is crocodile hunting," and a "Scotchman who lives at Inverness, and who is on intimate terms with the Lochness [sic] Monster."[39] Beyond featuring such exceptional characters, the program's overall design strengthened the institution's strategy of bringing television to its (potential) viewers by familiarizing the audience with television and its operation *and* filling airtime with free content.

Not all interviews took place trouble-free, however, as a letter from a participant in the 1939 program to the BBC testifies. For this participant the experience—although enjoyable—was somewhat disappointing, since he was interrupted by the "hostess" before he could repeat "a verse which [he] had adapted to bring in television." His letter furthermore alluded to a debacle of another sort: "With reference to the old gentleman who in 'Come and be televised' on Thursday morning complained about the cutting out of Picture Page during August. He appears to think that other people should not have a holiday so that his pleasure be not interrupted."[40] In other words, the "old gentleman" quoted in the letter had used his airtime to criticize the BBC for interrupting programs during summer months and taken advantage of the contingent character of liveness to communicate his dissatisfaction on-air. For both the participants and the institution the studio at Radiolympia thus formed a space to experience the unpredictability and potential surprise of live programming: inviting the audience into its production space, the BBC exposed itself to unexpected behavior and criticisms.

By opening the studio doors, "Come and Be Televised" expanded the glass studio's goal of revealing the medium's inner workings. Contrary to the latter, however, it created the possibility for an individual engagement of the audience with the medium and its institution. If earlier displays spectacularized television's machines and production processes through their framing behind a window, the new mise-en-scène undid the separation of spaces before and behind the glass. As a participatory exhibit it staged a physical encounter between the medium's (future) audience and its broadcasting institution, which implied a bodily experience of television, be it in the form of a hand gesture in the Westinghouse film or of storytelling and letter writing in the BBC's program.

FROM EPHEMERAL TO PERMANENT STRUCTURES

The ephemeral studio built for Radiolympia 1938 thus represented a new way to communicate the "behind the scenes" of television, to allow the audience to engage with the new medium, and to tie the latter's identity to the BBC. These increased public relation efforts accompanied the ongoing institutionalization of the new medium and constituted in particular an answer to the construction of permanent but (for the public) restricted studios. As one article in *Radio Times* explained, the Radiolympia studio's ultimate role was indeed to replace a visit to the BBC studios located in Alexandra Palace: "'Please may I visit the television studio at Alexandra Palace?' is a plea that is made many times every week by members of the public. Working conditions are normally such that a 'Sorry, quite impossible' is the only answer that can be given. The position is very different with the giant television studio in the National Hall at Olympia."[41] Thanks to its ephemerality, the studio offered an opportunity not available during "normal" service. To work in glass studios and with the audience would not be sustainable on the long haul for BBC's television crew; for the duration of a radio fair, however, it promoted the new medium, and its institution, by literally bringing in its potential audience. In other words, the ephemeral studio accompanied and consolidated the institutionalization of television taking place beyond the exhibition grounds.

For the general public the BBC's growing interest in television became visible in June of 1935, when the corporation announced it would install television studios in Alexandra Palace, a former entertainment venue in north London.[42] The transformation of Alexandra Palace into up-to-date television studios represented a break from the institution's previously reluctant attitude toward the new medium and reflected the national and international pressure exerted on the BBC to go forward with it. During the mid-1930s the Selsdon Committee had discussed the ideal placement for a new television building and assessed its most important features, among others its distance to Broadcasting House (BBC's headquarters in central London) and its elevation. The crumbling ruins of Alexandra Palace were eventually chosen from a list of four possible sites, which had also included the iconic Crystal Palace.[43]

The original plans for Alexandra Palace had been designed in the late 1850s by Owen Jones, who had been responsible for the Crystal Palace's decoration in 1851. The new exhibition building should again be made of glass, with a huge dome covering a winter garden, a concert hall, a theater, and vast exhibition areas. But after early financial difficulties, the original plans were modified and a less spectacular version of the palace was eventually opened in May of 1873.[44] Shortly after the inauguration, the building burned down, but it was rebuilt rapidly and used again as an entertainment and exhibition venue. In the interwar period the building and its premises went mostly unused. Through the BBC's occupation of the site in the spring of 1936, Alexandra Palace was revived as a center of modern leisure and information culture and as a symbol of England's leading position in television.[45] The BBC's occupation of the premises, however, redefined the building's function: as a popular site for mass events, it had drawn the city into its halls. As a broadcasting studio, it henceforth "radiated" signals from the hill outward to the city.[46]

This permanent structure simultaneously produced and epitomized television by creating a widely visible monument to the medium. The construction of a physical space for television anchored it within a concrete location and conferred on television a new authority that inscribed it into the official national media landscape. As with other architectural sites for (televisual) broadcasting, Alexandra Palace materialized the dialectics of media spaces, highlighting the space-binding *and* site-specific nature of communication.[47] Whereas exhibitions drew part of their attraction from their ephemerality, and thus exclusiveness and uniqueness, the erection of lasting studios, offices, control rooms, and other infrastructure symbolized producers' willingness to provide television with more stable forms and practices developed by

FIGURE 3.4. A televisual icon: Alexandra Palace, the new BBC television studio with its distinctive antenna. *Popular Wireless & Television Times* 30 (Sept. 12, 1936): cover.

engineers, producers, and performers. Very much like radio shows but as perennial sites, studios like Alexandra Palace participated in the shaping of television and, in particular, in its integration within the mass media industry.[48]

The announcement by the Selsdon Committee about the new site for BBC's television studios was widely echoed. The press enthusiastically embraced the new building and reproduced numerous photographs that transformed Alexandra Palace from the physical location of BBC's TV studios into a symbol of English television. Alexandra Palace was everywhere: on the magazine cover announcing the special issue for Radiolympia, in BBC's annual report, in the pages of radio journals, and on the cover of the 1936 television issue of *Radio Times*. Traveling around the country, its photograph provided the new "British" television service with a visible identity that went beyond the physical limitations of the service's transmission range. Drawings and photographs of the studio made sure to depict its impressive antenna (fig. 3.4). Representing the only distinctive feature of the new home for this new medium, the antenna signified technological modernity and progress, in stark contrast to the original structure's older forms of entertainment. Subsuming the double function of Alexandra Palace as a geographical location and a broadcasting center, the antenna synecdochally represented the whole building and stood as a metaphor for BBC's entire television service.

From its beginning Alexandra Palace thus circulated as an icon, existing simultaneously as a geographical location and an architectural shelter for television *and* as a mass reproduced image and symbol of the electronic medium.[49] Beatriz Colomina's incisive summary of modern architecture and its links to modern mass media—"The house is in the media and the media is in the house"—perfectly suits the BBC's television studios.[50] From the first transmission realized on its premises, Alexandra Palace became inseparable from its representations. As a concrete space photographed and circulated in the press, it participated in a network of signifiers that symbolically shaped the image of British television; as a space producing televisual representations, it created the images transmitted by British television.

TELEVISION AT RADIO CITY

In the United States NBC's glamorous television launch took place at the 1939 New York World's Fair, where the corporation presented a widely seen pavilion in the shape of a radio tube.[51] NBC's involvement with television had, however, been promoted one year earlier thanks to a sophisticated public studio at Radio City. Opened in 1938, the studio invited its visitors to a "television tour" similar to the radio studio tours it also offered. Already in 1933, the site at Rockefeller Center had been chosen as the future television location, and at the opening of the building complex, a "group of four studios on the ninth floor" had been reserved for television broadcasting.[52] The entrance hall to NBC's headquarters represented the company's activities in monumental photomurals by Margaret Bourke-White. Blown up to giant size, the photographs depicted fragments and singular elements of transmission and reception technologies, communicating the grandeur of the corporation. Included in this dispersed view of modern media-making was an enormous image of a cathode ray tube located just next to a huge radio antenna tower. In his discussion of Bourke-White's mural, Olivier Lugon argues that the artist commented on the power of the new means of communication by creating an analogy between wireless communication and the photographic mural. Like broadcasting—and, in particular, like television, the future cornerstone of NBC's empire—the photomural functioned as an amplification of visual information.[53]

From late summer 1938 on, visitors paying fifty-five cents could tour an actual television studio exclusively established for demonstration purposes. The press release issued on June 13, 1938, before the opening of the television tour, presented the future attraction "as a complete unit in itself":

> Three studios have been set aside for the benefit of the public. The first houses the Iconoscope camera, a "boom" microphone and other equipment for broadcasting sight as well as sound. . . . Once the camera has been inspected, the group will be taken to an adjoining studio separated from the telecasting room by a huge glass panel, a telephone connected to the studio, and the four RCA experimental television sets which will show the action taking place in the studio. A fifth receiving set, yet to be delivered, will be in an unfinished chassis, with all the works exposed. This

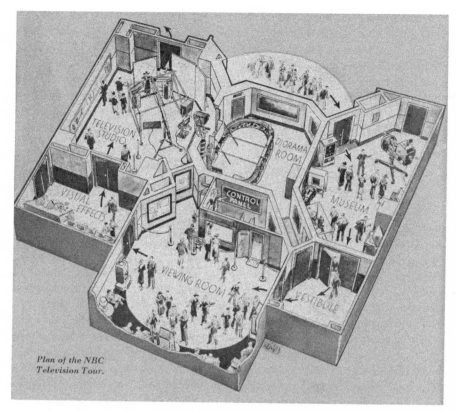

Plan of the NBC
Television Tour.

FIGURE 3.5. Map of the NBC television exhibition studio at Radio City. National Broadcasting Company, *America's First Television Tour: Demonstrating [and] Describing the Art and Science of Seeing at a Distance* (New York: National Broadcasting, 1939).

will be open for inspection by tour parties. In the second studio visitors will be able to see performers in the room they have just left, both on the screens of the receiving sets and, through the glass panel, in real life. Guides will converse with persons in the telecast studio so that their image, doubly visible in receiving set and through the panel, will be accompanied by their voices audible both through the loudspeaker and over the telephone. The third room will be the first television museum.[54]

The NBC television tour's objectives were obvious. By combining the display of progress (in the museum) with the unveiling of an outstanding technology (in the other rooms), NBC hoped to educate and inform its future audience about its new service. The tour revealed every aspect of television production and consumption as envisioned by the corporation, shaping television after its own image and presenting the medium as belonging to NBC. The press release notably emphasized the "huge glass panel" and the sets placed in close proximity, celebrating the visibility created by the transparency of glass and screens.

For the 1939 New York World's Fair, NBC promoted this visibility through a small booklet, *America's First Television Tour: Demonstrating-Describing the Art and Science of Seeing at a Distance,* which included a map of the different segments of the "show studio" tour (fig. 3.5). The map suggests that, except for the "large glass panels," no other windows existed: the world on view was the world produced within these walls. Following a predetermined path indicated by arrows, the visitor passed these transparent surfaces not as a flaneur in urban space but rather as part of a well-oiled machine that, in each room, revealed a new window onto its own workings. In the so-called viewing room the sights conflated with the television images, which showed in reduced size what was visible through the two windows opening onto the television studio. The demonstration studio no longer merely displayed television: its entire architecture was transformed into a technique of seeing, in which windows opened views similarly to those seen on screens. Whereas the combination of transparent surfaces and multiple screens created the impression of a surplus of visibility, the demonstration studio merely promoted itself. The visitors paying the entrance fee to "see at a distance" were brought into a space turned not toward the outside but to the inside of the corporation. From the booklet distributed to every camera on display, the television tour advertised television itself, not just its content, as NBC's product.

CONCLUSION: INTERWAR TELEVISION AND CONSUMER CULTURE

The exhibition of television studios during the interwar period thus aimed first and foremost at performing the medium and its makers. Be it the early displays of inventors and small entrepreneurs or the sophisticated mise-en-scène of public institutions and commercial corporations, the displays highlighted television's materiality and infrastructure. Organized around showings of televisual machinery rather than content, the medium's introduction to its first audiences was thus highly reflexive and pointed relentlessly to television itself. Following David Thorburn and Henry Jenkins, this "self-awareness" and "self-reflexivity" may be understood as inherent to the "periods of media change" and the particular "aesthetics of transition" they engender.[55] As a "new media," interwar television participated in a changing mediascape, and its reflexivity was linked to the moment of its emergence: the hypermediated exhibition displays explained its functioning to visitors and curious crowds, and, in doing so, coconstructed television as a means of instantaneous communication.

But television's reflexivity can also be understood as a result of the exhibition gesture. On display, each exhibit highlighted this very gesture of displaying, which in turn put the spotlight on the object shown. As Janet Ward writes, the act of displaying is "an act of unfolding, spreading out, in the sense of constantly calling attention to itself."[56] It is intrinsically exhibitionist and thus essential to the "culture of showing" characteristic of modern consumer society.[57] Interwar television's reflexivity indicates the medium's place within this culture, a place determined less by the commercial value of receivers and programs than by pleasurable—and commercialized—encounters with technological modernity. The entangled history of exhibitions and interwar television points to the ways in which the medium, despite lacking programs and audiences, participated in modern experiences of industrial and consumer culture. Built to exhibit television in the making, the ephemeral studio was at the heart of this experience.

NOTES

1. Boddy, *Fifties Television*, 1.

2. Delavaud, *L'art de la télévision*.

3. Standard histories of early television focus on the medium's technical development, but recent scholarship offers more diverse historiographical perspectives. See, e.g., Uricchio, "Television, Film and the Struggle for Media Identity"; Jacobs, *Intimate Screen*; Sewell, *Television in the Age of Radio*. Very recently, Doron Galili has adopted a media archaeological perspective to discuss the intermedial entanglements of television with other media, in particular cinema; see Galili, *Seeing by Electricity*.

4. This chapter is part of my book *Interwar Television on Display*, in which I analyze the entangled history of television and interwar exhibitions from a transnational perspective.

5. Exhibitions continued to play an important role in the medium's promotion and legitimization during the postwar period; see Wheatley, *Spectacular Television*, esp. chap. 1.

6. Arnheim, "Seeing Afar Off," 77.

7. For a discussion of these televisual imaginaries see Uricchio, "Television, Film and the Struggle for Media Identity"; and Galili, *Seeing by Electricity*.

8. See Udelson, *The Great Television Race*, 77–78; for an exhaustive technical and transnational history of interwar television see Burns, *Television*.

9. Albert W. Protzman, "Television Studio Technic," *Journal of the Society of Motion Picture Engineers* 33, no. 7 (July 1939): 26–40, 26.

10. "300,000 Visit N.Y. Show, See 1930 Design," *Radio World*, Sept. 28, 1929, 20.

11. On Sanabria see Udelson, *The Great Television Race*, 66–77.

12. "Television to Link Theaters in Test," *New York Times*, Oct. 14, 1931, 31.

13. Bolter and Grusin, *Remediation*, 174.

14. This display accompanied the launching of the first experimental television service in London, a cooperation between Baird Television and the BBC. For a discussion of the different starts of television services by the BBC see Medhurst, "What a Hullabaloo!"

15. Trenton, "Now! Where Do We Go from Here?" *Television: The World's First Television Journal* 2 (Nov. 1929): 451.

16. Trenton, 453.

17. Trenton, 451.

18. See Thompson, "Machines, Music, and the Quest for Fidelity," 131.

19. See Thompson; see also Sterne, *The Audible Past*, 261–65.

20. Thompson, "Machines, Music, and the Quest for Fidelity," 148–56.

21. Sterne, *The Audible Past*, 261.

22. Trenton, "Now! Where Do We Go from Here?" 451 (emphasis in the original).

23. See Burns, *British Television*, 351–59.

24. Noel Ashbridge, Controller (Engineering), "Report on Demonstrations of Television at the RMA Exhibition at Olympia," Sept. 7, 1936, BBC Written Archives Centre, Caversham Park, Reading (hereafter BBC archives), T 23 / 77 / 2.

25. "Television Demonstrations," *Radiolympia* (1937), 148.

26. "Wait for Radiolympia!" *Radio Times*, July 22, 1938, 16.

27. "News of the Week: Radiolympia. Television the Focal Point of the Show," *Wireless World* 43, no. 991 (August 25, 1938): 187.

28. For detailed discussions of televisual displays at the postwar *Ideal Home Exhibitions* see Wheatley, "Television in the Ideal Home"; and Chambers, "Designing Early Television for the Ideal Home." For a broader account of the history of the Ideal Home Exhibitions see Ryan, *The Ideal Home through the 20th Century*.

29. "Alexandra Palace Goes to Radiolympia," *Radio Times*, August 19, 1938, 7.

30. Jacobs, *Intimate Screen*, 43 (emphasis in original).

31. "Impressions from Olympia," *Wireless World and Radio Review*, no. 993 (Sept. 8, 1938): 228.

32. "Progress of Television," *The Times* (London), August 23, 1938, 8. See also TV Publicity Pamphlet 1938. BBC Archives, T 23 / 80.

33. Until December of 1936, 427 receivers were sold; in June of 1937 the British industry had sold a total of 1,444 television sets. Burns, *British Television*, 446.

34. See "Radio Notes," *Popular Wireless and Television Times* 31 (August 28, 1937): 579.

35. "Television—Facsimile—Radiotype," New York World's Fair 1939–1940 records, Manuscripts and Archives Division, New York Public Library, P1.44, box 401, folder 12.

36. Westinghouse Electric & Manufacturing Co, *The Middleton Family*.

37. Warren Susman observes that the idea of an "average" person was central to the vision and the rhetoric of world's fairs organizers. The Westinghouse film certainly sustained this discourse. See Susman, "The People's Fair."

38. Television program in *Radio Times*, August 19, 1938, 15.

39. "Come and Be Televised," BBC memo, Sept. 1st, 1938, provided by the Alexandra Palace Television Society. I thank Simon Vaughan for his kind assistance.

40. G. Makemson (?) to the BBC, August 30, 1939, BBC Archives, T 14 / 929 / 1.

41. "Alexandra Palace Goes to Radiolympia," *Radio Times*, August 19, 1938, 7.

42. "London Television Station Chosen," *The Times* (London), June 7, 1935, 13.

43. One reason for not choosing Crystal Palace was that it was already occupied by John Logie Baird's company, which had signed a lease in 1933. Like Alexandra Palace, the Crystal Palace offered sufficient space and was located on an elevated site: the two media—exhibitions and television—asked for similar localizations within the urban landscape. Installing its headquarters, including four television studios, in this most famous of all exhibition buildings, Baird's firm stayed until a fire in 1936 destroyed laboratories, studio, offices, etc. See Burns, *John Logie Baird, Television Pioneer*, 297–98, 325–26.

44. *Grand Opening Festival, Saturday, May 24th, 1873. Programme and Book of Words* (London: Burt & Co., 1873).

45. Burns, *British Television*, 409.

46. "Television To-Day," *Radiolympia* (1938), 37.

47. See Ericson, Riegert, and Aker, "Introduction," 1–18.

48. For more about American television studios' role in the promotion of the networks' corporate image and of the medium as a "modern" means of communication, see chapter 10 of this volume; and Spigel, *TV by Design*.

49. With regard to the importance of photographs taken of studio exteriors for the social shaping of a new medium, see Brian R. Jacobson's fine-grained analysis of Hollywood's early studios and their architecture of "fantastic functionality." Jacobson, "Fantastic Functionality," 60–65.

50. Colomina, "The Media House," 57. This is equally true for the Broadcasting House, BBC's headquarters in Central London, opened in 1932 and designed by a team of modernists including Wells Coates and Serge Chermayeff.

51. On television at the New York World's Fair see Becker, "'Hear-and-See Radio' in the World of Tomorrow"; and Fickers, "Presenting the 'Window on the World' to the World."

52. "Opening of Radio City, New York," *Nature*, Dec. 30, 1933, 998. In the early 1950s NBC would hire industrial designer Norman Bel Geddes to design entirely new production facilities, which, however, would not be built. See Gleich, "Lost Studio of Atlantis."

53. Lugon, "Entre l'affiche et le monument," 89–95.

54. "Television Exhibit Planned for Visitors to Radio City," press release, June 13, 1938, George H. Clark Radioana Collection, Archives Center, National Museum of American History, Smithsonian Institution.

55. Thorburn and Jenkins, "Introduction," 4.

56. Ward, *Weimar Surfaces*, 196.

57. König, *Konsumkultur*, 33.

PART TWO

Foundations

4

Estudios Churubusco

A Transnational Studio for a National Industry

Laura Isabel Serna

La historia de los estudios Churubusco es la historia del cine mexicano. (The history of Estudios Churubusco is the history of Mexican cinema.)
—CARLOS GARCÍA AGRAZ[1]

No physical space is linked more closely to Mexico's cinematic heritage than Estudios Churubusco, S.A. Situated on five hectares (approximately twelve acres) in southeastern Mexico City, the complex has been in operation continuously since 1945. The name carries a strong symbolic association with Mexico's Golden Age of cinema, the mid-twentieth century flowering of the Mexican film industry that birthed a cultural imaginary that was not only extremely popular in its day but continues to resonate across the hemisphere.

In 2017 the studio's past became the subject of an exhibition at the studio itself; it was the first time the studio had opened its doors to the public. The exhibition allowed visitors to engage in interactive activities, learn more about the history of Mexican films produced over the studio's long history, and appreciate—through objects such as cameras, costumes, and lobby cards—the work of the men and women who made films there. Material related to important films from Mexican cinema's Golden Age—such as some of the motorcycles used in filming *A.T.M: ¡A toda máquina!* (Ismael Rodríguez, 1951), starring midcentury heartthrob Pedro Infante—occupies space next to objects from more recent films, such as the car from *Amores perros* (Gonzalez Iñárritu, 2000). This exhibit provides access to one very important strain of Mexican cinematic history, identifying and documenting the films and figures that, it can be argued, constitute a national cinema, a project that, as the exhibit does, begins with the films and stars of the Golden Age.

The abundance of scholarship about this period has explored the range of films that contributed to the creation of a distinctly Mexican cinema, the star system that emerged, and the auteurs whose names are most frequently associated with the industry at its height of international acclaim. Much of this scholarship focuses on the ways in which films produced during this period reflected preoccupations with national identity and provided an alternative to Hollywood fare.

Much less has been written about the political economy and industrial infrastructure that emerged around that production and even less about the iconic studio whose name is so readily associated with the period. Scholarship focused on the political economy of the Golden Age reveals that not only did the state become increasingly interested in supporting Mexico's mass media industries but also that these industries were built on transnational cooperation. In this context nationalism emerges as frequently contested and, just as frequently, more rhetoric than reality. In his explanation of American magnate William O. Jenkins's virtual monopoly on motion picture exhibition in Mexico in the 1940s, historian Andrew Paxman asserts that Jenkins's long-standing relationships with Mexican politicians and businessmen encouraged government officials to turn a blind eye to his outsized role in this sector of the film industry.[2] Seth Fein, who has examined the broader political economy of the post–World War II Mexican film industry, concludes that despite nationalist rhetoric and what he characterizes as "moderate protectionist measures," ultimately, "the Mexican state chose to support its national film industry in a framework that did not directly challenge U.S. hegemony."[3] That is, the celebration of creative and aesthetic nationalism coexisted with an industrial structure that relied on foreign capital and political realism to shore up what had become a significant national industry.

The existing, albeit limited, scholarship on Estudios Churubusco and Mexican studios in general falls into two modes: celebrations of Churubusco as a "dream factory" or as a site of contestation between the Mexican film industry and Hollywood.[4] In the latter vein Francisco Peredo Castro mines US State Department correspondence to cast RKO's involvement in Churubusco's founding as part of a "ferocious struggle for the control of Mexican cinema."[5] Peredo Castro observes that many involved in the Mexican film industry viewed their labor as part of a nationalist project that should be supported by the state, while Hollywood studios remained invested in preserving their hold on Latin American markets. However, in casting Hollywood as the villain in a nationalist set piece, he neglects the transnational relationships at the core of the studio's founding.

This essay analyzes accounts of Churubusco's emergence in both the Mexican and North American press from early rumors about the studio's construction just after the end of World War II to RKO's quiet exit from the project in the early 1950s. A discursive analysis allows us to see Estudios Churubusco as a symbol not of a national industry at its zenith but rather a repository of the aspirations and interests of the major stakeholders in the Mexican film industry as it existed at mid-twentieth century: Mexican film producers anxious to have access to modern production facilities, technological know-how, and technology itself; Mexican investors and American expatriate businessmen hoping to make a tidy profit from the growing Mexican film industry; and US film studios seeking to adapt to the changing media landscape in Mexico and across Latin America. Though Churubusco has persisted in the Mexican cultural imaginary as the physical site that generated a vibrant and enduring national cinema, its origins speak to a national film industry whose nationalist rhetoric often masked complicated transnational relationships.

From the silent period onward, Mexicans dreamed about developing a domestic film industry that would nurture culturally specific representational practices and, perhaps most important, present dignified and "authentic" images of Mexico on domestic and global screens.[6] During the silent period, production was artisanal as filmmakers shot scenes on the street or on location or made do with improvised shooting spaces. Thus, the first studios did not appear until the late teens. Azteca Films, led by actress turned producer-director Mimi Derba and her associate director Enrique Rosas made a series of melodramas inspired by popular Italian films. The company had a studio with one stage for production, a laboratory, and an office. During the same period Ediciones Camus, owned by distributor and producer Germán Camus, had a stage, lab, dressing room, and warehouses that Camus rented out to other producers. These facilities were ephemeral, like Mexican production itself. The major studio still in operation at the end of the 1920s, Estudios Chapultepec, consisted of a shooting stage, laboratory, dressing rooms, and offices but could not accommodate the growing demand for production facilities after the introduction of sound.[7]

Despite later invocations of Churubusco as a "factory"—a rationalized, industrialized site of cultural production—studios in Mexico were not the integrated business entities we associate with the Hollywood studio system of the 1940s. The major Hollywood studios of that period were constituted as corporations, expected to generate revenue that would cover production costs and generate profit for investors, and, until the late 1940s maintained a stable of creative and technical personnel on staff. Frequently they developed a house style that might revolve around genre, stars, production design, and so forth. Importantly, Hollywood studios were, until the 1950s, vertically integrated and thus controlled the production, distribution, and at least first-run exhibition of their projects. In Mexico, in contrast, studios—the physical spaces where films were made—existed primarily as entities separate from the production companies that made films and from distributors and exhibitors.

The introduction of sound technology created opportunities for domestic producers and for technical and creative staff who returned to Mexico after working in silent-era Hollywood, creating an unprecedented demand for production facilities. After the initial success of the first sound film, *Santa* (Ramon Navarro, 1931), which was the effort of local capital and Hollywood-trained talent, including the film's director, production increased from two films in 1931 to sixty in 1936. Tomás Pérez Turrent describes how in the mid-to-late 1930s Mexico experienced "studio construction fever."[8] Some studios, like one a man named Roberto Farfán proposed building in Baja California, which had the advantage, he declared, of its "proximity to the biggest film center in the world, Hollywood," went unrealized.[9] But in Mexico City there was a flurry of studio construction. In an overview of Mexican film studios, Pérez Turrent identifies Estudios México, Estudios Industrial Cinematográfica, S.A., and Empire Studios as among the facilities built in the early 1930s. CLASA (Cinematografía Latino Americana, S.A.) Studios, built in 1934 with state backing, represented a significant advance in terms of film production facilities because it was outfitted with the latest technology. Notably, CLASA was the only studio from the period that functioned in the same fashion as a Hollywood studio by producing its own films. Built in 1937, Estudios Azteca, which rented its facilities to producers, became the other leading facility.[10] Despite this construction boom, there were still not enough well-equipped studios to handle projected or desired film production, which rose steadily over the course of the 1930s.[11] A 1943 press item asserted that existing studios could only make, at best, eighty films a year, which meant that the industry could not fill the demand for Mexican films, either domestically or internationally.[12]

For many the obvious answer to this dilemma was increased state support. Calls for increased state intervention circulated widely in the 1930s and continued through the 1940s.[13] For example, a brief, anonymous item in El Día in 1935 asserted that state support was a prerequisite for the industry's success : "if the government helps [the film industry], it will become a great national industry that will benefit everyone."[14] Such requests frequently dovetailed with declarations that the film industry serve the state's nation-building project, calls that frequently came from the state itself. As early as 1931, El Nacional Revolucionario called for investors willing to put their money to work "making Mexico the Cinelandia of Latin America," and in 1935 former president Emilio Portes Gil declared the importance of cinema to Mexico's national project, calling it "the expression of modern Mexico." In the 1940s both producers and film workers from all sectors of the industry—exhibition, distribution, and production—sought ways to generate support for an industry that employed a large number of workers but whose future seemed precarious.

The government had intervened in the film industry before. After sound technology was introduced in the late 1920s, the Mexican government instituted significant import taxes on films in English and their accompanying sound disks. At the same time tariffs on film-related raw materials and equipment were lowered.[15] This effort was quickly rolled back after threats by US distributors to withhold product from Mexican movie theaters and protests from workers in the distribution and exhibition sectors.[16] The issue of tariffs and quotas would reemerge throughout the 1930s, but such proposals met with immediate resistance from American distribution companies.[17] Most concretely, in 1942 the state established a funding mechanism, the Banco Cinematográfico, which gave producers access to a mix of private and public funds.[18] But, in general, as Seth Fein notes, state support for the film industry was provisional as the state was reluctant to take on the powerful North American interests, which provided films to Mexico's growing number of motion picture theaters and during World War II gave Mexican producers access to film stock and technology.[19]

The need for more production facilities and weak state support dovetailed with Hollywood studios' desire to use Mexico as a low-cost production center, whether for studio production or location shooting. This desire manifested itself in anecdotal musings like that of production manager Tom Kilpatrick, who came to Mexico in September of 1931 as part of a Metro-Goldwyn-Mayer delegation. Kilpatrick gushed over the money-saving possibility of using Mexican landscapes as the backdrop for films with jungle settings. In regard to Hollywood's Spanish-language film production—the industry's initial response to the problem of language presented by sound—Kilpatrick opined that shooting in Mexico could reduce production costs and provide easy access to necessary extras, "crowds," and ambiance.[20] Kilpatrick's observations represent a particularly colorful take on North American companies' interest in shooting films, whether in Spanish or English, in Mexico that persisted long after studios had abandoned Spanish-language production in the United States. In addition to Disney's activities in Mexico under the auspices of the Good Neighbor Policy, United Artists and the Poverty Row studio Republic Pictures both looked to Mexico as a site for production in the early 1940s, and rumors circulated about other studios' interest in filming there.[21] Even calls to make Mexico the center of film production in Latin America, which celebrated the possibilities of a robust national industry, nodded toward the participation of American companies.[22] In 1944, however, Universal Pictures' Mexican representative stated that "despite the many reports of contemplated production by American companies in Mexico, very little has crystallized to date."[23] But the idea continued to percolate. Its realization—in the form of Estudios Churubusco—began to take shape in 1943.

Churubusco was not, at least initially, a collaboration between Hollywood and Mexican investors. Turrent puts it bluntly: "The idea to build the studio [Churubusco] came from speculation in urban land values."[24] In the 1940s Mexico City was growing exponentially. Developers invested in the building of new housing tracts—more than seventy-one colonias came into existence during the early 1940s—and related amenities.[25] Though part of the Ávila Camacho administration's push to modernize Mexico, encourage home ownership for the middle class, and make Mexico City a cosmopolitan destination, funds for these projects frequently came from foreign investment.[26] As scholars of urbanization have noted, virtually all of this growth took place on the periphery of Mexico City, including in the suburban south, where there were still wide-open swathes of land, including the area where Estudios Churubusco would be built.

As in other industries, American expatriates played an important role in film production, distribution, and exhibition. Paxman has documented how William O. Jenkins, the American expatriate businessman who had made his fortune in textiles and sugar, used shell companies to acquire the majority of Mexico's motion picture theaters. Theodore Gildred, an American businessman who would later be the US ambassador to Argentina, held a controlling interest in a large motion picture circuit in Mexico City, COTSA (Compañía Operadora de Teatros, S.A.). In the early 1940s he collaborated on the building of Estudios Tepeyac. Gildred explained to the Mexico City daily *Excélsior* that he had come to the film business via real estate development. He had cannily included cinemas in some of the housing developments he invested in, but because these developments were suburban, rather than in the city's center, he had difficulty obtaining films to screen there. According to Gildred this made him keenly aware of the need for more film studios in Mexico.[27] Thus, in addition to the active presence of US distributors who had accompanied the expansion of US film companies into the Mexican market in the 1920s, American expatriates were eager to do business with their Mexican counterparts in the film business.[28]

At the outset, Estudios Churubusco was the brainchild of one such American expatriate, Harry Wright. In 1909 Wright and his brother, who had come to Mexico around the turn of the century as scrap-iron salesmen, cofounded the iron foundry La Consolidadora, S.A.[29] In 1920 he became the president of the newly reopened Mexico City Country Club, which had fallen on hard times during the revolution. In addition to being an avid golfer, Wright was an enthusiastic amateur cineaste.[30] Wright and a group of American expats held land adjacent to the country club and perceived ownership of a film studio as potentially lucrative in and of itself, as well as being good for business at the club.[31] Wright may have met his collaborator, Howard Randall, at the club or at another expatriate social club. Randall was an RCA engineer who the *Motion Picture Daily* noted had been "active in the sound phase of the business in Mexico for some time," initially as the head engineer at the CLASA studios.[32]

Thus, Churubusco was initially conceived of by American expatriate investors and technicians affiliated with American companies who brought their industry knowledge and technical expertise. Although the partners and a group of Mexican associates incorporated under the name Asociación de Productores Americanos, SA, the trade press in the United States initially associated the project with Randall. In the summer of 1943 his travels to the United States to acquire technology for the studios and the progress of "his" project were reported in *Motion Picture Daily* and *Motion Picture Herald*.[33] By the spring of 1944, however, neither Randall nor Wright was involved with Churubusco, although available sources make it difficult to assess why. Randall had shifted his expertise over to Theodore Gildred's

Tepeyac Studio project, while Wright simply disappears from the film scene.[34] (Two years later Randall had moved on to ventures in the Brazilian film market.) While Randall's participation in the project proved fleeting, his early role represents the value that transnational technical staff brought to Mexican cinema.

This is precisely the value (in addition to capital) that RKO Pictures brought to the table when it became a partner in the still-under-construction Estudios Churubusco in 1944 (see fig. 4.1). Wright and Randall sold their interests to a new entity, the Asociación de Productores Mexicanos. The press reported that, in accordance with Mexican law, 52 percent of the capital for this new corporate entity had come from Mexican investors, including the increasingly powerful cinema owner and radio entrepreneur Emilio Azcárraga Viduerreta and film producer Jesús Grovas.[35] In February of 1944 Peter N. Ravthon, RKO's chief executive, came to Mexico City and confirmed the studio's participation in the project. When construction was over, he declared, "Mexico would be proud to have the most modern [facilities] that exist and are comparable with the best in the United States, because they have been designed according to the most advanced techniques and at all costs."[36] Other news items stressed that RKO would be a conduit for the acquisition of American technology.[37] *Film Daily* noted that not only was American-made technology being installed but also that "Hollywood technicians are being set up as department heads."[38] By the end of 1945 the Asociación de Productores Mexicanos had invested a bit more than half of its reported initial capital of 13 million Mexican pesos (approximately US$4 million) in the studios' construction, including procuring the latest technology.[39] In this way RKO's involvement in the project represented a privately funded extension of the technological aid that the US had provided to the Mexican film industry during the war.[40]

It is no surprise, then, that press coverage of new studio construction focused on the technology that would be installed and available to producers and creative personnel.[41] In 1945 the fact that Charles Woram, RKO's representative and the general manager of Churubusco, had gone to the United States to acquire more equipment for the studio was reported breathlessly, emphasizing the amount of money reportedly being spent.[42] As Churubusco neared completion, press coverage consistently listed its many amenities. In comparison to what had been Mexico's state-of-the-art facility, CLASA, with its six sound stages, Churubusco was enormous.[43] Once finished, the complex would have twelve sound stages, multiple dressing rooms, and mechanical and construction shops.[44] More films could be made simultaneously than in any other studio. Other amenities promised to make filmmaking more efficient. Installed by Pathé, the laboratory featured all of the latest technology, including modern, mechanized developing equipment. For the first time, Mexican film production would not have to use the established, but time- and labor-consuming, rack-and-tank method. Other efficiencies included clear spatial division of labor. One profile of the studio mentioned what must have

FIGURE 4.1. Estudios Churubusco under construction, 1945. Fototeca Nacional INAH, Colección Archivo Casasola, VF 278177.

been a common practice at other Mexican studios—constructing set decorations on the floor of the sound stage where filming would take place—and expressed amazement that Churubusco was so large that it contained a "modern machinery [workshop] for the construction of sets, which are constructed in a shop separate from the stages."[45] Finally, the complex had "a private plant to give direct current," two fixed and eight mobile generators, which likewise promised efficiency.[46] During the 1940s, electrical power was often unreliable, and the capacity of Mexico City's electricity grid had not grown to keep pace with demand, making on-demand energy a prerequisite for regular, uninterrupted film production.[47]

Beyond space and efficiency, descriptions of Churubusco focused on its up-to-date technology—a factor that would allow producers to make more polished films and, hopefully, reduce the "gloss gap" between Mexican and Hollywood films.[48] Journalists took note of the complex's recording and dubbing studios, both equipped with RCA Victor sound systems and state-of-the-art soundproofing. A photo spread in the magazine *Mañana* presented readers with three images—one of an executive on the phone booking rentals—intended to illustrate that Churubusco offered producers "less noise, less cost." One of the images featured star Jorge Negrete shouting, above a caption that assured readers, "Be amazed! Not

FIGURE 4.2. An aerial view of Estudios Churubusco and the surrounding area, Tlalpan, Río Churubusco, and Club Campester (Country Club), Mexico City, Dec. 13, 1946. Aerofoto BRMA 4518, Fundación ICA.

even his resonant voice reaches the interior of the [sound] stages." And the text of the article noted that the studios had "made the dreams of the old producers a reality. In the Estudios Churubusco they have suppressed noise."[49] State-of-the-art sound technology was likewise emphasized in coverage of Tepeyac Studios, which it was reported had walls "recovered in various layers of asbestos to prevent sound from passing through them."[50]

But just as important as the studio's technology was the symbolic role that Churubusco played in 1940s Mexico City. It is instructive that in histories of architecture from this period Churubusco never appears as an example of the modernist aesthetic that could be seen everywhere, from multifamily housing developments to movie theaters and the university's new campus. Indeed, in photographs taken from above in the 1940s and 1950s, Estudios Churubusco looks like a massive set of airplane hangars set in a field (see fig. 4.2). Thus, though the building itself was an unremarkable example of midcentury Mexican industrialization, it became the backdrop for a range of activities beyond filmmaking. Churubusco formed an important part of the

FIGURE 4.3. Emilio "El Indio" Fernandez with the American cast of the RKO film *Mystery in Mexico* (Robert Wise, 1948) and other Mexican nationals, possibly cast members or studio personnel, Estudios Churubusco, 1947. Fototeca Nacional INAH, Colección Archivo Casasola, VF 93581.

capital's cosmopolitan film culture. As the project took shape, executives from RKO and other related companies traveled to and from Mexico City, sometimes accompanied by their wives.[51] The studio's Mexican staff likewise traveled to Hollywood.[52] This image of cosmopolitan mobility lent an air of sophistication to the studios, represented in one news item's report that these jet-setting media executives had flown American Airlines' luxury "Flagship" aircraft.[53] The studio also played host to groups associated with Mexico's burgeoning mass-media industries. For example, in November of 1945, before the studio had officially opened, Emilio Azcarraga hosted a luncheon in honor of a film business convention.[54] The next year, just after its opening, Churubusco hosted the screening of an informative documentary for the Interamerican Radio Diffusion Association, which was holding its meeting in Mexico City.[55] On a more quotidian level, the press frequently reported banquets, charity balls, and other events—frequently attended by RKO executives and their guests—that were held at the studio.[56] In these ways the studios functioned as social spaces where the transnational nature of the Mexican media industries could be put on display, celebrated, and nurtured (see fig. 4.3).

All of this conviviality could not obscure the fact that Mexican film producers and their American counterparts had distinct objectives. While Mexican producers saw the studio as an important step toward stabilizing domestic production, RKO saw Churubusco as a way to profit off of the increasing popularity of Mexican film in Spanish-speaking markets and generating a revenue stream through studio rental income. Lisa Jarvinen has documented how Spanish-language film production, the most enduring of Hollywood's multilingual experiments in the wake of the introduction of sound, ceased in Hollywood itself by 1939. She observes, however, that many companies shifted toward distribution and coproduction outside of Hollywood as less capital-intensive ways of maintaining a stake in the Spanish-speaking market.[57] Richard B. Jewell, who has written what is considered the definitive history of RKO's rise and decline, mentions Churubusco in passing as a pet project of studio head Ravthon, who ran RKO from 1940 to 1946. According to Jewell, although RKO, like its peers, experienced an upsurge in profits during wartime, it was followed by another dip, exacerbated by labor unrest, a lack of physical space, and increasing production costs, all of which may have motivated Ravthon's decision to invest in Churubusco.[58] "Ravthon," *Motion Picture Daily* reported in 1945, "characterized the studio and film production project as not only an investment for the company but also an effort to become part of the Mexican industry."[59]

With its investment in Churubusco, RKO attempted to establish a foothold in the Spanish-language market. First, RKO developed a separate production entity, Ramex, to make films in Spanish for Latin American audiences. These films were either remakes of RKO films—continuing a strategy of Hollywood's multilingual production—or were based on properties that RKO owned. Ramex was formed with capital of 4.5 million Mexican pesos (approximately US$1.3 million) in the form of forty-five thousand shares, the bulk of which were owned by Charles Woram, Churubusco's manager. *Motion Picture Daily* reported that the production company had completed two films by November of 1946 and four or five more were slated for 1947.[60] These two films seem to have been *Los que volvieron* (Alejandro Galindo, 1947), a Spanish-language remake of *Five Came Back* (John Farrow, 1939), and *Todo un caballero* (Miguel Delgado, 1947).[61] Of the four forecast for 1947 only two seem to have been made: *Hermoso ideal* (Alejandro Galindo, 1948) and *El casado casa quiere* (Gilberto Martinez Solares, 1948).

RKO also invested in prestige coproductions with Mexican and US independent producers and less frequently made its own films at Churubusco. Of the former, *La perla/The Pearl* (1947), which was made in both English and Spanish versions, is probably the best known. Emilio Fernandez directed both versions with a Mexican cast that included Pedro Armendariz and Dolores del Rio. The *Hollywood Reporter* noted that making both films cost a mere 2 million Mexican pesos (US$400,000).[62] John Ford's *The Fugitive* (1947), the story of a fugitive priest that was set during the Cristero Rebellion in the mid-1920s, which he produced through his own company,

Argosy Productions, featured American talent in some of the lead roles and Mexican actors in secondary parts. RKO made at least one of its own program pictures, *Mystery in Mexico* (Robert Wise, 1948), "the story of an American nightclub singer in a Mexican setting of music and mystery," at Churubusco.[63]

Finally, Churubusco studio's executives were also happy to welcome independent producers from the United States. The US trade press reported that Mexican studios were actively trying to recruit independent and major studios as clients because Mexican producers could not use all the available space.[64] In 1946 Ravthon told *Variety*, "Production costs there are much lower than in the U.S., which has been one reason for strong American film company interests in Mexican studios."[65] Films produced in Mexico and shot or developed at Churubusco by American film companies included 20th Century Fox's *The Captain from Castile* (Henry King, 1947), which featured Mexican performers in secondary roles; Sol Lesser's *Tarzan and the Mermaids* (Robert Florey, 1948), reportedly the best in the series because of its "beautiful backgrounds and native cast in supporting roles"; and Bryan Foy Productions' *Adventures of Casanova* (Roberto Galvadón, 1948).[66] In 1947 optimism about Mexico as a site for US production was at an all-time high. *Variety* reported, "A large number of pictures are on studio skeds for using Mexican locations later this year anywhere from one to eight weeks, which represents the largest utilization of a foreign country by Hollywood in a single year in the history of the studios."[67] This optimism was reinforced by a report by the Office of International Trade and Commerce Department, which claimed that "Mexico looms as a new film production center to be used by Hollywood for Latin stories." Mexico, the report noted, offered "background" and "authenticity" in "natural form."[68] For a moment, at least, RKO's goal of creating, as Jewell describes it, a "state of the art rental facility for Mexican filmmakers," and an opportunity for its own producers to take advantage of reduced labor costs in Mexico, seemed possible.[69]

Though RKO's Mexican collaborators were enthusiastic about the possibility of coproductions and independent productions, others were wary of how US influence would affect Mexico's domestic industry. Periodically, an alarming headline would appear in the Mexican press declaring that the entire industry was about to become a vassal of Hollywood. For example, journalist Carlos Denegri reported in *Excélsior*, "Our cinema is passing into foreign hands," a phenomenon he blamed on the failure of dubbing as a Hollywood strategy for appealing to Spanish-speaking audiences. After listing all of the production projects and studios being developed in collaboration with Americans, including Churubusco, Denegri observed: "This union of the Mexican and North American [film] industries will greatly benefit our own film investors and film art in Mexico, but it will put the economic destiny of one of our principal industries in Hollywood's hands."[70] This alarm was echoed by a feature in *El Nacional*, which predicted that the domestic industry would be absorbed by North American capital, arguing that the presence of US

investment was pitting Mexican laborers against their US counterparts.[71] Sometimes, such anxieties were even articulated in the US trade press.[72]

Many who were deeply involved in the film industry viewed the situation more
realistically. Descriptions of Churubusco in the North American trade press
emphasized that it was "a general service studio for Mexican as well as American
producers."[73] Journalist Roberto Cantú Robert reiterated this view in the pages of
Cinema Reporter. The Mexican film industry, he observed, had long been "at the
mercy of those who provide us with virgin material [film], equipment, etc.," in
other words American manufacturers of film-related materials.[74] Rather than having been established as national facilities for the domestic industry, studios such as
Churubusco had been constructed as rental facilities. The same logic governed
Estudios Azteca, whose management clarified that the studio was not a production
company but rather a production space. Jose U. Calderón, Azteca's manager, touted
the studio's 100 percent Mexican financing even as he acknowledged that the Mexican film industry was "not autonomous." "The film industry in general and the
studios in Mexico City in particular," he observed, "owe a great deal to the American government."[75] As had been the case with the railroad and mining industries in
the early twentieth century, the development of the film industry in Mexico was
based on the importation of both technology and technological know-how.[76]

Even as some segments of Mexico's film industry clamored for protectionist
measures and more state support, goals that would be realized in the 1949 Ley de
la Industria Cinematográfica, organized labor proved to be the most significant
roadblock to the success of the studio as RKO had imagined it.[77] RKO had invested
in Churubusco at a moment when labor unrest wracked the Mexican film industry, though Ravthon would publicly brush such concerns aside.[78] The studio
opened having signed labor contracts with the newly formed Sindicato de Trabajadores de la Producción Cinematográfica, which had split off from the Sindicato
de Trabajadores de la Industria Cinematográfica.[79] Both of these groups pushed
consistently for quotas that would guarantee screen time for domestic films and,
more importantly in the context of production, for wage increases. In the late
1940s, labor demands soon made American producers think twice about making
films in Mexico.[80] News outlets periodically reported threatened strikes.[81]

By the late 1940s, Churubusco had become a drag on RKO. It neither generated
the rental income the studio had hoped, nor had it become the remote production
site executives imagined. Though RKO designated a special sales manager to sell
Ramex films in Latin America and developed targeted sales materials, a dearth of
coverage either of box office or critical reception indicates that the films the company produced were unsuccessful.[82] Despite the fact that by 1948 Churubusco,
along with Azteca, was producing almost all of the American films made in Mexico, as well as a generous share of domestic production, the company signaled that
it wanted to get out of its commitments to the studio. Sunny prognostications

about the ways that increased capacity would put the Mexican film industry on solid footing aside, in 1946 fewer films had been produced than in 1945.[83] The trade press in the United States reported that the company was operating in the red, even as workers demanded a 60 percent salary increase and rentals to American producers failed to materialize.[84] As a strike loomed, Churubusco and Mexico's other US-Mexican owned studio, Tepeyac, merged, but even that move could not salvage RKO's investment.

By the fall of 1948 rumors circulated that RKO was looking for a buyer. Meanwhile, the studio continued to be used by American companies for the production of 16 mm films for television, dubbing, and independent productions. It also continued to make a significant share of the country's total output: thirty-three of eighty-two films in 1948. Churubusco, which had absorbed Tepeyac, would merge with Estudios Azteca in 1950. Stock of the new, merged company would be split three ways among RKO, Azcarraga, and Azteca.[85] This took place as the studios continued to try to lure independent producers from North America in order to better utilize all of the available facilities. The flurry of studio production that had animated the late 1930s and early 1940s had, ironically, resulted in "an excess of studio space and facilities."[86] Although it is unclear precisely when—both the press and histories of RKO are silent on the topic—sometime around 1951 RKO divested itself of its interests in the plant.[87] That did not, however, end the studio's relationship with American film producers. In 1953 *Variety* announced a six-picture deal between United Artists and an unnamed Mexican production company to make films in both English and Spanish under the terms of which UA would "provide the coin, world distribution, equipment, scripts, and directors, and for the Mexicans to supply technicians, scenery, and players."[88] And the following year another eight-picture deal between independent producers and their Mexican counterparts forecast using Churubusco's facilities.[89] That is, Mexico continued to be seen as an attractive place for independent production throughout the decade, even as Mexican cinema slipped into a long decline.[90] In 1957 Emilio Azcarraga threatened to shutter Churubusco and sell off its land to real estate developers. He cited the studio's lack of profit, which he claimed was due to "unfair competition and labor troubles."[91] Of course, the studio was not shut down. Instead, CLASA, which had been run by the state for many years, was closed, and the Banco Nacional Cinematográfica acquired Churubusco, the country's most well-equipped production facility thanks to RKO, placing it under government control.[92]

Thus, even after RKO, caught up in its own turmoil during the 1950s, exited the scene, transnational coproductions and the rental of studio space by US-based producers continued to be (and continue to be) vital to Churubusco. Lisa Jarvinen writes that Spain's, Argentina's, and Mexico's "film industries developed in ways shaped by Hollywood's dominance of world film markets."[93] Churubusco is a case in point. Nationalist histories of the studio gloss over the importance of the United

States in the form of expatriate investors, a major studio willing to gamble on an escape valve for backlogged production and a conduit to the increasingly valuable Latin American market, and technicians who brought their expertise to the studios. Even at the height of the Golden Age, film production was a risky endeavor for Mexican producers. They saw Churubusco as a way to increase the industry's production capacity and the quality of technology available to producers. In sum, Churubusco emerged not out of the triumph of the national film industry but rather out of anxiety about its future. Rather than a nationalist triumph, Churubusco might be thought of as a structure that contained the transnational relationships that undergird the Mexican film industry's development and trajectory.

NOTES

1. Quoted in "Estudios Churubusco muestra 72 años de cine a través de exposición," *El Mundo* (Las Vegas, NV), Dec. 6, 2017, www.elmundo.net/entretenimiento/estudios-churubusco-muestra-72-%C3%B1os-de-cine-trav%C3%A9s-de-exposici%C3%B3n.

2. Paxman, *Jenkins of Mexico*, 251.

3. Fein, "From Collaboration to Containment," 148, 155.

4. See Pérez Turrent, *La fábrica de sueños*; Pérez Turrent, "The Studios," 133–44; and Peredo Castro, "La batalla por los Estudios Churubusco," 134–52.

5. Peredo Castro, "La batalla por los Estudios Churubusco," 135.

6. For accounts of early Mexican filmmaking see Reyes, *Cine y sociedad en México*. Rielle Navitski provides a summary of these aspirations in *Public Spectacles of Violence*, 90. See also Serna, *Making Cinelandia*, 53.

7. This account of silent-era studios is based on Pérez Turrent, "The Studios."

8. Pérez Turrent, 137.

9. Roberto Farfán to Luis I. Rodríguez, June 11, 1936, Archivo General de la Nación (Mexico), Fondo Lazaro Cardenas, vol. 653, exp. 525.3/3.

10. W. V. Wolfe, "Report of the SMPE Committee on Progress: Film Production in Mexico," *Journal of the Society of Motion Picture Engineers* 48, no. 2 (April 1947): 315.

11. See, e.g., "Ya necesitan más estudios," *Excélsior*, Jan. 1, 1938, 10; "Una gran industria," *Novedades*, Feb. 5, 1943, 15; and "Va a ser la meca," *Novedades*, March 19, 1943, 15.

12. "Una gran industria," *Novedades*, Feb. 5, 1943, 15.

13. See, e.g., "La industria nacional," *El Día*, Oct. 2, 1935, 21; and "Ya se necesitan más estudios," *Excélsior*, Jan. 1, 1938, 10.

14. "La industria nacional," *El Día*, Oct. 2, 1935, 21. See also "El porvenir de una industria naciente," *El Nacional*, Oct. 18, 1935, 8.

15. "Películas cinematográficas—derechos de importación," *El Universal*, Jan. 30, 1930; "Aumento de derechos a las películas," *El Economista*, Sept. 16, 1930, 2; "El Asunto de las películas: Las antiguas tarifas arancelarias seguirán en vigor sólo provisionalmente," *El Nacional*, Oct. 22, 1931, 8. "Modificaciones a la tarifa de importación para fomentar la industria cinematográfica," *Boletín de informes de la Secretaría de Hacienda y Crédito Publico*, July 29, 1931, 29.

16. "El aumento de cuotas para la importación de películas" *El Universal*, April 22, 1932, 9; James Lockhart, "Mexico Theatres, Heavily Taxed, Fear New Impost Will Close Doors," *Motion Picture Herald*, April 16, 1932, 14; "High Tariffs Cripple Swedish Markets; Mexico May Be Totally Film-Less Aug. 20 for Same Cause," *Variety*, August 2, 1932, 13. Employees wrote to President Pascual Ortiz Rubio

outlining their case: Sindicato de Empleados cinematografistas del Dto. Federal to Pres. Pascual Ortiz Rubio, August 5, 1931, Archivo General de la Nación, Fondo Pascual Ortiz Rubio, C-69, vol. 15, exp. 8.

17. See, e.g., "Los alquiladores de películas se van," *El Universal,* Jan. 18, 1935, 9.

18. See Vega Alfaro, "The Decline of the Golden Age," 167. In 1947 it would change its name to the Banco Nacional Cinematográfico and shift to a primarily state funding model.

19. See Fein, "From Collaboration to Containment," esp. 155–57.

20. "México puede llegar a ser el emporio de los productores de films," *Excélsior,* Sept. 26, 1931, 10.

21. "Disney and Staff Guests of Mexico," *Motion Picture Herald,* Dec. 19, 1942, 25; "Latin America Builds Own Film Industry," *Motion Picture Herald,* August 5, 1944, 24; Don Pepe (pseud.), "Republic to Continue Production in Mexico," *Box Office,* June 16, 1945, 22; "El millonario Schenke ingresa al cine nacional," *Novedades,* Oct. 20, 1943, 15; "México atrae a los cineastas," *Novedades,* Oct. 25, 1942, 15; "US Majors Talk Mexican Production," *Film Daily,* June 16, 1943, 16.

22. See, e.g., "La Cinelandia de Latina América," *El Nacional Revolucionario,* Oct. 11, 1931, 8.

23. "Little U.S. Production in Mexico: Epstein," *Motion Picture Daily,* Dec. 26, 1944, 9.

24. Pérez Turrent, "The Studios," 138.

25. Canclini, Castellanos, and Mantecón, *La ciudad de los viajeros,* 24.

26. On Ávila Camacho's goal of fostering development in Mexico see Niblo, *Mexico in the 1940s,* esp. 1–73.

27. "Los Estudios Tepeyac colocan a México en primer plano de producción mundial," *Excélsior,* August 4, 1946, 10. See also Don Pepe (pseud.), "Mexican Studio Work Waits Federal Okay," *Box Office,* March 17, 1945, 35.

28. See Serna, *Making Cinelandia.*

29. Their trajectory conforms to that of the many North American technicians and salesmen who came to Mexico in the late nineteenth and early twentieth centuries. See Beatty, *Technology and the Search for Progress in Modern Mexico,* 66–68.

30. See Morales, "La importancia de llamarse Bolling y Harry Wright."

31. Oral History with Enrique Solis Chagoyan by Aurelio de los Reyes, Archivo de la Palabra, Proyecto de cine mexicano, PHO/2/8, Instituto Nacional de Antropología e Historia.

32. "Another New Studio in Work in Mexico," *Motion Picture Daily,* July 14, 1943, 1; "Boom in New Houses Continues in Mexico," *Film Daily,* May 23, 1941, 3. See also "NY Backing for New Mexican Film Studio," *Variety,* June 30, 1943, 25.

33. "Randall Studio Progress," *Motion Picture Daily,* July 23, 1943, 4. See also Luis Becerra Celis, "Plan New $1,000,000 Mexico City Studio," *Motion Picture Herald,* July 10, 1943, 36.

34. "Big Production Budget for Tepeyac Studios," *Film Daily,* August 28, 1946, 10: "Talk Merger of Top Mex Studio," *Variety,* Oct. 15, 1947, 16.

35. "RKO Buys into Mexican Studio," *Film Daily,* March 10, 1944, 1. "Industrias Cinematográficas," *El Nacional,* Dec. 24, 1945, 4.

36. "Inversión en nuestro cine," *Novedades,* Feb. 23, 1944, 15.

37. "16 New Stages to Swell Production in Mexico," *Film Daily,* March 10, 1944, 1.

38. Ralph Wilk, "Hollywood," *Film Daily,* Feb. 4, 1946, 11.

39. "Industrias Cinematográficas," *El Nacional,* Dec. 24, 1945, 4. Historical exchange rate generated using date at Lawrence H. Officer, "Exchange Rates between the United States Dollar and Forty-One Currencies," MeasuringWorth, 2018, www.measuringworth.com/exchangeglobal.

40. "Mexican Film Industry Getting Amer. Equipment," *Film Daily,* June 25, 1943, 2.

41. See, e.g. Roberto Cantú Robert, "Puntos de vista," *Cinema Reporter,* Feb. 26, 1943; "Los grandes estudios para el cine en Churubusco," *El Nacional,* Feb. 11, 1946.

42. "Don Carlos Woram," *El Porvenir,* Jan. 21, 1945, 11.

43. "Una visita de buena fe al Hollywood Mexicano," *El Universal,* May 10, 1942, 9.

44. "RKO Is Active in Mexico," *Motion Picture Daily,* Oct. 23, 1946, 1.

45. "Los Estudios Churubusco," *Mañana,* Jan. 19, 1946, 73.

46. "Private Power Plant for Churubusco Studios," *Film Daily,* August 21, 1946, 10.

47. See Wionczek, "The State and the Electric Power Industry in Mexico, 1895–1965," 540–41; and Tamayo, "La generación de energía eléctrica en México," *El Trimestre Económico* 9, no. 35 (Oct.-Dec. 1942), 405–39, 411. Wionczek writes, "As a result [of industry structure], well before the end of World War II, serious shortages of electric power appeared all over the country" (541).

48. Stephen R. Niblo uses this term to characterize the inefficiencies of the Mexican film industry in the 1940s. See Niblo, *Mexico in the 1940s,* 51.

49. "Los Estudios Churubusco," *Mañana,* Jan. 19, 1946, 73.

50. "Los Estudios Tepeyac colocan a México en primer plano," *Excélsior,* August 4, 1946, 10.

51. "RKO Execs Mex Trek," *Variety,* Oct. 9, 1946, 6.

52. "Hollywood," *Variety,* June 19, 1946, 55; "Coming and Going," *Film Daily,* July 2, 1946, 2; "Coming and Going," *Film Daily,* August 6, 1946, 2.

53. "Otros funcionarios del RKO de México, arribaron a esta," *El Nacional,* Oct. 12, 1946, 5.

54. "Clausura de una reunión," *El Nacional,* Nov. 30, 1945, 1.

55. "Como se hará la clausura," *El Nacional,* Oct. 6, 1946, 4.

56. Colmenares (pseud.), "Ritmo Fílmico," *Jueves de Excélsior,* August 8, 1946, 30; "American-Mexican 'Variety-Club Week,'" *Motion Picture Daily,* Nov. 18, 1946.

57. Jarvinen, *The Rise of Spanish-Language Filmmaking,* 146–47. Jarvinen notes that United Artists was a pioneer in coproduction with Mexican companies.

58. Jewell, *Slow Fade to Black,* 40–41.

59. "World Release for RKO Mexico Film," *Motion Picture Daily,* Dec. 21, 1945, 1.

60. "RKO Affiliate in Mexico Finishes 2," *Motion Picture Daily,* Nov. 7, 1946, 12.

61. "Film Reviews," *Variety,* August 13, 1947, 22.

62. "$400,000 'Pearl' Expected to Take $2,500,000 in U.S.," *Hollywood Reporter,* Oct. 22, 1947.

63. "Sales and Product," *Motion Picture Herald,* July 12, 1947, 13.

64. "Mexico to Campaign for U.S. Producers," *Film Daily,* May 20, 1946; and Peggy Le Boutillier, "Tourists Find Inflation Heavy in Mexico; Building Boom On," *Variety,* Nov. 20, 1946, 20.

65. "Ravthon Sees Small Chance for Mex 50% Quota; Tells RKO Prod. Plans," *Variety,* Oct. 23, 1946, 18. See also "H'wood Circles," *Variety,* March 31, 1948, 8.

66. "Tarzan and the Mermaids," *Motion Picture News,* March 23, 1948, 2; "Ravthon Sees Small Chance for Mex 50% Quota."

67. "At Least 8 Films Slated for Mex. Prod. This Year," *Variety,* June 11, 1947, 18.

68. "Mexico as New Film Production Center for Latin Yarns Forecast by Golden," *Variety,* July 23, 1947, 11.

69. Jewell, *Slow Fade to Black,* 31.

70. Carlos Denegri, "Nuestro cine pasa a manos de extranjeros," *Excélsior,* Feb. 12, 1946. See also "Magnates Americanos desean asociarse al cine nacional," *Excélsior,* Sept. 13, 1943, 10.

71. Ernesto Alvarez Nolasco, "El cine mexicano, a punto de quedar totalmente absorbido por capital norteamericano," *El Popular,* Feb. 6, 1947, 15.

72. See, e.g., Douglas L. Grahame, "Mexico City," *Variety,* Feb. 5, 1947. See also, "Mexico Cleans House in Reorganization," *Motion Picture Daily,* Nov. 7, 1946, 2.

73. "World Release for RKO Mexican Film," *Motion Picture Daily,* Dec. 21, 1945, 6.

74. Roberto Cantú Robert, "Puntos de vista," *Cinema Reporter,* April 15, 1944, 27.

75. "La Azteca hace declaraciones a lo dicho por el Sr. Grovas," *El Universal,* Nov. 28, 1943, 10.

76. See Beatty, *Technology and the Search for Progress.*

77. "Slowdown at RKO Mexican Studio," *Motion Picture Daily,* Jan. 23, 1948, 1.

78. "Labor Rows Won't Block RKO Studios in Mexico," *Film Daily*, March 27, 1946, 1, 8.

79. "El 'STIC' desea colaborar y modifica sus pretensiones," *El Nacional*, August 30, 1945, 2. Though deserving of a careful explication, film industry unions that had been established during the silent period by workers in the exhibition and distribution sectors grew stronger in the 1930s and 1940s as creative personnel and technical staff joined their compatriots, and the power of unions grew with the support of the state. In the mid-1940s the largest film-workers' union, the Sindicato de Trabajadores de la Industria Cinematográfica, experienced a very high-profile split as above-the-line creative talent and production workers, led by actor Mario Moreno (Cantinflas), formed their own union, the Sindicato de Trabajadores de Producción Cinematográfica.

80. "Slowdown at RKO Mexican Studios," *Motion Picture Daily*, Jan. 23, 1948, 7.

81. "Sin titulo," *El Informador*, July 4, 1945, 6; "*Cine*," *Mañana*, March 30, 1946, 96–97.

82. "RKO Latin-America Shift Includes Gomez Switch," *Variety*, April 16, 1947, 16; "RKO Radio Expanding Foreign Publicity Service," *Showman's Trade Review*, March 15, 1947, 15.

83. "Mex Film Strike Threat Spreads to 4 Studios; Both Sides Give Stand," *Variety*, June 23, 1948, 14.

84. "Mex Churubusco Studios to Fold under Pay Load, They Tell Federal Board," *Variety*, June 8, 1948, 3; "Wage Strike Threatens Two of Five Mex Studios," *Variety*, June 16, 1948, 15; "Mexico Studio for H'wood Usage Didn't Pan Out, RKO Wants to Unload," *Variety*, Oct. 27, 1948, 4.

85. "Churubusco and Azteca Mexican Studios Merger a 3-Way Split with RKO," *Variety*, March 29, 1950, 13.

86. "Churubusco and Azteca Mexican Studios Merger a 3-Way Split with RKO."

87. "Mex City Studio Boss Quits," *Variety*, August 22, 1951, 15.

88. "US, Mexican Group Set 6-Pic Production Deal," *Variety*, Jan. 21, 1953, 14.

89. "US Producers to Make 8 Pix in Mexico by January," *Moving Picture News*, Sept. 29, 1954, 15.

90. The causes of this lengthy decline have long been debated. Most scholars point to high costs, inefficient production, the insularity created by the STPC (which prevented new talent from entering the industry), and the recycling of themes. For a fresh perspective see Paxman, "Who Killed the Mexican Film Industry?"

91. See "Mexico's Churubusco Studio Forced to Close Down by Deficits," *Variety*, April 16, 1957, 1.

92. "Mex Bank Acquires Churubusco Studios," *Motion Picture Daily*, Oct. 1, 1958.

93. Jarvinen, *Rise of Spanish-Language Filmmaking*, 161.

5

Pinewood Studios, the Independent Frame, and Innovation

Sarah Street

British director Darrel Catling reported to the British trade press in February of 1948 on the Independent Frame (IF), a new system of film production that had been launched at Pinewood Studios. Catling had recently used it to make *Under the Frozen Falls,* a short children's film that had benefited from the IF's aim to "rationalize that which is largely irrational in film making."[1] He described how his film had been very carefully preplanned in terms of script, storyboards, and technical plans. Several scenes were prestaged and filmed without the main cast, who were later incorporated into scenes by means of rear projection. Special effects were of paramount importance in reducing the number of sets that needed to be built. Process work included hanging miniatures, glass shots, matte shots, and foreground transparencies. Sets were built on wheeled rostrums so that studio floors were never idle as one set replaced another, more or less instantaneously. These were the essential features of IF filmmaking, which aimed to reduce the time normally taken for a production while also reducing costs. The IF received extensive commentary in the trade press over the next two years, as several feature films were released that applied its techniques and philosophy of efficiency, planning, and integrated design. Heralded as a revolutionary approach, the IF promised to streamline British production methods and halt a series of serious economic crises that had beset the film industry following the end of the Second World War. While most of its key components were already in existence or had been mooted, such as "the pictured script" and a number of special effects involving projection, it represented a turn toward more mechanized and cost-effective methods for their deployment.[2]

Yet despite the excitement that accompanied its development and initial application, the IF has largely been recorded in film histories as a failure. Despite enthusiastic

endorsement from Michael Powell, who as early as 1945 advocated it as a "revolution
... [and] a big step forward" with "consequences as far-reaching as the introduction
of colour and sound," the IF was never applied to the production of more than a handful of British films in the late 1940s.[3] Most histories consider it as a bold experiment
that failed for a number of reasons, including bad timing, criticism from technicians,
uneven application, and having been used in films that were seen as unremarkable.[4]
This essay reconsiders the IF's history, focusing on its origins, application, the debates
it prompted, and its legacy for Pinewood Studios. I argue that even though in the
short-term it did not transform production, the IF was much more than an expensive
gamble by J. Arthur Rank, Britain's dominant film producer, who bankrolled its development. Rather, the IF was an innovative response to the problems facing the British
film industry at the end of the 1940s. It also helped to change Pinewood, both physically and in its production practices, contributing to its evolution into the effects hub
it is renowned for today; it is thus a key part of Pinewood's history.

The IF was devised by David Rawnsley, a British set designer with an engineering background who had worked with David Lean, Michael Powell, and Emeric
Pressburger. Although the IF was presented to the trade as a new system, it orchestrated a number of existing technical developments. During the Second World
War, disruptions to studio activity and a scarcity of labor and materials meant that
cost-cutting efficiencies spawned creative invention. Rawnsley had become concerned about "the crowded stages, the interminable delays, the chopping and the
changing, the noise and the confusion, and the other uneconomic aspects" of studio film production.[5] As art director on *In Which We Serve* (David Lean and Noël
Coward, 1942), he devised many ingenious effects to convey stormy seas by means
of a rocking process screen. Michael Powell's admiration for Rawnsley's work followed their collaboration on *49th Parallel* (Michael Powell, 1941) and *One of Our
Aircraft Is Missing* (Michael Powell and Emeric Pressburger, 1942). Powell recalled
how Rawnsley and production manager Syd Streeter, "practically single-handed,
built the submarine for *49th Parallel*. And, when we had to make *One of Our Aircraft Is Missing* with John Corfield on a shoestring, and we had to take six actors
across Holland and back to England ... there must have been about forty sets of
which at least half were on-the-spot improvisations, effects of light and shade,
cooked up by Ronnie Neame and David and me, and not only perfectly satisfying
to the public—it was a damn sight more satisfying to us."[6] Powell made an important point that influenced his subsequent approach to production design: "Realism
is one thing and naturalism another. I hate naturalism. I hate it when we have a
simulated exterior scene in the studio, and I see prop men bringing in great
branches of living trees, covered with leaves, which wither under the light and are
thrown out the next day."[7] This philosophy was implied with the IF, a point recognized by Dixon, who acknowledges that simplified sets had the potential for styli-
zation via emphasis on shadows and props that could become "part of an overall

system of imagistic substitution."[8] As we will see, a few of the films made with the IF showed such artistry. Macnab even goes so far as to argue that "in a sense the IF prefigures the 'total cinema' Powell sought to achieve" with productions such as *The Red Shoes* (1948) and *The Tales of Hoffmann* (1951).[9] These shared the IF's emphasis on preparatory drawings, preplanning, and the creation of a total, immersive world within a film studio.

The prevailing ethos of the IF was to place emphasis on the production team, whose efficiency was crucial for its success. As such, it was antiauteur in its promotion of the contributions of technicians, special effects experts, and set designers such as Rawnsley, who enjoyed the challenges of lower budget, independent filmmaking. Rawnsley had learned the benefits of detailed preplanning when he designed the sets for *They Were Sisters* (Arthur Crabtree, 1945). Claiming to have influenced Rawnsley, producer Harold Huth recalled how he perfected "a scheme of pre-planning every shot in a picture" by using charts that recorded camera movements, the movements of the actors, models and storyboards.[10] These were incorporated into the philosophy of the IF, which was also an intricate set of technical instructions designed to work in concert and with precision to achieve the most effective results. Sets, properties, and perspectives were built as a unit. They could be transported as a unit, used, and reused, in very little time. As Catling observed: "The system establishes a *set of rules* for the game of picture making—where previously no holds were barred; and if the system is to work, people must abide by the rules, and that's where the team spirit comes into play."[11] The *Kinematograph Weekly* described the IF as a challenge to producers and directors to adjust their practices to "factory conditions of film making; they must learn to coordinate their ideas with the technical methods offered by their heads of departments."[12] Essentially, it was "a system of pre-production planning—with a difference," in which effects, or "tricks of the trade," were fully utilized to speed up production and reduce costs. This meant deploying back projection, process shots, miniatures, and glass shots into a precise scheme of preproduction planning. Detailed storyboards informed the planning phase, as well as location shooting, using extras instead of principal actors.[13] These scenes would appear in the finished film, followed by interior scenes featuring the main stars, thus cutting costs on engaging major players for location filming. Techniques such as back projection, which had been used for decades in British studios, became central to IF productions. In addition, Rawnsley is credited with having devised new equipment, including hexagonal rotating stages; ingenious back-projection tunnels and direction booths set high above the studio floor; combined screen holders and light rails; and mobile rostrums and projection towers (figs. 5.1–3).[14]

The first production to use the IF was Catling's *Under the Frozen Falls* (Children's Entertainment Film and Gaumont-British Instructional, March 1948). Rawnsley left the Rank Organization's research department at the end of 1947 and established

FIGURE 5.1. Independent Frame Equipment:
Hexagonal rotating stage under construction.
The Engineer 119, no. 2 (August 26, 1949): 224.
Printed with permission from *The Engineer*,
www.theengineer.co.uk.

FIGURE 5.2. Independent Frame Equipment: Combined screen
holder and light rail in raised and lowered positions. *The Engineer* 119,
no. 2 (August 26, 1949): 223. Printed with permission from *The
Engineer*, www.theengineer.co.uk.

Aquila Films with Donald Wilson.[15] The IF was then applied by Aquila and Gains-
borough for the following feature films: *Warning to Wantons* (Donald Wilson,
Aquila Films, Feb. 1949); *Floodtide* (Frederick Wilson, Aquila Films, May 1949);
Stop Press Girl (Michael Barry, Aquila Films, July 1949); *Poet's Pub* (Frederick Wil-
son, Aquila Films, August 1949); *Boys in Brown* (Montgomery Tully, Gainsborough
Pictures, Dec. 1949); and *The Astonished Heart* (Terence Fisher and Antony Darn-
borough, Gainsborough Productions and Sydney Box Productions, March 1950).
All of these films were produced at Pinewood.[16] Rawnsley continued to develop
ideas related to the IF and is credited with being an IF/technical consultant on
Under the Frozen Falls, Warning to Wantons, Stop Press Girl, and *Floodtide.*[17]

Before we consider the IF and its application in more detail, it is important to
outline the prevailing economic and political contexts for its introduction. These
factors shaped its evolution, short-term impact, and reception by the film trade. The

FIGURE 5.3. Independent Frame Equipment (left to right): Mobile rostrum and projection tower. *The Engineer* 119, no. 2 (August 26, 1949): 225. Printed with permission from *The Engineer*, www. theengineer.co.uk.

postwar years were extremely difficult for the British film industry, when it faced fierce competition from Hollywood's films, which had historically dominated the domestic market. After 1945, Hollywood was keener than ever to export films to Europe and was determined to dismantle protective quotas, such as those enforced since 1927 to protect the British film industry. The British economy was handicapped by a shortage of dollars, particularly the large amount remitted to America for popular films shown in British cinemas. Film thus became an integral aspect of Britain's acute postwar balance of payments problems. A crisis came to a head in August 1947 when the British government imposed a 75 percent "ad valorem" duty on foreign films.[18] As a retaliatory measure, Hollywood producers boycotted the British market for just over six months. In the absence of the American films that exhibitors relied on to make profits, the British film industry made a valiant attempt to produce more feature films. But the boycott exposed the fragility of the film industry on many levels, not least conflicts between the production and exhibition sectors. A deal was struck in March of 1948 when the duty was removed in exchange for a blocking arrangement whereby American companies could remit up to $17 million a year, plus a sum equal to the dollar earnings of British films in the US. The intention was to encourage the use of blocked earnings from American films to finance productions in Britain. To encourage British production, in June of 1948 the British government increased the statutory quota to 45 percent of British first feature films to be shown by exhibitors; the quota for the supporting program was lower, at 25 percent.[19] In October of 1948 the National Film Finance Corporation was established to loan Treasury funds to producers via a distribution company, British Lion.

The immediate background to the launch of the IF, then, was inextricably bound up with these larger issues of the British government's film policy and also of Anglo-American film relations. The ability of British producers to supply cinemas with good quality films was at the heart of debates about available studio space, budgets, production methods, and how to turn out the best films in relatively quick succession. The American boycott created an opportunity for British films but the reentry of American films in March of 1948 once again subjected them to severe competition, this time from an industry determined to make good the lost months of overseas profits. It seems that during the key years of 1948 and 1949, British production held up better than might have been expected, but profits were falling, particularly for the Rank Organization, which provided research and development funds for the IF. Much was at stake for Rank, as owner of half of all British studios, including the largest, Denham and Pinewood. In 1947 Rank reported severe production losses and in 1948 a high bank overdraft and investments in uncompleted films.[20] Producers were thus challenged to turn the crisis around by revolutionizing studio methods and technical infrastructure. The 45 percent quota placed even more onus on them to deliver a greater number of profitable films, as noted in a contemporary production survey: "The whole problem of making films in all the studios *at the right price* must be solved at once. Reissues can only keep kinemas going for a few months at the most, and, if the full quota is to be met later in 1949 British studios will have to be making at the minimum 100 *first* features a year. And the maximum which can be made on available stage space (unless we revive the 'quickie') is 120. This can only be done with all the studios working all the time."[21] This judgment was based on the fact that British studios wholly completed sixty-three first features in 1948 and fifty-nine in 1947, figures considerably lower than one hundred.[22]

A survey of the output of the major studios gives a sense of Pinewood's capacity at this time. For most of the Second World War Pinewood was requisitioned for propaganda filmmaking by the Army Film and Photographic Unit, the RAF Film Unit, and the Crown Film Unit. After the war the studio was once again active for commercial filmmaking, and production increased. Rank's films cost less from 1948, and the average shooting schedule for first features was reduced. These conditions were conducive to the introduction of the IF, with its emphasis on economy, time management, and efficient use of studio space. Yet the industry's instability was signaled when unions became worried by closures of studio space in 1948, with dismissals reported at Denham and Ealing, British National, and smaller studios. Gainsborough Studios closed in 1950, and Rank was keen to concentrate production and technical innovation at Pinewood.

While the IF promised in the longer term to increase production, in the shorter term it felt threatening to some technicians who feared that its cost-cutting rationale might result in layoffs of studio labor. The aim of continuous production proved to be impossible even though production of first features rose slightly to sixty-six films in 1949 and the number of films produced by independents increased.[23] Despite Rank's continuing financial difficulties, Pinewood completed nine first-feature films in 1949, and Denham was responsible for ten. It should be noted that the majority of films made using the IF were filmed and released in 1948–49, placing emphasis on the role of the process in production activity during this crucial period. Indeed, the annual trade publication *The Kinematograph Year Book* took the opportunity to assess its record, while noting that it was "intimately associated with the problem of production costs." The arguments for and against the IF were neatly summarized: "It enables production costs to be reduced by a quarter, with no sacrifice of entertainment value. Against this, it is urged that it restricts the work of director and artistes and detracts from the realism which can be secured only by the use of genuine location photography and unfettered studio work."[24]

The technical innovations associated with the IF were widely praised, particularly the development of still and moving background projectors by British Acoustic. In addition, mobile lighting rails to carry lamps and crew were constructed by Vickers-Armstrong. Lighting setups were typically indirect: "An ingenious reflector system is employed which dispenses with light rails and reduces the candlepower of the normally lighted set by almost two-thirds."[25] Sets built on mobile rostrums could be moved through preproduction and production departments (fig 5.4). Some reconstruction had been necessary in Pinewood, including the erection of twin stages, each 200 × 175 ft. in area, with a collapsible insulated partition between them. The principle of the assembly line is evident in the rational, spatial flow for the organization of materials, construction stores, and the assembly bay, where sets were mounted on the mobile rostrums. A "waiting bay" next to the stage held the sets until required, when they would be flown into position by an overhead gantry. A similar approach had been applied in Hollywood when Fred Pelton, MGM's studio manager, used mobile sets. But they were too large and unwieldy to be fully effective, which convinced Rawnsley that the IF would work best with smaller mobile sets and rostrums. He also studied Disney's planning methods and was inspired by how the British Broadcasting Corporation's (BBC) technicians were effective in spite of working in cramped conditions at Alexandra Palace.[26]

The IF was exploited at a time when other significant technical innovations were being introduced to British studios, thus associating it with a wider culture of contemporary experimentation. This included Ealing's introduction of the Spellerroller, a device that could jack up and move with ease heavy pieces of scenery. Studio lighting equipment was also progressing in terms of compact-source lamps and the renowned 225 amp arc lamp produced by Mole-Richardson known as "The Brute." Other innovations included Venetian-type shutters with remote control, which enabled sets to be dimmed with great sensitivity and precision.[27] Pinewood producer Donald Wilson reported in April of 1949 that the first films to be

FIGURE 5.4. Independent Frame Equipment: Models and grid; scene with projected background; rostrum, screen, camera, and light bridge setup; reverse side of projector screens. *The Engineer* 119, no. 2 (August 26, 1949): 222. Printed with permission from *The Engineer*, www.theengineer.co.uk.

made using the IF had been largely successful in demonstrating several of its key features, including in *Warning to Wantons* evoking opulence for very little cost and in *Floodtide* conveying the signature of "authenticity in the production of a particular place—Glasgow and Clydeside—with large canvas, brought to the studio."[28] Other studios were urged to follow these principles, and toward the end of 1948 plans were publicized for the IF to be used at Ealing and Denham.[29]

The spin-off effect of the IF was notable as minds were concentrated on time-saving in set construction and preplanning. Terence Verity, an art director working for Associated British, devised a turntable technique to enable a set to be turned to face the end of the stage with the backings/backdrop. This saved shooting time and set construction, enabling continuous shooting for *The Hasty Heart* (Vincent Sherman, 1949), filmed at Elstree.[30] Kenneth K. Rick, second unit director on *The Gorbals Story* (David MacKane, 1950), considered how the IF might benefit studios smaller than Pinewood or Denham. He estimated that the film's twenty-day shooting time could have been reduced if a form of the IF had been applied in Merton Park studio. In particular, he drew attention to time-saving devices such as rolling-rostrum set construction, back-projection still plates using a Stereopticon and detailed shooting plans.[31] David Rawnsley kept his name in profile as a technical innovator with expositions of a new light-reflector system to provide greater control of light and shadow.[32]

A consistent feature of the debates surrounding the IF was the need to reduce the high costs of film production. This imperative informed the establishment of a committee chaired by Lord Gater at the end of 1948 on film production costs. The inadequacy of planning methods in British studios informed its unsurprising conclusions.[33] The IF can be read as a response to the idea that more films should be produced, faster and for less money. To some extent this was at odds with the desire, also prevalent in the postwar period, for quality, prestige films to conquer overseas markets, particularly the US market. Yet data published on the subject gave ambiguous results. While it was proven that cheaper, ingeniously made films such as Gainsborough's *The Wicked Lady* (Leslie Arliss, 1945) could make huge box-office profits, the trick was to systematize this as the modus operandi of British cinema. *In Which We Serve,* the film that gave Rawnsley his first opportunity to try out some of his innovative technical methods, cost a respectable £240,000. It did very well at the UK box office and also in America.[34] The debate questioned the idea that "high quality" production values, deemed to be necessary to impress foreign critics and audiences, should necessarily be equated with how much a film cost to produce. The inflation of production costs was much-publicized in the late 1940s, with high-budget films such as Rank's *Bonnie Prince Charlie* (Anthony Kimmins, 1948) costing £760,000 but recouping only £94,327 by April of 1950.[35] Better records were attained by "prestige" films, including *Hamlet* (Laurence Olivier, 1948), which cost £572,500 and *The Red Shoes* (Powell and Pressburger, 1948), budgeted at £505,600, both of which did well in the US.[36] Films made with the IF aimed for more modest budgets of £104,000 to £105,000, compared with the more typical £160,000 for lower-budget feature films in 1949.[37] The average length of an IF feature however was 7,840 feet, considerably longer than the average for second features of the period.[38] Records of releases on the Odeon circuit, owned by Rank, confirm that some IF films were billed as first features.[39]

Discussion of budgets and production methods accompanied the release of the first IF feature film, *Warning to Wantons*. Each IF release was designed to demonstrate a different aspect of the method. Scholarship has tended to group the films together as low-budget "quota fillers" aimed at working-class audiences.[40] But reviewing the films shows that each was quite different, suggesting a variety of generic possibilities enabled by the IF. *Warning to Wantons* was "designed to show that lavish settings with many luxury interiors and elaborate backgrounds, are at the disposal of even a moderate priced picture."[41] The film cost £117,000 and was shot in six weeks. Contemporary estimates calculated that had the film been made by normal methods at either Denham or Pinewood, it would have cost £250,000. From this perspective, "judged by present-day standards of price and production time the picture is a brilliant success."[42] As a light comedy, the film follows the adventures of Renée de Vallant (Anne Vernon), a wily young woman who has escaped from her convent school. She pretends to be a young ingénue, captivating most of the men she meets, including Max (David Tomlinson), the fiancé of Maria (Sonia Holm), who can see through her wiles.

The film's location is unspecified, but it is "abroad" in a generic sense, even to the extent of having characters from a village speak an unknown language. The use of location shots is fairly abundant, with actors doubling for the film's stars in the distance. But the film also has some quite opulent sets for a castle, ballroom, banquet, and fashion house. Even though the *Kinematograph Weekly*'s reviewer had reservations about the film's cast and box-office potential, its "rich staging" was praised as "spectacular" and "generously mounted."[43] The film's nonspecific "foreignness" can be related to one of Rawnsley's aims to make IF-developed sets and projections available to producers abroad. Rather than dub or subtitle a film for non-English speaking release, the "frame" of the film could in theory be applied with the addition of a different cast. Although this method has been criticized, in this case one can see how a film such as *Warning to Wantons* would lend itself to such transferability.[44] The idea is similar to the trend for multilingual versions (MLVs) of films that were popular in the early years of sound. American and European studios shot multiple versions of films in different languages and with indigenous stars, but the sets and crews were the same. The IF provided a means of rationalizing this process technically, and although there are no examples of this happening, the aim was to give the IF an international applicability in keeping with its ambitions to encourage cheaper films whose "frames" could, in effect, be recycled beyond the UK.

Warning to Wantons made use of the effects that were an integral part of the IF's signature. Back projection was frequently used, as in an early scene in which two girls and a nun are shot on a sparse set but with a background of a colonnade vista that has been projected. Another scene featured a large castle room, with a vast pillared background and glass doorway. The actors performed on a small raised platform in the studio, which was sparsely furnished with props. On the platform was a glass doorway through which the actors moved. Plastic projection screens surrounded this stage, onto which were projected photographs of the castle interiors that had been made in Portugal. In preplanning, technicians made sure that "the outline of the projected castle fitted exactly with the outline of the glass doorway from the camera's point of view. . . . [They] knew how to place another screen behind the glass door so that during the action, the camera picked up distance location shots through the studio door."[45] Transparencies, matte processes, and live action were coordinated in the backgrounds, using shadows strategically in the frame.[46]

Floodtide was set in postwar Glasgow and the Clydeside shipyards. Achieving authenticity of place and realism were important to the film's tale of David Shields (Gordon Jackson), a young man from the country who dreams of being a ship designer. His rise to the top brings conflict between his loyalty to former work-

FIGURE 5.5. Shipyard location shot and David Shields (Gordon Jackson) in a studio shot with projected background in *Floodtide* (Frederick Wilson, 1949).

mates and friends, and the very different social milieu associated with his upward career trajectory. The film did not do well at the box office, but its location shots of Glasgow and Clydeside are remarkable for their vivid capture of postwar shipyard work.[47] Indeed, the *Kinematograph Weekly*'s review referred to it as "a shrewd cross-section of life on Clydeside. . . . Honest, down to earth and showmanlike, it's the best and most entertaining 'regional' offering screened for many a day."[48] While the IF is in evidence in some scenes (the projected backgrounds sometimes appeared less in focus than the foreground action), the interior sets were generally successful in suggesting the different class positions of their inhabitants. The film definitely aimed to showcase how the IF combined location shots with process ones in a locale that lent itself to graphic imagery (fig. 5.5). A back projection of a shipping cradle in one shot, for example, was combined with a real girder in the foreground in the studio; the actors were then filmed to complete the action. As well as being of interest technically, the film's concentration on Shields's commitment to hard work, technical ingenuity, and engineering skill can be interpreted as a self-reflexive statement on the aims of the IF; working hard to obtain the best results was the film's message, as well as its method.

The next IF productions, *Stop Press Girl* and *Poet's Pub*, were comedies, a genre associated with lower-budget films, which could, as Chibnall and McFarlane acknowledge, provide "a laboratory for technological experimentation."[49] Producer Donald Wilson told the trade press that "even in a moderate-priced comedy, the director need not be restricted in the number of his sets and that extensive use of process work for comedy effects need not be too expensive an item."[50] *Stop Press Girl* employed a variety of sets for its story of Jennifer Peters (Sally Ann Howe), who has the power to stop machinery. Comedy is created around this basic situation involving her stopping cars, trains, a film show, the clocks in a factory, and an aircraft.

FIGURE 5.6. Jackie Knowles (Richard Attenborough) in cell and the Governor (Jack Warner) with Borstal inmates with projected background shot in *Boys in Brown* (Montgomery Tully, 1949).

Stop Press Girl had the advantage of many scenes taking place in confined spaces such as a railway carriage, a car, or plane. With an emphasis on dialogue and medium-close shots, less importance was placed on whether the IF succeeded in seamlessly "matching" different sets and locations. From many perspectives *Stop Press Girl* is perhaps the most successful of the IF films.[51] The film's presentation of successive comic setups works well, as does the escalation of public interest in Jennifer as a "miracle girl" heroine for Nature vs. Machine Age protestors. This anticipates some of the ideas in Ealing's more famous *The Man in the White Suit* (Alexander Mackendrick, 1951), a comedy that similarly deals with issues of overdependence on technology. The formula of combining gentle comedy with larger issues thus works well, and the IF seemed on course to deliver more effective comedies such as *Poet's Pub*, which also had a respectable afterlife on American television.[52]

The next IF film, *Boys in Brown*, has received more critical commentary than the others, perhaps because of its "social problem" genre, in this case a study of the British Borstal corrective institution for young offenders.[53] Its director, Montgomery Tully, is also notable for his work in directing "B" movie crime thrillers.[54] Although the film's ostensible message defends the Borstal system, the film can be read as being, as Raymond Durgnat noted, "ahead of its time in criticizing the running of Borstals."[55] To some extent this is an effect of the film's graphic imagery, rendered stark with harsh lighting contrasts in many scenes that evoke the pervasive Borstal environment as oppressive, prisonlike, and depressing (fig. 5.6). *Boys in Brown* follows the time spent in Borstal by Jackie Knowles (Richard Attenborough), who is depicted as a young man who has gotten in with the wrong crowd and once inside the institution gets caught up in an unsuccessful escape plan. The mise-en-scène contributes a disturbing picture of life in Borstal where the institution grinds down the young men with drills, the cold, chapel, exercise, and work.

Boys in Brown was conducive to the IF technique. As Dixon has noted: "The brown uniforms worn by the inmates readily lent themselves to easy 'matching' of close and distant shots, and they made substitutions between actors and stand-ins extremely easy to accomplish."[56] Stills of the interiors of corrective institutions were projected as backdrops for several scenes. Using stills in this way presented considerable technical problems, not least the buckling of slides under the heat of the projector.[57] This problem was somewhat ameliorated by water-cooling the light beam and also by air-cooling the slide.[58] While the artificiality was rather obvious, the foreground placement of the figures and action directed viewers' attention away from the IF mechanics of the scene. In this sense the film does not appear inauthentic since the character-focused drama establishes the internal regime of the setting, reinforcing an impression of its emphasis on conformity and regimentation. A model was built of the interior of a Borstal since the Home Office was reluctant to sanction filming inside a real institution; the model reproduced this in replica form and was photographed for still plates from many different angles.[59]

The escape scenes are lit darkly by Gordon Lang, emphasizing danger. As the inmates climb over the Borstal's high outside wall, the imagery of prison dramas is vividly recalled. Lang was full of praise for how using IF methods assisted the cinematography: "The most helpful aspect of the IF system was the full conference between planners, writers and senior technicians from the first stage of production."[60] Yet it seems the film was not particularly popular. Gillett argues that this might have been because actors Richard Attenborough and Jimmy Hanley are "not convincing as working-class delinquents."[61] Yet Attenborough had successfully performed such characters before, most notably in *Brighton Rock* (John Boulting, 1947). Perhaps the emphasis on Jackie being rather passive, even naive, made for a less compelling performance.

Production on *Boys in Brown* moved from Pinewood to Denham so that the next film using the IF, *The Astonished Heart*, could be produced at Pinewood.[62] This was a completely different type of film with a "higher class" profile because of its adaptation by Noël Coward from his own play. It starred Celia Johnson as Barbara Faber in a sort of reprise of her performance in *Brief Encounter* (David Lean, 1945), only this time with her fictional husband, Christian (Noël Coward), having an affair. The film was made only partly by using the IF techniques because, according to assistant director Gerry O'Hara, "the process was just too constricting."[63] It is also possible that the film's pitching as "quality drama" was thought to necessitate special treatment but whereby aspects of the IF could be beneficial. Back projection was used extensively, supervised by Charles Staffell, who had worked on other IF films. The *Kinematograph Weekly* always considered a film's likely audience in its reviews. *The Astonished Heart* was judged thus: "The acting is polished, but the characters are inclined to talk too much. Good theatre, if not ideal kinema, it, nevertheless, carries strong feminine appeal. Title and star values are, of course, exceptional. Attractive 'double bill,' but for the tiara rather than the bonnet-and-shawl brigade."[64] So this was entirely different from previous IF films in terms of locale and pitch, and the film's failings can hardly be attributed solely to its technical production. Even though the comedies *Warning to Wantons, Stop Press Girl,* and *Poet's Pub* also featured upper-middle-class characters, the tragic drama about a psychiatrist's obsession with another woman involves a very different, dark sensibility. The film failed to capture the melodramatic tension of *Brief Encounter,* perhaps because neither the romantic pairing of the central couple nor Barbara's angst at being betrayed by her husband created the depths of emotional intensity associated with the former film.

After *The Astonished Heart* no further films were produced with overt reference to the IF in advertising or in the trade press.[65] Rank had spent between £600,000 and £900,000 on the process, a high sum at a time when his company was in considerable financial difficulty.[66] But Rank had spent and lost more on the production of *Bonnie Prince Charlie,* while the IF productions' budgets were considerably lower. It would only have taken one of them to be successful to represent a good return on Rank's investment. While the problems facing the film industry presented producers with a challenge to innovate, they also stymied a systematic introduction of the IF.

One way to think of the experiments of 1948–49 is that they were part of a longer trajectory of how effects were being used in studios and how change depended on lessons learned over time. Wood notes how "the new 'travelling matte' process, evolved by the Pinewood technicians, largely superceded the Back Projection part of the IF technique."[67] This is important because it meant that actors and backgrounds could be photographed separately. Actors were filmed in a filtered yellow light against a blue background, and the two were married in the final print. The advantages over back projection were that the scale of the background could be enlarged and both actors and backgrounds would appear to be in sharp focus at the same time. As we have seen, back projection tended to have the effect of flattening out perspective. In addition, Barry Salt points out that the new form of traveling matte involved "a Technicolor-type beam splitter camera" invented in Britain in the early 1950s.[68] This is also referred to by Bryan Langley, a cinematographer who was involved in special effects at the time. He recalled: "Travelling matte had the great advantage compared with back projection in as much as you could shoot it now and put on the background at leisure, anywhere and any different background, if you didn't like the background you could change it."[69]

It has thus been recognized that the IF left a valuable legacy for Pinewood as part of an incremental culture of invention and, perhaps surprisingly, for television. Rawnsley's ideas involved collaboration with television, an environment that was conducive to the IF's principles and practices. He advocated the redesign of studios to enable continuous production, with much preparation achieved in advance of a production by means of the "framework" as had been established at Pinewood.[70] He also saw the potential of television cameras being used to assist film directors since their viewfinders permitted instant examination of what was being transmitted. The efficiency of the television studio in this respect made for quicker productions, as well as the incorporation of prerecorded back projection and matte processes into the finished program. Rawnsley hoped that electronic techniques used in television could assist film production environments.[71] He even speculated that eventually "the motion picture camera will be supplanted by television cameras."[72] Indeed, in the 1950s some US television shows were shot live in the studio using three 35 mm cameras with television cameras attached as "a sort of early video assist." This enabled framing and focusing through the television camera linked to the film camera, and via monitors the director could see what each camera was filming. *Stop the World: I Want to Get Off* (Philip Saville, 1966), a British feature film shot at Pinewood, used a similar multicamera system that enabled the director to plan edits in advance of rushes.[73]

There were additional IF spin-off benefits for television. Donald Wilson, producer of *Under the Frozen Falls;* director of the first IF short film, *Warning to Wantons;* and cofounder of Aquila Films, went on to a career in television production, including the BBC's *The Forsyte Saga* (1967). The series was extremely popular in spite of its "artificial and cost-conscious" style, in which videotaped interior shots were happily intercut with sequences that had been filmed on location. The BBC's technicians studied the IF equipment at Pinewood, which in turn informed television production.[74] As Rawnsley had predicted, aspects of the IF were thus successfully employed for the "assembly line" television production environment. To facilitate back projection, John Hawkesworth, a draftsman at Pinewood, worked on the IF's rostrums that lifted projectors located at the end of a long tunnel that had been built at the end of the stage. He later produced *Upstairs, Downstairs* (London Weekend Television, 1971–75), another British television series that achieved outstanding popular and critical success despite being made using cost-effective methods of combining location footage and studio sets.[75]

The physical legacy of the IF was considerable. As early as 1951, the IF rostrums were deployed at Denham to assist 20th Century Fox's production *I'll Never Forget You* (Roy Ward Baker). In praise of the rostrums Baker commented: "It's a joy to know that your sound isn't going to be spoiled by even one wooden creak, and you can move them without trouble."[76] For several actors, including Gordon Jackson, Richard Attenborough, Joyce Grenfell, and Sonia Holm, as well as technicians, the IF films provided valuable training for their future careers. Ronald Spencer, assistant director on *Warning to Wantons,* went on to work with Raoul Walsh, Edward Dmytryk, Carol Reed, Jack Clayton, and David Lean. As managing director of Pacesetter Productions, Spencer forged important production links with the Children's Film and Television Foundation.[77] Visual effects specialist Charles Staffell worked on all of the IF films and went on to do back projection for *2001: A Space Odyssey* (Stanley Kubrick, 1968). He planned and executed the effects on many other films produced at Pinewood, including *Superman* (Richard Donner, 1978) and *Aliens* (James Cameron, 1986). In his view the IF was a very good system, but it ran into problems because the film scripts and directors employed were not always good.[78] Another view on the IF's shortcomings was that a rigid production schedule stifled creativity on the set and prevented directors from devising ingenious solutions to problems as they arose during production.[79] The principles of mechanization that were at the heart of the IF were not always popular among art directors, including John Bryan and Alfred Junge.[80] It is worth noting, however, that Junge's early methods of working as a celebrated production designer in Britain resemble some of the tenets of the IF, including emphasis on preplanning for "total design," particularly the use of continuity sketches, photographic backgrounds, and back projection.[81]

In the final analysis the IF's aim to support continuous production in British studios was perhaps overambitious, in view of the problems experienced by producers. Unlike Hollywood, where the studios' infrastructures relied on top-down, producer-driven methods, which accommodated lower budget and prestige productions, British producers struggled to deliver the levels of productivity required to take full advantage of the IF's innovations. As such, the slate of films produced was very small in comparison with the total number that needed to be produced. The IF's high profile placed great emphasis on its potential at a time when there was immense pressure for the industry to deliver. Far from being similar, the films attempted to trail the IF in a number of genres, and the method proved particularly appropriate for comedies and for use in conjunction with remarkable location footage. For all its emphasis on time tables, precision, and efficiency, the IF was a harbinger of an adventurous spirit of research and development at Pinewood, involving continuous experimentation with effects such as back projection and the traveling matte process.[82] As we have seen, Rawnsley also had the foresight to see that television studios had much to offer film studio environments and technologies. With these and other considerations, even though the IF experiment lasted only a few years, in the longer term it contributed to the establishment of a robust technical infrastructure at Pinewood, which laid the foundations for the studio's subsequent outstanding reputation for technical excellence, as well as streamlined methods of production.

NOTES

1. Darrel Catling, "The Independent Frame," *Supplement to Film Industry* 4, no. 20 (Feb. 1948): 13–20, 13.

2. For a discussion of how graphic art was incorporated into filmmaking, see Edward Carrick, "The Pictured Script," *Kinematograph Weekly Studio Review* 26 (Jan. 1950): 29, 31.

3. Michael Powell to Rank, Feb. 1945, quoted in Macnab, *J. Arthur Rank*, 122.

4. The most extensive commentary is provided in Dixon, "The Doubled Image," 41–52. See also Wood, *Mr. Rank*, 180–84; and Macnab, *J. Arthur Rank*, 122–131.

5. G. R. Stevens, "Independent Frame—An Attempt at Rationalization of Motion Pictures," *Journal of the Society of Motion Picture and Television Engineers* 57 (November 1951): 434–42, 434–35.

6. Powell, *Million-Dollar Movie*, 79.

7. Powell, 79.

8. Dixon, "The Doubled Image," 49.

9. Macnab, *J. Arthur Rank*, 126.

10. Harold Huth, "Rawnsley *Was* Right but . . . ," *Film Industry* 6, no. 40 (Jan. 27, 1949): 5, 14.

11. Catling, "The Independent Frame," 19–20.

12. *Kinematograph Weekly* 383, no. 2175 (Jan. 6, 1949): 6.

13. *Kinematograph Weekly*, 8.

14. Ede, *British Film Design*, 70. For descriptions with photographs see Anon., "Equipment for 'Independent Frame' Filming," *The Engineer* 118, no. 2 (August 26, 1949): 222–25.

15. Rawnsley was head of Rank's research department from 1945 to 1949.

16. *Boys in Brown* began production at Pinewood but completed at Denham, as reported in *Film Industry* 6, no. 50 (June 16, 1949): 10.

17. Kenneth Bellman became managing director of the sponsoring company when Rawnsley left Rank, as noted in the *Kinematograph Year Book* (London: Odhams Press, 1950), 165.

18. The value of the commodity (film) for the calculation of the duty was one quarter of its gross value. The duty was then set at three times its dutiable value.

19. The quota was a controversial topic, with different interests in the film trade lobbying for lesser (exhibitors) or greater (producers) degrees of state protection. The quota was reduced to 30 percent in 1950. See Dickinson and Street, *Cinema and State*, 195–98.

20. P. G. Baker, "Production Survey," *Kinematograph Year Book* (London: Odhams Press, 1949), 151–59, 152.

21. *Kinematograph Year Book* (1949), 156 (italics in original).

22. *Kinematograph Year Book* (1949), 151.

23. Production survey by Baker, *Kinematograph Year Book* (1950), 153.

24. R. Howard Cricks, "Technical Developments in 1949," *Kinematograph Year Book* (1950), 165.

25. Stevens, "Independent Frame," 436.

26. Wood, *Mr. Rank*, 181–82.

27. This was exploited to great effect by cinematographer Ossie Morris in *Moulin Rouge* (John Huston, 1952). See interview with Morris in Brown, Street, and Watkins, *British Colour Cinema*, 77.

28. Donald Wilson, "How the Independent Frame Is Working Out in Practice," Studio Review Supplement, *Kinematograph Weekly* 386, no. 2191 (April 128, 949): 39.

29. See *Film Industry* 5, no. 35 (Nov. 18, 1948): 1; *Film Industry* 5, no. 37 (Dec. 16, 1948): 1; and *Film Industry* 5, no. 38 (Dec. 30, 1948): 1.

30. Terence Verity, "Turntable Technique for Space-Saving Sets," *Film Industry* 6, no. 40 (Jan. 27, 1949): 10.

31. Kenneth K. Rick, "Pre-Planning and the Smaller Studio," *Film Industry* 6, no. 50 (June 16, 1949): 10.

32. David Rawnsley, "Indirect Lighting," *Film Industry* 6, no. 43 (March 10, 1949): 10.

33. Dickinson and Street, *Cinema and State*, 205.

34. Street, *Transatlantic Crossings*, 94.

35. Figures quoted from Board of Trade records in Harper and Porter, *British Cinema of the 1950s*, 275.

36. Harper and Porter, *British Cinema of the 1950s*, 275. For details of the distribution and reception of *Hamlet* and *The Red Shoes* in the United States see Street, *Transatlantic Crossings*, 106–10.

37. *Kinematograph Weekly* 386, no. 2188 (April 7, 1949): 3. "Supporting Features" generally tended to have even smaller budgets and lengths, as noted in Chibnall and McFarlane, *The British 'B' Film,* 40.

38. Figures compiled from the *Kinematograph Year Book* (1950), 7–35.

39. See lists of Odeon releases in Eyles, *Odeon Cinemas 2,* 199–200.

40. Dixon, "The Doubled Image," 50. See also Perry, *Movies from the Mansion,* 78.

41. *Kinematograph Weekly* 386, no. 2191 (April 28, 1949): 39.

42. John Sullivan, "Rawnsley Was Right," *Film Industry* 6, no. 39 (Jan. 13, 1949): 7.

43. *Kinematograph Weekly* 383, no. 2175 (Jan. 6, 1949): 16.

44. Dixon's "The Doubled Image," 43, refers to this as "a metaphoric packing crate" but assumes that the locations in the films were all shot in the UK. *Warning to Wantons,* however, contains several foreign location shots, probably of the Riviera.

45. David Rawnsley, "The First Independent Frame Feature Film Comes to the Screen," *Kinematograph Weekly* 383, no. 2175 (Jan. 6, 1949): 8.

46. Stevens, "Independent Frame," 437.

47. This has also been noted in Gillett, *British Working Class in Postwar Film,* 100, 202, 203.

48. *Kinematograph Weekly* 385, no. 2185 (March 17, 1949): 17.

49. Chibnall and McFarlane, *The British 'B' Film,* 72.

50. Studio Review Supplement, *Kinematograph Weekly* 386, no. 2191 (April 28, 1949): 39.

51. Perry, however, describes it as "a disaster, a misfired comedy savaged by the critics and ignored by the public" (*Movies from the Mansion,* 78). The *Kinematograph Weekly*'s review was critical of Sally Ann Howes's performance and described the film as a "crazy comedy . . . mediocre light booking," *Kinematograph Weekly* 387, no. 2195 (May 26, 1949): 18.

52. For contemporary reviews see Chibnall and McFarlane, *The British 'B' Film,* 72–73. *Stop Press Girl* is reported as being shown on American television, especially before the 1970s: www.lovingthe-classics.com/by-title/s/stop-press-girl-1949.html. William K. Everson reviewed *Poet's Pub* in October of 1979, when he recorded that it was part of a TV package: "Although *Poet's Pub* wasn't a blockbuster in England and certainly wouldn't have been one here either, it was nevertheless quite superior to a number of lesser Rank comedies (*Marry Me, The Perfect Woman*) which somehow did get US exhibition." See Everson, "Review of *Poet's Pub.*"

53. Dixon writes about the film in "The Doubled Image," 44–51.

54. Chibnall and McFarlane, *The British 'B' Film,* 145.

55. Durgnat, *A Mirror for England,* 60.

56. Dixon, "The Doubled Image," 44.

57. This point is made by art director L. P. Williams, August 12, 1993, BECTU History Project, interview no. 381.

58. *Kinematograph Year Book* (1950), 165.

59. Robins, "Full Production at Pinewood Again," *Film Industry* 6, no. 47 (5 May 1949): 4.

60. Robins, 4.

61. Gillett, *British Working Class in Postwar Film,* 132.

62. *Kinematograph Weekly* 388, no. 2197 (June 9, 1949): 17.

63. Gerry O'Hara, "Working within the System: An Interview with Gerry O'Hara," interview by Wheeler Winston Dixon, Dec. 3, 2010, Screening the Past, www.screeningthepast.com/2011/04/working-within-the-system-an-interview-with-gerry-o'hara.

64. *Kinematograph Weekly* 396, no. 2232, Feb. 9, 1950, 16.

65. Rawnsley left film production and emigrated to Italy. Ede, *British Film Design,* 71.

66. Most sources say Rank spent £600,000 on developing the IF, but Ede has a higher figure of £900,000, quoted in *British Film Design,* 71. This figure is also quoted by Harper and Porter in *British Cinema of the 1950s,* 201.

67. Wood, *Mr. Rank,* 183.

68. Salt, *Film Style and Technology,* 321.

69. Bryan Langley, interview by Arthur Graham, BECTU Interview Part 1 (March 24, 1987), British Entertainment History project, https://historyproject.org.uk/interview/bryan-langley.

70. David Rawnsley, "Television Film Production by the Independent Frame," *Film Industry* 5, no. 33 (Oct. 21, 1948): 6–7, 18.

71. Stevens, "Independent Frame," 442.

72. Rawnsley, "Television Film Production by the Independent Frame," 7.

73. Cleveland and Pritchard, *How Films Were Made and Shown,* 339.

74. Wood, *Mr. Rank,* 183–84.

75. Langley, interview.

76. *Kinematograph Weekly* 408, no. 2280 (March 8, 1951): 38.

77. Threadgall, *Shepperton Studios,* 102.

78. Staffell, quoted in Macnab, *J. Arthur Rank,* 130.

79. Langley, interview.

80. Ede, *British Film Design,* 70.

81. Bergfelder, Harris, and Street, *Film Architecture and the Transnational Imagination,* 86.

82. *Kinematograph Weekly* 401, no. 2257 (August 3, 1950): 30.

6

Backlots of the World War

Cinecittà, 1942–1950

Noa Steimatsky

Nine kilometers southeast of Rome, following the main thoroughfare of Via Tuscolana, heavy with traffic as it passes through the working-class residential quarters that boomed here in the postwar era; along yawning patches of peripheral wasteland and ever-shrinking pastures where grazing sheep can be spotted to this day; in the vicinity of sacred springs that fed the fountains of Rome lie the remains of ancient aqueducts. Some of their arches still sustain improvised illegal shacks that have sheltered the homeless in this area, including those displaced by war, bandits, escaped prisoners, retreating German soldiers. After serving the Quadraro neighborhood, the road widens where the Seventh Municipality offices now occupy the original building of Istituto Luce, the documentary-propaganda wing of the Fascist regime. Across the street a bit farther down is the Centro sperimentale di cinematografia, the national film school, expanded after the war to house also the Cineteca nazionale—Italy's national film archive. Back on the east side of the road, where studio backlots once served big productions and sprouted weeds and wildflowers in between, there now sits a glass-encased shopping mall, CinecittàDue, and immediately past it a large area enclosed by walls. Following this wall, there finally looms the large entrance building, marked 1053, 1055, and 1057 Via Tuscolana, and topped with the familiar Rationalist lettering spelling Cinecittà (fig. 6.1). From here the road speeds on toward Frascati and the hills of the Castelli Romani, where popes go on holidays.

The traffic between Cinecittà and the *vecchia città*—Rome's old city center—has been reciprocal, with ideas, talent, and labor streaming from the city, while the fortunes and fame amassed here invigorate, in turn, the ancient *urbs*. The modern mobility, and mutability, of this media-industrial hub are joined here with a highly

FIGURE 6.1. Cinecittà façade. Photo by author.

controlled, enclosed space: a walled and gated miniature city, where artisanal craftsmanship, handled to this day through family traditions, has been so well employed by the most discerning filmmakers. The interplay between center and periphery, between inside and out, location and set, between material reality and the worldmaking powers of cinema, between disparate historical and fictional mise-en-scènes—one penetrating or enveloping the other, not always according to clear categories or a stable hierarchy—is this essay's recurring trope. The regional features of the zone—its pastoral setting, its archaeology, its traffic with the city—intertwined with the quintessentially modern powers of the movie industry, but also with far greater political and historical forces, and of a global scale—all these have given rise to an intricate psychogeography. For history became entangled here within a warped, slippery space, which mutated incessantly with the violent circumstances of the mid-twentieth century but also affected whatever entered it. The movie studio determines, to a greater or lesser degree, what takes place within it: it is not just a receptacle or passive setting but exerts pressure on reality, effecting transformations, prompting actions, at times—we will see—giving rise to the most unlikely scenarios. The first part of this essay will offer an overview of Cinecittà's vicissitudes through the 1940s, joining well-known landmarks in its official history with lesser-known, or forgotten, events. I will subsequently retrace one chapter in this history, putting together new findings from recent research to uncover hitherto repressed events from the midst of wartime Cinecittà. For the controlled mise-en-scène of film production masked here a vaster historical drama, itself consisting of several acts, with consequences and meanings well exceeding the concerns of cinema alone.

CINECITTÀ: PRE- TO POSTWAR

It was Mussolini's grand vision of cinema as "the strongest weapon," which joined with his son Vittorio's desire to deprovincialize Italian cinema, and with the entrepreneurship of Luigi Freddi, who understood how international investments could augment the Italian film industry. Here was a new sort of cultural capital that could, and did, revitalize the Eternal City. Constructed in record time, Cinecittà was deemed an achievement of Rationalist architecture, with up-to-date technical equipment and services to support all stages of film production and some twelve hundred people under regular state employment. At once removed from the city yet close enough, the original Cinecittà occupied a plot of six hundred thousand square meters (150 acres)— about double its present area. These strengths were further boosted by Rome's friendly climate and a wealth of attractive locations within reasonable distance: from the villas of Tivoli to the dunes and beaches of Sabaudia and Ostia, and from the monumental aqueducts to the snow-capped Abruzzi Apennines.

The conception of centralized studios erected on the city outskirts, following a modern industrial design ethos, translated to an Italian Rationalist idiom, evolved thanks to Freddi's preparatory work. Freddi—soon to become the most powerful figure responsible for cinema under the Fascist Ministry for Popular Culture (MinCulPop) and Cinecittà's president—had traveled to Hollywood and seen its big studios sprawl over land beyond the city. This, indeed, is how Cinecittà came to exceed in scale all European studios of its time, Ufa included. Its closest European counterpart, Denham Studios, some fifty kilometers outside of London, was being constructed at the same time but following a far more modest utilitarian-industrial plan and lacking the assertive stylistics of self-presentation sought by the Fascist state. As Sara Martin observes, Freddi and architect Gino Peressutti valorized the proud address of Cinecittà's front entry and the studio's symmetrical disposition along a central axis, with two parallel roads projecting from the front area, with its administrative offices and formal lawns. Cinecittà most resembled in this regard the First National Studios in Burbank, refurbished for sound in 1929.[1] Unlike the American timber structures, however, the Roman establishment was constructed largely of reinforced concrete, steel, and brick, resistant to vibrations and noise: here was a studio expressly engineered for the age of sound, and it was built to last.

Erected in record time and inaugurated by the Duce in 1937, Cinecittà consisted of sixteen soundstages and a pool for marine sets, as well as executive offices, bars, and restaurants, all within a network of streets, piazzas, and flowerbeds. Beyond these, the backlots for exterior set constructions spread over the greater part of the territory. Certainly Cinecittà's fabricated sets and colossal rhetoric were deeply imbricated in Fascist ideology, aspiring to overcome Hollywood's earlier permeation of the market and persisting in this effort following the iron pact with Hitler and the onset of war. But the war then invaded the scene of film production and transformed it in ways quite different from the uses for which it had been intended. In the first years production continued at full steam, including Cinecittà's participation in what has been called the "cinematographic Axis." Several German productions made use of the Roman studios even as they complained, periodically, of Italian disorder. Joseph Goebbels himself expressed some distrust, even contempt, of Italian cinema, closely inspecting the reciprocal distribution of films in the two countries and their relative success, expressing some dismay in view of the fact that Italian films garnered greater international success than did German ones. Still, he continued his dealings with top Italian film executives, enjoyed the company of Italian divas, and visited the Venice Film Festival. His special message offering congratulations for the festival's opening and praising the spiritual affinities and happy collaboration of the two nations and film industries was published, in German and Italian, in the September 1940 issue of the magazine *Cinema*.[2] It was one of the many twists of Italian Fascist culture that *Cinema*, edited by Vittorio Mussolini, also brought to print in those same years some of neorealism's earliest expressions. The Venice Film Festival was itself, of course, a Fascist invention, catering in that period especially to Axis films and routinely distributing prizes in a self-congratulatory manner.

It was only with the September 1943 armistice and the German occupation that film production in Cinecittà truly came to a halt, and, with all workers dismissed, the place was abandoned. The German military occupied the studio, using it to store ammunition and as a transit camp for prisoners. Only few documents survive to hint at what went on exactly inside the studios during those nine months of Rome's occupation. A handful of messages from late March to mid April 1944, addressed from Bern by the American minister to Switzerland, Leland Harrison, to the secretary of state in Washington, report that more than one thousand Allied prisoners of war (likely captured in the Battle of Anzio early in 1944) were being held in Cinecittà, with restricted food rations.[3] These bits of information were procured via escaped prisoners who likely made contact through the Vatican. Tracking the few names cited in these messages, one finds army veterans' testimonies about conditions of lodging in Cinecittà's big soundstages, as well as feats of escape: hiding in warehouses among movie sets and props, climbing the studio walls, and receiving help from peasant families in the vicinity.[4] Indeed, the neighborhood of Quadraro, surrounding Cinecittà, was known both for sheltering people—soldiers and civilians—escaping Nazi-Fascist capture and for partisan activity, some of it interlaced with the local banditry. The central event in this regard was the killing, at a local trattoria, of three German soldiers who served as guards at Cinecittà. This led to a German order to eradicate what they called Quadraro's "wasps' nest." The immediate consequence was a Nazi-Fascist raking of the neighborhood on April 17, 1944: all men between the ages of sixteen and fifty-five—basically the entire male population of working age, 947 men—were locked up for a couple of days in Cinecittà.[5] Those identified as Jews were sent to their death; the rest were labeled political prisoners and deported to labor camps, which many did not survive. This was a traumatic episode—second in magnitude only to the October 18, 1943, deportation of the Jews of Rome—but only little known beyond the Quadraro neighborhood.

The Allies, for their part, continued bombarding this industrial zone with its railway and munitions depot. There was no proper signage on the roofs, as required, that POWs were housed there. The army veteran interviews relate that, indeed, every morning at 10 a.m. sharp there were bombardments—after which it was their job to rebuild the tracks. Some soundstages, warehouses, and hangars, as well as Istituto Luce, suffered substantial damage. Not only Allied bombardments, however, but direct German vandalism inflicted extensive and partly lasting damage. Cinecittà was sacked and wrecked: equipment and films—including precious prints from the collection of the Centro sperimentale—were looted, some designated for the puppet Republic of Salò, where Luigi Freddi set up his *Cinevillaggio* (cinema village) in Venice, others designated for Germany but apparently lost for good.[6] The damages were considerable. A report published soon after the liberation describes how

> tanks and cannons circulated in the soundstages, with little benefit to the isolating wooden floors; in others they amassed hundreds of horses. Wehrmacht corporals slept in the divas' dressing rooms, and improved their leisure time smashing the bathrooms, sinks, and toilets with hammers. In the meantime, they stole whatever possible: they stole vehicles and fake beards; tens of thousands of bricks, nails, screws, iron wire, string and various stuffs in the amount of 2 million; they stole chainsaws, pots, tables and plates from the restaurants. . . . They uprooted trees. . . . They broke glass, smashed doors, demolished expensive equipment with pickaxes. When they departed . . . they left behind 36 million in damages, and the desolate spectacle of a great structure in ruins.[7]

On the night of June 4, 1944, after nine months of traumatic occupation, the Allies entered Rome and immediately, on June 6 (D-Day), the Allied Control Commission took possession of Cinecittà, drawing up a property requisition paper. A British Intelligence headquarters including a special prisoners' camp was set up in an area surrounded by barbed wire, making use of some existing structures. Nazi and Fascist prisoners of high rank and consequence were held here for interrogations. Among them were Marshal Graziani, one of Mussolini's most faithful generals all through the African colonial misadventure and the days of Salò; Guido Leto, chief of OVRA, the Fascist secret police (which also had big files on subversive elements within the Italian movie world); General von Vietinghoff, chief commander of the Wehrmacht in Italy; General Karl Wolff, chief SS officer in

Italy and a major actor in the secret negotiations with the Allies for the German capitulation in Italy; Herbert Kappler, the SS colonel who, having already deported Austria's Jews, had also sent the Jews of Rome to Auschwitz, this among other atrocities; Eugen Dollmann, translator between Hitler and Mussolini; as well as two women soon moved to a separate house in the vicinity: Margaret Himmler and her daughter Gudrun—it is here that they learn of Himmler's suicide. Records of these prisoners' interrogations and, above all, transcriptions of their clandestinely recorded personal conversations in the dressing rooms of the Fascist-era divas, are replete with dramatic detail: accusations, manipulations, and efforts at self-reinvention. This special intelligence camp was cleared by October of 1945, on the eve of the Nuremberg trials.[8]

Separated from it, and occupying the greater part of Cinecittà, there evolved, in the meantime, a huge displaced-persons' (DP) camp (I have told its story before and offer here only a summary of its complex structure and history).[9] Thousands were housed in the Cinecittà DP camp: the survivors of local bombardments and of distant concentration camps—people who had lost everything, among them a vast number of children. To one side was an international camp, soon managed by the United Nations Relief and Rehabilitation Administration (UNRRA), and housing people of more than forty nationalities, including Yugoslavs, Poles, Russians, Chinese nationals, Egyptians, Iranians, and Ethiopians, among many others. In Cinecittà's sculpture workshops were concentrated Romani Gypsies.[10] There were Jews from everywhere: initially those who made it past the German lines, then the survivors from distant concentration camps, waiting in Cinecittà for two weeks or for four years for visas to North or South America or for British certificates to enter Palestine.[11] Across a fence was the Italian camp, where conditions were significantly worse. But both sides suffered from overcrowding, and reports abounded on epidemics, theft, black market trading, political tensions, violence, and suicide. This must be why one of the few reporters on the camp titled her article "Valley of Josaphat" and snapped some photos before the place was blocked to the press.[12] Under pressure from Italian undersecretary Giulio Andreotti, the Italian camp was dismantled in fall of 1947, but the UNRRA camp, which was eventually shifted to the International Refugee Organization, continued to occupy part of Cinecittà until the summer of 1950.

Few images exist of the Cinecittà camp, with one notable exception: an UNRRA propaganda fiction feature coproduced with Istituto Luce and the Italian Ministry for Postwar Affairs. Titled *Umanità* (*Humanity*, Jack Salvatori, 1946), it is a comedy of remarriage making use of the camp as its central location and revealing snippets of the life therein. Presumably the place was perked up a bit for the production, but the images are revealing all the same: several high-angle shots disclose a vast interior space, subdivided into units, with narrow passages—a labyrinth of uncovered boxes that serve as elemental refugee housing (fig. 6.2). Yet we are within one of

FIGURE 6.2. Refugee housing within Cinecittà's great soundstage, Teatro 5, as it appears in *Umanità* (Jack Salvatori, prod. Istituto Luce, 1946). Frame enlargement.

the world's greatest soundstages: Fellini's legendary Teatro 5, which housed as many as fifteen hundred people; other soundstages were similarly used. The interior cubicles were put together and partly furnished with the remains of studio equipment and movie sets, including Classical-style plaster columns and a range of props. What this means is that Cinecittà's infrastructure, edifices, and even sets and gadgets, which had once lent themselves to colossal constructions of everything from Roman temples to society boudoirs, were morphed here into basic refugee habitation.

The displaced-persons' camp, with its ad hoc architectural *bricolage*, emerges here as a strange heterotopic counterpart to the movie studio: each is, in its way, a placeless place, real and unreal, a controlled artificial environment set apart from the ordinary run of life.[13] But while the enclosed world of the studio would deliver us to extravagant spectacles, fantasy worlds exported worldwide with substantial profits, internees of the DP camp are removed from territory and state conditions, from work and the freedom of movement and choice. The phantasmic world of the movie studio is transfigured into an altogether different kind of ghostly place, a shadow of the life outside. Different orders of mise-en-scène thus converged in

Cinecittà: the spaces, props, and denizens/users of the movie-studio-turned-camp joined here in what amounts to an allegorical tableau of its historical moment— one that could not fit, however, into any of film history's neorealist narratives or the official chronicles of Cinecittà.

THE AFRICAN SUMMER OF '42

What follows—a striking, earlier episode uncovered in my recent discovery of Italian military documents from the midst of the war era—opens up an altogether new perspective on Cinecittà's transmutations in the 1940s. It is, in a sense, a prequel— not simply in that it takes us back to an earlier point in time but in that it reveals forms and motifs already discerned in the *later* phases of this history, the phase already told. It is in the spirit of such a prequel scenario, then, that I launch this narrative with some conjectural elements, securely anchored, however, in military history, which delivers us back to 1939 or 1940, on a different continent, far far away, more than twelve thousand kilometers south of Rome, in what was then the Union of South Africa. Imagine now an impoverished neighborhood in Cape Town, or a rural village in the Northern Transvaal, where a drought, or grand promises to see the world, encouraged local tribesmen to join the Native Military Corps (NMC).[14] Black men were thus recruited to be deployed as "supporting units" in the South African military, itself part of the British Commonwealth forces in World War II. They were not given weapons because they were considered disloyal, or it was deemed "inappropriate" that they engage in direct combat against white Europeans. This meant they often could not defend themselves and were to be kept in the rear, although some of their roles inevitably brought them under fire. Eventually some of the soldiers at El Alamein, for example, were armed, but they mostly served as builders, drivers, stretcher-bearers, or as "boys" in the service of white officers, and they were paid less than white soldiers of equivalent ranks.

At this point one might trace the footsteps of one actual person: Lance Corporal Nzamo Nogaga, who published an account of his experiences in a South African journal for "missionary and racial affairs" shortly after his return home in 1945.[15] It is a brief but precious text: some of the horrific details are tempered by considerable irony and humor, while gaps and background information may be conjectured through data from the history books. Nogaga was likely subordinated to the South African Second Infantry, which took part in several actions in the North African Desert Campaign against the Italian forces, themselves supported by Rommel. Along with other Allied troops, the Second Division went through the nine-month siege in Tobruk. Relieved at the end of 1941, they remained militarily unsustained, however, and surrendered to the Italians. This is how Nogaga, among 1,753 soldiers of the NMC, was taken prisoner in Tobruk. He describes how he was held captive in a cage under atrocious conditions, escaped into the desert wild, and suffered burns, sores, thirst, and hallucinations before being recaptured by the Italians and kept in chains near El Alamein. With fellow prisoners he was taken from place to place in North Africa, then shipped from Tripoli to Sicily, suffered Allied bombardments, and was subsequently moved to Naples, Capua, then to Rome.

No history, certainly no film history, mentions the existence of a prisoners of war camp inside Cinecittà in 1942, while film production is still in full swing, but the evidence makes it clear. A founding document of the POW Office of the Italian Royal Army General Staff, dated March 23, 1942, actually establishes Cinecittà as "Concentration Camp number 122" at military post 3300, instructing that it be ready to receive four hundred prisoners by the end of that same month. A quick glance forward to a March 31, 1943, register reveals a count of 793 men, significantly exceeding the formal capacity of four hundred originally established.[16] This is not a negligible number of people who must have been held in a secluded area in one of the backlots, surely surrounded by barbed wire. A four-page report of the International Red Cross, dated October 14, 1942, describes conditions in the camp as it already functions, indicating that it actually opened on May 9 and that it currently houses 409 prisoners, specifying "all Negroes, soldiers":

> The Camp is situated on a plain in the immediate vicinity of a group of cinematographic studios. . . . It is a Labour Camp. The dormitories comprise 5 huts of double planking, roofed with tarred roofing felt. These huts, which are 32 metres long by 6 metres wide stand on a foundation of well-aerated cement. The prisoners sleep on two-tier bunks. . . . Everything is in perfect order and spotlessly clean. The dormitories, which each contain 80 beds have an adequate number of windows, all supplied with shutters. Electric light is installed. . . . The prisoners do their own cooking. . . . The general health in the camp is excellent. There have been no deaths. . . . The latrines are in a concrete building, very well constructed and there are enough of them. . . . The prisoners would very much like to receive some out of door games, such as Association and Rugby football sets; also jazz musical instruments. . . . Books in English, Afrikaans, and Sesuto would be welcome. (Books in Zulu are not yet allowed by the Censor). . . . According to the Commandant 70% of these prisoners are illiterate (only 30% can sign their names).[17]

All major points of the 1929 Geneva Convention are addressed in the report, also indicating that Red Cross parcels are distributed. Nogaga's own testimony, however, stresses that these parcels are what kept them alive since they were not given a subsistence diet in Italy.

It is also as per the Geneva Convention that Nogaga and his mates can work. Under the subsection of the Red Cross report titled "Work," we find this: "Prisoners work in the cinematographic studios nearby. On the days when they are working prisoners receive double rations . . . and they are paid 3 liras a day. The employers also give them a few extras, such as cigarettes and trifling gifts."

But deeper insight is offered by an earlier document at the Italian Army Archives, dated May 7, plus an addendum dated May 16, 1942. It is a directive from the POW Office of the General Staff of the Royal Army to the War Ministry. Its object: "Use of negro [*negri*] POWs in film work": "Having established preliminary contacts with the Fascist Federation of Entertainment Industrialists, this Ministry is of the opinion that for the employment of negro POWs in the film 'Bayer 205,' currently in production at Cinecittà, and generally for all future requests of this sort and by other cinematographic studios, the following administrative criteria should be followed."[18] Guidelines are then laid out in seven brief articles, cross-referencing other military regulations. The addendum forwards this directive not only to the Seventeenth Army Corps and the POW Camp 122 commander but to the general director for cinema at the Ministry of Popular Culture; this would be Luigi Freddi, Cinecittà's founder and historian (although none of it is mentioned in his postwar two-volume autobiographical history of the studios). The prisoners' pay is set at 3 lire per day per person (approximately US$1.85 at today's exchange rate), but a sum of forty lire (about US$24) per day per prisoner is to be paid by the production to the army treasury, with the explanation that it is the army that covers the prisoners' expenses in the camp. Other provisions are made for a minimum number of days' employment, that the entire group of four hundred must be hired, that they be insured against accidents, that any damages to their clothing be charged against the prisoners' own pay, nor will the military be held responsible for any damages caused by these POWs to cinematographic equipment.

It is important to note that the camp's founding document of March 23, 1942, already has as one of its addressees the cinema office of the MinCulPop. Moreover, the May 7, 1942, document permitting and regulating the "use of negro POWs in film work" itself precedes the actual opening of the camp on May 9 (cited in the Red Cross report). This could well mean that the decision to locate a camp in Cinecittà in the first place, and with this particular choice of population, was made in tandem with the plan for their film labor and with some advance negotiation and coordination among the various entities: the General Staff, the War Ministry, and Luigi Freddi, acting both on behalf of the MinCulPop and the Cinecittà studio administration. Strengthening this hypothesis is the note made in the document's first paragraph, stating that the prisoners' employment will be for the film "'Bayer 205,' currently in production at Cinecittà," while the second article further notes "the importance of the film." Something was at work here that mobilized an entire apparatus of political and military entities invested in this particular POW camp and in this particular film. It's probably safe to assume that the fact that its director, Max Kimmich, was Goebbels's brother-in-law gave the real push to the extraordinary provisions of the production: the cheap labor of hundreds of POWs at a time when, surely, black extras would not be easy to assemble in Nazi-occupied Europe.

Indeed, already on May 20, a week and a half after the camp's opening, a German correspondent visits the set, and some days later, an article extolling the adventurous production in progress, and accompanied by plenty of photographs, is published in Berlin's popular *Film-Kurier:*

> Spring in Cinecittà, Rome's film city. Roses and jasmin are blooming on the paths that connect the sprawling area's various buildings. A few green spaces, circled by singing sprinklers, are populated with red poppies. From the fragrant sea of flowers, the brown studio building is lifted into relief against the polished blue of the sky. Behind the studio halls, the free space is extensive. In the distance, it is framed by the panorama of the Alban hills. We pass the oriental exterior sets for Genina's new movie *Bengasi,* the shoot of which is now almost concluded. . . . Squat negro huts lie in the shade of palm trees. All around, you can see natives as black as ebony. . . . The Italian ministry for *Volkskultur* [namely the MinCulPop] has obligingly seen to it that enough negroes are available.[19]

In all, a sunny and altogether agreeable moment in wartime Cinecittà, which affords the German correspondent the luxury of complete oblivion (or pretense thereof) of the actual goings-on—for the war has, in effect, *already* entered the studio in the person of hundreds of POWs, those "ebony" extras who had been kept, until very recently, in chains and cages at the North African theater of war. Rather, the correspondent's attention is naturally focused on the film's most popular star, Luis Trenker, on the animal trainer, and on a leopard—all of whom provide sufficient distraction. Clearly, this production was not a minor enterprise but a major affair attracting all sorts of special investments: capital, sets, stars, labor force, and advance promotion.

Bayer 205—as it is named in the document authorizing the use of POW labor for the production—was the working title of a German propaganda fiction produced by Ufa, with exteriors shot in Cinecittà and its environs in the summer of 1942, and released the following year under the title *Germanin.* Both titles refer to a vaccine against the sleeping sickness, the development of which—a fictionalized and ideologically adjusted *Story of a Colonial Deed,* as per the film's subtitle—was based on bits of medical history that become the movie's ostensible concern. There is, in fact, a happy moment in the plot when the Bayer product is thus rebaptized as the more patriotic name. With such proud flourish around the German pharmaceutical brand (which, likely, contributed to the film's production), one now recalls Bayer's other claims to fame, from aspirin in the nineteenth century, and chemical weapons in World War 1, to its merging into the IG Farben conglomerate—among the Nazi regime's greatest supporters and profiteers, with a hand in the production of Zyklon B, and benefiting from slave labor and experiments on prisoners in the Auschwitz complex in the same period with which we are concerned.[20] In fact, the film's dramatic substance is predicated on German scientific

FIGURE 6.3. Extras in *Germanin: The Story of a Colonial Deed* (Max Kimmich, prod. Ufa, 1943). Luis Trenker appears on the right. Frame enlargements.

superiority over British efforts, comprising issues of medical ethics. It thus tells the story of a scientist and his pretty assistant in the heart of Africa of the early 1910s. A charismatic game hunter joins them. He is played by Luis Trenker, a notable figure in Nazi cinema: actor, director, and alpinist who was involved, we will see, in other functions of the production. The outbreak of World War I sends these protagonists back home to unhappy Germany, where after a hiatus they reassemble, return to the bush, and heal the multitudes. A spectacular tribal celebration scene follows with all the nativist trappings. Having thus demonstrated German superiority and magnanimity, and following the noble doctor's self-sacrifice to save a repenting British officer who begs to be cured, the film projects a great German future in Africa with the triumph of *Germanin*, even as the doctor perishes.

In an essay on colonial cinema of the Third Reich, Sabine Hake analyzes the film's ideological and racist attitudes through the triangulation of power relations among Germans, British, and black Africans. She reads the film in the context of contemporary features exploiting the primitivist fascination with the "dark continent," while observing that the horrifying scenes of suffering and dying, uncannily reminiscent of concentration camp scenes, might have been taken from contemporary documentaries on tropical illnesses.[21] The Roman summer, Italian expertise with exotic sets, and a large group of black prisoners would come in handy for the production (fig. 6.3). The Italian Ministry of Popular Culture, along with the War Ministry and the Royal Army, clearly sought to accommodate (indeed, impress) Goebbels's brother-in-law, Kimmich, who was the first but, in fact, not the last to profit from the arrangement. The Italians had their own substantial colonial movie trend, but for them, too, shooting on actual locations was interrupted by the war so that productions eventually migrated into Cinecittà's backlots.[22] Augusto Genina's *Bengasi* of 1942, wrapping up production at that time as

FIGURE 6.4. *Harlem* (a.k.a. *Knock-Out,* Carmine Gallone, prod. Cines, 1943). Frame enlargement.

per the *Film-Kurier* correspondent's report, set in Libya but shot in Cinecittà, certainly did not make use of these same prisoners (who would also be unsuited physiognomically). But at least one other production, immediately following *Germanin,* must have made use of this group: Carmine Gallone's *Harlem* (a.k.a. *Knock-Out,* 1943), a Fascist-propagandistic boxing flick boasting not only major writers (who will shine in the neorealist era) like Sergio Amidei and Emilio Cecchi but big stars, including Massimo Girotti, Amadeo Nazzari, Vivi Gioi, Osvaldo Valenti (who would be executed by partisans some years later), and the boxer Primo Carnera playing himself. With the plot triangulating in this case Italians, Italian Americans, and African Americans, the movie struggled to emulate American boxing and gangster films with rather pathetic results, expressing scorn for America, especially its black population and its boxers—although a revised dialogue track was put in after the war to turn around its anti-American spirit. Stock footage of Madison Square Garden was intercut with a set reconstruction in what is surely Cinecittà's big Teatro 5, and a crowd of black extras was needed to cheer the black boxer, who loses to Massimo Girotti (fig. 6.4). This film, specifically its circumstances of production, deserves a separate study.[23]

But what is notable in *Harlem,* as in *Germanin,* is certainly also the presence of numerous black women, as well as some children, that we find among the extras. Where did these come from, in the midst of war in Italy, itself already committed to racial laws? Clearly a realistic African village was a high priority for *Germanin*. But excellent Cinecittà set constructions and strong summer sunlight were not enough: a basic condition of verisimilitude necessitated that these populations not be made entirely of men! Luis Trenker's 1965 autobiography elaborates precisely on this aspect of the production. While his brand of humor is no longer appealing, Trenker does offer some invaluable detail:

> For these negro soldiers, being an extra was a welcome break to their monotonous lives. . . . The film was supposed to show Africa as it lives and breathes, and that included, other than apes, palm trees, elephants and leopards . . . also negroes, and also women and children. Negresses, however, at this time existed neither in Rome nor in Berlin, and so the assistant director . . . traveled with two Nazi minders to find some in Paris. Frequenting bar after bar, [they] eventually located roughly 100 pure-bred [*rassig*] negresses of all shades and social standings, some of them very pretty. . . . They agreed to relocate to Rome for a stint of several weeks with their kids. However just before the scheduled departure, the black women suddenly went on strike. Somebody had warned them that Hitler intended to shoot all blacks. Only after long negotiations it was agreed to take a train that would not touch Germany, but rather go directly to Rome via Nice.[24]

The Political Archive of the Foreign Office in Berlin has registers of incoming posts to the Reich's Foreign Ministry, where it is noted that on June 7, 1942, on the 11:35 a.m. train from Paris—it is, of course, occupied Paris—seventy-two "Negros" were transported to Rome in third-class cabins. Also in these registers is a record of permission for a black actor and dancer, Albert Köhler, who had been living in bohemian circles in Berlin, to travel to Rome for this film.[25] Yet another Berliner, Louis Brody, a black actor who had been acting in German films since the early 1920s, participated in *Germanin* as the stereotypical native chief.[26] But Trenker focuses on the women:

> No hotel was allowed or willing to accommodate 80 colored [*farbig*] girls. The city's police chief told the production to house the group somewhere outside the city and under supervision. The strange troupe consisted in part of rather respectable Parisian citizens, whose men were in captivity as French soldiers. But it also included exotic dancers, ordinary harbor prostitutes from Marseille, and some extraordinarily slim and beautiful Nubians. . . . I had learned of a catholic girls' convent in Frascati, not too far from Cinecittà, that was not occupied during the summer months. . . . I told [the mother superior] that we needed accommodations for roughly 100 actresses from Paris. The women would not be allowed to go out after 8 p.m. They would be picked up daily to shoot at Cinecittà and then return to the convent later the same day. We agreed on the price. . . .
> When the three buses arrived at the convent in Frascati and the catholic nuns saw all the dark-skinned, ember-eyed negresses with their French and African floods of

words, the mother superior almost fainted. Of course, I had not mentioned in the discussions that we were talking about lots of colored actresses.

"All these women are good Christians," I told the mother superior so as to calm her down. With a sigh, she said: "Va bene."—Alright, we all are poor Christian souls!—"Siamo tutti poveri cristiani!" and with touching care, the exotic flowers [*exotische Pflanzen*] were directed to their rooms.

It was funny to observe how distinctly polite the brother-in-law of the National Socialist propaganda minister was in treating the black women during the shoot. More than once he [Kimmich] had to apologize because he had accidentally said a rough word. Because these black French women would not be bossed around. Frequently they went on strike. They knew full well that there was no replacement for them in this film.[27]

One does not know whether to laugh or cry and can only begin to imagine the encounter, on the set, of all these different people, men and women of different provenances from around the globe, in the midst of war, in a strange land—indeed the strangest land of Cinecittà's backlot dressed up as the African bush.

Nogaga's mention of the men's experience of the shoot is brief but revealing, and it contradicts Trenker's assumption that the prisoners enjoyed it: "we were employed making bioscope films. We did not like these stunts as we were made to go naked all the time."[28] Clearly, Nogaga and his mates understood very well the incongruities of their situation in history: in relation to the South African and British military deploying them as second-class persons in a war so removed from their own reality; in relation to international agreements and organizations (like the Geneva Convention and the Red Cross) attempting to salvage some semblance of "human rights" under impossible conditions; in relation to the primitivist fantasies that they were supposed to reenact. Nogaga makes no mention of the African French women: he might have been a modest family man, returning home to domestic existence. In any event the incredible scene was certainly more than what could be told in a POW memoir published in a missionary journal!

It must have been a hallucinatory scene indeed on that Cinecittà backlot and then, with the production of *Harlem*, also inside Teatro 5, where so many human paths and experiences converged, propelled on the one hand by the mobilities of war, occupation, captivity, and exile and, on the other, by the workings of modern media and its own mobilities and makeovers.[29] Germany's subjugation of the European continent and Italy's glorious studio, celebrated for its sets and reconstruction know-how, were jointly boosted by military control, political favors, and shady business. Axis propaganda, with its quintessentially modern colonialist exoticism, basically exploited the havoc and misfortune of war and played itself out in this unreal city, nine kilometers from the Trevi Fountain, or from Mussolini's balcony in Palazzo Venezia—and apparently not *too* far from Paris or from Cape Town. *À la guerre comme à la guerre* is what the Parisiennes must have said among themselves.

THE STUDIO'S RECURSIVE STAMP ON HISTORY

In the convergence of the studio's suspended, controlled, and remade reality and the reality of war and crisis in the mid-twentieth century—itself a violently, atrociously remade reality—certain patterns seemed to recur. Only a few years after the events just described, as we catch up with Cinecittà's spinning chronicles to find ourselves in the displaced persons' camp at its later phases, people confined therein—under now-altered circumstances—were entangled again in the machinations of the movie studio. Between the two different moments—connected, however, by historical, spatial, and institutional logic—Cinecittà's first use as a POW camp and its postwar use to house refugees, many cataclysmic events took place. Nogaga tells, in few words, of his transfer along with his mates to camps in Germany and, following the German surrender, the roundabout ways that led him finally back home. But numerous POWs perished in camps where they should have been safe, and millions of civilian deaths in Europe and beyond will never be fully told. But history seems to have been stamped, several times over, in Cinecittà, by the setting, or indeed by the *set,* in which it was caught and some of whose functions it absorbed. The spatial systems and functions of the studio are such that they afforded, or indeed determined, the convergence of disparate mise-en-scènes, historical and fictional, in Cinecittà.

For the movie studio did not cease to be a studio, did not dissolve its structures and functions, once the POW camp and, in turn, the DP camp occupied it in whole or part. In the late 1940s Hollywood was beginning to invest in Cinecittà as part of the American commitment to European reconstruction, with a view to American influence in postwar-turned–Cold War Europe and, naturally, with a view to profits. A major instrument of its investment was the production of MGM's Technicolor extravaganza *Quo Vadis?* (1951) in Cinecittà—a venture that also contributed to the recovery of the studios and provided one of the big models, and inspirations, for the era of Hollywood on the Tiber. This movie's mythicized tale of the beginnings of Christianity in Rome, with the forces of good triumphant against the excesses of Nero, was certainly an allegory of the liberation of Rome, of Italy, and of Europe from tyranny. The production boasted not only a fat budget, spectacular sets, and big stars but also an unprecedented fourteen thousand extras. Costumed in rags, they streamed through Roman alleys and crowded the Forum and Coliseum, all reconstructed in Cinecittà. As mentioned earlier, while the Italian part of the camp was dismantled in the fall of 1947, the international camp continued to occupy part of Cinecittà through the summer of 1950, while the MGM production was in full swing. Interviews confirm what we have already suspected as part of the inevitable logic of the coinciding of camp and movie studio: that among the movie extras of this colossal film are some of the camp refugees, mingled with numerous persons of all ages fortunate enough to earn a meal here in this time of shortage.[30] The Technicolor images of *Quo Vadis?* thus both conceal *and* reveal the real-life refugees in rags. Once again, the painfully real situation of the war (and postwar) has become intertwined with the spaces and demands of cinema.

Yet a certain denial was at work, as it was to be in film history. Not only Hollywood on the Tiber but neorealism before it failed to acknowledge this reality and could not incorporate it into any of their founding narratives. The second half of the 1940s was, indeed, the high season of neorealism, which turned its back on the studio—above all this *particular* studio contaminated by Fascism. Neorealism aspired to reveal "real life" on location, in the backstreets of Rome and in other peripheral landscapes. But real life was happening right here, entangled with the very stuff of cinema: sets and props for elemental housing arrangements, cheap refugee labor benefiting big movie production. Cinecittà emerges in this story as a kind of microcosm where the disasters of war threw people from around the globe, together, into the most unlikely settings. Their stories, stranger than fiction, became intertwined: from the enlisted men of poor Cape Town neighborhoods to black communities in Paris struggling to survive under the Nazi occupation, and from local Italian lives shattered by the bombardments of Cassino and of Roman working-class neighborhoods, to the survivors of distant concentration camps, people torn from communities, people who had lost everything but bare life. Cinecittà seems to have repressed these events from memory. But in some sense they were being represented *in the flesh,* in *Germanin,* in *Harlem,* in *Quo Vadis?,* in the person of these mostly anonymous POWs and refugees, hidden in plain sight.

Certainly, film production and the interests of entertainment exploited these situations and profited from them in much the same way that other wartime sectors of labor, from farming and mining to industry at any scale, exploited prisoners in that same time—whether POWs, who should be protected by international law, or countless civilian inmates, exploited by slave labor while being systematically deprived, starved, or frozen to death. But the coordinates confronting us here, in the relatively less-severe circumstances of Cinecittà, add up to a uniquely intricate and edifying ensemble or, indeed, a quasi-allegorical tapestry, in which it becomes impossible to extricate one thread, one role, one mise-en-scène from another. Exceeding questions of representation and context, the novel art and industry of cinema, with its powerful material and imaginative resources, and with its fictional apparatus, became directly engaged on these grounds in a recursive *pas de deux* with war itself—comprising situations of occupation, incarceration, violence, suffering, and destruction—and persisted right through it. Both studio and camp—Hannah Arendt would say, *any* camp—are, in principle, set apart from the life outside: enclosed, defined, restricted but at the same time placeless places, where reality is on some level suspended and remade, or manufactured.[31] Places as controlled and pressured as these give rise to actions involving the use, but also the misuse, of bodies and people. It is as if, having entered Cinecittà, these various actors on the greater stage of history—indeed, a transnational history with meanings and implications well exceeding Rome and Italy and this particular war but truly spanning the globe and mingling with other histories—must become *other* than they are, must inhabit roles dictated by the studio. Yet through the coinciding of camp and studio in Cinecittà, war and cinema also reveal, each, something of the reality of the other. Nor was this an isolated passing episode, to be cast aside as an anomaly, but a recursive pattern running through the different situations, with one phase appearing to reproduce itself in a string of variations, and at different scales, like a fractal system, following the model of the movie studio itself and its own structures and functions.

The greater social, military, and political events and historical agents, or players, are seen here not simply as casually intersecting with film history but as invading and partaking in it, transforming, in the process, our conception of these histories and how they might be told. The mutual imbrication of studio structures and functions with an urgent historical reality, the interlacing of the spaces and circumstances of film production with those of war—all suggest a breakdown of boundaries and hierarchies in a period of crisis, a morphing of spaces, materials, and people within this particular setting, giving birth to the chimeric phenomena described here, a yoking of functions routinely delegated in separate disciplines and separate history books. No generalized picture of POW or DP camps can fairly account for the particular experiences of its denizens; no film history can be extricated from the spaces and circumstances of its production. The invasion of the war into the movie studio and the studio's entry onto the historical stage manifest here the most glaring instance of the permeability of cinema and history, of modern media and politics—of the sort that, by now, we almost take for granted. The Cinecittà movie studio thus stamped history with its own image but with far more direct and concrete material, social, and political implications than its own cinematic representations—as well as its representation in film history—were willing to admit.

NOTES

Parts of this essay draw on my earlier research published in "The Cinecittà Refugee Camp, 1944–1950," *October* 128 (Spring 2009); and a longer Italian version, "Cinecittà campo profughi, 1944–1950," pts. 1 and 2, in *Bianco e nero* 560 (Nov. 2008) and 561/562 (May 2009). New research developments were made possible via a fellowship from the American Council of Learned Societies (2017–18) and advanced with the kind support of Roberto Cicutto and Cristiano Migliorelli at Istituto Luce-Cinecittà, Mario Musumeci at the Centro sperimentale di cinematografia and the Cineteca nazionale, Pasquale Grella and Riccardo Sansone in Quadraro. I am grateful to Brian Jacobson for such constructive feedback. Presentations of this research in the SCMS conference in Toronto (March 2018), at the University of Vienna (May 2018), and at Johns Hopkins (Nov. 2018) yielded productive discussions. The input of John

Belton at the Columbia Seminar for Cinema and Interdisciplinary Interpretation (Oct. 2018) and of David Forgacs at the Columbia Seminar in Modern Italian Studies (March 2019) were most rewarding.

1. See Freddi, *Il cinema*, vol. 2, 177–317 and Martin, *Gino Peressutti, l'architetto di Cinecittà*, 89–97. See also Crafton, *The Talkies*, 195.

2. See Argentieri, *L'asse cinematografico Roma-Berlino*, esp. 145–47, on Goebbels's dealings with Italian film personalities and his diary citations. For the message to the Venice Festival see "Il ministro Goebbels per la manifestazione di Venezia," *Cinema*, no. 101 (Sept. 10, 1940): 161. See also Marco Spagnoli's documentary film *Cinecittà Babilonia: sesso, droga e camicie nere* (*Cinecittà Babilonia: Sex, Drugs, and Blackshirts*, 2016). While it takes some liberties, the film is research-based and probably does not exaggerate the ways in which Cinecittà pandered some of its starlets to men high up in the regime's power hierarchy.

3. Harrison's reports are in NARA RG 387, Entry 460A, Box 2152, Camp Cinecittà folder; and RG 59, Entry Dec. File 1940–44, Box 2232. Another testimony, which further confirms the existence of a massive Allied POW camp in the "cinema-city," is that of British Army veteran Private Alfred Charles Lowe, who was captured in Anzio; see the Imperial War Museum Sound Archive, Cat. no. 25200, reel 5. Lowe describes the paucity of food and poor conditions in the "dumps" where they were held—certainly soundstages since he associates them with "big aircraft hangars" full of straw. The paucity of documents relating to POWs in Italy is explained by a January 22, 1946, counterintelligence report of a fire that broke out ten days previously in "the building jointly occupied by the Central Records Bureau and the Prisoner of War Information Board at Prisoner of War Enclosure 339 at San Rossore, near Pisa. The building, which contained an estimated 97 per cent of all the records on prisoners of war in this Theater, was completely destroyed with all of its contents." NARA RG 226, Entry 174, Box 240, Folder 12 (1377).

4. Based on escaped prisoners' names cited in the NARA State Department files in College Park, Maryland, I have located the following American veterans' interviews online: Albert Pistelli, www.youtube.com/watch?v=hxJnrBiVpoA; and Floyd J. Dumas, www.youtube.com/watch?v=FIOArV9I9ZA. The Dumas interview is indicated as published by the New York State Military Museum, July 16, 2015.

5. See "La resistenza al Quadraro," in Majanlahti and Guerrazzi, *Roma occupata, 1943–1944*, 127–31. Above all, I have learned about Quadraro from Mario Musumeci, chief film conservator at the Cineteca nazionale, whose family has resided in the neighborhood for generations.

6. A British Foreign Office correspondence from early 1946, reporting on investigation of this loot all the way to Berlin, is in the National Archives of the UK (Kew), FO 371/53142. Among the films thus lost was Nino Martoglio's fatefully titled *Sperduti nel buio* (Lost in the dark, 1914), reputedly one of Italy's greatest silent films, from which only few clips and stills now survive.

7. Adriano Baracco, "L'amante grassa," *Star* 1, no. 1 (August 12, 1944): 3. All translations from the Italian are mine unless otherwise noted.

8. It was in Dollmann's autobiography, *Nazi Fugitive*, 1–35, that I found the first substantial clues about the existence of the intelligence center, which I then confirmed with War Office documents at the National Archives of the UK (Kew). A separate essay based on these discoveries is under preparation.

9. The following segment is based on my essays, where illustrations may also be found: Steimatsky, "The Cinecittà Refugee Camp, 1944–1950," 23–50; and the longer Italian version, Steimatsky, "Cinecittà campo profughi, 1944–1950."

10. This information is compiled largely from the Allied Control Command files, which I consulted in microfilm at the Archivio Centrale dello Stato, Rome. Some details I found in del Buono and Tornabuoni, *Era Cinecittà*, 22.

11. Italy was a major transit country for Jewish DPs. Files of the YIVO Institute for Jewish Research, NY, indicate a Central Committee for Liberated Jews, under UNRRA, headquartered in Rome.

12. Paola Masino, "Valle di Giosafat," *Crimen: documentario settimanale di criminologia*, no. 1 (Jan. 26, 1945): 14–15.

13. On the placelessness and irreality characterizing diverse kinds of camps in that era, see Arendt, *The Origins of Totalitarianism*, 278–89, 296–97, 444–45. In *Studios Before the System*, especially 205–6, Brian Jacobson reads the spatial dynamic and modern malleability of the movie studio through Foucault's notion of heterotopia.

14. On this topic I have consulted Killingray's *Fighting for Britain*, Grundy's *Soldiers without Politics*, and Botha's "Warriors without Weapons."

15. Lance-Corp. Nzamo Nogaga, "An African Soldier's Experiences as Prisoner of War," *South African Outlook* 75, no. 894 (Oct. 1, 1945): 151.

16. The founding document, titled "Campo di concentramento per pg. di Cinecittà," is at the Historical Archive of the Army General Staff: Archivio de l'Ufficio Storico dello Stato Maggiore dell'Esercito [AUSSME], fondo N-1/11, b. 667. In this same archive is the document of March 31, 1943, reporting on the numbers in POW camps, "Situazione prigionieri di guerra nemici," AUSSME, fondo L-10, b. 32.

17. "Prisoner of War Camp no. 122, Visited the 14th October 1942 by Dr. de Salis," trans. the London Delegation of the International Red Cross Committee, National Archives of the UK (Kew), WO 361 1915. Subsequent quotation is from this same document.

18. "Utilizzazione pg. negri nella lavorazione di filmi," directive from the Ufficio prigionieri di Guerra dello Stato Maggiore dell'Esercito, addressed to the Ministero della Guerra. AUSSME, fondo N-1/11, b. 667.

19. Günther Schroark, "*Germanin* entsteht im Süden," *Film-Kurier*, May 26, 1942, 1, 4. My thanks to Gregor Quack for translations from the German here and in what follows.

20. Emile Weiss's documentary *Criminal Doctors, Auschwitz* (2013) cites a correspondence between Auschwitz commanders and Bayer negotiating the purchase and delivery of 150 women for experiments, noting that they were emaciated, then reporting that the experiments were not successful and, since all subjects died, Bayer requests another shipment.

21. Hake, "Mapping the Native Body," esp. 170–71. Hake describes the film's population of male extras as forced laborers from Libya—only, we now know, a half-truth since these South African POWs were merely captured there. But her essay's chief objective is, of course, different from my own.

22. On the subject of the Italian colonial films see the definitive work by Ben-Ghiat, *Italian Fascism's Empire Cinema*.

23. Little has been written about *Harlem* other than a chapter in Alberto Zambenedetti's "Italians on the Move," 51–68, as well as a peculiar detective novel *(giallo)* by Umberto Lenzi, *Terrore ad Harlem*, which incorporates some scattered elements from the film's actual production circumstances. Speculations about the provenance of the film's black extras have been, to date, consistently mistaken.

24. Trenker, *Alles gut gegangen*, 402. I have followed Hake's clue to this remarkable episode in Trenker's autobiography.

25. Elsewhere in the register there is a note that Köhler's children were sterilized. The following documents have been consulted at the Bundesarchiv Berlin, Foreign Office Political Archive: PA AA, AB 1, Sachbuch, Abt. Inf III C, 1942, entries 1–2999; 2060.2, 2140.0, 2141.9, 1610.1, 2330.2, 2331.4, and PA AA, AB 1, Journal, Abt. Deutschland, Referat D III, 1943, entries 1–2790; 2001, PA AA, AB 1, Journal, Abt. Deutschland, Referat D III, 1941, entries 5461–9909; 8249, PA AA, AB 1, Namensregister, Abt. Deutschland/Inland II A/B, 1939–1944, PA AA, AB 1, Journal, Abt. Deutschland, Referat D III, 1941, entries 5461–9909; 5891.3, PA AA, AB 1, Namensregister, Abt. Deutschland/Inland II A/B, 1939–1944. I am grateful for Westrey Page's excellent assistance in researching these sources.

26. See Nagl, "Louis Brody and the Black Presence in German Film before 1945," 109–35.

27. Trenker, *Alles gut gegangen*, 402–3.

28. Nogaga, "An African Soldier's Experiences as Prisoner of War," 151.

29. Noting a "convergence of crisis and spectacle" in modern Italy, Ruth Ben-Ghiat and Stephanie Malia Hom explore "mobility" as a historical concept in their introduction to *Italian Mobilities,* 10, 1, respectively.

30. Two persons interviewed in Marco Bertozzi's 2012 documentary film *Profughi a Cinecittà / Refugees in Cinecittà,* confirmed the participation of DPs as extras: Angelo Iacono, who was thus employed while a teen, living with his displaced family inside Teatro 5, and Adriano De Angelis, whose family specialized in plasterworks for four generations in Cinecittà and who witnessed the goings-on at that time. I have collaborated on Bertozzi's documentary, itself inspired by my research, cited in note 9, and elaborating on it—particularly with these striking interviews.

31. I remain uncomfortable with Arendt's drawing of continuities, in *The Origins of Totalitarianism,* between all camps, including extermination camps, but agree on some aspects of the analogy around the notion of placelessness within a circumscribed space and reality, set apart from workaday existence.

PART THREE

Alternative Routes

7
___

The Film Train Stops at Mosfilm

Aleksandr Medvedkin and the Operative Film Factory

Robert Bird

MOSFILM 1938

Mosfilm Studio's internal newspaper *Za bol'shevistskii fil'm* (For Bolshevik film) greeted the first day of Soviet cinema's twentieth year by publishing Isaak Shmidt's two-panel caricature with accompanying verses celebrating the studio's star directors and their latest successes (fig. 7.1). On the left of the first panel the caped Sergei Eisenstein bears aloft the standard of Mosfilm, riding the triumph of *Alexander Nevsky*, his first release for a decade. Behind him rides Mikhail Romm, atop the armored car of *Lenin in October,* followed by other star directors with their latest Mosfilm productions. The second, more crowded panel, continues the panorama with, from the right, screenwriter Viktor Shklovskii and director Vsevolod Pudovkin pulling onstage their historical epic *Minin and Pozharskii* (in the form of the monument to the two seventeenth-century warriors that still stands on Red Square); Ol'ga Preobrazhenskaia and Ivan Pravov sailing ashore on their historical drama *Stepan Razin;* and Aleksandr Ptushko preparing his puppets for the stop-motion animated fairy tale *The Golden Key.*

These witty vignettes barely conceal the grave tensions of the moment. Positioning itself as the major rival to Hollywood, for years the entire Soviet cinema industry had been under intense pressure to produce more films with improved efficiency. At the start of 1938 Stalin personally joined the charge, ominously declaring: "The cinema is a powerful instrument of mass education. It is our duty to take matters into our own hands."[1] Accordingly, on March 23, 1938, Stalin's cabinet, the Council of People's Commissars, decreed the latest reorganization of the industry, which was now to be managed by the Committee on Cinema Affairs,

FIGURE 7.1. Isaak Shmidt, untitled satirical sketches, *Za bol'shevistskii fil'm*, Jan. 1, 1939, 2–3.

answerable directly to the council. The stated rationale related mostly to alleged mismanagement and even corruption by longtime industry head Boris Shumiat-skii, including the wasting of 2 million rubles expended on Eisenstein's film *Bezhin Meadow* before the completed film was shelved in 1937 and subsequently destroyed.[2] At this time of Terror, accusations of administrative impropriety frequently presaged more grievous (and, usually, wholly fictitious) charges, and in January of 1938 Shumiatskii was arrested on accusations of espionage and the attempted assassination of party leaders (he had once inadvertently dropped a rectifier and spilled mercury in Stalin's presence). Further down the ladder, two successive directors of Mosfilm were arrested in 1937 and executed in 1938; similar fates befell an untold multitude of professionals, from directors to projectionists. Recounting 1938's great harvest of films, Shmidt's caricature also celebrates Mosfilm's emergence from this extended paroxysm of violence. In confirmation of the new dawn, on February 1, 1939, Mosfilm and many of its leading lights—including Eisenstein with his cast and crew—were honored with prestigious state awards.

None of this triumphalism addressed the basic administrative fissure in the Soviet cinema system, exemplified by the March 1938 decree and unwittingly captured in Shmidt's caricature: the Soviet cinema was an increasingly centralized state system of commissioning and distribution that was driven, at the very same time, by an auteur-based system of production.[3] In particular, for all of its proximity to central government, the film studio—or "film factory," as it was commonly known in Soviet parlance—was organized around small and relatively stable creative teams, for which directors recruited congenial screenwriters, directors of cinematography, and production designers. The most vivid illustration of this contradiction is the system's dependence on and intolerance of its greatest star, Sergei Eisenstein. The fall of Shumiatskii laid the way for Eisenstein to return to the cinematic fold after the debacle of *Bezhin Meadow*, together with key members of his team who had worked with him for more than a decade.[4] But as one of only forty-odd films completed in 1938, few of which achieved lasting acclaim, the exceptional triumph of *Alexander Nevsky* confirmed the rule of systemic failure: not everyone was an Eisenstein.

Striking a singular note, to the far left of the second panel director Aleksandr Medvedkin sits at the helm of an incongruous double-decker bus-palace pulled by two scared horses, against the background of a classically columned and domed building flanked by more modern-looking structures, some in markedly Constructivist style. While his vehicle associates him with the blockbuster productions of the first panel, all of which involve symbolically resonant modes of transport, its patchwork construction suggests comedy—namely *The Miracle Worker* (1936), which controversially featured a fire engine hitched to an old nag that arrives too late to put out a fire.[5] From his precarious perch Medvedkin barks out a challenge to fellow director Konstantin Iudin, who drags along the recalcitrant titular character of his *Girl with a Temper* (1939): which of them will finish his film first and most economically, to their factory's and industry's greater glory? But of all the Mosfilm directors, Medvedkin is the only one pictured alone, without collaborators or actors. The lonely builder of a socialist cinema system—thus was Medvedkin's tragic fate.

Specifically, Shmidt caricatures the incongruities of Medvedkin's latest film, *The New Moscow*, a musical comedy heavy in studio-generated special effects, which confirmed Medvedkin's transition from a militantly ideological and aesthetically unconventional filmmaker into a rank-and-file employee of Mosfilm.[6] After shooting to fame on his Film Train in 1932, in his first two Mosfilm productions Medvedkin had crafted two satirical comedies—*Happiness* (1934) in addition to *Miracle Worker*—both of which were set in the backward Soviet countryside, signified by his nags. Another of Medvedkin's folksy screenplays, *Accursed Force*, lay fallow, despite having been approved and included in the studio's production plan, never to be made. Now, however, Medvedkin had taken on a more conventional musical comedy in order to represent a Moscow that was not only "new" but still masked in the mists of the future. Where is this unlikely pioneer driving the Soviet cinema? Where is it driving him?

Despite favorable advance reviews in *Pravda* and *Izvestiia*, the two most important central newspapers, *The New Moscow* never reached Soviet screens, for reasons that always remained opaque to Medvedkin.[7] Although Medvedkin stayed at Mosfilm as an activist and innovator, producing a color short on the 1939 physical culture parade and subsequently serving as head of the studio's party organization, *The New Moscow* proved his final bid to establish himself as a director of feature films on par with the other star directors—one, moreover, entrusted to direct his own screenplays (even Eisenstein had been assigned cowriters). If the shelving of *The New Moscow* was a relatively typical demonstration of the institutional maladies afflicting the Soviet film industry, paranoid of the very creativity it demanded from directors, for Medvedkin it was tantamount to being cast aside by a system only he truly believed in.

Working against simplistic oppositions between the Soviet avant-garde of the 1920s and socialist realism of the 1930s, in this essay I examine Medvedkin's experiments in the decade leading up to 1938 as episodes in a single effort to define an alternative ontology of cinema, differing not only from the dominant modes of Western cinema but also from those commonly associated with Soviet cinema of the time (i.e., montage, factography, and eccentric comedy). In the first part of this essay I present Medvedkin's Film Train as an experiment in operative realism, which Medvedkin understood as a cinema embedded not only in production but also, crucially, in the broader discursive environment of socialism that informed his odd synthesis of factography, satire, and whimsy. In the second part I briefly consider how Medvedkin adapted his operative cinema under the conditions of the centralized film factory and the aesthetic paradigm of socialist realism in his mid-1930s satires *Happiness* and *The Miracle Worker*, before returning, in the final section, to *The New Moscow*, which I present as a critique of Soviet studio practices (especially in light of the 1938 decree) and an appeal to remobilize socialist realism, even in its centralized and institutionalized form, as an operative film aesthetic.

OPERATIVE REALISM 1932: THE FILM TRAIN

Throughout texts about the Film Train, especially those penned by its first head, Aleksandr Medvedkin, one encounters the notion of an *operative* cinema, a word that today evokes immediate associations with Sergei Tret'iakov's factography and Walter Benjamin's related essay "The Author as Producer." In his 1931 essay "The Writer and the Socialist Village," Tret'iakov defined an "operative relation" as one that exceeds simply reporting on sites of socialist construction, like the collective farm *(kolkhoz)*, and becomes a form of "participation in the life of the material": "Side by side with my heroes, I struggle for the reorganization of their life, I make efforts to further their development, and together with my fellow workers on the kolkhoz, I assume complete responsibility for the paths that are chosen, for their successes, mistakes, and flaws."[8] Similarly, Medvedkin boasted of his Film Train that "it was frequently possible to measure the results of our work in statistics of mined coal or harvested grain."[9] The Film Train also served as an experimental laboratory for new methods of cinema production; it confirmed, for instance, the quality of the new Soviet film stock and challenged other filmmakers to adopt it.[10] But even more than the material production of industrial goods and films, Medvedkin's operative cinema also shouldered responsibility for the production of a nationwide discursive environment for socialism.

Born in 1900, Medvedkin came of age with the October Revolution of 1917 and, especially, with the ensuing Civil War, in which he served with distinction in the Red Cavalry. Here he came into contact with the agitational trains (or agit-trains) that took newsreels and other media to the war-wracked provinces, which served as a school for Dziga Vertov and Eduard Tisse, among other Soviet film professionals. Having shown himself a zealous and effective military organizer, authoring countless projects that were shot down by skeptical superiors—after the war's end in 1921 Medvedkin became a director in the Red Army theater, staging rough-and-ready dramaticals for troops. From 1927 Medvedkin learned filmmaking in the Red Army film agency (Gosvoenkino), beginning with simple training films, into which he injected homespun humor through imaginative montage and witty intertitles. As evident in *Mind Your Health* (1929), the sole surviving film of Medvedkin's six known Gosvoenkino titles, where the demonstration of sound bathing technique is intercut with footage of cats grooming themselves, Medvedkin addressed his films to relatively uneducated and unsophisticated soldiers and peasants, whom he endeavored to amuse, even while instructing.[11]

Medvedkin's military experience prepared him well for the onset of the First Five-Year Plan in 1928, when the Soviet Union shifted to a planned economy. As he later wrote:

> It was as if this vast country was in turmoil. The trains were packed to overflowing—with the builders of [the massive construction projects] Turksib, Magnitka, Dnepro-GES; with kulaks on the run; with mobilized Communists. . . .
>
> The days were grim, the nights anxious . . . while in the evenings (as if nothing had changed in the world) the flat shadows of "heroes" flitted across the screens of movie theaters, infecting the revolutionary spirit of the people with domestic dramas and the venom of tawdry happiness. . . .
>
> I came to film from the Red Army without any intention of getting caught up in this kind of "art." I came with people of a like mind and commitment, determined to overthrow it, force it into open battle, and drive it off the screen in order to replace it with a real revolutionary art of film![12]

Far from alone in positing for socialism a militant media system that would be fully engaged in economic and social processes, Medvedkin's distinction was in identifying satire as a primary mode of "real revolutionary art" and brevity as a formal key to its potency. Moving to the Moscow film factory, in 1930–31 Medvedkin produced five satirical shorts that countered the Soviet penchant for feature-length productions that often arrived on screens too late to intervene in the issues they targeted. By contrast, Medvedkin's militant principles of composition and production allowed him to complete his films in ten to fifteen days each. The result, he claimed, was more like "a proverb, an aphorism or a fable," or like a poster or caricature, which defined both the films' pointed effect and their short-comings, among which Medvedkin confessed to "schematism, cliché, isolation from a real environment, etc."[13] While these films were evidently crude in conception and execution (none has survived), and were punningly excoriated by the central cinema newspaper as "Medvedkino" (*medved* means "bear," so the term implies a degree of ham-fistedness and fuzzy thinking), Medvedkin cannot be dismissed as a naive artist; at least three of the five featured the actor Vladimir Maslatsov, a veteran of Vsevolod Meyerhold's avant-garde theater.

By mid-1931 Medvedkin decided to refine his films' "environment" and narrow their "aim" by mobilizing his cinema, in a literal sense, as a Film Train. Unlike the agitational trains of the Civil War, now not only the demonstration but even the entire production of film was to be taken on the road, with the material and logistical support of the People's Commissariat for Railways. Three disused long-distance train carriages were equipped as a mobile film lab, editing room, animation studio, archive, screening room, and printing press, all in addition to living quarters for the personnel (six or eight four-person compartments—accounts differ), a dining room (featuring a piano and radio), a kitchen, and a shower.[14] For short-range travel a one-and-a-half-ton truck was personally contributed by the sympathetic Sergo Ordzhonikidze, people's commissar for heavy industry.[15] A separate storage carriage held sixteen lighting units and two portable electrical generators, in addition to three professional cameras, three automatic cameras, and five portable projectors for showing both the train's own production and other films distributed by Soiuzkino (the name of the state body responsible for all aspects of the cinema industry between 1930 and 1938). The compartments and technical units were all linked by an internal telephone circuit and, during stops, with the national telephone network. The trains carried a staff of up to thirty-two, led by Medvedkin as head (*nachal'nik*) and lead director but featuring also a political editor, three directors, three cameramen, a screenwriter, and a photographer.

For 294 days, from January to October of 1932, Medvedkin's Film Train toured the country on six separate expeditions, producing seventy short films, all silent. Eighteen of them were explicitly presented as "operative" releases of a "film newspaper" documenting on-site events, critiquing local production practices, and offering slogans for their improvement.[16] The remaining fifty-two films were scripted and addressed to wider audiences; during Medvedkin's year in charge of the Film Train at least twelve films out of the seventy were approved for nation-wide distribution. Answering to the central People's Commissariat for Railways, which mandated its destinations and topics of coverage, the Film Train was unique in Soviet practice for having its own political editor, who bore responsibility for approving the films for local demonstration. Once they reached Moscow, these films became subject to the same centralized system of editorial control and distri-bution (i.e., censorship) as regular studio productions. The extent to which they were screened is unknown; in August of 1932 one reviewer complained that a five-day festival of newsreel cinema in Moscow had included none of the Film Train's available titles.[17]

Like Dziga Vertov's Cine-Eye and Tret'iakov's factography, Medvedkin's Film Train was premised on the need "to take the [film] factory on location [*natura*]"[18]—that is, for media to register the new world at the very site and moment of its crea-tion rather than fabricating its images at some central site of production. Just as Vertov found himself shunted from studio to studio, and eventually exiled to the Central Studio of Documentary Film, so also the Film Train could not be run from within the Moscow film factory. At the same time, each distant location was repre-sented as a node in the centralized and overlaid networks of Soviet industry and communications, exemplified by its ability to plug its internal telephone circuit into the national network. Fittingly, the Film Train's first destination was the rail industry itself (literally known in Russian as "paths of communication"—*puti soo-bshcheniia*), specifically "the transport hubs of the Donbass region," where the Film Train was charged with the following "themes": "shipping in autumn-winter; the struggle against traffic jams; [the struggle] for transport's operative work; for the acceleration of loading and unloading operations; for the standardization of routes; for better upkeep of locomotives (the quality of repairs, timely departures); for paired work teams; for the rational use of the train depot."[19] This first expedi-tion resulted in nine films shown to 35,300 viewers at 105 local screenings.[20] On February 21, 1932, three production groups "entirely shot, developed, printed, edited and released onto the workers' screens of Dnepropetrovsk the film *The Storm*," which highlighted problems at a locomotive factory.[21] Requiring a mere twenty-six hours of nonstop labor, from screenplay to completion, this production was touted as "the first experiment in storm brigade cinema labor," one that fully integrated film production into the material and imaginary networks of the Soviet system, visually representing and materially intensifying the fluid circulation of goods and ideas around the Union. Although the ideological and aesthetic results could be disputed, observers agreed with Medvedkin that "operativity is the main quality of the Film Train's work."[22]

Since electricity was the central force in the Five-Year Plan and its concomitant imaginary, in October of 1932 the Film Train headed to the Dnieper Hydroelectric Dam (known as DneproGES), where it filmed the final preparations and launch of

FIGURE 7.2. Aleksandr Medvedkin (left) and Garri Piotrovskii at the
Dnieper Hydroelectric Dam, 1932. Courtesy of the State Central
Museum of Cinema, Moscow.

a signal industrial installation of the First Five-Year Plan (fig. 7.2). In Medvedkin's
words, this was "the most operative journey of our 'traveling film studio.'"[23] A
thirteen-hundred-foot film was released in six prints on the very same day as the
events it documented.[24] Five copies were flown to Ukrainian cities, and one positive print accompanied the negative by airplane to Moscow for demonstration the
day after the launch and with an eye to nationwide distribution. Near-constant
press coverage represented the Film Train as a force akin to electricity itself, flowing almost instantaneously over the distribution grid, accelerating production at
nodes distant from the points of material extraction.

Although the Film Train shared the avant-garde's challenge to centralized cultural institutions, Medvedkin's "operativity" was markedly distinct from Tret'iakov's
or Vertov's. In addition to shooting and exhibiting on location, Medvedkin stresses
the speed and mobility of production rather than Tret'iakov's notion of prolonged
observation. According to Medvedkin, the Film Train sought to begin filming
immediately after it arrived at each "hot spot" of socialist construction, to develop
the film overnight, edit it the following morning, print copies and demonstrate it
in situ by evening. "Shoot today, show tomorrow," was the slogan. These conditions of production made the Film Train a constant test of workers' abilities and
endurance, as well as the crucible of a tight production crew. In addition to being
head of the train and director of thirteen films, Medvedkin also served as screenwriter, editor, and cameraman for other directors. This collective principle distin-

guishes the Film Train equally from Tret'iakov's singular "operative author" and from Dziga Vertov's later proposals for organizing documentary film production around a stable production unit, which he called the "experimental laboratory," under the director's firm leadership.[25] At times it is impossible to establish the precise authorship of Film Train products. More than for his actual films, Medvedkin's name became attached to the train for his organizing role and for his dogged promotion of its legend in subsequent years.

Medvedkin's concept of operativity also differed by consistently situating film production at the center of a broader discursive environment. The mobile film factory not only produced films on-site but also screened them there as centerpieces in discussions, "conduct[ing] all its mass work in living, operative contact with activists, and with Party and union organizations."[26] "Almost every screening," reads one contemporary account, "turned into a production meeting."[27] Critic Lev Vaks characterized the Film Train's films themselves as "speakers" (dokladchiki), as if at an all-Union multimedia conference. When distributed beyond the immediate context, the films were also frequently envisioned to be accompanied by lectures. Moreover, the Film Train proved surprisingly dependent on print media, including a factory newspaper, Temp, and other materials produced in its printshop but also the central press. The overall impression is one of multiple feedback loops, embedded one within another, in which the silent film shorts powered the ceaseless circulation of verbal discourse overlaying ramped-up industrial production.

This rather utopian vision was subject to all manner of stochastic disruptions. One Dnepropetrovsk worker described the visit of the Film Train at his factory as proceeding "chaotically," with films produced without input by the workers, the factory leadership, or party organization, and with screenings held without sufficient notification or preparation. When a screening did occur, workers were shown not a film shot at their own factory but random reels of "blast furnaces of a metallurgical factory and shots of a train arriving late at Rostov."[28] After the Film Train departed, two crew members returned with Medvedkin's *A Camel Visits the Dnepropetrovsk Steam Locomotive Repair Works,* his first thematic title, which was deemed a failure for using the material supplied by the factory (which showed "concrete culprits of the production shortfall") in too selective and generalized a way. "In this form the film doesn't help the factory, and therefore it isn't worth a penny," the worker complained. Further objections arose in general release. After watching Medvedkin's *About Love*—"a cinematic comedy created on local material and only for a local viewer"—reviewer E. Sheval' wrote, "some moments . . . prove memorable, but I don't recall any viewer laughing at the screening."[29]

Despite the crude production and haphazard demonstration, from a formal standpoint the emphasis on discursive environment enhanced the Film Train's value as an experimental laboratory. Vaks noted that "although it was intended not for inventive and experimental, but for purely operative, production-based work, [the Film Train] achieved variety in the genres of its cinema."[30] Among the Film Train's stylistic innovations are not just an authenticity of location but also an intimacy of address. As Emma Widdis notes, "New genres such as the 'socialist reckoning,' 'film reports' and 'film-letters' were used to document and criticize the everyday life in the communities visited," turning the representation of labor into an imperative addressed to the viewer.[31] In his own films Medvedkin continued the line of his brief proverb- or poster-like satires, which appear to have been quite distant from, possibly diametrically opposed to, a documentary sensibility, and which compensated in part for the "grim" tonality of the bulk of the Film Train's films, especially with Maslatsov's eccentric acting in *About Love, Hole, Titus*, and *The Trap*.[32] The press credited Medvedkin with inventing new methods of animation and shadow photography, which he seems to have deployed quite generously.[33] Based on an idea he elaborated long before the Film Train actually set off (the screenplay is dated September 6, 1931), in *A Camel Visits the Dnepropetrovsk Steam Locomotive Repair Works* an animated camel—a standard image of stubborn Oriental backwardness in films like *Turksib* (1929)—wanders around still photographs of the rail yard, identifying shortcomings in operations and shaming workers into collaborative action.[34] The camel was intended to become a serial character à la Mickey Mouse, endowed with "a good, pointedly Soviet name," with the same prefabricated clichés superimposed onto location-specific photographs, but it featured in only one more known film, Boris Kin's *Adventures of a Camel on the Railway*.[35]

In line with the heroic myth of the Film Train, recent responses have tended to gloss over the less savory aspects of its interventions on what Medvedkin referred to as "the front line of class war," especially during the third expedition to southern Ukraine, which was at the time wracked by state-enforced famine known in Ukrainian as *Holodomor*.[36] The very word *operativity* has prosecutorial connotations, which Cristina Vatulescu has highlighted as a feature of the Film Train's activity.[37] True to the military background of Medvedkin and some of his collaborators, the Film Train appears to have conceived of itself as a tool of battleground justice. As Medvedkin later recalled, "Still-breathing *kulaks* obstructed at every step, trying to put sticks in our wheels. . . . This was the cinema of 'dagger-like action.'"[38] The Film Train's "police aesthetics" are evident in other slogans for the project, such as "Don't leave a site until laggards reform. Hold them under the Eyemo lens like under the sights of a machine gun!"[39] Film Train films were credited with helping to identify wrongdoers, who were subsequently excluded from party ranks, imprisoned, or even shot.[40] Here too, though, the primary intent appears to have been the generation of corrective discourse rather than actual punishment. As Medvedkin commented, "By organizing socialist competition, the Film Train adopts the role of a referee, undertaking to film the results of the battle for primacy and establishing through films a socialist exchange of experience among the best brigades of coalfaces, mines and activist organizations."[41] For Medvedkin and his subsequent acolytes the Film Train represented an alternative cinema ontology, occurring largely outside of both commercial and administrative command structures, sustained by the enthusiasm of a tight and egalitarian professional collective, and embedded in a broad discursive environment, generating operative realism as a material and discursive environment of socialist planning.

MEDVEDKIN AT MOSFILM

While Medvedkin was driving the Film Train from site to site, overseeing the production of operative realism, the Soviet cinema industry was undergoing rapid transformation in a very different direction. Under the First Five-Year Plan, which reached its conclusion in 1932, a year ahead of schedule, Soviet cinema was increasingly perceived as a self-sufficient economic, technological, and creative system, free of imports of raw film stock or even, ideally, of foreign releases. After the first successes of 1931, especially Nikolai Ekk's *A Ticket to Life* (from the Mezhrabpomfil'm factory, a Soviet-German venture that closed in 1936), feature-film production was incorporating synchronic sound and special effects produced in the studio. In February of 1932, while the Film Train was on its first expedition, Soiuzkino opened a new Moscow Unified Film Factory on the outskirts of the city, in the village of Potylikha, allowing for indoor filming on extensive sets. The central location ensured advantageous servicing from other central institutions, most crucially the electrical grid, but also ensured proximity to central political power so that Stalin, for one, could personally supervise production at every stage.

Soon after, on April 23, 1932, the Central Committee of the Communist Party decreed an end to the existing artistic system and its "reconstruction" as a set of professional unions based on more inclusive principles. By the end of the year the new system acquired a name—socialist realism—and, in early productions like Fridrikh Ermler's *The Counterplan* (from the Leningrad film factory), the system quickly acquired material form. Although frequently reduced to a caricature by later observers, in its first years socialist realism heralded neither an obligatory and unimaginative artistic style nor the enslavement of artists to direct political control. Quite the opposite, as Harold Swayze first argued, socialist realism signaled the recognition that socialism required an exuberant "thinking in images" alongside a more disciplined "thinking in concepts."[42] In the cinema socialist realism was in part a campaign to mobilize the aesthetic and affective power of synchronized sound technologies to construct and disseminate an attractive cultural imaginary for socialism. In the words of former Constructivist Kornelii Zelinskii, the task of socialist realist film was to provide "cine-models of our immediate future."[43]

The ambitions of socialist realism exacerbated the material obsolescence of the Soviet industry. A shortage of lighting equipment meant that only one production could be active at any given time, and the factory newspaper frequently bemoaned the general disrepair of the studio and its surrounding amenities.[44] How could a studio that couldn't heat its own premises produce compelling "cine-models" of a brighter future? Most egregiously, although built during the advent of sound cinema, the Moscow factory was not designed for sound productions, requiring constant and extensive retrofits to the physical plant. As late as 1935, when the USSR hosted its first international film festival, the Moscow factory (now renamed Mosfilm) lagged far behind its older Leningrad counterpart (renamed Lenfilm), which garnered top honors for its recent productions *Chapaev* (1934), *Maksim's Youth* (1934), and *Peasants* (1935). (Mosfilm received honorable mention for Aleksandr Ptushko's stop-motion animated film *The New Gulliver* and Iulii Raizman's live-action *Pilots*, both from 1935.) Despite these handicaps, however, the competition between central factories for critical acclaim and box-office receipts helped to fuel a continual stream of formal and technological innovations under the aegis of socialist realism.

As a centralized system of film commissioning, production, and distribution, with an emphasis on the feature-length fiction film, early socialist realism might seem the antipode of an operative realism embedded in rapid, brief, and local production. In other respects, however, socialist realism continued to deploy the rhetoric of operativity. An extensive campaign was waged in the press in favor of stable production groups formed on the principle of "creative proximity" in a tacit acknowledgment that, to become self-sufficient, the system relied on the initiative and labor of established collectives, which would be encouraged to experiment in film style and form.[45] As Viktor Shklovskii wrote in the industry newspaper: "the main thing is we have to put an end to the dream of producing the absolute film. . . . We are people who are still en route."[46] Genre was a case in point; far from falling into rigid generic categories, films like the first socialist realist blockbuster *Chapaev* or *The New Gulliver* straddle multiple categories and ultimately defy categorization, except as "models of our immediate future"—and of a possible future cinema. Among this experimentation, the Film Train was also hailed for "developing a popular, accessible and expressive cinema language" in its eclectic syncretism.[47] Like many previously marginalized artists, Medvedkin took advantage of the advent of socialist realism as an opening back into the central cultural system.

Joining the Moscow Unified Film Factory as a staff director, alongside such established masters as Eisenstein, Pudovkin, and Dovzhenko, Medvedkin faced two major challenges in adapting his idiosyncratic style and institutionalizing his operative cinema. First, having created the genre of the satirical short, he was now expected to produce feature-length films. Second, having cut his teeth on site-specific filmmaking, he would now be constructing sets in the central factory's studio lot. For his first feature-length production, *Happiness,* Medvedkin tried as hard as he could to maintain the Film Train's sense of spartan comradeship, hiring Film Train veterans for key roles, most notably G. A. Troianskii as director of photography and actor Petr Zinov'ev in the lead role of Khmyr', a hapless country bumpkin who is eventually, after the revolution, shamed and cajoled by his forward-looking wife into working for the collective good. Like much of Medvedkin's work, the film seems at once archaic and innovative. Made and released without sound, one of Medvedkin's folksiest flourishes—the peasant Khmyr''s dream of himself in the form of an icon—allegedly occasioned the first experiment with color filming at Mosfilm (although the sole surviving positive print lacks this flourish).[48] In a defense that subsequently served Medvedkin as a safe conduct, although it was not published at the time, Eisenstein favorably contrasted *Happiness* to Chaplin, claiming that if Charlie was always "heading off into the distance," Medvedkin's Khmyr' eventually "arrives from all [Chaplin's] distances."[49] For *The Miracle Worker,* another unconventional comedy about a nutty female collective farmer, Medvedkin once again drew on his Film Train comrades: director of photography Igor' Gelein and assistant directors German (Garri) Piotrovskii and Lev Saakov. Neither film enjoyed much acclaim, but for Medvedkin they succeeded as radical experiments that marshaled broadly accessible, socially constructive laughter from within the studio system. He pressed on with a new screenplay in a similar vein, "Accursed Force," which was approved but never entered production, despite Medvedkin's lifelong efforts and to his undying frustration.

As on the Film Train, Medvedkin's signature contribution was not defined solely by his films but also by the activist discursive environment around the films. Always the inveterate reformer, Medvedkin was full of proposals and complaints about the film factory's physical plant and the organization of labor, which he voiced through the studio newspaper, as well as in memos and letters. He advocated "economic operative independence" for production units, cultivating a sense of responsibility for expenditures and productivity.[50] He attributed the studio's failure to develop "new cadres" to "the unhealthy moral state of our creative collective and the lack of real, creative criticism."[51] In August of 1938, during work on *The New Moscow,* Medvedkin condemned Mosfilm's training of actors outside of cinema production, claiming that this leads to a "theatrical leaning."[52] Throughout these interventions runs a line, leading back to the Film Train, that positions the film factory as an autonomous unit of production, where all workers pull together in close cooperation and competition—operatively—for the common goal of producing vibrant discourse about socialism. Institutionalized Soviet cinema, Medvedkin insists, could still produce operative realism.

THE NEW MOSCOW

The hybrid train-cart-fire engine-city that Medvedkin rides in Isaak Shmidt's caricature betrays a widely shared anxiety about Medvedkin's militant Film Train shorts and homespun satires as vehicles of Stalinist modernity. This anxiety is also evident in an earlier caricature from the Mosfilm newspaper, which shows

FIGURE 7.3. M. Miloslavskii, "At the Cine-Mayday," *Kino-gazeta*, May 1, 1938, 4.

Medvedkin (front and center, just to the right of a pirouetting Eisenstein) surrounded by buildings of the new Moscow, which dance around the befuddled director (fig. 7.3).

Medvedkin's evident confusion is caused not only by his unfamiliar topic—the new communist metropolis—but also by his still-new surroundings: the central film studio. Instead of going out into the world to capture its socialist transformation on location, here the Soviet cinema creates miniature models of possible worlds all on the same grounds, in the very shadow of the Kremlin towers: the frozen lake on which Eisenstein-Nevsky prances to victory; revolutionary Petrograd, where Romm-Lenin again rides his armored car; the Volga River, where Grigorii Aleksandrov rides the pleasure boat of his latest musical comedy *Volga-Volga*. (Not pictured, for understandable reasons, is the German concentration camp, "a precise copy of Dachau," constructed for Aleksandr Macheret's *Peat-Bog Soldiers*.)[53] The world is in motion, but the filmmaker stands still, passively registering Stalin's fantasies about it.

Like many films of the time, *The New Moscow* was commissioned from above, to celebrate the Haussmannesque reconstruction of the capital city. The project was not in Soiuzkino's thematic plan for 1938, which had been finalized in April, but was added in August and rushed into production. The film responds to the government's March 1938 decree not only by taking up a contemporary topic but also with the intensive use of special effects, which was encouraged in the report "On Improving the Organization of the Production of Cinematic Pictures," published alongside the decree above the signature of Viacheslav Molotov. Among other cost-saving measures, Molotov stipulated that studios "decrease the number of sets, widely deploying the method of painted backgrounds, and also lessening the time needed to construct sets, using at all stages the systematic implementation and use of mobile and modular sets."[54] On October 11, 1938, during the production of *The New Moscow*, Molotov's report was echoed by a Committee for

Cinema Affairs decree creating a special effects workshop at Mosfilm and urging its incorporation into regular production. Thus, special effects were presented more as instruments of central economic—and, by extension, ideological—control over the image than as a technology for modeling the future. Accordingly, many of the films made in the year after the March resolution, including *Alexander Nevsky*, made ample use of special effects, from rear projection to scale models, ostensibly for reasons of economy and efficiency.

The New Moscow was undoubtedly an economical production; although set in locations from the Far Eastern *taiga* to the Moscow metro, the action frequently looks like it transpires in a dank basement, lacking extended sightlines and perspectival sound. (Playing the granny, the august Mariia Bliumental'-Tamarina died before the film was completed, having caught her death of cold on the frigid set.)[55] But its deployment of practically every special effects technique in use at the time—from mechanical models shot against rear projection to matte shots—goes far beyond the pragmatic and marks the film as an almost unrivaled exercise in world-modeling; together with Vasilii Zhuralev's *Cosmic Voyage* (1935), it is the closest Soviet cinema ever came to Fritz Lang's *Metropolis* (1927). The effects were produced by a veritable army of special effects artists and cameramen. The architectural "motifs" were designed by Dmitrii Bulgakov, a former student at Vkhutemas of Aleksei Shchusev (the main planner of the Moscow reconstruction), who at the time worked in the Moscow city government, and were executed in three dimensions by Andrei Nikulin. In addition to codirector for "trick photography" Valentin Kadochnikov, the credits list eight trick cameramen and a separate cameraman, Fedor Krasnyi, to shoot the scale models.

The very multitude of contributors ensured that the film's special effects were polymorphic and polystylistic. The first shot places a log cabin against a flat *taiga* landscape, probably painted by Nikulin, who began as a landscape painter in Siberia. In a matte shot the engineers are shown admiring the workings of a tabletop apparatus in which miniature cranes assemble model buildings, photographed in stop-motion animation against a painted background (fig. 7.4). This mise-en-abyme immediately invites the viewer to contemplate the mechanisms by which cinema integrates heterogeneous two- and three-dimensional source images into a single flat plane. On the train ride to Moscow the young engineer Alyosha demonstrates the models to his accompanying grandmother and other passengers, while the scenery beyond the windows is generated by rear projection, as are the initial shots of Moscow, where the characters circulate against a backdrop of modern buildings. A composite shot superimposes a miniature banner for "Carnival Night" over a rear projection of Manège Square. The characters quickly end up at the carnival—the scene that seems closest to Medvedkin's usual aesthetic—which features matte shots of fireworks and composite shots with scale models. The young artist Fedia—who comically rushes to paint the old Moscow as it disappears

FIGURE 7.4. *The New Moscow* (Aleksandr Medvedkin, 1938).

before his very eyes, pettily lamenting his thwarted artistic ambition—is intercut with a cityscape of scale models and drawn skylines and then shot against a rear projection of this composite cityscape. The result is a disorienting proliferation of perspectives that complicate—and possibly compromise—any claim to realism on behalf of the world being modeled. When the granny visits her sister, the cityscape beyond the windows begins to move: "Where is our building going?" the sister exclaims. The shot plays both with our expectation of stationary domiciles and with the already-established conventions of rear projection to establish a new, cinematic principle of relativity. This is a world lacking any stable point of reference, a world in which the primary camera might be static, but it is not passive or unselfreflective. The camera's agency is part and parcel of this very world's motivity.

The motive world becomes spectacular in the closing scene, when Alyosha and Zoia finally reach the hall to demonstrate their "living model of Moscow." Previously, they were shown working on a room-sized three-dimensional electromechanical model with an intricate (albeit mystifying) set of relays and wires. But Medvedkin was evidently after a much more magical effect. In the screenplay, after Zoia announces (somewhat ominously), "Now we will show you, comrades, what the Bolsheviks will do with Moscow tomorrow," Medvedkin describes the new buildings as "arising," or "growing," and streets as "dressing themselves in asphalt," all "with amazing effect." In a report on the screenplay Mosfilm's chief editor is similarly vague, explaining only that the film "is supposed to show [the transformation of Moscow] by means of volumetric animation," adding that "in the model, streets, buildings and squares really move; it shows what the Party has done in recent years and what remains to be done. Old disorganized Moscow is also shown to comic effect."[56] These accounts continue to suggest stop-motion photography of miniaturized city models, which sounds appropriately low-tech and quaint for Medvedkino.

As produced, however, the "living model" consists mostly of a screen, surmounted by the painted profiles of Stalin and his city-building henchman Lazar' Kaganovich. True, across the semicircular stage in front of the screen there stretches a static, raised map of Moscow, as if the film is to serve as a rear-projected backdrop to a mechanized model, like an enlarged version of the engineers' initial tabletop model. But what Alyosha and Zoia actually demonstrate is not a mechanical model at all but a film that incorporates all of the special effects techniques that have been deployed so far to produce the live action: stock footage of old Moscow and its demolition linked through dissolves, drawn landscapes animated through stop-motion photography, and matte shots with scale models against photographed or drawn backgrounds. Live actors are inserted into shots either through rear projection or mattes. No doubt there were considerations of money and time, and Medvedkin was at the mercy of his team of special effects artists and cameramen, each of whom had his own signature techniques and style. But the overall effect is one of fixing the multidimensional and collaborative processes of world-modeling in a rigidly edited and projected sequence—one that can be reversed with the flip of a switch but cannot be altered, let alone inhabited.

Certainly, this world is distant from that of the Film Train, which embedded its films in the material and discursive worlds it modeled. Questioning whether operative cinema can be adapted to the material conditions of the central studio, the genre conditions of the musical comedy, and the institutional conditions of a centralized industry, Medvedkin turns his satirical aim away from the world itself and toward its cinematic modeling.[57] By presenting the three-dimensional model world alongside and in contrast to its flattened and static cinematic transcription, the finale of *The New Moscow* critiques the ways in which the socialist realist project was beginning, by 1938, to become inoperative. Henceforth, special effects would be marshaled for the production of pure fantasy, as in Grigorii Aleksandrov's *Radiant Path* (1940).[58] But *The New Moscow* also demonstrates that, as late as 1938, socialist realism continued to host radical experiments in making time-based media responsive to their concrete discursive environments. The Film Train still runs through Medvedkin's Mosfilm. Perhaps this sufficed for the Soviet authorities—perhaps Stalin himself—to pull *The New Moscow* from Soviet screens.

CODA

Soon after the German invasion in June of 1941, Medvedkin began to propose to the central authorities a mobile Film Truck Studio *(avto-kino-baza)*.[59] Nothing came of that; instead, Medvedkin was sent to Baku to serve as Grigorii Aleksandrov's deputy at the Azerbaijan film studio. In late 1943, after two years of frustrating bureaucratic struggle far from the front lines, Medvedkin was entrusted with a group of newsreel cameramen at the Third Belorussian Front, with whom he remained to the end of the war, contributing to newsreels and compilations documenting the victorious Soviet advance through Latvia, Belorussia, and Prussia. He was credited with adapting a rifle mount for Eye-mo cameras stripped from US warplanes and sent to the USSR through Lend-Lease. As before, this new mobilization of cinema gave rise to a new genre in Medvedkin's work, what he christened the "film-pamphlet," which combined a trenchant ideological critique of the USSR's rivals (not only the capitalist imperialists but also Mao's China and other perceived apostates from communism) with inventive montage and first-person ironic commentary. Medvedkin first displayed this method in a one-reel short from 1945, *A German's Apartment,* writing a wry commentary to accompany a pointed montage of a Nazi bureaucrat's sacked home in Soviet-occupied Königsberg.[60]

In its purest form Medvedkin's operative realism was possible only under the extreme conditions of a military campaign. This is why Chris Marker and his confrères mobilized Medvedkin in their activist cinema around 1968 and why, in his *tombeau* for his recently deceased friend, Marker called Medvedkin "the last Bolshevik." But the lesson I draw from Medvedkin's story is that operative realism can also persist within an institutionalized cinema, even one as rigidly institutionalized as Soviet cinema became after the initial, experimental upsurge of socialist realism. Medvedkin may have been one of the last to believe in socialist realism as a discursive system, oriented not to the creation of exemplary masterpieces but to the working through of an operative cinema for socialism. His isolation on the Soviet cinematic landscape—like that of Vertov, Esfir' Shub, and others—was not merely a personal tragedy but also a figure of the entire system's tragic failure.

NOTES

The author is deeply grateful to Peter Bagrov, Brian Jacobson, and Christina Kiaer for their invaluable help in preparing this essay.

1. *USSR in Construction,* no. 1 (1938): 2. The entire issue was dedicated to the Soviet cinema, written and "planned" by writer Valentin Kataev and director Aleksandr Macheret.

2. [Dmitrii] Koroptsov, "Navesti bol'shevistskii poriadok v Mosfil'me," *Za bol'shevistskii fil'm*, April 2, 1937, 2.

3. For a comprehensive analysis of this tension see Belodubrovskaya, *Not According to Plan*.

4. Shumiatskii was executed on July 29, 1938, just as Eisenstein was completing the filming of *Alexander Nevsky*. Later that year Eisenstein's director of cinematography Eduard Tisse stridently condemned Shumiatskii's leadership and hailed the March resolution as enabling "Stakhanovite tempos" of production; E. K. Tisse, "Aleksandr Nevskii," *Za bol'shevistskii fil'm*, Nov. 7, 1938, 3; cf. Krivosheev and Sokolov, *Aleksandr Nevskii*, 79–83.

5. S. Stemasov and N. Naletov, "Pis'mo v redaktsiiu," *Izvestiia*, April 24, 1937, 4.

6. The shift in Medvedkin's poetics is also the topic of an earlier caricature by the same artist, Isaak Shmidt, over the poetic caption

From now on he's decided
To betray his usual topic
And dedicate his newest creation
To our capital city.
(*Za bol'shevistskii fil'm*, Nov. 27, 1938, 4)

7. In late March the new director of Mosfilm was still listing *The New Moscow* among the studio's recent successes; K. A. Polonskii, "Nashi itogi," *Za bol'shevistskii fil'm*, March 23, 1939, 2. At exactly the same moment Dziga Vertov and Elizaveta Svilova were fighting the unexplained shelving of their latest film *The Three Heroines* (1938), produced at the Central Studio for Documentary Film. Like *The New Moscow*, *The Three Heroines* was never released in the USSR but has survived in the archives (unlike Eisenstein's *Bezhin Meadow*).

8. Tret'iakov, "The Writer and the Socialist Village," 69, 70; Mierau, *Erfindung und Korrektur*; Fore, "The Operative Word in Soviet Factography," 95–131.

9. Medvedkin, "Razdum'ia," 23. Unless otherwise noted, all translations are my own.

10. Temin, "Poezd vyzyvaet," *Kino-gazeta*, March 12, 1932, 1.

11. A. S. Deriabin, "Ves' Medvedkin," *Kinovedcheskie zapiski* 49 (2000): 88–89. See also Kirn, "Past Activism."

12. Medvedkin, "Satire: An Assailant's Weapon," 246.

13. Medvedkin, "Pozitsii ne sdadim!" *Proletarskoe kino*, no. 9 (1931): 18–19.

14. T. Andreeva, "Kinopoezd v puti," *Proletarskoe kino*, no. 2 (1932): 37–38. The variance in recorded figures for the Film Train's equipment and capacity is explained in part by its periodic refurbishment between expeditions.

15. Medvedkin, "The Kino-Train," 32.

16. [A.] Medvedkin, "Kinopoezd v boiakh za rudu," *Kino-gazeta*, May 12, 1932, 1.

17. V. D., "Piat' dnei kinobezobrazii," *Gudok*, August 30, 1932, 4. Only one release of the Film Train's *Kino-gazeta* has survived, whereas at least eleven thematic films survive in whole or part from Medvedkin's year in charge of the train. Of all Medvedkin's titles for the Film Train, only the second reel of *An Empty Place* is extant.

18. V. Plonskii, "Chetvertyi reis," *Proletarskoe kino*, nos. 17–18 (1932): 38.

19. Andreeva, "Kinopoezd v puti," 39.

20. Widdis, *Alexander Medvedkin*, 24.

21. Temin, "Na shturm," *Kino-gazeta*, Feb. 24, 1932, 1.

22. Temin, "Nekotorye itogi," *Kino-gazeta*, March 18, 1932, 1. See also Medvedkin, "The Kino-Train," 72–74.

23. Medvedkin, "Vosstanovit' kinopoezd," Russian State Archive of Literature and Art (RGALI), f.2749, op.1 (R. G. Grigor'ev), no. 377, 1–2.

24. Lev Vaks, "Reisy kinopoezda," *Sovetskoe iskusstvo*, August 11, 1933, 2.

25. See Tode and Wurm, *Dziga Vertov*, 197–98.

26. Plonskii, "Chetvertyi reis," 38.

27. Renov, "Fil'my delaiutsia v poezde," *Gudok*, May 14, 1932, 4.

28. Shevchenko, "Kinopoezd v Dnepropetrovske," *Kino-gazeta*, May 24, 1932, 2.

29. Evg. Sheval', "Pro liubov'," *Kino-gazeta*, July 12, 1932, 3.

30. Vaks, "Reisy kinopoezda," 2.

31. Widdis, *Alexander Medvedkin*, 26.

32. Medvedkin, "The Kino-Train," 45.

33. See "Kinopoezd ukhodit," *Kino-gazeta*, Jan. 15, 1932, 1.

34. Widdis, *Alexander Medvedkin*, 32. Medvedkin credited poet Aleksandr Bezymenskii with creating the character; see Medvedkin, "The Kino-Train," 30. Medvedkin's screenplay "The Camel" is held in his archive at the Central Museum of Cinema in Moscow.

35. Aleksandr Deriabin, "Kinopoezd Soiuzkinokhroniki," *Kinovedcheskie zapiski* 49 (2000): 132. Medvedkin also mentions a release of the *Kino-Newspaper* with the camel; see Medvedkin, "The Kino-Train," 39.

36. Medvedkin, "The Kino-Train," 27. See Medvedkin's troubling account of their expedition to "the battle for grain," when "for the first time in the history of agriculture, the peasants were discovering the amazing joy of collective work" (53–64).

37. Vatulescu, *Police Aesthetics*, 92–99.

38. Medvedkin," Vosstanovit' kinopoezd," 3 (see note 23 above).

39. Medvedkin," 4.

40. Anonymous, "Kogda kino razoblachaet," *Gudok*, Dec. 24, 1933, 4; Medvedkin, "The Kino-Train," 87.

41. [A.] Medvedkin, "Kinopoezd v boiakh za rudu," *Kino-gazeta*, May 12, 1932, 1.

42. Swayze, *Political Control of Literature in the USSR, 1946–1959*, 13–14.

43. Kornelii Zelinskii, "My vybiraem budushchee," *Sovetskoe kino*, no. 1 (1934): 88.

44. *Za bol'shevistskii fil'm*, Sept. 7, 1934, 3.

45. See *Kino-gazeta*, May 18, 1932, 1; and *Kino-gazeta*, May 30, 1932, 4.

46. Viktor Shklovskii, "Kto vinovat?" *Kino-gazeta*, May 30, 1932, 3.

47. D. Pakentreiger, "Reis v piatiletku," *Kino-gazeta*, Sept. 18, 1932, 1. The tendency toward a more popular cinematic idiom continued after Medvedkin's departure, when under the leadership of Iakov Bliokh, over three years the Film Train produced approximately 105 films of increasing length and sophistication—e.g., with the addition of synchronic sound; see I. Lidinov, "Kinofabrika na kolesakh," *Gudok*, June 2, 1933, 4; Aleksandr Medvedkin, "Razdum'ia," 24; Widdis, *Alexander Medvedkin*, 34.

48. Nikolai Izvolov, "Aleksandr Medvedkin i traditsii russkogo kino: Zametki o stanovlenii poetiki," *Kinovedcheskie zapiski* 49 (2000): 29. See also Firsov, "Za polnometrazhnye trekhtsvetnye kartiny," *Za bol'shevistskii fil'm*, April 11, 1938, 3.

49. Eisenstein, "[Happiness]," in *Alexander Medvedkin Reader*, 264–65; translation adjusted from S. M. Eizenshtein, *Izbrannye proizvedeniia*, vol. 5 (Moscow: Iskusstvo, 1968), 232.

50. *Za bol'shevistskii fil'm*, Feb. 21, 1934, 2.

51. *Za bol'shevistskii fil'm*, Jan. 16, 1936, 2.

52. *Za bol'shevistskii fil'm*, August 11, 1938, 2.

53. R. M., "Val'ter"; undated clipping from *Kino-gazeta*, 1938, in the file for *Peat-Bog Soldiers* at Gosfil'mofond, Moscow, Russia.

54. V. Molotov, N. Petrunichev, "Ob uluchshenii organizatsii proizvodstva kinokartin," *Pravda*, March 24, 1938, 1.

55. RGALI, f. 2450, op. 2, no. 262, 57. Medvedkin doesn't appear to have accepted responsibility, although he did add his signature to a letter mourning Bliumental'-Tamarina's death; see *Kino-gazeta,* Oct. 17, 1938, 3.

56. RGALI, f. 2450, op. 2, no. 262, 70.

57. On the tabletop apparatus see Schmalisch, *Mobile Cinema,* 9; see also Marina Vishmidt, "The Humorous Dimensions of Time," in Schmalisch, *Mobile Cinema,* 65–69.

58. See Salys, *The Musical Comedy Films of Grigorii Aleksandrov,* 281–340.

59. Medvedkin, "The Kino-Train," 71–72.

60. See Bird, "Medvedkin na voine," 295–313.

8

_____

Postindustrial Studio Lifestyle

The Eameses in the Environment of 901

Justus Nieland

The short film "901: After 45 Years of Working" (1988) features a lengthy tracking shot into one of the more unconventional film studios of the mid-twentieth century—the Eames Office, located at 901 West Washington Boulevard in Venice, California. The Steadicam takes us from the street outside and the building's unassuming facade, through the front door, and into the open design and production space of the studio's flexible interior. As the camera floats, tracking forward and backward through the superabundant space, it pans and tilts, allowing us to appraise all manner of now-empty Eames furniture, designed over the course of the studio's working life, often on-site. The furniture sits among other evidence of past, now-abandoned work product still hanging on the studio's walls as the iconic, lasting yield of the Eames Office's research program. Love at last sight.

The film's occasion was the death of Charles's design partner and wife, Ray Eames, who stipulated that the teeming contents of "901"—as the Eames Office became known—be catalogued, boxed, and then shipped to various museums and archives. The melancholy shot appears late in the film, which was made by Eames Demetrios, Charles's grandson, as a kind of elegy to the life in work contained by this creative environment. It's a knowing enactment of Charles Eames's long-standing commitment to what he called, borrowing from Buckminster Fuller, the "feeling of security in change."[1] The well-engineered fluidity of the long take performs temporal continuity as an homage to the studio's long and storied life, which has come to an end, its material remains now en route to the Library of Congress. We see this more transitory process in several shots of accelerated motion, one of the Eameses' own recurring filmic techniques. Speedy sorting and packing are the film's formal nod to the style, and lifestyle, of the Eameses' own early furniture films—their way of commenting on the time of work, of media, and of creative work in media.

The Office may have ended in the archive, as information and accumulated research product, but 901 began in the brave new object world of plywood—first at war, then converted to the stuff of postwar domestic comfort. The studio was also born at the historical moment when the function of the designer, sparked by wartime mobilization, expanded from the making of consumer objects to participation in the creative, knowledge-based, information-saturated operations of a nascent postindustrial society.[2] This change placed 901—and the more than one hundred films the Eameses made there—at the heart of the Eames Office's postwar investigations into education, its experiments in the communication of information and ideas, and what John Harwood has called its "sustained interdisciplinary research conducted in tandem with the central scientific institutions of the postwar period, public and private."[3] Over the course of the Eameses' career at 901, this ever-widening research agenda included work for IBM, the RAND corporation, ARPA, the Westinghouse Electric Corporation, and various governmental bodies and institutions: the United States Information Agency, the Departments of State and the Interior, and the Smithsonian, to name just a few. In this way 901 was also implicated in what Caroline Jones and Peter Galison have identified as a broad shift in the postwar studio from the centralized "aggregative and social mode of production" of work of the wartime factory to a decentralized, dispersal of production "among multiple authors at multiple sites" and in "the spectacular and discursive realms of print, film, and photographic media."[4]

In this essay I approach 901 as a studio environment for the kind of tech-savvy, postwar production that, for the Eameses, constituted happy, creative living in the mid-twentieth century. Eamesian happiness has been understood as one of the period's more powerful normative horizons for orienting consumers at home and abroad toward designed objects and "ways of life" that circulated—as did images of the studio lifestyles of the Eameses—as signs of the postwar good life. I've argued elsewhere that Eamesian happiness is more instructive as a model of production, a medial and technical process of working with objects and images, than as the reified promise of any particular good.[5] The logic of production informing the Eameses' design practice requires a more fine-grained account of the technological and scientific environments of the postwar period in which they worked. These environments radically transformed what seemed taken for granted or "natural" in the unfolding of the good life. And the film studio, of course, was one such technical environment—as excellent materialist film history by Brian R. Jacobson and others has recently argued.[6]

The environment in and around 901 during the studio's forty-five years of operations was, in its origins, devoted to experimental plywood manufacture during the war. It was the site where that technomarvel of postwar nonnature—the

plywood chair, announced to the world as "the Eames chair" in March of 1946—
was researched and developed, prototyped, and filmed in a collaborative, democratic atmosphere of wartime interdisciplinarity. I say "in and around" because
one of the axioms of Eamesian production—amply borne out in plywood's contemporary media culture—was its sheer extensivity and promiscuity. Such making
refused to be contained in one space, or practice, or medium, or discipline; it
insisted that *all* spaces of creative life and making are studio spaces.

Many of the Eameses' films have a way of announcing this fact. Consider *Kalei-
doscope Shop* (1959), produced after 901's laboratory of wonder had become famous
internationally. When Charles was invited to give a lecture at London's Royal College
of Art, and asked to offer an illustrated tour of the Eames Office, he responded with
a visual surrogate for 901's relentless productive activity. Charles's four-minute film
dissolves a site of organized collective production into play and sensation, asking the
tourist-spectators to see work by looking through a toy: here, a kaleidoscopic camera
that Charles built at 901 with the help of Parke Meek and Jeremy Lepard. Graphic
layout room, film editing room, conference room, darkroom, furniture shop—all
the spaces of the Eameses' wide-ranging media practice are presented to the viewer
as part of a relentlessly active visual field in which the eye, like these designers, never
rests. In asking us to view their kind of creativity through dispersed, technically
fabricated views of a famous office-turned-playground, the Eameses announce their
design practice and its material infrastructure as a studio *lifestyle*. In it, filmic experimentation becomes play, and both are embedded in the times, speeds, and sensa-
tions of postindustrial production and its quasi-utopian transformations of the
spaces of private life, its reworking of the boundary between leisure and work.[7]

This lifestyle is most associated with 901 and the broader artistic and political
ferment of wartime Los Angeles. But as I will argue, 901's studio environment had
multiple determinations. Its far-flung sources of cultivation stretched from suburban Detroit to Hollywood, and its models included new kinds of things and people, from molded plywood and compact sofas to computers and Billy Wilder, an
Eames intimate and, for them, an exemplary studio professional. As the material
infrastructure for the more intangible shape of postindustrial lifestyle itself, 901
came to embody a flexible mode of work—of creative, corporate production; it was
a node in a network that extended beyond the Eameses and the talented, increasingly numerous members of the Eames Office staff. This essay's approach to 901 as
a studio, therefore, moves centrifugally, thinking outward from the various studio
environments, scales of studio production, and media cultures that the plywood
chair, and the lifestyle it materialized, seemed to require, as the chair's increasingly
famous designers found themselves more and more working and living in all manner of studios. In the process the Eames Office produced films that allegorized the
conditions of the studio environments that made them—and indeed, that remade
life in the mid-twentieth century itself.

PLYWOOD'S STUDIO CULTURES AND THE BIRTH
OF POSTWAR DESIGN

The journey of 901 from garage to factory to laboratory to world-famous design studio began after the honeymooning Charles and Ray Eames moved to California from the Cranbrook Academy of Art in the summer of 1941 with a plan to mass-produce the plywood furniture designs that had won Charles and Eero Saarinen awards in MoMA's famous "Organic Design in Home Furnishing" competition in 1940–41. At Cranbrook the Eameses were first encouraged to understand film-making and furniture experimentation, plywood and celluloid, within an interme-dial and interdisciplinary design practice (Fig. 8.1).

A telling photograph of Charles at Cranbrook, taken by its Photography Department, features Eames seated on an armchair prototype for the MoMA com-petition. The image insists on the experimental proximity of mechanical recording media and plywood furniture through a superimposition that dissolves, organi-cally, human into technological form. At Cranbrook Charles worked in furniture design, film, and exhibition design simultaneously, but also collaboratively, and within the broader communicative agendas of the esteemed educational institu-tion that employed him, and he had quickly learned the lessons of the PR revolu-tion.[8] Eames tended to refer to the administrative unit he led at Cranbrook as the department of "experimental design," and he made repeated trips to László Moholy-Nagy's School of Design in Chicago to consult with the Bauhaus master on the scope of a vanguard pedagogical practice. At the school this included film, and so, too, at Cranbrook. In 1939 Charles produced *Academy Film*, his first work of useful cinema and, effectively, his first sponsored film, designed to promote and publicize the educational activities and aesthetic aspirations of the Academy of Art. He followed this with footage assembled as *New Academy Movie* (1941). The film documents a range of student activities, visiting speakers like Frank Lloyd Wright, and esteemed faculty like ceramicist Maija Grotell, whose studio process of happy, expert making is shown in admiring close-ups of the shaping and firing of a series of vases. The film's subjects are design objects and practices, from Gro-tell's ceramics or Eliel Saarinen's tea urn to Eames and Saarinen's chair prototypes. This preoccupation with studio process extends, of course, to Cranbrook itself—its campus a living collection of studios and an object of total design, and its educa-tional mission and abiding lifestyle overlapping design processes demanding com-munication. The film concludes with a sequence featuring an exhibition of student work across media: textiles, painting, sculpture, photography, and photomontage. In the process it enacts film's own exhibitionary power as a medium about media, materials, and the studio environments that put them to use.

As an assemblage of bodies, tools, and techniques, 901 emerged in Venice in the early 1940s at the locus of the intersecting itineraries, social networks, and agendas

FIGURE 8.1. Charles Eames superimposed in an armchair prototype, June 1941. Courtesy Cranbrook Archives, neg. 5702-1.

of various studio personnel and practices. These agendas and actors operated at various scales, extending from the experimental Cranbrook classroom to the sets and locations of the Hollywood majors and, beyond that, to theaters of global war. Moving from Michigan to Los Angeles, Charles took a job as a set designer at MGM and worked for several months for the studio's legendary art director Cedric Gibbons as a draftsman on *Johnny Eager* (1941), *Random Harvest* (1942), *I Married an Angel* (1942), and *Mrs. Miniver* (1942). A midwesterner with no friends in California, Charles made his first connection to the Hollywood studio system through Cranbrook sculptor Frances Rich, the daughter of film and radio actress Irene Rich. With Eero Saarinen and his wife, Lily, Charles had in fact visited California to design a studio for the sculptor, with whom he was said to be romantically involved, in 1940. It was Frances Rich's close friendship with Katherine Hepburn that Eames traded on when he contacted Hollywood agent Leland Hayward (Hepburn's erstwhile lover) about a job with MGM.

For Eames, the gig in MGM's prestigious dream factory would be short-lived, a steady paycheck as he and his new (second) wife, Ray, pursued the experimental promise of molded plywood from the makeshift home studio of their Richard Neutra–designed Westwood apartment. Let's consider Charles's MGM day job as an encounter with another studio environment caught up in epochal change. As Jerome Christensen has argued, with a signature production like *Mrs. Miniver,* MGM was not just serving up a well-crafted story of a middle-class British family's fateful involvement in World War II.[9] In the wake of the 1940 Consent Decree, *Mrs. Miniver*'s war-mobilization plot constituted an artful, morale-building studio allegory of MGM's own claim to continued excellence in the uncertain postwar future of Hollywood's oligopoly. Read as a work of anticipatory planning, *Mrs. Miniver*'s narrative affirmed the inevitability of choice in liberal society, linked liberal-democratic choosing to styles of consumption, and positioned the studio's abiding commitment to quality as best equipped to handle potentially threatening postwar change—here, "in the conditions of production, distribution, and exhibition."[10] Security in change. The responsibility to choose. Commitment to goodness. Eamesian lessons, all.

Eames may have readily understood Metro-Goldwyn-Mayer's corporate allegory, since he was, at night, in his home studio, performing his own commitment to quality and making a similarly risky wager on postwar styles of consumption and taste—not in the goodness of film, but furniture, another product of studio magic. In his apartment's spare bedroom, Eames constructed a homespun contraption for prototyping and refining the plywood molding processes that he had begun at Cranbrook with Saarinen and designer Don Albinson. Because of the transformative wonders it worked in wood veneer, Eames dubbed it the "Kazam! Machine," scaling down the standard wood molding technologies then finding wartime applications in the aerospace industry.[11] MGM by day, Kazam! Machine by night (and early mornings!): in 1941 the Eameses moved from one studio environment to the next, inaugurating a pattern of a life in work that would become typical in the years to come.

The couple lived in the Westwood apartment for the next eight years, before moving in 1949 into an eventually more-famous home of their own design—Case Study House No. 8. It included, across a small courtyard from the home, a one-thousand-square-foot studio in a separate, two-story building, with storage and sleeping space above and a bathroom and darkroom below. Eames and Saarinen's accompanying briefs for Case Study Houses No. 8 and 9, respectively, enshrine the very logic of efficient modern spaces, in which one lives and produces in time and media, that the Eameses had first enacted by living with the Kazam! Machine: "'House' in these cases means center of productive activities."[12] The Eameses are

described anonymously in the brief as "a married couple both occupied professionally with mechanical experiment and graphic presentation"; this requires an
environment in which "work and recreation are involved in general activities: Day
and night, work and play, concentration, relaxation with friend and foe, all inter-
mingled personally and professionally with mutual interest."[13] In the Eameses'
house, as in their Westwood apartment that preceded it, play dissolves into work,
work is the stuff of enjoyment, and professional and personal investments blur in
the domain that Charles Eames dubbed "serious pleasure." The house itself—as an
envelope for living—becomes an unobtrusive stage or frame for a lifestyle in which
everything is interesting.

The key mediating figure between these two Eames homes (and home studios)
was erstwhile MGM writer John Entenza, who had just purchased and begun to
reinvent the small lifestyle magazine *California Arts & Architecture,* formerly a
"genteel regional publisher of homes, gardens and theatre reviews," as the Eameses
arrived in Los Angeles.[14] A committed liberal, Entenza had worked in an experimental film production unit at MGM in the late 1930s under Paul Bern and eventual blacklist victim Irving Pichel. Throughout the wartime period, and into the
nascent postwar heralded by *Arts & Architecture*'s Case Study House program,
Entenza was Charles Eames's most fervent promoter and most reliable source of
financial support. He was also Charles and Ray's gateway to LA's thriving art, architecture, and design communities featured in the magazine, which fomented its own
plywood culture. Entenza constituted the link between plywood's industrial development as revolutionary material—molded in the technical objects at 901 whose
sophistication increasingly outstripped the Kazam! Machine—and *plywood as
image,* a more intangible harbinger of a postwar Eamesian lifestyle distributed in a
variety of media platforms: first print and photography, then film and television.

A twelve-thousand-square-foot former garage located in an industrial area of
Venice two blocks from the Pacific Ocean, 901 began its storied life as the home for
the Evans Products Company's expanded wartime plywood manufacturing, which
came to include the Eameses' revolutionary designs. Its location was scouted by
one Norman Bruns, an electrical engineer who came to Evans via the Lockheed
Corporation at Burbank, where he worked on the support team for P-38 fighter
planes. Bruns was introduced to the Eameses through Entenza, and his contacts in
the aerospace industry gave Eames access both to technical information from the
industry, crucial to his plywood research and development, and to materials
restricted to noncivilian use during the war, without which the Kazam! Machine
would have no magic.[15]

Plywood's demand soared during the metal shortages of the global war. Months
after the US's entry into the conflict, Eames quit his job at MGM in the summer of
1942 to devote his energies to this experimental material, and the navy eventually
ordered 150,000 molded plywood splints from his recently established Plyformed

FIGURE 8.2. Molded Plywood Division staff members with a blister for a glider nose section. © 2017 Eames Office LLC (eamesoffice.com).

Wood Company (fig. 8.2). Formed in late 1942, the plywood "cooperative" (as it would be initially understood) included Entenza, the socialist architect Gregory Ain—a friend of Entenza's invited into the group for his engineering expertise in the building of plywood molding machines—and two of Charles's associates at MGM: Griswold Raetze, one of many US architects who found employment in the Hollywood studios during the Depression, when commissions were scarce; and English set designer Margaret "Percy" Harris, who left London in 1940 to find work in the United States. In 1943, to help scale up production, that original company moved into 901 as the Molded Plywood Division of the Evans Products Company. During the war, 901's two-hundred-dollar-per-month lease was paid by Evans, the first manufacturer of the Eameses' plywood furniture before Herman

Miller began marketing and distributing it, and eventually took over its manufacture in 1949. Evans's Plywood Division also included crucial personnel from Cranbrook's studios: first, the wood sculptor Marion Overby, whom Charles had met in Carl Milles's sculpture studio, and pressed into the war effort; then, from the metal studio, Italian sculptor Harry Bertoia; and later, in 1946, following his stint in the air force, Cranbrook alumnus Don Albinson. And from 1943 to its dissolution in 1946, the Plywood Division also drew extensively on the talents of the celebrated Swiss designer and photographer Herbert Matter, the Division's "in-house staff photographer and darkroom technician" and the figure most responsible for the visual documentation of the wartime plywood experiments.[16] Having worked as a fashion photographer for *Harper's Bazaar* and *Vogue,* Matter was well-positioned to preside over plywood's swift conversion from experimental object to postwar glamour image in *Arts & Architecture* and elsewhere.

Plywood was 901's first interdisciplinary object. Drawing on technical expertise from the domains of sculpture, art, architecture, graphic design, engineering, the military and aerospace industries, electronics, metallurgy, set design, fashion, film, and photography, the Plywood Division exemplified the kind of collaborative, research-driven activity, "enriched by an exotic mix of disciplines," that typified 901 throughout its working life as a studio.[17] While the term *interdisciplinarity* had emerged in the 1920s, it matured as a practice in the forms of collaboration and communication demanded by wartime mobilization.[18] It would enjoy its heyday in the Cold War period of the designer's newfound global prestige, when the idiom of "design" took on a larger and more expansive meaning, often becoming a kind of shorthand for managing, and providing security within, change itself. Whether practiced at 901 and RAND or enshrined in period-specific theories of general education and late-Bauhaus aspirations toward holistic training across media, both of which decisively shaped the Eameses' media practices at 901, interdisciplinarity became a crucial Cold War habit of mind.[19] It was defined by the putative "democratic" character traits of tolerance and open-mindedness, nonconformity and creativity, and especially "flexibility": the capacity to cope with complexity and ambiguity and to find security in change.

In the case of the Eameses the key disciplinary solvent was "communication," a centrifugal domain encompassing the wartime study of information-handling, propaganda, and the mass media. Communication's period-specific prestige in influential interdisciplinary assemblages like the Rockefeller Foundation–funded "Communications Group" led to the consolidation of mass communications research as a social-scientific discipline, and the first PhD programs in Mass Comm, but also to a redrawing of the parameters of the Eameses' design practice at 901.[20] In the early years of 901 the most obvious instance of this investment was the film *A Communications Primer* (1953), an illustration of postwar communications theory based on Warren Weaver's introduction to Claude Shannon's *A Math-*

ematical Theory of Communication (1949). But the indifference to disciplinary pro-
priety evident in the transdisciplinary aspirations of cybernetics is also apparent in
the galley proofs of an ad for the film *A Communications Primer* in the Eames Collection at the Library of Congress that cross-promotes the film with the plywood
furniture group: "Low cost chairs designed by Charles Eames will quickly turn
your selling floor into a center for universal modern seating." Presumably targeting furniture dealers, the advertisement betrays the inkling that the stuff of modern furniture and au courant theories of information processing might share a
similar logic or partake in the same aspiration toward universality or boundary-
crossing interdisciplinarity. This, we might say, was a postwar lesson anticipated by
the Plywood Division at war.

This compressed wartime history of 901—linking factory, lab, and design
studio—reminds us that plywood's interdisciplinary world was not limited to
Evans's machine shop but overlapped significantly with the media-savvy environment of wartime and postwar Los Angeles, with the personnel of the film industry,
and with liberal technophilic visions of a happy postwar future. Plywood experimentation was always part of 901's broader terrain of media practice. In the Eameses' case the proximity in LA of machined wood and modernist media experimentation in a visionary program of arts integration was most evident in the pages of
Arts & Architecture. Entenza's magazine played a pivotal role in the articulation of
a California modernism with speculative designs on the future and abiding technologies of the postwar good life most famously in its sponsorship of the Case
Study House program.

In *Arts & Architecture*'s September 1943 issue Ray Eames made her own pitch
for plywood's centrality in the integrated technoaesthetic terrain later dubbed the
"new subscape" by George Nelson, who would hire the Eameses in 1946 in his
capacity as director of design for the Herman Miller Furniture Company.[21] Preceded in the magazine by an ad for the George E. Ream Company promoting
"Plywood For War . . . Later For Peace," Ray's photomontage depicts an Eames
chair in an expansive terrain of production, including works of painting (Picasso's
Guernica) and sculpture but also oil derricks, military helmets, contemporary
skyscrapers, airplanes, and the reels of a film-editing table.[22] The collage is accompanied by a short prose manifesto that announces a contemporary aesthetics
"influenced by the world in which we live and by the synthesis of the experiences
of the world by all creators," including "the engineer mathematician physicist
chemist architect doctor musician writer dancer teacher baker actor editor the
man on the job the woman at home and painters." In the September 1946 issue the
Eameses' own plywood furniture designs were treated to a lavishly illustrated
twenty-page feature, written by Eliot Noyes. It contained a number of stunning
illustrations by Matter. Within the magazine's liberal editorial vision of integrated
arts, Noyes's gushing account of the inspired democratic vision of the Eameses'

furniture was prefaced by Entenza's own column insisting on the power of the citizen's vote in the country's upcoming midterm elections.[23] It also shared space with Robert Joseph's "Cinema" column—here about the US Office of Military Government's recently finished concentration camp documentary *Die Todesmühlen/Death Mills*. Joseph's praise for this landmark work of German political reeducation, much of it done by Billy Wilder at the Film Section of the Information Control Division, summons the power of US propaganda in "all mediums of communication—radio, theater, newspapers, magazines, books and motion picture films" to "acquaint the German people with the horror of these terrible murder factories."[24] Its communicative aspirations lodged between technologies of mass death and techniques of postwar happiness, the media culture of Eames-era plywood in 1946 was wildly capacious.

S-73 | POSTINDUSTRIAL STUDIO LIFESTYLE

The 1946 feature in *Arts & Architecture* precipitated the breakup of the interdisciplinary plywood cooperative that same year. For some members its "great man" account of plywood prototyping and production marked a betrayal of the collective's founding commitment to shared credit and profits.[25] The Eames Office proper came into being at 901 shortly thereafter, in 1947, when Evans Products moved its plywood manufacturing operations to Grand Haven, Michigan, allowing Charles to create a studio first called "The Office of Charles Eames" and staffed in part by a few remaining members of the Plywood Division. In 1950, after having opened a Los Angeles showroom (designed by the Eames Office) the previous year, Herman Miller established a West Coast manufacturing plant and assumed the lease on 901, relocating its factory operations to the front and rear sections of the building, where the Office designed and produced the Eames Storage Units (1950–53), the fiberglass plastic armchair with Zenith Plastics (1950–53), the wire mesh chair (1950–53), the Sofa Compact (1954), the Eames lounge chair and ottoman (1956), and much more. From 1950 to 1958, 901 housed some three dozen employees of Herman Miller and the Eames Office, described by one Eames associate as "all comingled in an energetic, mutually interdependent, cooperative, and democratic mix of designers, clerical and management personnel and factory workers." Accounts of the atmosphere of 901 by its talented staff and visitors describe a space of wonder: "like a film set," one staff member observed, "901 possessed an informal and almost magical quality quite different from the quietly restrained design offices of the period"[26] (fig. 8.3).

While Charles Eames happily wrote of being able to leave MGM in 1942 to focus on the work of furniture design, he wasn't so much leaving the film studio as he was beginning to reconceptualize its Fordism within a culture of postindustrial image production and consumption. As a physical space whose plywood products had just begun to find a vanguard audience and international distribution as tech-

FIGURE 8.3. Eames Office staff, working at 901. Dec. 1951. © 2017 Eames Office LLC (eamesoffice.com).

nically mediated objects and images, 901 remained a modest, unassuming building with brick walls, a concrete floor, and no architectural distinction whatsoever. It was nonetheless a studio in the process of transformation and expansion. But perhaps "expansion" is too mild; it doesn't capture the explosion of experimental activity within what Catherine Ince has described as the Office's dual "condition as both shop (in the American sense of the word) and studio set."[27] Film—like photography—was at the heart of 901's wide-ranging design activities across media as of 1950, when the Eameses made their first, unfinished film, *Traveling Boy*, with a camera borrowed from screenwriter Philip Dunne.

Indeed, 901's ambitions to be a *film* studio, specifically, grew as the Eameses' interdisciplinary interests in communication expanded over the course of the 1950s and 1960s. "More and more," Charles remarked in 1957, the Office "has come to be concerned with the way information is handled."[28] This meant increasingly

FIGURE 8.4. Eames Office staff, at 901 on the set of *Introduction to Feedback,* 1960. © 2017 Eames Office LLC (eamesoffice.com).

more of 901's work was spent on the production of films, graphics, and exhibition design, pursuits that "eventually eclipsed furniture design and production as the principle [*sic*] office activity" in the 1960s and 1970s. This reorientation from the domain of objects to images, information, and knowledge work was fully under way by the end of the 1950s, following the Eameses' IBM-sponsored film *The Information Machine: The Creative Man and the Data Processor* (1958), made for the IBM Pavilion at the Brussels World's Fair, and its famous multiscreen experiment in informatic saturation *Glimpses of the U.S.A.*, commissioned by the USIA for the American National Exhibition in Moscow in 1959. As both a sign and catalyst of this change, Herman Miller moved its California offices from 901 to Culver City in 1959, an office reorganization that freed up more studio space for film production. By this time, all of the film production was done at 901; the office had subsumed for the Eameses many of the functions of home and studio.[29] A representative shoot is captured in a photograph of the Eames Office staff on the set of *Introduction to Feedback,* the IBM-sponsored sequel to *A Communications Primer,* which appeared in a 1959 feature in *Vogue* (fig. 8.4). The next, and final, major change to the physical space of 901 came in 1971, with the construction of a two-story building to house the models and work product for the large exhibition *A Computer Perspective*, also for IBM. Following the exhibit, the structure became a dedicated shooting stage and slide area, and its balconies held the "overflow of objects, film storage, and records from the main building," now fireproofed.[30]

If 901's studio interior thus bore the traces of the Office's increasing embeddedness in the rhythms of postindustrial culture and its modes of media production, the foundational condition of this environment was postindustrial *flexibility*, its most prominent structural feature. "Magic" and "wonder" were secondary affects that followed from the studio's more primary architectural receptivity to relentless change. The otherwise unremarkable interior of 901 was a fully demountable space, subdivided by Celotex panels attached temporarily to the old garage's wooden bowstring trusses above by c-clamps. This reliable old technology became the binding stuff of vanguard interdisciplinarity, as 901's layout changed often between 1943 and 1978, remaining ever ready for new spatial configurations to suit the specifications, necessary personnel, and collaborative activities required of any given job. In this rough-and-ready way 901 materialized the recombinatory principles of many of the Eameses' furniture designs and toys such as *House of Cards* (1952) and the *Revell Toy House* (1959). But it also served as a "heuristic environment"—embodying the normative conditions of work and play, knowledge production, and creativity, as an endlessly iterative feedback-driven process of problem-solving within conditions of constant change.[31] In its flexibility such postindustrial studio lifestyle performed "the feeling of security in change," the affective condition that Charles Eames called—again summoning Bucky Fuller—the most important product that any education can provide.

These conditions were addressed in the IBM commissions, most obviously, but also in 901's less-well-known sponsored films for Herman Miller, which united postwar objects and moving images in an overtly pedagogical agenda. The furniture, like the films made about them, were studio products but also midcentury allegories of flexible production.[32] In fact, the Eames Office films often implicate its furniture's materiality—plywood, fiberglass, steel, aluminum—in expansive technical environments that extend both to their films as canny, self-aware technologies of postwar modernity and to filmmaking itself as a mode of participation in the communicative, systems-oriented work of a nascent information society. Because this lifestyle required studio practice, we should not be surprised to find in the furniture films the flexible creative environment of the studio itself.

Take the couple's first surviving film about a furniture design, *S-73: Sofa Compact*, one of eight works of nontheatrical, "useful" cinema made for Herman Miller between 1954 and 1973. The film was made to explain the design and function of the Eames Sofa Compact to Herman Miller's sales force, dealers, and merchants. Like other Eames films, it was also screened at Herman Miller showrooms, which

blurred film exhibition and product display in movie nights featuring the designers' work. The Eames Office, beginning with a seemingly modest film like *S-73*, was
not only teaching its client—and its client's clients—how to use this piece of furniture; in fact, it was enacting how the filmic apparatus itself might be put to corporate use as a flexible communicative device, its technological mobility basically of
a piece with the film's ostensible subject. From the start, the film *S-73*'s future life
of exhibition and display is conceptualized as a kind of metapedagogy in a corporate circuit extending from Herman Miller's production and distribution networks
to their own clients, who can show the film to their own sales staffs.

The film's opening montage frames the sofa's compact design as the materialization of the solution to a problem in and of modern systems—the problem of shipping as both the manufacturer's responsibility and the "designer's problem." The
film's graphic play with boxes of various kinds—trucks, trains, cubes, packages,
and grids stretching from floor tiles to living-room drapes—announces its position at the dawn of "containerization" itself—the mid-1950s standardization of
shipping containers and the transformation of freighting from the "break-bulk"
method to the aggregation of cargo into identical, corrugated steel boxes that
could be moved directly from ship to truck or train. The film thus comments on
the extension of modularity as a principle of furniture design and production to its
equally flexible networks of distribution and their traffic flows.

As an exploration of postindustrial lifestyle, the film turns from boxing to
unboxing, from questions of distribution to the product's "life of service" in the
hands of the consumer. Now, the film performs its pedagogical lesson about the
handy assemblage of the sofa by showing its "de-compacting" by two "average couples," and *in two speeds*—fast and slow. First, through the filmic magic of stop-
motion (scored to classical music), one couple puts together the sofa in a snap.
Then, "a couple less experienced in such matters" takes "a little longer." We need to
see the decompacting twice because in being repeated, it communicates itself as a
variable *process* of becoming acclimated to a system of new equipment for modern
leisure with which couples can be more or less "experienced." To master this habi-
tus, we will need to go through the motions, perform the requisite gestures, build
the kit more than once. But we also see in the two iterations of assembly how the
Eameses link the *S-73*'s feats of compacting and decompacting to film's own capacity for temporal compression, abstraction, and elongation in forms of duration.
The film is the first in a series of the Eameses' attempts to think together the mobile
time of modern furniture and the times of moving-image technologies, and
beyond that, the broader forms of "space-time compression" that are the hallmark
of a postindustrial society of consumption oriented toward a "life of service."

Against these forms of temporal compacting, *S-73* also works to thicken or
stretch the time of this sofa by embedding its time- and money-saving design solution in a longer history of care and planning, thought and experimentation—

which is to say, in 901's environment of happy making. As if anxious to correct the misperception about creative authorship fomented in the wake of the Plywood group's collapse, S-73 works to materialize the value of human labor and scenes of production that have informed it. As Eames's voice-over insists that the S-73 is a "product that is the result of much thought and research on the part of the designer," we cut to a close-up of a smiling Charles, eyes closed, resting his face on the seat of the sofa and then to a fast-cut series of seven close-ups of the faces of various members of the Eames Office involved in the longer history of this product's manufacture. The lesson, humanized by the faces of studio labor, is a kind of design flashback that chronicles all the "problems and decisions that go with planning and preparing a product for production," including some of the important mock-ups and models" of S-73. Embedding the sofa in collective work of its planning in this way also nods to another peculiarity of 901 as a design studio: by keeping the furniture workshop and machine shop in the back third of the building, 901 maintained an unusually close, organic proximity between model and prototype production and the design process.[33]

Continuity of design process, the film insists, coincides with flexibility, in both the sofa's making and its future uses. In fact, the final segment of the film makes clear that this seat—and its abiding time—isn't really for lounging. Instead, the S-73 exemplifies a more restless, mobile time, as we see it featured in a sequence of different environments: a dentist's waiting room, an art museum, and airy living room, facing a TV, where a sleeping housewife is roused from her slumber by her son. The scene clarifies S-73's suitability for brief moments of *vulnerable repose*—the time of waiting rooms, bourgeois leisure, a housewife's interrupted catnaps. The film ends with the wish for a kind of long-lived happiness of the sort the S-73 can provide, but it has labored to show us that this temporal continuity of "service and pleasure" exists alongside the other, more vulnerable times of the midcentury media environments materialized by the sofa: the abstract time in which it is boxed and shipped, the habit-forming time of domestication it takes to incorporate this new technology into one's lifestyle, the time of labor that produces it, the downtimes between what counts as eventful in one's day, even the press of contingency that only synthetic upholstery can manage. "There is no predicting what may happen in the life of a sofa," Eames's voice-over observes. The S-73, like 901 itself, materializes the conditions of security in change. Carving out any time for leisure, and the designed spaces of restive repose that allow us to take pleasure in it—this, S-73 clarifies, takes work: it calls for logistical control, discipline, and predictive capacities. When does the life of service begin and end? Do designers ever sleep? In asking these questions, S-73 is less a chair or a film than a plea for systematicity, for better modes of time management. Beginning with the box, the grid, and the shipping container, it is a film not just about a sofa but about that broader and largely neglected category that John Durham Peters has dubbed "logistical media"—media that "organize and orient," that "arrange people and property" into time and space; it attests to the place of flexible sofas and speedy film production at 901 within what media historian Alexander Klose calls the ascendancy of "the container principle."[34]

S-73 demonstrates that the Eameses had begun to think hard about the relationship between modern furniture, filmic time, and the postwar incursion of television into the domestic interior that would, in fact, prompt the broadcast of their first furniture film. In the film's concluding vignette the *S-73* finds itself in a living room reoriented around a television set, which it faces. The momentary pleasure the sofa offers to the napping mother seems to depend on both mom and TV being, for a time, turned off, removed from broadcast television's ongoing space of abstract flows. *S-73*'s way of bringing flexible modern furniture and TV together is canny, since a rising cultural fascination with the Eameses' furniture and its lifestyle provided the couple access to the television studio itself. The best-known instance of this came when the Eameses unveiled their famous lounger in a charming two-minute Herman Miller promotional film, *Eames Lounge Chair,* broadcast on April 14, 1956, as part of a lengthy spot on NBC's lifestyle show *Home,* hosted by Arlene Francis. But the couple had made their television debut several years earlier on *Discovery,* a public-service program on *Creative Arts Today,* sponsored by the San Francisco Museum of Art and broadcast on station KPIX in December of 1953. Producer Allon Schoener pitched to Charles a program on furniture design, apparently, in which Eames would "explain the evolution of some of [his] designs, demonstrate their uses, and possibly include a film section showing how they were made in the factory."[35] With "no experience with television," Eames warmed to the notion of using prefabricated filmed modules as stand-alone "answers" to questions posed to him on-air by the program's emcee: "from what I hear," he wrote, "it might be best to get a certain amount on film and avoid studio panic."[36] Sending Eames a rough outline of the program, Schoener insisted that the filmed material—however much it allowed the Eameses control over the show's content—not betray television's essence as "carefully planned and rehearsed spontaneity."[37] He thus cast the show as both an experiment in itself and a kind of summation of Eamesian research and development: the program, Schoener insisted, would be "much more interesting if you felt it could be your own presentation and the result of your experiments"[38]—from one studio to another.

Schoener's initial request for a film about the making of the Herman Miller furniture—a short, lost film about the molded plywood chair titled "Chair Story" in the program's drafted script—precipitated the inclusion of several filmed modules: an animated sequence illustrating some principles of design evolution; a two-minute film labeled "Toys, Other Designs" in the script's final version; and two filmed sequences of stills shot in and around the couple's already-famous home in the Pacific Palisades—material later recombined into *House: After Five Years of*

Living (1955).[39] Ostensibly about furniture design as a creative art, the TV program effectively showcased, while expanding, the studio-based terrain of the Eameses' media experimentation. Within it, the processes of making a toy or a chair, or filming its manufacture, or broadcasting that activity on television connote the same mobile, happy studio lifestyle enacted in the couple's modern home. "Chair Story," then, is both a film about the revolutionary processes of molded-plywood manufacturing and a testing ground—like the TV appearance itself—for the Eameses' ongoing, overtly communicative experiments. It is one part of a flexible, studio-based media kit. While the *Discovery* program may have featured furniture designs, those designs were, within the context of the Eameses' contemporaneous interests in television, already folded into a broader, multimedia pedagogical practice in a network of studios, with 901 its central node. In it, their films would be explained to the TV audience as "the logical continuation of the design program."[40]

BILLY WILDER, STUDIO PRO

A midcentury episode in convergence media, the *Discovery* program's basic format was repeated in May of 1956, and the "Chair Story" module repurposed, when Charles Eames was invited to appear on CBS's "prestige" public-affairs program *Omnibus*. Then occupied with second-unit location shooting for his friend Billy Wilder's film *Spirit of St. Louis* (1957), Eames notes his and Ray's admiration for this experimental program:

> Perhaps a painless way of doing a program about "myself" would make little reference to *things* we have done but explore a few of a great *variety* of things that will help shape a real human scale environment of the future—this would include many of the things in which we have been interested, from toys and kites to electronic calculators and games of strategy. . . . Inasmuch as this is for a television *workshop* I would not feel right unless we could give special attention to the "production"—some things we would have to shoot, cut, and score here. . . . I doubt we would want to use much of our existing films.[41]

Eames insists not on autonomous things but on their sheer variety and networked relations, not on himself as expressive maker but rather on the scenes of happy studio making that augur the productive horizon of the "human scale environment of the future." As its modular schema clarifies, the *Omnibus* program reused some films from the *Discovery* broadcast, including "Chair Story" and "Toys," and presented alternative versions of others, including *House*. The schema also includes films labeled "Kite Film," "Feedback Film," and "ABC." In the first draft of the script, however, the Eameses proposed an alternative final section, which would follow the six-minute "Chair Story" and a station break. Here, "Feedback," a working version of *Introduction to Feedback* (1960), the IBM-commissioned sequel to *A*

Communications Primer, would be "replaced with some film and short (twenty second) pertinent statements by Eero Saarinen, Billy Wilder, and Norbert Wiener."[42]

What is an appropriate show-biz segue from the production of plywood chairs
to Billy Wilder and cybernetics? The goal of the third part was to model just such
connections—to "point out that what was shown in the chair film marked just the
beginning of designers' responsibilities." That this terrain of expanded production
might appear disconnected, or seemingly unrelated to the stuff of furniture, is
indicated by notes penciled on the proposed conclusion of the *Omnibus* script:
"somehow should end up with a chair if it's about a chair."[43] Indeed: the chair's
"aboutness" is at stake. Is it an isolated thing or systemically defined? The filmed
statements from the unlikely trio of Saarinen, Wiener, and Wilder provide the
conceptual logic that would explain to *Omnibus*'s TV audience why the program
about a chair is not *just* about a chair—why the designers' thinking ranges so
widely across media and studios and seemingly disparate zones of inquiry, a scalar
flexibility provided through the disciplinary solvent of communications theory
and the universal aspirations of cybernetics. Saarinen's oft-cited quip about the
designer's centrifugal expansion of attention to "The Next Larger Thing" (from a
chair, to its room, to the building that houses it, to its site, etc.), the script explains,
"leads to communication through graphics and through film." Wiener would offer
a caveat about "the danger of abandoning the seemingly unimportant outposts of
thinking." And Wilder, it seems, would explain "the help that comes through communication theory and how this is often at a very human scale."[44]

By 1957, Wilder had found his way into the thick of the Eameses' studio practices, and vice versa. We might pause on the strangeness of this fact, born from a
lasting and perhaps unlikely friendship hatched in Hollywood of the early postwar, about the time that Wilder's *Death Mills* and the Eameses' plywood experiments were discussed in the same 1946 issue of *Arts & Architecture*. We can think
of them as discrepant signs of the Janus-faced power of wartime technics and contrary harbingers of the future of "modern man." While Wilder's most famous studio productions in Hollywood seemed to be the noir riposte to Eamesian postwar
sunshine, Wilder himself functioned as an important model for the Eameses' studio lifestyle. In a 1950 profile of the Eames house in *Life* magazine, for example,
this modeling work was quite literal. Wilder appears in a multiple-exposure photograph, seated in a prototype Eames plywood chair. The previous year, the Eameses had designed a home for the director in the Hollywood Hills. Meant to be a
flexible, "unselfconscious" enclosure for a creative artist and his expanding art collection, the home was never built, but the Eameses created a detailed architectural
model of the structure at 901 and photographed Wilder and his wife, Audrey,
admiring it. The Eames-Wilder friendship fostered a series of exchanges, gifts,
favors, and acknowledgments of shared tastes that epitomized the overlapping of
901's studio lifestyle across various locales. In 1962 Wilder would be quoted in an

admiring profile of the Eameses on this particular aspect of the couple's productive genius: "The usual arbitrary and unfortunate division of life into Home and Office ceases to have any meaning in their case. . . . Their friend Billy Wilder has said, 'They are One.'"[45]

And Wilder himself fostered this "enviable continuity" that became the hallmark of the Eameses' studio lifestyle. Around the time Ray designed the title sequence for Wilder's *Love in the Afternoon* (1957), for example, the director gave the Eameses a toy Ives locomotive that prompted Charles to collect a series of toy trains and thus inspired the production of *Toccata for Toy Trains,* a film shot entirely on an eight-foot tabletop in the Eames house with the help of 901 staff members. And the Eameses would consult with Wilder frequently on their various projects. The Eames archive at the Library of Congress contains a Paramount lot pass for Charles, dated August 14, 1950, as well as a letter from Charles to Billy in March of 1953, as Charles, George Nelson, and Alexander Girard embarked on the Art-X multimedia experiment at the University of Georgia: "We leave today for the GEORGIA panic—and *what* a panic."[46] Wilder also encouraged the Eameses to visit the Conditorei Kreutzmann pastry and coffee shop in Munich during their 1955 cultural exchange trip with Nelson, Robert Motherwell, and Richard Neutra, and they were so impressed by the shop's nonstop inner workings throughout the night that they produced a three-screen slideshow, *Konditorei* (1955), dedicated to the "ritual forms and organizational harmony of the pastry shop." A few years later, the Eameses called on Wilder's own expertise in the art of democratic propaganda as they, and the USIA's Jack Massey, consulted with him on the design of their five-screen *Glimpses of the U.S.A.* (1959). And the Eameses returned this favor by including in their flowing display of soft power, alongside shots of industrial processes typifying daily life in the US (milling, refining), a clip of a smiling and winking Marilyn Monroe from *Some Like It Hot* (1959).

What Eames seemed to admire about Wilder's studio operations was their own organizational form, as disciplined and logistically orchestrated as a German bakery—or the circus. The montages Eames shot for *The Spirit of St. Louis* are a paean to collaborative productive process on a tight deadline. They occur at a crucial moment in the film, just after Lindberg (James Stewart) meets the engineers who will build the titular plane. In a comic bit Lindberg walks into the unassuming garage and asks for the "executive offices" and to see "the boss." He is directed to a man wearing goggles while cooking fish on an improvised grill heated with a blow-torch, his own kind of Kazam! Machine. Wilder's mise-en-scène makes clear that the designers and office personnel capable of delivering the product in a compressed window of time work collectively in an unpretentious shop, much like 901 itself, and the director was likely thinking of Charles Eames's own St. Louis roots and his by-then-famous history of experimental airplane design when he invited him to shoot the montages documenting the team's production of the titular craft.

Eames's montages include various sketches and models of the plane, as the workers in the design office whir into orchestrated production. Structured by a series of close-ups of objects, tools, machines, and "unselfconscious" materials brought into rhythmic beauty, the montages, unsurprisingly, pay special attention to wood: glued, hammered, curved, sanded, and fashioned into a series of delicate lattices comprising the *Spirit*'s wings (fig. 8.5). It is as if Eames scaled the widescreen Warner Bros. star-vehicle down to the kind of modest, honest design process enshrined at 901 and allegorized, on another scale, in *Toccata for Toy Trains*, shot in the Eameses' home studio that same year. *Toccata* opens by explaining why the film features "real" and "old" toys and not scale models. "In a good, old toy," Charles's gentle narration explained, "there is apt to be nothing self-conscious about the use of materials. What is wood is wood. What is tin is tin. What is cast is beautifully cast." That film asks viewers to take pleasure in the sincerity of toys, but of course the Eameses became famous for the bravura of their experimental technical interventions into wood and plastic, for the seeming insincerity of plywood and fiberglass. Like many of the Eameses' films, *Toccata*, like *Spirit*, allegorizes the relentless multimedia productivity of the Eames Office itself, offering "a clue," as Eames's narration says of the old trains, to "what sets the creative climate" of any time.

Wilder's work on *The Spirit of St. Louis* had its own creative lessons to offer; indeed, it would become a model in the Eameses' ongoing parables of production and knowledge work.[47] While working with Wilder on *Spirit*, Eames produced a slideshow whose narration, addressed to the picture's audience, begins: "It will look easy on the screen, we hope—yet in order to shoot even this simple scene, it took the equipment, and organization of a combination military campaign and traveling circus."[48] The narration lauds the producer (with "the responsibility of overall planning") and the director (responsible for "the end result of the whole company's activities") of any film as "the two men who drive a picture to a successful conclusion." But the demystifying narration makes clear that their executive "responsibilities" are just part of a teeming network of interlinked "on-the-spot decisions" and "somewhat frantic," cascading responsibilities in the collective endeavor of a studio film like *Spirit*. By the time its far-flung location shooting is finished, "and ready for you to see, more than 20,000 people will have been in some way involved." Eames summons his own montage as an example not just of the decisions and responsibilities sustaining any organization, and, for him, liberal democracy itself, but also such an organization's abiding fuel, communication: "All this activity," he observes, "is directed at THE CAMERA. It is the prima donna of objects and becomes the center of all communication. Through the camera is filtered every form or motion or color you see on the screen—through equipment linked to the camera pass the sounds you will hear." The script frames Wilder not as a romantic auteur but rather as a node in the dispersed sites of a studio production like *Spirit* and thus an Eamesian lesson in efficiently networked communica-

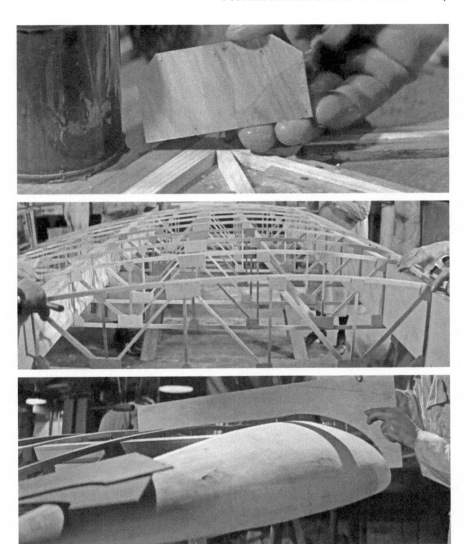

FIGURE 8.5. Unselfconscious materials. Plane design in *The Spirit of St. Louis* (1957).

tion as 901 itself expanded. And it helps us understand why Eames might have asked Wilder to provide a blurb on communications theory for *Omnibus*.

Eames wasn't quite done with Wilder's model. Images of Wilder at work on the set of *Spirit* and other films were later incorporated into the Eameses' three-screen slideshow *Movie Sets* in the last of Charles's six Norton Lectures at Harvard

University in 1970–71. Following Lionel Trilling, Eames's turn as Norton chair was preoccupied with the organizational impulses of liberalism and the problem of happy making, though neither were directly named as such. Rather, their contours were modeled, in content—as lectures *about* models—and in form, as multimedia environments that turned the lecture hall itself into a performance of 901's expanded operations over a more than a quarter century of working. As Franklin F. Ford, dean of the Faculty of Arts and Sciences at Harvard noted in his letter of invitation to Charles, "'poetry' is interpreted as all forms of poetic communication," and the intention of the foundation was to offer the Norton post to "men actively engaged in creation."[49] Eames's lectures comprised primarily slideshows and films representing a broad cross-section of the Eameses' work at 901 and their conceptual preoccupations to date. Two key ideas ran as leitmotivs threaded throughout the lectures: the centrality of models and modeling in the Eameses' media practice and the use of visual material, including film, as means of structuring and disseminating information and knowledge.

As the apex of this modeling of modeling, Eames's final Norton lecture clarified, and defended, the organizational tropism of the Eameses' work at 901, and the Eames Era more broadly, even as the studio's operations increasingly dispersed. The problem with administration, his lecture notes indicated, is "centralization" and a centripetal concentration of decision-making power.[50] This could be combated, the Eameses hoped, by distributing the technical, infrastructural, and institutional resources for informed decision making, and unimpeded transmission of covetable ideas, as democratically as possible.[51] The problem facing society was "not so much a lack of scientific, or technical, or sociological knowledge" but a lack of "ways of transmitting existing knowledge to people as they need it, in forms they can readily grasp and use."[52] Similarly, the challenge to liberal-democratic happiness in the late 1960s was not "a lack of values" but rather a vexing excess of conflicting ones. Indeed, Eames continued, "our present discontents . . . show that we do have quite a range of values and that we still feel strongly about them. The difficulty is in accepting that we have no choice but to choose!"[53] At the end of the day, then, values had to be chosen, preferences made, distinctions of quality asserted. This, for the Eameses, was the basic ontology of liberal political life and the law of every studio they worked in. It acknowledged the ongoing necessity of life's organization: "If human nature is viewed as changeable, then armies, police, and *administration* will be seen as interim necessities, not immutable requirements."[54]

The final lecture began with *Movie Sets*, featuring on-location photographs of Billy Wilder in the studio, at work, on various films, including *Spirit, Ace in the Hole* (1951), *Sabrina* (1954), *Irma la Douce* (1963), and *Avanti!* (1972) (fig. 8.6). The film studio's technical environment, Eames submitted, was a "model of the environment of the professional process" in a lecture about the role of such models in democratic knowledge work and the capacities of the computer as a tool of mod-

FIGURE 8.6. The camera as the "center of all communication." Wilder on location in Eames slide show *Movie Sets*. © 2017 Eames Office LLC (eamesoffice.com).

eling and political decision making. Wilder's studio, in other words, had, like 901, made its final turn toward the condition of postindustrial dispersal. The slideshow was followed by some of the Eameses' more famous films about the computer: the recent *A Computer Glossary* (1968) and the earlier *Information Machine*. About the latter, then twenty-one years old, Eames felt obliged to note its age, and its "impossibly naive/wide-eyed" attempt to describe the possibilities of a once-alien technology.[55] A drawing by Ray mapping out the sixth lecture's themes connected the Eameses' rhetorical work of modeling, and issues of "machine use," to the ongoing task of meeting the "universal sense of expectation" ushered in by World War II. That devastating war made people aware of "the promises, and powers, of technology." And the long postwar boom to follow in the promise of plywood offered "immediate exposure to different ways of living, and a catalog of possessed and possessable objects," producing the widespread "feeling that he could, even should, have all those things he has seen the others have." Can the world, Eames asked, still "be arranged so as to fulfill" these "universal expectations"?

The Eameses' career-long answer to this question was a resounding yes. But not without understanding—as Ray's diagram put it—that the use of such technology is a "political choice," one not up to manufacturers but rather redounding to that broader administrative unit of society, as "the real test of Jeffersonian democracy."[56] And not without films. Ray's drawing also included a quotation by Lillian Gish that "films are the mind and heartbeat of this technical century."[57] And not, as I've argued here, without organizational media like the computer, or plywood, or the efficiency of a node in a professional process named "Billy Wilder" by his intimates. And certainly not without that far-flung studio environment encasing the production of films and toys and exhibits and all of the stuff of Eamesian making called "901."

NOTES

1. Eames, "Design, Designer, Industry," 99.

2. Vallye, "Design and the Politics of Knowledge in America, 1937–1967."

3. Harwood, "R and D: The Eames Office at Work," in *Explorations in Architecture: Teaching, Design, Research*, ed. Reto Geiser (Basel: Birkhäuser Architecture, 2008), 200.

4. Galison and Jones, "Factory, Laboratory, Studio," 512, 498.

5. See Nieland, *Happiness by Design*. Portions of this chapter appear in a different form in chapter 2 of that book, "Happy Furniture: On the Media Environments of the Eames Chair." My thanks to the University of Minnesota Press for permission to reprint that material here.

6. See Jacobson, *Studios Before the System*.

7. See Riesman, "Leisure and Work in Postindustrial Society"; and Riesman, "Abundance for What?"

8. CAA Publications, *Academy News*, May 1939. Cranbrook Foundation RG 1: Office Records, Box 27, Folder 15, Cranbrook Educational Community.

9. Christensen, *America's Corporate Art*, 109–32.

10. Christensen, 133.

11. See Neuhart and Neuhart, *Story of Eames Furniture, Book 1*, 305–31; "Plywood Flies and Fights," *Fortune*, March 1942, 145–54.

12. "Case Study Houses 8 and 9, by Charles Eames and Eero Saarinen, Architects," *Arts & Architecture*, Dec. 1945, 43–51, 44.

13. "Case Study Houses 8 and 9," 44.

14. Goldstein, introduction to *Arts & Architecture*, 8.

15. See Neuhart and Neuhart, *Story of Eames Furniture, Book 1*, 296.

16. Neuhart and Neuhart, 34.

17. Neuhart and Neuhart, 33.

18. See Frank, "Interdisciplinarity," 91.

19. See Nieland, *Happiness by Design*. See also Cohen-Cole, *The Open Mind*, esp. chap. 3, "Interdisciplinarity as a Virtue." On the Bauhaus's interdisciplinary ambitions see Alexander, "The Core That Wasn't"; and Alexander, *Kinaesthetic Knowing*, 167–201.

20. See Gary, *The Nervous Liberals*.

21. Nelson, "The New Subscape" (1950).

22. *Arts & Architecture*, Sept. 1943, 16.

23. Eliot Noyes, "Charles Eames," *Arts & Architecture*, Sept. 1946, 26.

24. "The Germans See Their Concentration Camps," *Arts & Architecture*, Sept. 1946, 14.

25. Neuhart and Neuhart, *Story of Eames Furniture, Book 1*.

26. Ince, "Something about the World of Charles and Ray Eames," 13.

27. Ince, 13.

28. Neuhart and Neuhart, *Eames Design*, 223.

29. Neuhart and Neuhart clarify that the Eameses increasingly dined, socialized, and hosted at 901—which had a kitchen and full-time cook—rather than at home, despite many famous photos of parties at the Eames House.

30. Neuhart and Neuhart, *Story of Eames Furniture, Book 1*, 29.

31. On the creation of "heuristic environments" in the Eameses' work, especially for IBM, see Harwood, *The Interface*.

32. I borrow the phrase "allegories of production" from David James, *Allegories of Cinema*.

33. Neuhart and Neuhart, *Story of Eames Furniture, Book 1*, 31.

34. Peters, *The Marvelous Clouds*, 37; Klose, *The Container Principle*.

35. Part II: Box 190, Folder: *Discovery* television program (1953). Charles and Ray Eames Papers, Manuscript Division, Library of Congress, Washington, DC. Hereafter EP.

36. II: Box 190, EP.

37. II: Box 190, EP.

38. II: Box 190, EP.

39. II: Box 190, EP.

40. II: Box 190, EP.

41. Excerpted from a handwritten letter from Charles Eames to someone at *Omnibus*; undated, but likely 1956; II: Box 190, EP.

42. II: Box 173, EP.

43. II: Box 173, EP.

44. II: Box 173, EP.

45. II: Box 173, EP.

46. Davenport, "Chairs, Fairs, and Films," 228.

47. II: Box 22, Folder: Wilder, Billy, 1950–57, EP.

48. This new category of labor was coined by Peter Drucker and Fritz Matchlup nearly simultaneously in 1962. See Matchlup, *Production and Distribution of Knowledge in the United States.*

49. II: Box 191, Folder: *Spirit of St. Louis* film montage, EP.

50. II: Box 217, Folder: 1970–1971 Charles Eliot Norton Lectures, Miscellany, EP.

51. II: Box 217, Folder: 1970–1971 Charles Eliot Norton Lectures, Notes, Lecture 6, EP.

52. Schuldenfrei, *Films of Charles and Ray Eames,* 199.

53. Eames, "Smithsonian Lecture Notes," quoted in Schuldenfrei, 202.

54. II: Box 217, Folder: 1970–1971 Charles Eliot Norton Lectures, Notes, Lecture 6, EP.

55. II: Box 217, Folder: 1970–1971, EP.

56. II: Box 217, Folder: 1970–1971, EP.

57. II: Box 217, Folder: 1970–1971, EP.

9

The Last Qualitative Scientist

Hollis Frampton and the Digital Arts Lab

Jeff Menne

It is possible to tell the story of postwar modernism in the US—in particular the role the artist's studio played—through the person of Hollis Frampton. In his early twenties he paid ongoing visits to Ezra Pound at St. Elizabeths Hospital, seeking the tutelage of one of the great figures of literary modernism. After this he moved to New York City in the twilight years of abstract expressionism, the movement that had "stolen" modern art from Paris.[1] Frampton and friends hung out at the Cedar Tavern to be in the midst of the city's venerated artists, but they would, in their turn, repudiate the romantic individualism of this movement and help install in its place minimalism and pop art. Meanwhile, he became involved in the New American Cinema, the postwar film avant-garde that Jonas Mekas had helped to organize, which led Frampton in the mid-1960s to transition from still photography to filmmaking. He then joined the faculty of Media Study that Gerald O'Grady was recruiting at SUNY Buffalo, and there Frampton's focus oscillated between film and video and, in his final days, personal computing. From poetry to the digital arts, he spanned the modernist century.

An aesthetic trajectory such as his might hold interest of several kinds, but this essay will put an accent on the artist's studio in telling the story. The gambit is that when we let the studio frame our inquiry, we foreground the political economy of the arts. A studio is an economic site, of course, in the banal sense that it's a site of production, but in a more rigorous sense a studio is a material cost, just as an artist's other media (paints for painters, film for filmmakers) are material costs, and these costs must be offset in whatever bargain is functionally struck in any given art. What we might expect, then, is that as such costs rise with the evolution of media from tools readily at hand to industrial and then postindustrial machinery,

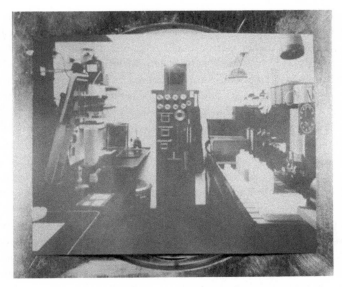

FIGURE 9.1. The unremarked photograph of Hollis Frampton's dark room in *(nostalgia)* (1971).

the arts will come to depend on different patrons. In this essay I consider how, within the framework of the postwar economy, the university became a patron of the intensified media experiments in film, video, and personal computing. Because the Center for Media Study at SUNY Buffalo experimented in each of these media, oftentimes in combination, I take it for my case study, and in particular I focus on the Digital Arts Lab (DAL) that Frampton and video artist Woody Vasulka helped establish there at the end of the 1970s.

My attention rests on Frampton specifically (rather than Vasulka, say, or colleagues Paul Sharits or Tony Conrad) because his passage into the university was accompanied by a critique of sorts. Frampton's interest in what he called "metahistory"—a modernist interest, it should be said, in aesthetic self-reflection—meant that his work was focused on the conditions of its making.[2] One of his most famous films, *(nostalgia)* (1971), begins on a still photograph of his darkroom (fig. 9.1). The voice-over says nothing about it because the film, in accordance with its structure, shows an image but cannot address it in the moment: the voice-over, that is, narrates the *next image,* the one yet to be shown onscreen, which happens to be a photograph of the minimalist sculptor Carl Andre. But the photograph of Frampton's darkroom goes all the while unremarked. The explanation of it, we might say, comes before the film: it is the infrastructure of art-making and is simply presupposed.

The structure of the film, moreover, is anticipatory, future-oriented. Themati-
cally, this makes sense, given that what it narrates is Frampton's passage from still
photographer to filmmaker. But in its self-reflexivity the film is situating Frampton's own transition from photography to film within the history of media forms,
modeling the succession of one dominant media form by another—first the word
(in the form of the voice-over), which anticipates the image, which "burns" and is
replaced by another image—that is, moving images. This staging of media forms
in their historical perspective, from old media to new, is what so many of his films
do, including *Zorns Lemma* (1970), the Hapax Legomena series—of which *(nostalgia)* is a part—and the Magellan series. In the closing pages I will discuss a film
from Magellan, *Gloria* (1979), in terms of Frampton's personal passage from ana-
log film to digital computing within a historical succession whose narration was
his life's work.

Frampton gives us in *(nostalgia)* a brief, witty history of media forms but one in
which their infrastructure must be suppressed. I say this not only because he
shows his darkroom without speaking of it but also because several photographs
displayed are of his art-world friends such as Andre, Frank Stella, and James
Rosenquist. Frampton's job, early on, was to make publicity photographs of artists
for exhibition catalogues. Hence, *(nostalgia)* reckons with his implication in the
commerce of art, the artist's image, and so on. In part this is because the emergence of minimalism and pop art from abstract expressionism was predicated on
an art-world self-awareness of its own economic infrastructure. In *The Painted
Word* Tom Wolfe had satirized the "boho dance" that artists did for *"le monde"* as
the evolutionary upshot of modern art, a process that had carried the artist from
the court to the *salon* to the *cénacle*.[3] The artist, Wolfe says, had always worked in
relation to patrons, but in modern art the relationship had to be dissimulated for
its own health. Sarah Burns has discussed the early phases of this bohemian life in
turn-of-the-century New York City, which was centered in Greenwich Village—
the "artistic colony," it was called—and became a "zone of tourism" for those seeking a glimpse of "disorder, irregularity, and rambling unpredictability" that otherwise "found no space in modern America, where discipline, punctuality, and
responsibility were paramount in carrying on with business and moneymaking."[4]
Though this bohemian spectacle might be displaced by neighborhood (from
Greenwich Village to the Lower East Side, say), what Burns described in the early
1900s took roughly the same form in the midcentury fascination with Jackson Pollock's *Life* magazine profile. But the next generation of NYC artists, the minimal-
ists and pop artists, from Andre and Stella to Claes Oldenburg and Andy Warhol,
would ironize their practices in turn. Oldenburg set up "The Store," a combined
studio and gallery space that stitched his commoditization into its architecture. He
ironized distribution, stacking all his art on shelves, "the leitmotif of shop-window
display," in Julia Robinson's words, whereas Warhol would ironize production.[5] He

set up "The Factory," a loft space that he gave a "nineteenth-century inflection," as Caroline Jones puts it, in which he was "absent manager," employing "mechanical means" and inducing "total Marxist alienation."[6]

I will argue that Frampton continued this tradition of self-reflexive studio construction, but his project looked different from Oldenburg's or Warhol's because he was not interfacing as directly with the market forces of the art world as they were but rather with a funding structure that was more socialized. In part Frampton's self-reflexivity stemmed from the fact that he was entering an institution—the university—riven by what C. P. Snow had called the "two cultures" of the sciences and the humanities. In the 1970s, as Richard Florida et al. have demonstrated, the model of "cold war science" had become pervasive, seen in the uptick in industry funding for "academic R&D," which rose between 1970 and 1990 "from 2.6 to 6.95."[7] When this model was established in the postwar years, Clark Kerr had explained it under the rubric of the "multiversity," which was "not really private and . . . not really public; it is neither entirely of the world nor entirely apart from it" insofar as it triangulated industry, state, and higher education.[8] In the meshing of industry and university, the disciplines of "engineering and applied science" were the obvious targets of funding. But SUNY Buffalo was an interesting case, as I will show, because in the DAL it carried forward experimentation that had begun at institutions such as MIT and the University of Utah but now in a humanistic key.

Frampton was the ideal agent for this, since for him the paragon of intellectual activity was James Clerk Maxwell, whom he described as "either the last qualitative physicist or the first quantitative physicist."[9] In the DAL Frampton was hoping to build a "new media studio," designed to reconcile in its form and function the traditions of qualitative and quantitative reasoning, and—most significant for him—how they were mediated. His friend Michael Snow would say of Frampton that he was among the last avatars of an "ancient tradition," embodied by him as a kind of "poetic scientism." Frampton was not hyperspecialized but polymathic, and it was his "love of systems, his literariness, his sculptural sense, even the influence of radio," Snow says, that enabled him to conceive the DAL as an architectural and institutional hybrid, born of the experimental protocols of the artist's studio and the scientist's laboratory alike.[10] Such a space as Frampton imagined would, in practice, incite a certain amount of category confusion, given that in it the standards of the art world's investment culture and the applied science's funding bodies would be muddled together. It's possible that Frampton was uniquely capable of producing a language for such institutional encounters, and in retrospect it seems that his habit of paradoxical thinking provides us with a powerful understanding of the aesthetic possibility of the mathematized realm of computer art, the promise of which, he believed, was (and perhaps still is) to redeem in a single practice the resources of intellectual traditions that had otherwise been sorted into separate jurisdictions.

HOW BUFFALO STOLE THE IDEA OF MEDIA ARTS

Gerald O'Grady has said of his program-building that his "secret" was "to be involved in funding and administration, but somehow to maintain my roots in what's happening outside."[11] What was "happening outside" was happening in New York City. O'Grady had originally been in Houston, where he founded the Media Center at the University of St. Thomas in 1967. Next, he took a job in the Department of English at SUNY Buffalo, which allowed him to bounce around in visiting positions among NYC universities, such as Columbia, the New School, and NYU. It was NYC's status within the world of media experimentation that drew him there from Houston in the first place. In this capacity he befriended many of the artists—film and otherwise—connected to its art world. But he was all the while operating inside the academy, which in the main did not dignify media such as film and video as objects of study. When he began the Center of Media Study at SUNY Buffalo in 1973, therefore, the main constraints on it were on the one hand the prejudices against the field, which to colleagues in "physics, anthropology, or music" seemed reducible to the industries of Hollywood or commercial television, and on the other hand the terms of "media," which had already been "organized into traditional 'departments,' such as painting and sculpture (art), the language (literature), etc.," and thus led O'Grady to claim whatever fell outside this codification. Practically, what this meant was that he would bring the avant-garde, once the province of the art world, into the ambit of the university. If the subject wasn't yet codified, if it was in the process of being formed, the only pedagogy O'Grady could imagine was to have the artists teach it. "The State University of New York at Buffalo," O'Grady remarked, "was one of the first schools to invite practicing artists to be professors, such as Robert Creeley and John Barth in literature, and Morton Feldman and Lukas Foss in music." And because "there were no trained scholars" in the fields of film and video, he said, "the only persons I could find to explain these new media were the practitioners."[12]

There were multiple reasons that O'Grady deemed Buffalo a congenial site for centering media studies in the academy. "New York State is a large state, and a sophisticated and wealthy one," he would say. "This is my logic: SUNY at Buffalo is the largest component of the 72 centers in the state system. We have a tradition at this university—with the Creative Associates in music, with a strong English Department, of inviting creative writers for residencies."[13] New York had the state system it had, O'Grady explains, because Governor Nelson Rockefeller had built it out in emulation of Pat Brown's expansion of the California system.[14] Amid this boom, research money was there for the taking, and O'Grady, the *Buffalo Courier-Express* would say, had a "magical expertise in the fund-raising area."[15] In 1973, thanks to state and federal funding, he established Media Study Inc. as a community center with a mission of training local residents in media technology and affordably renting them equipment. It was not associated with the university but ran in parallel to its Center for Media Study. In 1975 Media Study Inc. received $75,000 in grant money from the New York State Council on the Arts, plus more than $37,000 from the National Endowment for the Arts (NEA), which allowed it to move from its location on Bailey Avenue to the "luxuriously large quarters in the Sidway Bldg. at Main and Goodell." In the same year it received $150,000 in grant money from the National Endowment for the Humanities (NEH) for the documentary *America Lost and Found: A Social History of the Depression Years*. So Buffalo had a robust cultural scene, beyond the reach of the university, and a current of that scene that Frampton and Vasulka would accentuate in the later years of the 1970s was its activity in electronic arts. Robert Moog's company, R. A. Moog Inc., moved its manufacture of Moog synthesizers to Buffalo in 1971, and Lejaren Hiller, known as the first composer to write music on a computer, had been drawn from the University of Illinois to Buffalo in 1968 to codirect SUNY's Center for the Creative and Performing Arts. Before his Slee Lecture series, Hiller told the *Buffalo Courier-Express* that "the composer must reflect his time and place," and it was "only natural that the composer, like everyone else in the society, has felt the impact of electronics—radio, television, phonograph records."[16] Frampton would later sound the same theme in his argument for establishing computer art in the SUNY curriculum: "Our traditional so-called *cultural* education is at best inadequate," he wrote in a university proposal, "and can really act as a form of enforced disenfranchisement of our students from the emerging planetary *culture* of the 21st century."[17]

The planetary culture, indeed, is what O'Grady understood media to be. In this, O'Grady was thoroughly McLuhanite, believing the ultimate effect of media expansion was a fundamental reorientation of space. It had made a "common place," he said, "a mediated video environment which is now being referred to as 'videospace.'"[18] Notions of space, it turns out, figured heavily in O'Grady's approach to media study. For a MoMA audience he imagined the horizons of the moving image, its power to "transform the pedagogical function of the museum in a new world without walls."[19] What he was talking about ("videospace," "a world without walls") is virtual and futuristic, but it should be noted that for all the talismanic concepts he lifted from media theory, he remained institutionally pragmatic as he planned the spaces of the Center for Media Study. In the very name of the center— indeed, *study* rather than *studies*—he signaled an interest in the relation between space and media. He opted against the plural *studies* because he wanted to draw on the etymology of *study*, its original sense of zeal or focus, but also its relation to *studio*. Media production, he explained, had "extended" the sense of studio because it required a "soundproof place to focus"; O'Grady's interest lay in this kind of "intensity" but in "metaphysical" rather than industrial terms. On the face of it, it might sound less than pragmatic that he should invoke metaphysics, but what he meant by this was that the other programs then in development—he mentions Temple and Iowa, in this regard—had started by building studios, incurring "huge expenses, 35 mm," and in following such an industrial model they were already accepting the metaphysics built into this infrastructure.

To turn away from this model, O'Grady looked to Hollis Frampton and his experience from the NYC art world. Frampton was one of the first two hires in the program and hence was called on for ideas in the redesign of the upper floors of the Richmond Quadrangle. He was expansive in his advice: "I don't know how many square feet are normally allotted to such things as ordinary classrooms," he said, "but the *shape* of a space can be extremely important, as well as its area." He rooted his authority in his "years of lab experience," which refers to the livelihood he made between 1961 and 1969 as a lab technician for dye imbibition color. This gave him "some notion of how much can be got out of floorspace providing it's well designed." The faculty, he insisted, must have "more than a little say" in the facility design.[20] O'Grady asked both Frampton and filmmaker James Blue to detail the equipment that should be acquired for the Center, and each was eager to share his expert opinion in the matter, Frampton preparing a two-page list and Blue itemizing the program's needs more expansively in an eleven-page document. In this sense, as Media Study moved from Richmond to Wende Hall, from the more Brutalist buildings of the North Campus to the more Georgian buildings of the downtown South Campus, Frampton, Vasulka, and their colleagues, all drawn from different corners of the art world, would encode their needs as artists into the very architecture of the research university. In the transplant of the artist's needs from art world to university, though, what strikes me as most deserving of study is how extensively the art world had been shaped by the theatricalizing of the relationship between artist and marketplace and how, in turn, the university's indirect relationship to the marketplace would reshape the projects of the artists it recruited.

"NOMADIC HUNTER TO URBAN FARMER": NYC TO BUFFALO, ART WORLD TO UNIVERSITY

Hollis Frampton had been moving, step by step, from the art world to the university throughout the 1960s. After having taught at the Free University of New York in 1966 and 1967, he joined the faculty at Hunter College, where he offered courses in still photography between 1969 and 1973 and then began teaching film courses at the School of Visual Arts (1970–71) and Cooper Union (1970–73). When O'Grady got two lines approved for the Center for Media Study, he called Stan Brakhage and asked him to recommend someone. Brakhage said Frampton, and in the fall of 1973 Frampton began at Buffalo. In this period, too, he had left NYC and bought a small farm in Eaton, New York, in 1970. This means he had been commuting to Manhattan and would continue the same in his first years at Buffalo. In part his drift was steered by the capital-intensiveness of his preferred media forms. He notes that when he started working in film in 1962–65, he "underwrote" the commitment by buying camera equipment. This was all very expensive, and Frampton, as he told MoMA curator Donald Richie, had witnessed Maya Deren's penury from afar as she suffered from "genuine need" and "beg[ged] for money" in order to finish *The Very Eye of Night.* "That won't happen to me," he said, "nor any other artist I know."[21] What is interesting about his turn to the aegis of the university, though, is not simply that it would underwrite his projects henceforth but that it would also permeate his film work and inform his aesthetic. His films, as I have noted, can be read in terms of their site of production. This is true in an uncomplicated way about every film, thanks to the indexicality of the medium— Ernie Gehr's *Serene Velocity* (1970), for instance, is about Binghamton University insofar as he shot the film one night in the corridor of a campus building. The physical setting of *Serene Velocity* is treated differently as raw material, though, than the Empire State Building was treated in Andy Warhol's *Empire* (1964): Gehr's film is largely indifferent to its content—that is, the campus building—but is concerned rather with the formal reconstruction of it (it has "minimal exterior subject matter," P. Adams Sitney says, the better to concentrate on an "interior rhythm" produced by alternating the zoom lens every four frames), whereas Warhol's film is largely indifferent to the formal treatment of its content, the Empire State Building, preferring to let it feature as a "star."[22] For Frampton, however, the mediation of the site of production was raised to such a level that it might be called the subject of his work. Take, for instance, the short, playful film *Carrots & Peas* (1969), in which images of the titular vegetables are shown in succession, sometimes separated and other times mixed, sometimes in color and other times in black and white, tinted here, overlaid with red polka dots there. It was conceived, Frampton said, as a "set of ironies upon the form of the art history slide lecture." The voice-over, which is played backward, is meant to be the voice of a lecturer, as it might sound to a bored student. Frampton made a film about the form of the lecture, in other words, as he was beginning to make his living as a lecturer; hence, the discursive limits and the formal conditions of his work (teaching) have been ironized in his work (art-making). This is just one example. Other examples, such as the systematic character given his work in series—such as Hapax Legomena and, later, Magellan—will bear the institutional mark of the university more philosophically, as I will explain in my closing paragraphs.

The university is a system, made of "higher" and "lower" faculties, as Kant would say, and to the extent that one plans to mobilize its resources, as both O'Grady and Frampton did, one must think of it on this model.[23] O'Grady was obliged to speak of it in these terms in his effort to establish a "center," one that sat between disciplines, and he did so in a twelve-page letter to President Robert Ketter dated

September 26, 1974. In it he imagines the interaction between departments, such as Speech Communication and Instructional Media, History and English, but he also envisions how these will interrelate with the university-owned and -operated public radio station, GEMS-ITV (a closed-circuit television), and with his own nonprofit center, Media Study Inc. The internal memo is the genre for theorizing such a totality, and while it might be thought that O'Grady wrote so ably in this genre because he was a creature of institutions, what I wish to demonstrate is that Frampton mastered this genre, too. He believed the university's function should be "derived from common argument in confrontation rather than from a nominal consensus of independent memoranda"—which is to say he didn't want decision making entrusted to department chairs and deans alone—but he did consider the latter, the "independent memoranda," to be the theoretical channels that were laid down for the university's self-understanding.[24] Because Frampton was such a great essayist, a skill he began cultivating from 1971 onward (publishing in *Artforum* and elsewhere), he had an easy time adjusting to intrauniversity communication.[25] O'Grady has insisted, indeed, that all the artists on faculty—Frampton, Vasulka, and Paul Sharits—excelled, too, in the genres of institutional writing, namely internal memos such as curricular proposals and grant writing. It is my sense, though, that it was the confluence of Frampton's training (his art-world credentials, his polymathic aptitudes, and his adapted essay-writing skill) that enabled him to lobby for the funding and construction of the DAL. Beginning in 1977, when he started to work, "both alone and with a small group of students," "to formulate the hardware and software requirements for a hospitable computing environment for the arts," Frampton bent his energies to establishing the DAL and implementing its courses, both practical and theoretical, in the program curriculum. Existing "programming languages," he explained, "were designed, from economic necessity, to accommodate the scientific and business communities."[26] That he should specify the need to formulate computer environments for "the arts," however, reveals the Kantian dimension of his thinking about the "higher" and "lower" faculties in the university: they depended on each other, but whereas the needs of the former were determined by the society external to the university, the needs of the latter (including philosophy and the arts) were determined by their own internal logics. A medium, whether in thought or expression, must achieve some self-understanding. Frampton, in effect, was casting his pitch for the DAL in the terms of medium-specificity when proposing it to the university and appealing to the NEA for funds. "It has never before been possible for an artist to explore the uses of the computer," he would explain, "with the intimacy and flexibility that the painter or writer takes for granted and finds the necessary condition for creative work."[27]

In Frampton's NEA proposal he stressed that the interest of the DAL would lie in computers as "manipulators of symbolic systems" rather than as "number crunchers." Their "entire emphasis," he said, "has rested upon the notion of the computer as a personal expressive tool, at once general and intimate." His proposal for the 1979–80 academic year, in the amount of $25,000 with "in-kind matching," was successful.[28] It is interesting, in this light, to compare his proposal to Woody Vasulka's National Endowment for the Humanities (NEH) proposal for the same time frame. Vasulka's was rejected, and in the NEH response they explained that his request fell outside their "purview" because its "basic theory" was "mathematical," to which they added: "else a computer would be of no use in the study."[29] It's a fascinating response, not only because they impute a quantitative ontology to the computer but because it implies that Vasulka's project would struggle to find federal grants of any kind because its hybrid of mathematics and art did not fit the very structure of funding. Vasulka was trained as an industrial engineer, it's true, but his concerns could only be categorized as artistic. The thrill of the Center for Media Study, on principle, was how mixed the training of its faculty was. Tony Conrad, who was hired in 1976, was a mathematician originally. Brian Henderson had studied law; Sharits was a designer; and Frampton, by his own account, had trained in "classical and modern languages" and "mathematics."[30] Moreover, the students they began attracting to the Digital Arts courses, as Frampton told O'Grady, were from the assorted fields of "Electrical Engineering, Computer Science, Mathematics, Psychology, English, Music and Art," as well from within the Media Study program itself. What Vasulka's NEH rejection suggests is that the intrauniversity realignment of the quantitative-qualitative ratio that they hoped the digital arts might provoke was still at odds with the interuniversity culture wherein the quantitative-qualitative segregation was deeply entrenched. Despite letters of protest from both O'Grady ("His study is philosophical and involves the semiotics of culture") and Buffalo's director of Academic Computing, Jay Leavitt ("It would seem that the attitude of the N.E.H. is that Humanists can ignore the presence of technology" and that "support for any technically related subjects belong to the National Science Foundation"), the NEH still opined that Vasulka's project lay "outside the domain of the humanities."[31] All things being equal, Frampton was a better practitioner of the grant-writing genre because he managed the prejudices a humanist audience held against computers. He softened them by using the art-world language of medium specificity, which Caroline Jones has argued was already geared to rationalized institutions.[32]

With funding secured, the Digital Arts Lab was set up in Wende Hall on the downtown campus. The DAL comprised two different classrooms, actually, one on the second floor and another on the fourth. Both rooms were sites of sociality, but their functions differed. The second-floor room was Frampton's classroom, and there he had a computer workstation that served both as his on-campus home (his Eaton farmhouse was a three-hour drive away) and his productive space. This room can be characterized as a studio, I will explain, if anachronistically understood. The fourth-floor room was dedicated space for the program's core graduate

FIGURE 9.2. Bob Coggeshall at work in the "sonic hippie" space of the fourth-floor DAL. Courtesy of Bob Coggeshall.

students, where they all had independent workstations, furnished with kit-assembled microcomputers (fig. 9.2). This was the "sonic hippie" space, according to former graduate student Bob Franki, and it was treated as something of an "electronic music studio."

I will focus on the second-floor classroom, because that was where they organized work on a general-purpose graphics package, which included the frame buffer designed by Bob Coggeshall and the IMAGO software designed by Franki. But I want to note the significance of both rooms as sites of cross-traffic between academic disciplines. Room 404 was important because students from electrical engineering, music, and media study collaborated there, and this collaboration, in turn, put the faculty of the respective programs in contact. Franki, for instance, did his master's project with sponsorship from media study, electrical engineering, and computer science. In a less formal project students worked with Tony Conrad on a "video freak-out," feeding recordings of a Conrad jam session in NYC through a Hearn device keyed for video processing, which they coupled to a synthesizer with inputs from microphones in the room that were picking up a student jam session. They were producing, in short, the multimedia environments that Conrad and Sharits had learned in their Fluxus participation but now in a classroom rather than in the East Village, and to accomplish it, they were calling on resources typically siloed in departments across campus. Faculty in the music program, too, worked with DAL students on the design of electronic hardware. Lejaren Hiller and Frampton cosponsored Coggeshall's master's work, and in 1984, when the United States Information Agency approached Hiller about showcasing the creative potential of computers in the American Pavilion at the 1985 International Exposition in Tsukuba, Japan, Hiller's student Charles Ames worked together with Coggeshall and Franki to build a hosting system for Hiller's automated compositions, namely *Circus Piece* and *Mix or Match*. This is all to say that while each site of the DAL functioned somewhat differently, they both in their own way helped form an institutional nexus for disciplines that in the day-to-day beat of the university were kept apart.

Frampton's second-floor classroom, though, might be analyzed as a special case within the historical evolution of the artist's studio. In this room, perhaps 50 × 25 feet in area, an oblong layout with Frampton's workstation in the front corner, he taught the "Digital Arts Workshop" to graduate students. Frampton would usually camp out at his computer, and in the adjacent section at the front of the room were couches and armchairs for congregating. The environment was casual and relaxed, with students socializing there throughout the day, as did Frampton himself. Because he commuted to campus, he put in long days, from roughly 9:00 a.m. to 9:00 p.m. on Tuesdays and Thursdays. He treated the room as he would domestic space, smoking and drinking Genesee beers ("Genees," his students say) as he worked on his computer, and his students did as well, leaving the room only long enough to attend their classes. In the back half of the room were long tables, "old-style science class tables," as Franki describes them, which had sturdy wooden legs and hard rubber tops. In this sense the room looked like a "lab." Otherwise, the space was undistinguished: though the architecture of Wende Hall gave the appearance of a more traditional university building—a late nineteenth-century Georgian facade with cornices and a bell tower—the interior, redesigned in 1957 by the firm James, Meadows, and Howard, was unornamented and institutional in style. The floors were a composite material, and the walls were cinderblock. But Frampton's classroom was like a lab or studio in the customary sense that it was disorganized, with books and chips and tools of whatever kind at hand. Franki has described it as "a science lab run by artists." There was "a pretty good library," Franki has said, with primers on computing such as Donald Knuth's *The Art of Computer Programming* and Fredrick Brooks's *The Mythical Man-Month*. This library was the by-product of Frampton's self-education in computing. There was no such thing as a Digital Arts program outside the invention of it taking place among Frampton and his students, and in this respect the sociality of the environment, hardly classroom-like in any conventional sense, came to evoke an older model of the artist's studio forged around the master's experimentation and the emulation of techniques carried out by apprentices. For Franki it was very much "an old-world apprenticeship," which, he jokes, involved "indentured servitude" in the form of running personal errands. But such was the dailiness of the undertaking, which often ended in Frampton treating those students who hung around the DAL until closing hours to a dinner at the Sign of the Steer restaurant down the block from Wende Hall. Over dinner and drinks Frampton extended the work of the classroom in discussion of the day's ideas. He "held court," Franki says.

The work of Frampton's DAL was consecrated to making the computer not a "number cruncher" but a "manipulator of symbolic systems," and the symbolic unit that concerned him was the image. As Andy Uhrich has observed of the early

1980s, computer kits were available, but "there were few, if any, off-the-shelf programs to manipulate sound and images."[33] Sound, as noted, was the province of the
fourth-floor lab. The second-floor lab, by contrast, was given over to the building
of a frame buffer, GOLEM, and the coding of software, IMAGO. The design was
team-based, but the chief architect of the frame buffer was Coggeshall. Production
was based in the university's economy: labor was paid in credit hours and in the
fulfillment of thesis requirements. As Coggeshall engineered the frame buffer,
Franki and others wrote the software for what at the time was only a theoretical
machine. They had to theorize as they were working, that is, whether the machine,
once complete, could execute the code they were writing. It did, eventually, and
they were able in the last years of the lab (before Frampton's untimely death) to
perform some relatively sophisticated real-time video processing. Coggeshall executed a series of frame-manipulation experiments, and others wrote a program for
"instant flicker movies," an "app," Franki explains, that made one "Paul Sharits at
the touch of a button." Much of this happened, however, beneath the radar of the
university. The computer they built, in fact, was later misplaced by the university.
Today there are "146 obsolete eight-inch floppy disks" without the computer tools
to read them; they are now just artifacts. Coggeshall explains that they did such
work in an era before the university aggressively claimed ownership of whatever
was produced in its labs. Though Frampton never fully integrated these digital
tools into his art-making, this may have been their more appropriate fate. Having
only a "theoretical machine" for so long meant there were no practical applications: knowledge was produced, yes, but they had no product to commodify. Thus,
their work was indifferent to market uses. This left them the freedom vouched only
to pure researchers; they were theorists, imagining tools of the future, not market-
ers or technicians of present-day tools.

Throughout the 1970s Frampton had theorized his preferred tool—the
cinema—as one oriented by the past. He called it the "Last Machine." It was the
obsolete if "exceptional machine" from the "Age of Machines," Frampton wrote,
and its "subset of still photographs" was a psychic aid to our cognition of history
even as the physical aid that machines had provided us was superseded. Don't be
"misled by the electric can opener," he warned; "small machines proliferate now as
though they were going out of style because they are doing precisely that." What
would replace the Last Machine, however, was a point of debate when he wrote
these words in 1971: some thought it would be video, but Frampton turned to radar
because it "replaced the mechanical reconnaissance aircraft with a static, anonymous black box."[34] We might think, in retrospect, that the "black box" was Frampton's prefiguration of the computer. How this black box let him see differently the
way "things looked" and "worked," and "how to feel and think," was a project oriented not only in time but in space. If the future was new tools, and the novel
mode of tool-being they would induce in us, then the space for devising it was

Frampton's DAL, wherein the film studio was transformed into the new media studio. Svetlana Alpers has imagined the studio, in this respect, as parameters for seeing the object world. When painters retreated into studios, she says, they took up "a condition" that was more "a matter of mind" than a matter of what was "actually there before the artist's eyes and body," such that Cezanne, for instance, came to paint landscapes "as if they were still-life motifs."[35] Likewise, Frampton understood film to be a "principle of intelligibility," one that made the world appear to us consecutive and "anisotropic with respect to time," so it made good sense that the studios built to service this medium were consecutive in their operations, like assembly lines in a factory. Hollywood, he said, was the "Detroit of the image."[36] In this light the computer might allow its user to understand history differently, not "anisotropic" but in all directions at once, as though historical eras were overlaid on each other or circled back on themselves. Thus the anachronism of the DAL, with Frampton a Rembrandt teaching his workshop of apprentices. In an interview with Lucy Fischer, Frampton explained it this way: the "passage from film to video to digitally processed images is a figurative passage from 'nomadic hunter to urban farmer,'" a passage that mapped onto his own from NYC to Buffalo, from a documentary mode of image gathering to a digital mode of image processing. "My thrills from roaming the hills are not what they once were," he said. "Bagging the live shot was always fused with the pleasures of dragging home the carcass and cooking it."[37]

METAMACHINES FOR METAHISTORIANS

Frampton's movement from the art world to the university meant that rather than satirize the art world and its fatal assimilation to commodity culture, as did Oldenburg and Warhol, he had a share in foretelling the forms of digital culture. In doing so he was not a digital utopian but, as he would put it, a metahistorian. The cinema suggested a metahistorical form, Frampton argued, from its original coordinates, which, in his telling, were the following: the play *Woyzeck,* by Georg Buchner; Évariste Galois's group theory; the invention of photography by Talbot and Niépce; and Joseph Plateau's invention of the phenakistiscope. From these historical forms, Frampton says, we can tease out the "infinite cinema," and the work of its "polymorphous camera" that "has always turned, and will forever turn, its lens focused upon all the appearances of the world."[38] Conceiving metahistory in the figure of an endlessly turning camera, however, means in turn that we conceive our historical being in consecutive and mechanical terms. But the computer proposed something different, subsuming into itself even the infinite cinema and producing as it did a kind of isotropic historical time. The computer was the metamachine, and as such it required a studio constituted variously from studio ideas throughout history. If today the computer has become the "studio" for much

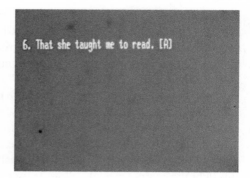

FIGURE 9.3. A frame of computer green
screen from *Gloria* (1979).

artistic practice—in the sense of Adobe Studio, Macromedia Studio, Microsoft Visual studio, and so on—those virtual forms needed a material one as their prototype, and Frampton's legacy is to have fashioned it from a deep, reflexive engagement with the studio's long history. Though he left these projects unfinished as a result of his premature death, we are licensed nonetheless to extrapolate from what he left since his was an extrapolative project in the first place.

A film from which we can extrapolate is Frampton's *Gloria,* a fragment that he intended as one of the final installments of his Magellan series. It gives us the theory, we might say, or the virtualization of the practice that occupied him during his last years in the DAL. The film begins with an optically printed version of "Finnegan's Wake," possibly taken from the Library of Congress's paper print collection of early cinema, and it ends with another version of it.[39] Between these two prints we see nothing but the green screen of a computer monitor. In effect seven-plus minutes of the film are given over to a computer screen. At first computerized text appears on the screen, putting forth a series of "propositions" that are coded twice, once numerically and a second time alphabetically. The first codes the order in which the propositions occurred to Frampton, and the second indexes their value to him. For instance, the first proposition states that he and his maternal grandmother were related by blood, and its numeric priority is matched by its alphabetical value (A), indicating that their biological relation greatly matters to Frampton. But the second proposition states that "others belonged to the same kinship group, and partook of that tie," and though numerically this has high priority, its alphabetical designation (Y) suggests that it matters little to him. What is being established, here, is the fact of consecutive priority in confrontation with priority of another kind, which we might call metaphysical value. Frampton's grandmother came before him, as did many closely and distantly related people, but she assumes personal importance for him in the quality of their relation. In part this is because she taught him to read, a transmission between them that he assigns the highest possible value, (A) (fig. 9.3). In teaching him to read, she taught him a form in which experience of the world might be mediated for him.

But the form given to *Gloria* invites us to dwell not only on its mediation of facts and experience for us, its audience, but as well on the very historical character of mediation. The film contains various media forms in sequence, including early cinema, computerized text, and an Irish jig that plays subsequent to the text and presumably is the fulfillment of "a tune" mentioned therein as having been played at his grandmother's wedding. In part Frampton has done this to suggest that the temporal character of cinematic mediation is consecutive (i.e., we watch the parts of the film one after the other), whereas for computer mediation it is recursive (i.e., in the digitized propositions we are asked to compute them in recombinatory series). The film's more interesting commentary, though, is addressed to mediation as such. Though we hear the tune his grandmother recalls only after its mention—after, that is, the text stops and the screen is empty—we are induced to project the moment of our hearing back onto its mention, in the same sort of temporal lag he had earlier used in *(nostalgia)*. We must coordinate in a cognitive act the Irish jig and the grandmother's description of it, sounding "like quacking ducks." Then, too, we realize in the final section of *Finnegan's Wake* that the revelry of its characters could fittingly be scored to the tune of "quacking ducks." The separateness of our mediated experience, in short, can be reassembled as a whole within the mind, suggesting two orders at play—a consecutive, secular one, and an imaginatively whole, metaphysical one.

What this film enacts on a small scale, I propose, is Frampton's total project, which was as boldly ambitious as a "Tour of Tours," as he would put it, "of all knowledge."[40] Frampton was drawn to the aesthetic programs of modernism, namely its encyclopedism (e.g., James Joyce's *Finnegans Wake*), just as he was drawn to the university's institutional charge "to summarize the culture and encapsulate it." But in constructing a new media studio within the university, he hoped to thwart the worst tendency of this institution, which was to "academicize" the discoveries of the arts and sciences by reducing their vibrancy and dynamism into "dry, sterile, prescriptive formulae." A new media studio would not merely be a site for computers but rather a site for the examination of media in the emergent moment of their newness, as well as a reintegration into such a process of the functions made dormant by media oldness. It would be a site, Frampton thought, whose forging must be entrusted "to creative artists and creative mathematicians."[41] That computers were in fact the tool they devised and deployed in the DAL was for Frampton, self-reflexive as always, an occasion for him to reflect on the omnidirectional sense of history to which this tool gave rise. He did this in films such as *Gloria,* which was the virtual or theoretical side of his project, and he did it in studio spaces arranged for their making, which was the concrete or practical complement.

NOTES

1. See Guilbaut, *How New York Stole the Idea of Modern Art.*

2. In his essay "For a Metahistory of Film" Frampton suggests that the "class of verbal artifacts" used for recording history did not "substitute" for it but instead "made up an open set of rational fictions within that world." These "fictions were what we may call *metahistories* of event," which "remain events in themselves" (131, italics in original). This essay appeared in *Artforum* originally and has been reprinted in *On the Camera Arts and Consecutive Matters.*

3. Wolfe, *The Painted Word,* 13–23.

4. Burns, *Inventing the Modern Artist,* 251, 273.

5. Robinson, "Before Attitudes Became Forms—New Realisms, 1957–1962," 36–37.

6. Jones, *Machine in the Studio,* 198.

7. Cohen et al., "Industry and the Academy," 173.

8. Kerr, *Uses of the University,* 1.

9. Frampton made this remark in an interview with Michael Snow published in *Film Culture,* no. 48 and 49 (Winter and Spring 1970): 6–12.

10. Snow, "On Hollis Frampton, 1984," 242, 248.

11. Roberta Plutzik, "O'Grady: Nonstop Work in Serious Films," *Buffalo Courier-Express,* Sunday, March 18, 1973, 4.

12. Sei, "Malcolm X, McLuhan, Media Study," 137.

13. Plutzik, "O'Grady: Nonstop Work in Serious Films," 4.

14. Much of the background on SUNY Buffalo was gathered in interviews that I conducted with Gerald O'Grady on July 7, 2017; with Bob Coggeshall on July 5, 2017; and with Bob Franki on November 20, 2017.

15. *Buffalo Courier-Express,* Sunday, Sept. 28, 1975.

16. Levine Packer, *This Life of Sounds,* 85.

17. Hollis Frampton, "Proposal for Bachelor of Arts in Media Study," *Department of Media Study: Records, 1959–2009,* Box 1, Folder 1, University Archives, SUNY Buffalo.

18. "Media Study History," *Department of Media Study: Records, 1959–2009,* Box 8, Folder 1.

19. O'Grady, "Sound-Track for a Tele-vision," 83.

20. Hollis Frampton to Gerald O'Grady, memo, July 30, 1973, *Department of Media Study: Records, 1959–2009,* Box 1, Folder 1.

21. Frampton, "Letter to Donald Richie," 160–61.

22. Sitney, *Visionary Film,* 400–401.

23. See Kant, *Conflict of the Faculties.*

24. Hollis Frampton to Gerry O'Grady, memo, Dec. 27, 1977, www.vasulka.org/archive/Artists2/Frampton,Hollis/corresp.pdf.

25. Beginning in 1971, Frampton published essays regularly, most often in *Artforum,* including "For a Metahistory of Film," "Eadweard Muybridge: Fragments of a Tesseract," "The Withering Away of the State of the Art," and others.

26. Frampton, "Proposal: Hardware and Software," 269.

27. Frampton, 269.

28. Frampton, "Proposal to the Media Panel at the NEA," *Department of Media Study: Records, 1959–2009,* Box 45, Folder 5.

29. Woody Vasulka has gathered his 1979 NEH grant proposal and the ensuing correspondence on his online archive: www.vasulka.org/archive/Vasulkas1/Grants/NEH/general.pdf.

30. For Hollis Frampton's self-description, but more generally for his vita and those of his colleagues, see Frampton, "VITA" and Frampton, "Hollis Frampton in His Own Words."

31. O'Grady's letter and Leavitt's letters are gathered in the document cited in note 29 above.

32. See Jones, *Eyesight Alone*.

33. Uhrich, "Pressed into the Service of Cinema," 20–21.

34. Frampton, "For a Metahistory of Film," 136.

35. Alpers, *The Vexations of Art*, 44, 40, 39.

36. Frampton, "For a Metahistory of Film," 136, 133; Frampton, "The Invention without a Future," 178.

37. Fischer, "Frampton and the Magellan Metaphor," 58–63.

38. Frampton, "For a Metahistory of Film," 134.

39. Michael Zryd suggests that one of the two films is likely Murphy's Wake (Am & B, 1903), but the other has not been positively identified. See Zryd, "History and Ambivalence in Hollis Frampton's Magellan," *October* 109 (Summer, 2004): 119–42.

40. Frampton, 138.

41. Hollis Frampton, interview by Esther Harriot, SUNY Buffalo, 1978.

PART FOUR

Studio Futures

Made-for-Broadcast Cities

Lynn Spigel

When searching through the papers of former ABC president Leonard Goldenson, I came across artworks he painted in 1977 toward the end of his thirty-five-year reign at the broadcast network. Like other executives and government officials who rose to prominence at midcentury, Goldenson was a "weekend painter" whose artistic aspirations resulted in a range of subjects and styles, including the one that interests me here: a painting he called *Communications Center* (fig. 10.1). Goldenson presents a fantasyscape of the then three dominant network headquarters lined up next to each other on Manhattan's Avenue of the Americas. Rendered in blue, white, and yellow, with the CBS, ABC, and NBC corporate logos drawn whimsically on each, the skyscrapers rise in the foreground as the Empire State Building, Chrysler Building, and the (then-still-standing) Twin Towers (all homes for the technical infrastructure that carried the city's broadcast signals) fade on the horizon. As Goldenson explained, even while he took some poetic liberties (NBC was actually housed in Rockefeller Center's RCA Building, and CBS and ABC were not directly next to each other on the street), he did so in order to "convey the unity of the three buildings as the TV and Radio Communications Centers of America."[1] Envisioning the city block as a communications grid for the nation, Goldenson's skyscrapers demonstrate something of the mind-set of the old network chiefs, who, together with visionary architects, engineers, and urban planners, mapped out a new media landscape over the course of the twentieth century.

This essay explores broadcast "cities," a conceptual framework and a generic term that architects and industry executives often used to describe a range of built and unbuilt plans for studios devoted to radio and television production. Much more than a single building, broadcast cities were designed as "cities within cities,"

FIGURE 10.1. *Communications Center*, Leonard H. Goldenson, 1977. Courtesy of Loreen (Goldenson) Arbus and USC Cinematic Arts Library and Archives.

self-sustained environments capable of producing entertainment and information in unprecedented volumes and speeds. "Radio City" is, of course, the name of NBC's first major radio studio, opened in 1933 in New York's Rockefeller Center. The city concept carried through to television with, for example, CBS Television City and NBC Color City, both of which opened in the Los Angeles area in the 1950s. Moreover, as a conceptual framework, the broadcast "city" expanded beyond large metropolitan areas to studios across the country, which were housed in broadcast stations. Even if they did not always call themselves radio or TV "cities," local radio and TV stations often presented themselves in the image of the city, as the ultimate in modern design.

Broadcasters and networks used the city concept to mark their value as urbane, civic, and, above all, *modern* environments for addressing and gathering publics through the wires. Mayors and governors hailed broadcast studios as boons for civic pride, but studios were also commercial meccas for tourism; and, most important, on the airwaves they served as showrooms for sponsors' products. Here I trace the city concept back to US radio studios in the 1930s and 1940s, and I focus on several speculative and realized designs for television cities in the mid-twentieth-century period—especially, given its prominence, CBS Television City. In all their manifestations broadcast studios were distinctly modern forms of media architecture that created material spaces for the flow of commerce and communication while offering audiences new mental maps through which to navigate an increasingly mediatized nation.

GENEALOGY

To be sure, the "city" concept is not the invention of the broadcast industry. It dates back to modern industrial environments and utopian dreams for the future. The broadcast city is contemporaneous with Le Corbusier's plans for an urban utopia in *Towards a New Architecture* (first published in French as *Vers une architecture* in 1923) and *The City of To-morrow and Its Planning* (1929).[2] Le Corbusier imagined machinelike, efficient, yet decongested noise-free cities with glass and steel skyscrapers, centralized transport (with "aero-taxis"), and large parks that promoted healthy lifestyles. In *City of To-morrow* Le Corbusier calls the skyscraper the "city's brains, the brains for the whole nation," and communication devices including radio are key to the skyscraper's intelligent operation. "Everything is concentrated in them: apparatus for abolishing time and space, telephones, cables and wireless."[3] Le Corbusier's unrealized plans for a "Radiant City" (first published in 1933) were modeled on similar goals of machinelike efficiency with business and residential towers, an underground transport system, and abundant green space and sunlight; moreover, many of the street's functions were internalized in buildings. All of this would ideally contribute to the creation of a better society.[4] The broadcast city also developed in the context of more traditional designs for "radial" cities, which by the twentieth century were applied to the modern metropolis. (For example, the 1909 Burnham Plan in Chicago, first outlined in 1903, featured streets designed as "arteries" that radiate from the central civic center core.) The Latin root word *radiare*—"to beam, to shine"—speaks to the enlightenment project at the heart of the city of tomorrow. Radio, of course, is not far from this etymological and cultural equation. As Shannon Mattern claims in her work on cities and sound, "The 'spatial ontology' of radio is radiant, spherical, and lends itself to graphic representation in the form of expanding ripples."[5]

The first major broadcast city, NBC Radio City studios in Rockefeller Center, was modeled on the city-of-tomorrow concept. In early planning stages Rockefeller Center was named "Rockefeller City," in line with the more general language of utopian cities on which it was based.[6] Its chief architect, Raymond Hood, was in dialogue with visionary architects and city planners.[7] He had read Le Corbusier's publications and Hugh Ferriss's visions of futuristic cities in *The Metropolis of Tomorrow* (1929), and he formulated his own dreams for the ideal city while working on skyscrapers in Chicago and New York.[8] Hood was also a veteran in the field of radio architecture. His firm, Hood, Godley and Foulix, designed the first NBC radio studios that opened in 1928, just blocks away from what would become the more advanced studios in NBC Radio City.[9] In 1931 Hood drafted visionary schemes for a "City under a Single Roof," depicting vast complexes where industries "united into interdependent developments with clubs, hotels, stores, apartments and even theaters."[10] Hood's concept materialized in a slightly different form in 1931 with the opening of Rockefeller Center, the largest urban complex of its time. As it grew over the course of the 1930s, Rockefeller Center housed radio studios, theaters (including the spectacular Radio City Music Hall), international buildings, restaurants, and office buildings. A subway led into the complex; on top, the roof garden afforded skyline views. Comparing the latter to Le Corbusier's Radiant City, Rem Koolhaas claims Rockefeller Center represents "'the maximum of congestion' combined with the 'maximum of light and space.'"[11]

The conundrum that Koolhaas suggests was embedded in broader ironies of the utopian city. As Fredric Jameson notes of utopian programs more generally, they are always already failures. The city of tomorrow belied the paradox of a social vision in which forms of collective association are nevertheless forged through separation, what Jameson calls "utopian enclaves." Intended to produce collectives, utopias wall out social difference and dissenting voices to achieve group consensus.[12] As should be obvious, the utopian cities were primarily the visions of white men in powerful situations. It is worth pausing to remind readers that *utopia* is a loaded word. The broadcast cities of the twentieth century were financed by male industrialists—network chiefs—who reigned over and hoped to control a new media landscape. Hood's Rockefeller Center was the first megacity complex to house these industrialists' dreams.

In 1930 NBC and its parent company, RCA, became Rockefeller Center's first investors and prospective tenants. When it opened in 1933, NBC Radio City was a modern marvel, what historian Emily Thompson describes as an immense planned environment for the production of the modern soundscape.[13] Occupying eleven floors and one hundred thousand square feet of Hood's art deco RCA building, the complex featured audition rooms, performer lounges, engineering stations, and twenty-seven studios of different sizes, including the "largest auditorium studio . . . in the world," seating 250 audience members and a stage big enough to accommodate a one-hundred-piece orchestra.[14] Designed for optimal sound, the studios had the latest innovations in noise-abating "floating construction in which the walls, ceilings, and floors were mechanically isolated from the surrounding structure," as well as quiet air-conditioning systems (that cooled heat generated by machines).[15] Art and interior design paid tribute to the new medium. An abstract rendering of radio, Margaret-Bourke White's photomural adorned the grand circular lobby. Entrances to the RCA building welcomed visitors with, for example, Gaston Lachaise's sculptural relief that presented modern civilization with radio waves depicting the "Conquest of Space."[16] Promoting the public's curiosity about the new medium, the NBC Studio Tour (which began in 1933) gave visitors a behind-the-scenes look at the technical and architectural marvels inside.[17] Just three years later, in 1936, NBC honored "Mr. and Mrs. Million"—the millionth couple to purchase tickets for the tour.[18]

But NBC Radio City was not designed just for tourists and studio audiences; it was also fashioned with home audiences in mind. As Thompson explains, the galleries were "wired for sound, so what the members of the audience heard there was not very different from what they heard at home; an electroacoustic reproduction of the live performance that they observed through a glass curtain. When 'audience noises' were desired 'to give the production a stamp of authenticity,' the [studio's] glass curtains were raised so that microphones in the studios could pick up the laughter and applause."[19] Although Thompson does not focus on this, for the home audience, this "stamp of authenticity" was central to the aesthetics of radio as a cultural form. The studio setup elicited what Raymond Williams calls "mobile privatization"—broadcasting's affordance of connection with, and imaginary transport to, an urban center for people listening or watching in the privacy of their homes.[20] Broadcasters' emphasis on live transmission and on "liveness" (as an aesthetic appeal) ideally turned mobile privatization into a listener and (with television) a spectator experience by giving home audiences a sense of being on the scene of presentation.[21] In this respect Radio City, and its "authentic" soundscape, was designed to negotiate the paradox of telepresence—the vexing relationship of absence and presence entailed in media communication. Speaking of NBC's architectural and engineering triumph, Koolhaas argues, "NBC conceives of the entire block . . . as a single electronic arena that can transmit itself via airwaves into the home of every citizen of the world—the nerve center of an electronic community that would congregate at Rockefeller Center without actually being there. *Rockefeller Center is the first architecture that can be broadcast.*"[22]

In all aspects NBC Radio City served as a model for other studios, and telepresence continued to be a main architectural concern for the midcentury television city. In fact, NBC Radio City already anticipated television by creating conditions for future expansion in a rapidly changing industry. In the 1930s, Radio City was a home for experimental telecasts and tests for the RCA color system. In this regard the studio was a "house of the future."

As such, the broadcast studio also finds its genealogy in the utopian environments of world's fairs and exhibitions, which often featured new media technologies (including radio and TV) as part of their wonderous attractions.[23] It is no coincidence that some of the major architects of radio and television cities also designed exhibition spaces for the fairs. Hood codirected the architectural commission for Chicago's Century of Progress Exhibition and designed the "Communications Court" for its International exhibition. Swiss émigré William Lescaze designed radio studios (several for CBS) before codesigning the aviation building at the 1939–40 New York World's Fair. Industrial designer John Vassos (who was on staff at CBS and worked for RCA) designed media exhibitions at numerous venues, including the 1939–40 New York World's Fair and the 1958 Brussels World's Fair. As a young man, William Pereira (one of the chief architects of CBS Television City) helped draft the master plan for the Century of Progress Exhibition; his partner, Charles Luckman, designed the US Pavilion at the 1964–65 New York World's Fair. Sol Cornberg, who worked for NBC in the 1950s and designed speculative plans for television cities, created television viewing carrels for library use that were first displayed at the 1964–65 New York World's Fair. In the early 1950s, when NBC hired industrial designer Norman Bel Geddes to create a television studio, he was already famous for his futuristic designs, especially the General Motors "Futurama" exhibit at the 1939–40 New York World's Fair. Indeed, the world of tomorrow and the world of broadcasting were never far apart.

Some of these same architects (including Pereira, Bel Geddes, and Cornberg) also designed film sets and stage effects for motion pictures and theater. Their experience in film studios and theatrical venues speaks to the more general relationship between broadcast cities and film cities such as Universal City, which opened to visitors in 1915. As Brian Jacobson argues in his history of early film studios in both the US and European contexts, film studios were cutting-edge spaces for the invention and use of building technologies and materials, especially glass, concrete, and lighting technologies, which were also "changing the character of the modern built environment."[24] With the coming of sound, film studios joined radio studios in the development of architectural acoustics. And, like Le Corbusier's utopian cities, Hollywood studios were machinelike places, often calling themselves "plants" for efficient production. Moreover, as Jacobson demonstrates, film studios constructed "unreal cities" and "artificial worlds" (like miniatures of Paris or New York). In Los Angeles film studios helped turn Hollywood (and surrounding areas) into a destination by serving, like Universal City did, as tourist venues. As Mark Shiel argues, "film studios had utopian aspirations and an EXTRA LARGE presence in the [LA] landscape."[25]

Although broadcast studios borrowed ideas from film studios, they were fundamentally different from their movie predecessors. They had unique technological requirements for lighting, sound engineering, and staging. As with Radio City, many broadcast studios were designed with auditoriums for studio audiences and with the experience of home audiences in mind. The sheer number of programs it took to fill a daily schedule, and the fact that programs were often broadcast live, required unprecedented volumes and speed of production. Broadcast studios operated more on a transport model (of the train schedule) than on the film studio's theatrical model of distribution and exhibition. Moreover, unlike the film studio, radio and television studios sprang up in multiple places across the country, housed in local stations that dotted the US map.

MAPPING THE BROADCAST CITY

In recent years scholars have focused on material geographies and media infrastructures, detailing how media and communication technologies have influenced the design and experience of modern environments, often focusing on cities as media spaces.[26] Scholarship on the media city is less concerned with studio architecture per se, however, than with the ways in which the rise of new media—especially telephones, radio, and digital media—have helped create urban communication routes and the experience of everyday life in different parts of the world. Much of the existing scholarship on media cities focuses on major metropolitan areas. Similarly, the relatively scarce literature on broadcast studios is generally concerned with major cities; in the US the focus has been on network studios in New York and Hollywood.[27]

But, rather than just big city architecture, the broadcast studio was also a form of vernacular modernism throughout the nation. Over the course of the twentieth century the city concept permeated the entire US map. The advent of radio broadcasting was in itself a reinvention of place as geographical locations and their populations were reorganized into broadcast "markets" where citizens were increasingly addressed as consumers. Attempting to convince sponsors of the wide consumer populations within their reach, stations often advertised themselves with images of maps that displayed their signal coverage over the borders of local towns and even states.[28] In this context the architecture of broadcast stations and their studios became a major opportunity for local economies and for forging audience pride in being part of a newly mapped broadcast community. Even before NBC's Radio City, newspapers and popular magazines like *Radio in the Home* reported on the construction of radio towers and studios. Such stories may well have responded to public curiosity about the mysterious "ether" by locating the airwaves in material places and concrete architectural sites, but they also spoke to a utopian future. By the 1930s and 1940s studios around the country boasted of their cutting-edge technologies, and broadcasters frequently used the term *ultramodern* to describe their wondrous forms. For maximum coverage and to avoid interference with their signals, industrial cities like Chicago, Detroit, and Cleveland housed studios in their tallest buildings (often hotels, department stores, or office towers). The CBS network placed its first major radio studios in its newly built Madison Avenue skyscraper near the transmitter on top of the Chrysler Building.[29]

Many studios were built from the ground up or housed in converted buildings that were turned into palaces of modern design.[30] In 1933 CBS affiliate station WCAU in Philadelphia relocated from its original 1922 station to a new headquarters with seven studios (the largest of which accommodated a one-hundred-piece orchestra). The studios employed the latest technologies and materials, including sheet steel wall coverings, sound-enhancing fabric imported from Germany, and floating floors for soundproofing. Calling it the "last word in modernity," *Broadcasting* enthused about its "100-foot glass tower [that] rears above the eight stories of the building, adding to the beauty of the striking blue finish of the structure."[31] The tower gleamed with neon lights, a beacon in the night. Complementing the tower, WCAU's interiors were adorned with modern art and design (fig. 10.2). In 1934 industrial designer John Vassos (by then a regular employee on the CBS staff) filled WCAU's lobby with an abstract mural composed of swirling geometric and cylindrical shapes that indicated radio towers, skyscrapers, and technical mechanisms.[32]

While New York's Radio City and the WCAU tower represented the height of vertical modernity, other studios—from Florida to Montana to Arizona—were often low one-to-five-story buildings designed in the streamline or art deco style. They were typically white or pastels, color choices that worked in conjunction with modern air conditioning systems to keep the buildings cool. But their color palettes were also in keeping with the whiteness of architectural modernity more generally, and they especially recalled the white pavilions and monuments at world's fairs, marking their "world of tomorrow" status.[33] Meanwhile, like NBC Radio City, their architectural acoustics delivered the utmost in noise-free modern sound. Local studios used equipment and studio layouts designed by Western Electric and RCA, which consequently standardized the modern sonic environment for a broadcast nation.[34] Yet, despite architectural and technological standardization, building designs and decor varied with local iterations.

Even radio stations located in small cities promoted themselves as major urban attractions. In 1937 NBC affiliate KGNC boasted of its "ultramodern radio city" in

A Visitor Tours WCAU

By KENNETH W. STOWMAN, In Charge of Public Relations, WCAU

AS A casual passer-by walks along the busy and fashionable Chestnut Street in Philadelphia, he sees a handsome blue building on the south side between 16th and 17th Streets. This new structure stands as a symbolic monument to the radio industry and is noted for its striking beauty. The front of the new home of WCAU is trimmed with stainless steel in designs created by the architect to express impressions of radio.

After sundown the large glass tower atop the building, illuminated from within by mercury vapor lamps, casts a blue light throughout the center of the city and can be seen twenty-five miles away.

A visitor entering the portals of WCAU for the first time is greeted at the entrance with beautiful stainless steel doors and overhead are architectural designs depicting Drama, Music, Literature and Comedy.

The interior of the entrance lobby is of Italian marble with indirect lighting overhead casting a silver glow. As we await the arrival of the elevator to the studio reception room on the seventh floor, we notice a

A PERFORMANCE IN PROGRESS IN STUDIO E. ARTISTS WHO HAVE PERFORMED AMID THESE PLEASANT AND UNUSUALLY BEAUTIFUL SURROUNDINGS AGREE THAT HERE THEY FEEL INSPIRED TO PUT FORTH THEIR FINEST EFFORTS AND THAT SUITABLE ENVIRONMENT IS OF GREAT IMPORTANCE IN ENABLING THEM TO ACHIEVE THE BEST RESULTS.

STUDIO B, LOOKING TOWARD THE "DEAD END." CONSIDERING THE BRILLIANT COLORS AND THE CHROMIUM METALLIC TRIM EMPLOYED IN THE DECORATION SCHEME OF THIS STUDIO, THE ABOVE VIEW IN BLACK AND WHITE HARDLY DOES JUSTICE TO THE SUBJECT.

copper cut plate on the outer doors of the elevator. Here the architect has created a masterpiece in the figure of a man holding a WCAU microphone with radio waves emanating from the transmitting station.

As we step into the elevator we are impressed with the unusual interior decoration of the car itself and we imagine that we have been transferred into a new world of modern and artistic conception. The

FIGURE 10.2. John Vassos's *Radio Tempo* mural pictured in an article on radio station WCAU in *Broadcast News*, April 1933. Courtesy of the Hagley Museum and Library.

downtown Amarillo, Texas, a white one-story building fashioned in the streamline style with glass tiles decorating its marquee-like corner window (the high point of the plan). Interiors included "a large studio for audiences and . . . the latest acousti-cal treatment . . . western electric throughout."[35] That same year in Fort Wayne, Indiana, the WOWO-WGL station replicated the striking modern photo mural collage in the lobby of NBC Radio City with its own "modern motif" collage set off by an eggplant-colored linoleum floor with a "sixteen point star of tan and terra-cotta."[36] Opened in 1940, WMBG in Richmond, Virginia, was fashioned in the streamline style but this time with a white limestone and glass brick exterior. *Architectural Record* named WMBG one of the "most noteworthy examples of modern architectural design in the vicinity."[37]

With even grander visions, in 1937 the Crosley Broadcasting Company drew up blueprints for WLW's million-dollar building that would relocate the historic Cincinnati studio to an area just outside the city's core. As featured in a promo-tional sketch, WLW echoes the "city within a city" concept, housing the "latest in modern improvements" with twenty-eight offices, twelve studios, a theater accom-modating six hundred people, stages capable of handling shows with sixty to sev-enty performers, employee lounges, a "modern lunchroom," a vast music library, and a "radio post office"—all in a three-story building with a five-story glass-paned tower in front. As a twist on the gleaming tower of WCAU, this all-white building was to be bathed in an "ingenious system of floodlighting . . . visible all day and night for miles throughout the neighboring Ohio and Kentucky area."[38] According to the logic of this speculative design, the studio would bring the shining city on the hill to the heartland. Unfortunately for its owners, the plan did not materialize. Instead, in 1942 WLW moved into Crosley Square, a converted Elks Lodge in downtown Cincinnati. Yet, despite this downsized vision, Crosley Square was still a monument to architectural modernism. William Lescaze (known for his promi-nence in the International Style and his designs for previous CBS radio studios) was the chief architect for the Elk Lodge building conversion, overseeing the sta-tion's sound design, interior design, and principal furnishings.[39] Although not as spectacular as the floodlit building that Crosley had previously planned, Lascaze's spectacular design for the president's suite showcased radio's radiance with "lumi-nous large panels of glass block that transmitted daylight in two directions."[40]

By the mid-1930s, as Hollywood became a production center for radio program-ming, the major networks moved west, where they built their own streamlined megacomplexes. In 1935 CBS hired Bel Geddes, who drafted plans for a huge CBS entertainment center, yet another self-sufficient "city within a city" with performing and visual arts facilities, athletic fields, restaurants, and gardens. While that never materialized, in 1938 CBS hired Lescaze to build CBS Columbia Square, which he designed in the modern International Style with streamlined motifs, ribbon win-dows, and a large glass facade (fig. 10.3). When the studio opened in Hollywood on

FIGURE 10.3. Exterior view of the CBS Columbia Square building on Sunset Boulevard, Hollywood, California, 1938. © CBS via Getty Images.

April 30, 1938, CBS broadcast *A Salute to Columbia Square,* a star-studded program featuring Bob Hope, Al Jolson, and Cecile B. DeMille. Remarking on its futuristic look, Jolson joked, "Columbia Square looks like Flash Gordon's bathroom."[41]

In 1938 NBC replaced its already outgrown Melrose Avenue studios (built in 1935), with Radio City West, a streamlined building constructed by the Austin Company (a major builder of film, radio, and, later, television studios). Calling the studio a "modern plant for a modern institution," promotional materials touted its "attractive appearance," especially its thirty-foot terrace wall, its magenta "zeon" light trim, and its three-story glass-bricked lobby (the highest point on the edifice) that wrapped around the corner of Hollywood and Vine. But NBC especially emphasized the studio's "functional" layout and cutting-edge technical systems (including "complete air conditioning," "new standards of lighting," automatic switchers that provided "split-second timing," and sound-absorbing surfaces). Rather than CBS's focus on celebratory spectacle, NBC purposely opened "without premiere or fanfare" and sought instead to position the studio as the "ultimate scientific development in broadcasting facilities." (Even the pale blue paint used for the exterior "was chosen scientifically to reduce the California sun glare.")[42] Nevertheless, with live production for studio audiences, NBC Radio City West soon courted the public. By 1939 both Columbia Square and Radio City West offered studio tours to eager fans, helping to expand Hollywood's influence as a national tourist destination.

More broadly, across the country stations welcomed studio audiences, and they publicized themselves with studio tours and forms of civic engagement such as fireworks shows, parades, or exhibits at local and state fairs. Despite their media modernity, these events often spoke to regional folk customs such as WREC's "sweet potato festival" in Dresden, Tennessee.[43] In these ways the studio was more than an abstract transmission zone; it became a local place. By publicizing the broadcast studio as a community center, stations encouraged local citizens to think of themselves as faithful audiences (and consumers) in the market. Some of the place-marking publicity tactics went beyond the spectacle of architectural and technological modernity to other more blatantly erotic attractions.

BROADCAST GIRLS

On a regular basis broadcast studios promoted a sense of local place through a specifically female form: the radio and TV "girl." Often also known as "Miss Radio" or "Miss TV," these young women appeared in pinups used for station and studio publicity, and they competed in station beauty contests. Perhaps evolving out of the 1920s radio "hostesses" (the young women who welcomed visitors into early radio stations), the radio and TV girls were sites of attraction for studios. On the one hand, they were a simple exploitation tactic used to appeal to program sponsors and male employees, and they also served to promote new technological innovations. (In their famous color patent wars, RCA/NBC and CBS each promoted their systems with a "Miss Color TV.")[44] On the other hand, the broadcast girl was also a means to charm audiences and to generate local pride in the station.

In 1931, when CBS debuted its new radio studio in its Madison Avenue skyscraper (built in 1929), the network announced the occasion in newspapers by featuring a photo of Olive Shea, its "CBS Girl" and "Miss Radio of 1929."[45] As the practice evolved at local stations, radio girls spoke to the specificities of place. At radio station WHO in Des Moines, Iowa, broadcast girls decorated a 19 1/2 foot cornstalk. (The stalk had just won the National Tall Corn Sweepstakes prize in a competition with other stations in the region.) As depicted in a 1940 issue of *Broadcasting*, the cornstalk is placed next to a ladder with five young women in bathing suits straddling each rung. In this local articulation of the radio girl, the cornstalk and its bathing beauties form a farmland version of the looming radio towers located in cities like Chicago and New York.[46]

FIGURE 10.4. Miss Television finalists in *Miss Television U.S.A* (TV pilot, produced by David Wolper, 1965).

By the TV age, the conceit had become a standard practice.[47] Stations used specifically salacious titles like San Francisco's Miss K-RON (the station called her "36-24-36 WOW"), and Sally Ardrey, Miss WSPB, "Winter Cheesecake" of Sarasota, Florida. In station ads featuring TV girls (or cartoon renderings thereof), the slippage between signal "coverage" and clothing "coverage" on female bodies was a constant pun. In a 1954 promotional pinup Los Angeles's Channel 7 "KABC Girl" Maxine Marlow sits on a gigantic number "7" (studio prop), wearing a costume reminiscent of pinups in the then scandalous men's magazines—a black strapless bathing suit, with cleavage, black hose, and high heels.[48] (The station manager next to her wears a business suit.) While she was not dubbed Miss TV, Marilyn Monroe (then Norma Jeane) appeared as a pinup in a studio portrait shot at Hollywood's pioneering Don Lee Television Studios in which she posed seductively in a revealing (for the time) two-piece bathing suit.[49]

In more family-friendly versions broadcast girls were billed as attractions at fairs. The RCA Pavilion at the 1939 New York World's Fair featured several Miss TVs. At the 1950 Chicago Fair TV girls from local stations across the country competed for the Miss US Television prize (fig. 10.4). The contest was televised live on the DuMont Network.[50] Serving as host, the Grand Finals chairman periodically called attention to a map featuring station locations while judges (all men) ranked the various Miss TVs as they pranced around in swimsuits and talent competitions. (The winner, Edie Adams—Miss New York—would go on to TV fame with her husband, Ernie Kovacs.) In 1965, TV producer David Wolper resumed the practice with his unaired television pilot *Miss Television U.S.A.* The winner, Miss Orange Grove, California (a.k.a. UCLA student Pam Bennett), walked down the runway as host Byron Palmer serenaded her with a song that began: "A vision for television you are . . ."[51]

Given their ubiquity as a symbolic marker and popular attraction of the broadcast studio, radio and TV girls were as central to the mapping of broadcast cities as were the studios' technical and architectural wonders. In that sense the utopian modernity of the studio revealed itself as a "technology of gender" in which women were feminine decoration, functioning much as the murals and sculptures did in the otherwise clean empty soundproof spaces of modern studio design. Moreover, even in their more family-friendly versions broadcast girls evoked the red-light district of the modern metropolis. Just like the burlesque queen, the broadcast girl was modernism's sideshow—but one that nevertheless endured at broadcast studios for at least five decades.

THE IMAGE OF THE CITY: TELELOCATION AND VIRTUAL TRANSPORT

While radio and TV girls recalled the erotic sideshows of city life, just as typically, stations promoted themselves as urban centers, hoping to convince sponsors of the densely populated consumer markets in their locations. Ads in *Broadcasting* often featured images of skyscrapers, crowds, and busy streets. A perfect example is a 1941 ad for KNOX radio in St. Louis. Bragging of the station's strong signal, the copy tells prospective sponsors that KNOX covers the entire sweep of the "River Valley Market" (which comprised not only downtown St. Louis but also outlying suburbs and farms). Yet, despite this heterogeneous landscape, the ad presents the station and its studio as a thriving vertical urban center with a sketch of modern skyscrapers dotting the banks of the Missouri River. All sorts of modern transport—spiraling highways, a freight train, a cargo boat, trucks, and cars—adorn the city, picturing it as a space of mobile modernity. But the most striking visual detail in the ad is a huge hand that literally covers the image of the city, which is presented in Lilliputian proportions from an aerial perspective. With its larger scale, the hand appears to manipulate the city as one might arrange a dollhouse miniature. In this way the image evokes the sponsor's ability to capture what the ad calls a "money maker market."[52]

Images of cars, trucks, and trains—as well as aerial (helicopter) views of cities—appear over and over again in station and studio ads. As in Le Corbusier's city of tomorrow, traffic circulation was a key aspect of the modern broadcast city and its image. Studios were often planned according to preexisting transport routes and included ample parking and easy access from streets so that people and vehicles (such as delivery trucks or mobile radio and TV units) could move fluidly inside and outside the buildings. More generally, the station publicity reminds us that "telecommunications has historically been interrelated with transportation," and often their routes were overlaid on each other.[53] The intertwined fates of media networks and transport routes is signaled by the very language used to name them. The word *station*, for instance, applies equally to transportation systems (bus stations, train stations) and to broadcast stations. For much of the early part of the twentieth century, the *Statistical Abstract of the United States* measured communication and transportation under one heading, suggesting the close association of the two in practices of governmentality.[54]

In the postwar period the urban iconography of skyscrapers and mobile transport remained central to TV stations. An ad for CBS affiliate WMAR in Baltimore presents an aerial view of the downtown city core, telling prospective sponsors to "look at the very center of the picture. See the tall buildings dominating this prosperous area? . . . See the ocean-going ships docked right in the downtown area? . . . See the railroad terminals? . . . Look very closely and maybe you can see just a few of the television aerials leading to the more than 40,000 homes in the Baltimore area that now have television receivers."[55] With its triple focus on skyscrapers, family houses, and transportation, this ad indicates how the midcentury TV city stretched beyond the urban landscape per se into the outlying areas marked by suburban developments. Ads for television studios evoked an increased emphasis on mobile privatization that was key to the postwar commuter suburb, as well as to television's appeal.

In a related way broadcast stations engaged local audiences by offering an experience of imaginary transport to the broadcast studio, providing the sense of telepresence so important to radio from the start. On the airwaves, studios took on the qualities of *lived* places through discursive and representational cues. The space of the studio has always made itself present, not only via the "noise" of the studio audience but also through the voice of the station announcer. During much of the broadcast era (roughly, through the 1980s), when programming was not an around-the-clock affair, the local station greeted viewers in the morning and put them to bed at night with sign-ons and sign-offs. (For example, "On behalf of the management and staff at KTUL TV in Tulsa, Oklahoma, we wish you a very pleasant night and good morning.") Such salutations typically stated the address of the broadcast station, and on TV this was usually followed by the station's local iteration of the national anthem (often a waving flag intercut with sites of the local city or landscape).[56] In this sense the studio became what Benedict Anderson (referring to newspapers) calls an "imagined community" that joined people together through a common language of nation, location, and place.[57]

URBAN DILEMMAS AND TV STUDIO SPECULATORS

Ironically, given the history of radio cities, it was the city—and specifically the vertical industrial city—that created the major hurdle for television executives. In the earliest years of commercial TV, television was mostly an urban affair. In 1948 the FCC put a freeze on station allocation, which lasted until 1952. While intended to provide time to resolve technical vexations and patent disputes, the "freeze" also had the effect of limiting local station and studio construction. This meant that television was confined to preexisting outlets, many of which were CBS and NBC affiliates in major urban areas on the East Coast and in Chicago, Los Angeles, and a smattering of locations in between. So, too, in the late 1940s and early 1950s the production of live network prime-time dramas and variety shows usually took place in New York theaters, whose stages were too small for the vast amount of camera technology, sets, lighting, boom mikes, and other necessities of television production.[58] Television producers, performers, and industry executives complained about the theaters' effect on the development of TV art, especially the static feel of programs resulting from restrictions on camera mobility, set design, blocking, and performer movements on the small stages. As *New York Times* television critic Jack Gould put it, television producers were "working in a closet."[59] Network executives also decried the exorbitant rental and subleasing costs incurred by theater owners. To solve the space shortage, ABC, CBS, NBC, and the short-lived DuMont network began to acquire (via ownership or lease arrangements) theaters, concert halls, hotel ballrooms, skating rinks, and even a Coca-Cola bottling plant. In Chicago, which was also a vibrant production center for early television, NBC affiliate station WNBQ converted its radio studio, located in the expansive space of the Merchandising Mart, to accommodate TV production.[60] In New York CBS converted the vast space above a waiting room in Grand Central Station, located across the street from its transmitter in the Chrysler Building. Despite such solutions, a dedicated television studio complex seemed a much better choice.

As early as 1948, the networks and broadcast stations began to contemplate plans for expansion, and designers drew up speculative prototypes they hoped would be adopted as industry standards. In 1951 NBC hired Bel Geddes, who created a series of models, the first of which he called "Atlantis." As Joshua Gleich describes in detail, the Atlantis studio took the form of a Manhattan skyscraper (TV's answer to NBC Radio City), equipped with "the 14 largest stages in America" and a wondrous system of overhead mobile grids "that moved sets and lighting up and down the multiple stories of the building" to the shooting stages. While Atlantis was a spectacular display of designer showmanship, Bel Geddes nevertheless called it a "television factory" that promised to produce the maximum "number of shows to sell to advertisers" and to cut labor costs through mechanization. Atlantis also remedied the static feel of television programs by eliminating the proscenium altogether, minimizing the distance between the spectator and the performer and drawing "both the live and home audiences closer to the program."[61] While this had the potential to enhance the industry's much desired sense of liveness and telepresence, for a variety of reasons (including the sheer complexity of the mechanical devices) NBC eventually deemed the plan imprudent.

About the same time that Bel Geddes first imagined Atlantis, NBC's Sol Cornberg created his own designs. Departing from the Manhattan skyscraper model altogether, Cornberg produced sketches that were published in a fourteen-page article titled "Television City" in a 1951 issue of the design journal *Interiors*. Cornberg's plan was one of the earliest television cities on record and the first (as far as I know) to garner intense interest from the design community.[62] Cornberg was the multimedia renaissance man of the moment. An influential theater stage designer, by 1951 he had joined the staff at NBC, where he created sets for the network's innovative schedule of live programs, *Tonight, Today* (with its glass observation window looking out on Manhattan), and *Home,* a women's program whose rotating circular set—which NBC called a "machine for selling"—showcased the latest consumer products.[63] By 1955, Cornberg was the director of studio and plant planning at NBC.

Although designed independently of the network, Cornberg's television city was a grand vision for the industry. It featured "five buildings in one": a central circular tower with four blocks situated around the core. As *Interiors* described it, the tower "command[s] a scenic field that broadens as it radiates outward." In other words, this television city was designed on the model of a radial city for efficient circulation of the vast number of things, people, and "complicated activities required to televise a day's programs."[64] The studio features business offices, craft shops, storage facilities, dressing rooms, business offices, screening rooms for sponsors, underground parking, and employee amenities, including a cafeteria, a library, a dispensary, a rooftop sun deck, and a recreation area. It also contains vast stage spaces for camera mobility and plans for TV's unprecedented growth (fig. 10.5).

Media specificity is central to the design. Cornberg explains: "Technical ability in the transmission and reception of television has far outstripped its literary, histrionic, and artistic development. Vital to the hastening rapport between the technical and artistic facets of the medium is a clear understanding of what television is not. It is not Living Theater! It is not Cinema! It is not Radio! *IT IS TELEVISION!*" He continues: "A prerequisite . . . toward a genuine television form is . . . television plant design and production approaches, divorcing the industry from Lilliputian ideals and work habits."[65] By way of illustration, Cornberg presents graphic comparisons that superimpose designs for a TV studio over those for a living theater, a radio studio, and a film studio. The blueprints collectively demonstrate the need for expansive stage spaces and unique seating arrangements.

Cornberg especially focused on audience experience and spectator psychology. In each graphic he presents a "schematic" of a human head, and he calculates the "eye, ear, and brain activity of audience members as they participate in each medium."[66] While he sites no actual scientific principles, the important point for Cornberg is the creation of a new media architecture that will produce an ideal spectator experience. Television, he suggests, must "compensate" for the losses of previous media. The television "medium as it now functions would deprive the audience of all the opportunities for satisfactory participation which the older media afforded: mental: via suggestion and imagination [as in radio]; physical—

the studio floor . . . . .

FIGURE 10.5. Sketch of the expansive stage space for a prototype "Television City," Sol Cornberg, 1951.

which going out to the theatre or motion picture afforded; not to mention the exciting proximity to mass emotional contagion."[67] In other words, like the radio cities before it, Cornberg's television city is a place designed to negotiate the paradox of presence and absence through an architecture of telepresence—this time with TV in mind.

Even if Cornberg's television city remained speculative, many of its features continued to inform television studios that began to materialize in the early 1950s, especially after the lifting of the FCC freeze. As NBC art director Robert J. Wade observed in 1953, "Vast efficiently articulated, spacious television cities for New York, Hollywood and possibly other production centers are no longer mere dreams of the future—architects and engineers are beginning to sharpen their pencils in earnest."[68] In that same year *Progressive Architecture* ran a special issue on some of the first television studios in the country. The editors' analysis resulted in general principles of design. Primary among these were "sufficient space," "flexibility and expansion" to serve future growth, and the "need for speed and split-second timing in production." The editors also noted that "placing the television station in the right location is *all-important* and critical."[69] CBS Television City was the first, and most coveted, example featured in the issue.

CBS TELEVISION CITY: THE VIDEO TEMPLE OF HOLLYWOOD

Confronted by the shortage and cost of studio space, and lured by the prospects of radio and film talent, CBS, NBC, and the then fledging ABC network moved from the vertical downtowns of New York and Chicago to the horizontal sprawl of Hollywood locales. By far, as the *New York Times* reported, CBS was the most "spectacular" of the "the video temples of Hollywood," a model of "revolutionary design."[70] At midcentury the studio was *the* TV city, synonymous with the CBS brand.[71]

CBS Television City was an extension of the company's focus on defining itself as the "Tiffany" network—a quality brand achieved in large part through modern graphic and architectural design.[72] For the Los Angeles project CBS chairman William S. Paley and network president Frank Stanton employed the firm of William Pereira and Charles Luckman, architects who created much of the midcentury Southern California environment, including iconic structures such as the original Disneyland Hotel (1955) and the Los Angeles theme building at LAX (1960).[73] Fashioned in the International Style, with clean simple lines and the requisite concrete and steel "floating" construction, Television City occupied twenty-five acres in LA's Fairfax District. Construction began on December 29, 1950, and moved at a remarkably rapid pace. When it opened in November of 1952, the facility contained four studios (the largest to date, and two created for live production), as well as business offices, film storage facilities, screening rooms, a master control area, rehearsal and dressing rooms, craft shops, employee lounges, and related amenities. The architects spoke often of the building's "complete flexibility" with "demountable walls and movable lighting and wiring grids," which allowed for malleability in production areas and adaptability for television's future expansion (fig. 10.6a).[74]

The building promoted the Tiffany label through design elements. Like TV at the time, Television City is mostly black and white. The name "Television City" appears black-on-white on one edifice and white-on-black on another, and the two edifices meet at a sharp corner so that the overall effect is high contrast and sharp focus (two of the most desirable qualities in TV reception). A canopied ramp with a marquee exclaiming "CBS Television City" (in clean Didot Bodoni typeface) led into the building. The CBS eye figures prominently both outside and in. The lobby alone featured a wall of CBS eyes (thirty-six thousand eye tiles) that could be seen through the building's most spectacular feature—a demountable curtain wall composed of more than twelve thousand sheets of glass (one of the largest glass installations of its time) on the facade of the four-story service build-ing. The glass glowed by night like a television screen to broadcast the company image.[75] Publicity photos of Television City, most of which were taken by architec-tural photographer Ezra Stoller, emphasize all of its televisual features. Both in its depiction in media publicity and in relation to its material status as media, Televi-sion City is the perfect example of Beatriz Colomina's famous claim: "Modern architecture is all about the mass-media image."[76]

Even before the studio opened, CBS promoted Television City with a two-ton interactive model known as "the monster" that toured the nation via department stores (fig. 10.6b).[77] The ribbon-cutting ceremonies on November 15, 1952, featured network executives and stars (including CBS's top draw, Lucille Ball), Mayor Fletcher Bowran, religious leaders, and the "Spirit of Television," a TV girl don-ning a tin-foil headdress shaped as an antenna. Declaring it "Television City Day," Mayor Bowran enthused about the studio's boon to tourism and the local econ-omy. On the same day, CBS televised a network special, *Stars in the Eye*, which not only featured CBS celebrities but also displayed the vast stages, technical wonders, camera mobility, and (for the time) rapid scene transitions that the studio afforded. One year later, on November 15, 1953, CBS newsman Edward R. Murrow hosted *Inside Television City*, a TV special that gave home audiences a tour of the studio's main attractions.[78] The building had become a CBS star in its own right.

Studio interiors had expansive stages meant to solve the "working in a closet" dilemma. Pereira and Luckman used what they called a "sandwich-loaf" principle: four large rectangular studios (two of them for live productions) divided by serv-ice doors. The live studios were designed for televisuality, configured to accom-modate the maximum number of seats (350) without disturbing the performance in front of the cameras. The audience was "placed between the center camera

FIGURE 10.6a (above). CBS Television City by night, 1953. © CBS via Getty Images.

FIGURE 10.6b (below). Actress Betty Luster pushing a toy truck on the parking lot of CBS Television City architectural model, 1952. The curtain wall facade is also featured. © CBS via Getty Images.

range and the stage floor," and the audience section began at a lower level than the stage, rising halfway back in the auditorium to the stage level. Pereira and Luckman proposed that "with the camera platforms in the midst and on the sides of the audience, the spectators will feel that they are actually a part of the production that is taking place."[79] From the point of view of CBS executives, that feeling of participatory spectatorship would ideally translate to the small screen, giving home audiences the sense of "liveness" and "being there" that the network considered the optimal television experience (and the one that differentiated CBS's TV products from those of film studios). Like NBC Radio City, but now through a careful coordination of cameras, spaces, and sight lines, Television City was (to borrow Koolhaas's phrase) an architecture that could be broadcast.

Pereira and Luckman also considered television's temporal demands. While Paley and Stanton often called Television City a "plant" designed for efficient production, the building also had to address televisual (rather than just architectural) time. Television City's vast stages allowed for swift transitions between scenes. Wide hallways afforded rapid transit of sets, props, costumes, and talent. "This emphasis on split-second timing," said the architects, "has not been a major consideration in architectural planning for any other medium [but] becomes mandatory in television, where the volume of production surpasses anything [yet] achieved, and where production costs can become uneconomic unless the most optimum conditions for efficient operations are provided."[80] State-of-the-art technologies like the automated Izenour Lighting Board (originally designed for theaters by Yale drama professor George C. Izenour) memorized and delivered technical cues on demand, leading *Variety* to dub the plant "the ultimate in push button entertainment."[81] The building was a material manifestation of what Paul Virilio calls telecommunication's collapse of time and space into "speed."[82]

Outside the complex, the aesthetics of speed, mobility, transport, and, especially, automobility were communicated through landscape design. Set back on the intersection of Beverly Boulevard and Fairfax Avenue (two main traffic arteries), Television City was meant to be witnessed and accessed not by pedestrians (as with NBC's New York Radio City) but by drivers. A vast parking lot constructed of twenty-six thousand yards of asphalt wrapped around the building and secured it from the street.[83] CBS publicity photos and the two-ton model showcased the parking lot as if the huge expanse of cars was more impressive than the building itself. Murrow's televised tour began with a zoom out from the building to the parking lot, followed by a pan depicting cars driving through the lot. He observed, "This building has enough concrete in it to build twenty-eight miles of a four-lane highway." The imagery of modern transport in station advertising had become an architectural ideal. CBS Television City helped to usher in a new national imaginary in which Los Angeles, the car, and speed became the quintessential alternative midcentury modernity to the dense urban metropolises of the first half of the twentieth century. Moreover, CBS Television City served to make LA and its mid-century autotopia a national state of mind. Central to the studio style was the announcer's voice introducing programs with the tagline, "Live from CBS Television City in Hollywood." (The actual Fairfax District location would not have had the same ring!)

The opening of CBS Television City coincided with the construction of NBC Color City, and, not surprisingly, the tale of these two TV cities is one of dramatic conflict. In a desperate push to catch up with CBS, NBC completed partial construction of the studio on a forty-eight-acre lot in Burbank. "To cope with the quick deadline" (imposed by the race with CBS), "the structural designers [used] . . . pre-cast concrete columns and wall panels . . . hoisted in place in three weeks' time." The wall panels were punctuated by simple decorative "scorings" impressed in the concrete.[84] Although a modern building, it never aspired to Television City's spectacular vision. Instead, as with Radio City West, Color City was built by the Austin Company, which emphasized functionality and the research and design agenda of NBC and RCA. As the name suggests, NBC Color City served RCA and NBC's goal to own the future of color TV. In 1955, a little more than a year after RCA emerged the victor in the color patent wars with CBS, Color City was complete. As Susan Murray explains, despite its nondescript look, the facility was a high-tech mecca with "three times the amount of lighting . . . required" for black and white studios. Designed (like the CBS facility) with a mix of film and live studios, Color City had a "fifteen-by-twenty-foot large screen RCA color projector" that allowed the studio audience to experience color TV onscreen.[85] Although with diverging agendas, both NBC Color City and CBS Television City materialized in relation to early network business goals and visions of what television might be. But, as it turned out, the future did not go exactly as planned.

BROADCAST CITIES IN SLOW DECLINE

By the early 1960s, the great broadcast cities were already in decline. The live production model at the core of the CBS complex was petering out. Increasingly, telefilm and videotape production spread across the LA area, and CBS moved much of its production to Burbank. It seems *Architectural Forum* was right when it claimed in 1953 that "the most striking feature of the [CBS] building is its impermanence."[86]

Rather than a sudden death, the demise of the broadcast city was a slow and uneven decline. Even while their use value for the television industry was more limited than originally imagined, the CBS and NBC studios continued to be a viable network model, and both buildings expanded. With the lifting of the FCC freeze, broadcast studios with live facilities materialized around the country, several designed by Pereira and Luckman before they parted ways.[87] Built by other architects, many fashioned themselves on the model of the television city (although they typically called themselves "centers"), and seeking space, they moved to suburban locales. One of the earliest to do so was CBS affiliate WCAU, which left its gleaming tower of 1933 for a ten-acre site in the Philadelphia suburbs. Praised in the architectural trades, the new WCAU Television and Radio Center (built by the Austin Company) had a curtain wall facade, smaller than but similar to the one featured at CBS Television City. The glass wall facade became a marker of midcentury broadcast modernity in numerous stations around the nation.

Speculative designs for megacomplexes also persisted. After Atlantis, Bel Geddes envisioned two more TV studios for NBC, both of which emphasized live production with studio audiences. The "Pilot Studio" (1952–55) and "Horizontal Studio" (1956–57) were spectacular science fiction–like spaces in line with Bel Geddes's "Futurama" sensibilities.[88] In 1955 Cornberg followed up his 1951 Television City with his own sci-fi "Space-Control" studio, which was illustrated in a full color futuristic design on the cover of RCA's inhouse journal *Broadcast News*. "The ultimate in automation," the studio had "remote control floors, walls, and scenery flying equipment for operating purposes." The pièce de résistance was its "one-tenth scale model of the Space-Control production areas" that allowed technicians to calculate programs before they were shot. The calculations and output could "be recorded on tape or electronic calculator for re-use at any future date."[89] The Space-Control Studio was a computational space for a utopian space-age future.

Even in 1985, the television city was still a viable utopian concept, albeit in the more neoliberal corporate form of late twentieth-century urbanism. Most noteworthy today for its famous visionary, then real estate magnate Donald Trump, "Trump Television City" was a mixed-use complex to be located on seventy-six acres of redeveloped land from the old Penn Central rail yards. According to a recent story in *Politico*, Trump "intended to build nearly 8,000 apartments and condominiums . . . almost 10,000 parking spots, some 3.6 million square feet of television and movie studio space, and some 2 million square feet of 'prestigious' stores." There would be "no fewer than six 76-story towers, and looming atop it all, one unprecedented skyscraper twice that height" that, Trump claimed, "would be the world's tallest building. . . . And he was going to live at the top."[90] Things, of course, turned out differently both for Trump and for the future of the broadcast city.

DEMOLITION

Today, in an era marked by digital transformations, the broadcast city exists in vestigial forms. NBC's New York Radio City is revamped as the NBC Studios, and the RCA Building is now the Comcast Building. Many of the old local stations still dot the map, with studios converted for digital systems. The broadcast city concept informs London's recent plans for a mixed-use residential and television complex in its White City district (which exists in the context of London's own separate history as a broadcast city). Yet despite such recent iterations, the ultramodern twentieth-century broadcast city is no longer a central fascination. NBC Radio West was the first to go, demolished in 1964 and replaced by a bank. More recently, from 2013 to 2016 CBS Columbia Square was redeveloped into a mixed-use office, retail, and residential complex. After CBS moved its primary studio facility to Studio City in 2008, Television City was the next logical target. Under threat of destruction, the studio was rescued by preservationists. In June of 2018 the Los Angeles City Council granted the studio landmark status, ensuring that iconic portions (but not all) of the complex will remain for future generations.

It seems somehow predictable that when finishing this essay, I learned that CBS sold Television City to the real estate developer Hackman Capital Partners. When the sale was announced in December of 2018, Hackman Capital (which also recently purchased the historic Culver City studios) promised to maintain the historically protected parts of the CBS studio, as well as the Television City trademark name (minus the "CBS" brand designation). Marking the end of this grandest of television cities, the sale is the material manifestation of the waning of the three-network broadcast era over the course of the last thirty years.

Like other utopian cities of modernity, Television City has become what Koolhaas calls "Junkspace"—the detritus of the twentieth-century metropolis—which he variously describes as "authorless yet authoritarian," places of "terminal hollowness," and "a tyranny of the oblivious." Junkspace piles uses on top of uses, styles on top of styles. "Restore, rearrange, reassemble, revamp, renovate . . . rent: verbs that start with re- produce Junkspace." He laments, "Junkspace will be our tomb."[91] With his exhilarating prose and doomsday observations Koolhaas evokes the derealized branded landscapes of a Philip K. Dick novel, ending (maybe all too predictably?) with the ultimate "junky" object of dystopian tales: TV. After his voyage through all sorts of environmental disasters, Koolhaas winds up in a TV studio. "TV studio-sets," he writes (in stream of consciousness prose), are "real space edited for smooth transmission in virtual space, crucial hinge in an infernal feedback loop . . . the vastness of Junkspace extended to the edges of the Big Bang."[92] Although in less earth-shattering terms, Television City's simultaneous demolition and reuse by the authorless Hackman Capital does resonate with Koolhaas's Junkspace vision. Still, it is also the case that the old broadcast cities continue to have affective resonance as "places" in contemporary times, especially for the TV generations who will miss them.

Following CBS's sale of Television City, the internet exploded with posts nostalgically recalling Television City as its bits and pieces came falling down. One month into the demolition, blogs and news sites posted "ruin porn" (a random piece of Television City's studio marquee; some Didot Bodoni "C" "B" "S" letters on the ground). Many of the posts are maudlin—even angry—expressions of longing not just for the architecture but also for the virtual sense of place and generational bonding that the studio provided for so many years. For these bloggers and posters (most of whom appear to be boomers and Gen-Xers), it was as if Mom and Dad had sold their homes. One post presents a CBS eye with a tear streaming down.

But perhaps not all is lost. It may be that every television city that once was will rise again—if only in digital form. Attempting to monetize the CBS wreckage, Hackman Capital is leasing space—and Google is about to move in. (Amazon already leased offices in Hackman Capital's renovated Culver Studios.) Indeed, the Junkspace of the broadcast city is now an anonymous rental opportunity for digital corporations and their flexible workforces. Unlike the old broadcast cities with their gleaming towers, ultramodern styles, studio audiences, thrilling tours, and architecture of telepresence, the place of digital media remains so elusive that most people have no idea where Netflix, Amazon, or Hulu are, save for a spot to select on a remote control and digital menu. To be sure, newly planned digital cities, powered through tech giants like Google, offer extravagant utopian plans for the twenty-first century's increasingly mediatized social life. But radio and television producers don't typically mark their territories through the city concept. In this sense my tour of the broadcast city leads somewhere else altogether—to anonymous transmission zones and data storage sites, spaces that chart a future that no longer seems to need the modern city as a utopian concept at all.

NOTES

1. Leonard H. Goldenson, quoted in Slight, Exhibition Catalog, n.p.
2. Le Corbusier, *Towards a New Architecture*; Le Corbusier, *City of To-morrow*.
3. Le Corbusier, *City of To-morrow*, 187.
4. The plans for the Radiant City began in the 1920s and were published in French as *Ville Radieuse* (1933), but Le Corbusier continued with the concept. It is reprinted with some revisions in English as *The Radiant City*.
5. Mattern, *Code and Clay*, loc. 822 of 3893, Kindle.
6. Gordon, *The Urban Spectator*, 108.
7. Hood collaborated with many other designers, engineers, urban leaders, industrialists, and, most important, John D. Rockefeller Jr., who financed the complex. For histories of Rockefeller Center see Gordon, *The Urban Spectator*; Koolhaas, *Delirious New York*, 161–230; and Okrent, *Great Fortune*.
8. Ferriss, *The Metropolis of Tomorrow*. Koolhaas discusses Hood's familiarity with Le Corbusier in *Delirious New York*, 164. In that same book (109–17) he explains Ferriss's influence in the period.
9. See Hood, "National Broadcasting Studios."
10. Hood, quoted in Koolhaas, *Delirious New York*, 174.
11. Koolhaas, *Delirious New York*, 207.
12. Jameson, however, still values what he calls the "utopian impulse." See Jameson, *Archaeologies of the Future*.
13. "NBC Begins Occupation of Radio City," *Broadcasting* (Oct. 1, 1933): 20; Thompson, *The Soundscape of Modernity*, 303–4.
14. Thompson's *Soundscape of Modernity* provides a seminal history of modern sound. Its principal features include a "commodified nature," a "direct and non-reverberant quality," an "emphasis on the

signal and its freedom from noise," and the ability to transcend traditional constraints of time and space." See Thompson, 284.

15. Raymond Hood, quoted in Thompson, *The Soundscape of Modernity*, 266.

16. Thompson, 299, 301.

17. "NBC Begins Occupation of Radio City," 20. For more about the public curiosity for television during the 1930s and the role studios played in profiting from this desire to see the infrastructure beyond the televisual frame, see also chapter 3 of this volume.

18. "Mr. and Mrs. Million," *Reception Staff Review* 2, no. 4 (April 1936): 1.

19. Thompson, *The Soundscape of Modernity*, 304.

20. Williams, *Television*, 26–28.

21. For liveness and telepresence in radio and early TV see, e.g., Scannell, *Television, Radio, and Modern Life*; Boddy, *Fifties Television*; and Sconce, *Haunted Media*.

22. Koolhaas, *Delirious New York*, 200 (emphasis in original).

23. Chicago's Century of Progress Exhibition (1933–34) demonstrated a large-screen television set, and the city's radio stations maintained offices on the site from which they broadcast fairground thrills; the 1939–40 New York World's Fair, with its "World of Tomorrow," featured RCA's TV system in the company's radio tube–shaped building; and the 1964–65 New York World's Fair exhibited everything from the Bell System's picture phones to IBM's computer to RCA's color television studio that, following a similar tactic from the previous fair, allowed the public to see themselves on TV (this time in full color) and to witness the operations of the TV studio. Note, too, the dazzling electric lights at nineteenth-century fairs and world expositions is a precursor to the twentieth-century fair's media exhibitions. See Nye, *Electrifying America*, 37; and McQuire, *The Media City*, loc. 1866–90 of 3609, Kindle.

24. Jacobson, *Studios Before the System*, 15; Jacobson, "Fantastic Functionality," 52–81.

25. Shiel, *Hollywood Cinema and the Real Los Angeles*, 130 (emphasis in original).

26. See, e.g., McQuire, *The Media City*; Mattern, *Code and Clay*; Packer and Crofts, *Communication Matters*; and Parks and Starosielski, *Signal Traffic*.

27. For scholarship on broadcast studios see Ericson and Riegert, *Media Houses*; Spigel, *TV by Design*, 110–43; Gleich, "Lost Studio of Atlantis"; Doordan, "Design at CBS," 8–12; Thompson, *The Soundscape of Modernity*, 226–306; and Harwood, "Wires, Walls, and Wireless." For studios of the major networks see the wonderfully detailed collaborative blog *Eyes of a Generation: Television's Living History*, hosted by Grady School of Journalism, University of Georgia, at https://eyesofageneration.com.

28. See, e.g., ads for WEEI, Boston, MA, in *Broadcasting*, Nov. 15, 1933, 36; WHAS, Louisville, KY, in *Broadcasting*, Sept. 1, 1939, 8; and KGW, Portland, OR, in *Broadcasting*, March 15, 1951, 41.

29. For more on CBS's studios see Grady School, *Eyes of a Generation*, https://eyesofageneration.com.

30. Material shortages during WWII put much of the station construction on hiatus; however, designers still devised visionary plans.

31. "The New WACU: A New Standard in Radio," *Broadcasting*, Feb. 1, 1932, 9.

32. *RCA Broadcast News*, Feb. 1934, 21.

33. For whiteness in architecture see Wigley, *White Walls, Designer Dresses*.

34. In the 1950s RCA sold do-it-yourself TV studio planning kits for purchase by local stations. See, e.g., *Broadcasting*, April 20, 1953, 19.

35. *Broadcasting*, August 1, 1937, 45; *Broadcasting*, July 15, 1937, 14.

36. *Broadcasting*, August 1, 1937, 88.

37. *Architectural Record*, cited in *Broadcasting*, Nov. 15, 1940, 34.

38. "WLW Plans Million Dollar Structure," *Broadcasting*, Sept. 1, 1937, 12.

39. William Lescaze, "Offices and Broadcasting Studios, Station WLW, Crosley Corporation, Cincinnati, Ohio," *Pencil Points*, July 1944, 42.

40. Lescaze, 50.

41. Jolson, quoted in "Columbia Dedicates Coast Radio Center," *New York Times,* May 1, 1938, 7; see also "New Broadcast City Dedicated," *Los Angeles Times,* May 1, 1938, A8.

42. David Glickman, "Hollywood Radio City an Ideal Plant," *Broadcasting,* Nov. 1, 1938, 22–23, 58; Noel Corbett, "Preview of Hollywood's Radio City," *NBC Transmitter,* Sept. 1938, 2; "Hollywood Radio City to Have Studio Tour," *NBC Transmitter,* Nov. 1938, 1.

43. See the ad for WREC in *Broadcasting,* August 1, 1937, 29.

44. Although the networks used them for promotional tactics, the "Miss Color TV" girls served primarily as models for network color tests. Their use as test models helped establish racialized standards for color (the women were chosen for their white skin tones). See Gross, "Living Test Patterns"; Sterne and Mulvin, "Low Acuity for Blue," 118–38; and Murray, *Bright Signals,* 110–11, 117, 119.

45. C. E. Butterfield, "CBS Soon Will Broadcast Moving Pictures by Radio," *Galveston Daily News,* June 7, 1931, 6.

46. *Broadcasting,* Oct. 1, 1940, 18.

47. *Broadcasting,* Oct. 11, 1954, 41.

48. The ads are respectively in *Broadcasting,* Feb. 7, 1955, 75; *Broadcasting,* March 2, 1953, 21; and "KABC Girl," *Broadcasting,* March 1, 1954, 82.

49. Shot (c. 1948) most likely by the studio pinup artist Joseph Jasgur, this is likely a publicity photo for the studio but circulates now as a star pinup of Monroe.

50. For the program see www.youtube.com/watch?v=K28fAaae6s4.

51. The judges included stars like Agnes Moorehead and Jane Meadows.

52. *Broadcasting,* Dec. 19, 1941, 21–22.

53. Forrest Warthman, "Telecommunications and the City," *Annals of the American Academy of Political and Social Science* 412 (March 1974): 127.

54. Perhaps it's no coincidence that Don Lee Broadcasting (a major station group in LA and parts of the West Coast) began as an offshoot of Lee's California automobile dealerships. His branch dealership model for auto showrooms up and down the coast operated much like his eventual merger with CBS for his networking of radio stations. After his death the company created TV stations. For more see Fischer, "Don Lee and the Transformation of Los Angeles," 87–115.

55. *Broadcasting,* March 7, 1949, 41.

56. This announcement can be viewed along with other similar examples at www.tv-signoffs.com. Note, too, the voice of the station announcer (and in TV also "station identification" graphics) punctuated program flows throughout the daily schedule.

57. See Anderson, *Imagined Communities.*

58. For more on early theaters, as well as the use of set design to create an illusion of space and depth onscreen, see Spigel, *TV by Design,* 112–17.

59. Jack Gould, "Working in a Closet: Cramped Settings Destroy Video's Perspective," *New York Times,* August 16, 1953, X9.

60. Before New York's Radio City opened in 1933, NBC's Merchandising Mart studio billed itself as the nation's largest radio facility. The TV conversion took place in 1949.

61. Gleich, "Lost Studio of Atlantis," 5–6. Bel Geddes was actually more interested in creating a TV studio that also served as a public venue for live events that people might attend much as they went to the movies or theater.

62. Sol Cornberg, "Television City," *Interiors* 110, no. 12 (July 1951): 93–108.

63. For discussions of Cornberg's design for *Home* and his later designs for university media, see Harwood, "TV University ca. 1964," 24–31.

64. Cornberg, "Television City," 93 (these statements are in the introduction by the *Interiors* editors).

65. Cornberg, 95.

66. Cornberg, 97.

67. Cornberg, 101.

68. Wade, *Designing for TV,* 26.

69. Editors, "TV Stations," *Progressive Architecture,* Sept. 1953, 90, 86.

70. Florence Crowther, "The Video Temples of Hollywood," *New York Times,* July 27, 1952, X9.

71. For my more detailed discussion of Television City see Spigel, *TV by Design,* 110–43. The first to go west was the fledgling ABC network, which purchased the old Vitagraph lot from Warner Bros. in East Hollywood in 1948. The studio was essentially two film stages rather than an expansive television city. Later, in 1972, ABC established (now demolished) West Coast business headquarters in Century City on land that had once belonged to Twentieth Century Fox. Century City, which opened in 1962, was itself conceived as a "city within a city." For more on ABC TV studios see Bobby Ellerbee and Eyes of a Generation.com, "ABC Studios—West Coast," https://eyesofageneration.com/studios-page/abc-studios-west-coast; and Anderson, *Hollywood TV,* 138.

72. See Spigel, *TV by Design,* 68–109; and Doordan, "Design at CBS."

73. Separately, Pereira's designs dominated the look of the Southland for the next thirty years. See Steele, *William Pereira.*

74. William Pereira and Charles Luckman, "CBS Television City," *Arts & Architecture,* Jan. 1953, 21.

75. When president of Lever Brothers in the 1940s, Luckman commissioned and worked with architects for Manhattan's Lever House, a classic midcentury curtainwall skyscraper. In his analysis of the midcentury curtain wall, Reinhold Martin likens the glass facade to a television screen. See Martin, "Atrocities," 70–72.

76. Colomina, "Media as Modern Architecture," 66, 68.

77. David J. Jacobson, "I Remember a Monster," *Variety,* Nov. 12, 1952, 29.

78. An ad for the program is in the *Los Angeles Times,* Nov. 15, 1953, D12. The program is available at www.youtube.com/watch?v=Q5YdyY8IM9M.

79. William Pereira and Charles Luckman, "Take a Sandwich Loaf Idea, Add Some Imagination, and Presto—CBS TV City," *Variety,* Nov. 12, 1952, 29, 54; Pereira and Luckman, "CBS Television City," 22.

80. Pereira and Luckman, "CBS Television City," 22.

81. Carroll Caroll, "The Ultimate in Push-Button Entertainment Needs Writers Too," *Variety,* Nov. 12, 1952, 23. See also, Val Adams, "The Izenour Board: TV's Lighting Wonder," *New York Times,* Jan. 31, 1954, X13; and "TV City: A Picture Report," *Architectural Forum,* March 1953, 148.

82. Virilio, *Speed and Politics.*

83. "Some Vital Statistics on CBS Television City," *Variety,* Nov. 12, 1952, 36.

84. "NBC Studios," *Progressive Architecture,* Sept. 1953, 111. NBC purchased the land from the City of Burbank and Warner Bros., adding to the then ongoing archaeological layering of TV architecture on top of Hollywood's cinematic past.

85. Murray, *Bright Signals,* 158. As Murray notes, NBC had already opened less elaborate color studios in New York by the time the Hollywood location was completed. NBC publicity was a carbon copy of the CBS fanfare. For its opening in 1955 NBC aired the star-studded variety show *Entertainment 1955.* California governor Goodwin Knight welcomed the studio by declaring "NBC color week."

86. "TV City: A Picture Report," *Architectural Forum,* March 1953, 146–49.

87. See Spigel, *TV by Design,* 140.

88. See Gleich, "Lost Studio of Atlantis."

89. Sol Cornberg, "Space-Control Production Area," *RCA Broadcast News* 86 (Dec. 1955): 33, 44.

90. Kruse, "The Lost City of Trump."

91. Koolhaas, "Junkspace," 319, 125, 202, 273.

92. Koolhaas, 421.

11

The Nature of the Firm and the Nature of the Farm

Lucasfilm, the Campus, and the Contract

J. D. Connor

In "The Nature of the Firm" (1937) Nobel Prize–winning economist Ronald Coase asked the foundational question of why firms exist at all. "If production is regulated by price movements, [and] production could be carried on without any organization at all, well might we ask, why is there any organization?"[1] The answer is uncertainty. In an uncertain environment there are costs to reaching the right conclusion (searching for answers, making mistakes). Price regulates competition between firms; within them, the "entrepreneur coordinator" allocates resources. If it is more efficient to organize internally, firms that leave organization to the market will be at a disadvantage. If it is more efficient to allow the market to rule, firms that internalize such decision making will be at a disadvantage. At the margin, then, the entrepreneur has to decide whether to "make or buy."

What Coase casts as a theoretical question is, for the studio—particularly for the post-*Paramount* studio—a recurring, practical problem: should this transaction be internalized or farmed out? Own or lease? Build or rent? Develop or acquire?[2] As those decisions accumulate, they congeal in patterns of action, and those patterns become characteristic of the firm for those who work there and those who work in its orbit. Those patterns compose a great deal of a studio's "corporate culture." At the same time, such decisions leave behind material residue even as they marshal material support. Such material concerns exert a degree of power over the firm's decision making. Sometimes they seem decisive; other times they are intentionally ignored; and still other times they are taken into account but ultimately granted only a limited influence on the events that make up the studio's course of action. In this essay I explain how that fundamental, iterated contingency and its attendant patterns of material and social deposition have taken form in postwar studio facilities. While there has been productive work on the legacy studios in Los Angeles—particularly Stephanie Frank's study of Fox—I concentrate on the history of Lucasfilm as an independent company, from its origins in temporary spaces in the mid–1970s through its Bay Area–constellations in San Rafael, Skywalker Ranch, and the Presidio.[3]

At the core of this approach is the claim that ultimately the spatial dispositions of modern studio facilities figure evolving contractual relations—the socialized materializations of creative labor and its attendant supports. To be sure, those dispositions are inflected by a host of other forces operating more or less visibly across longer and shorter timelines. Technology changes; communications infrastructures are built out; communities of practice ("scenes") form and dissolve; labor becomes tractable or resists; governmental agencies undertake regulatory operations; and the whole assemblage interacts with an ecological "base." All of these factors have shaped the sorts of places Lucasfilm has made and been part of, and we might approach the studio through any one of them in particular. But by combining corporate history with economic geography, we gain a better sense of why it might be that Lucasfilm has taken the forms that it has, what made them possible, and what converted those possibilities into actualities.

A theory of the firm here joins a theory of "the farm," understood in two dimensions. First, and most essential to the operation of Lucasfilm, is farming as an industrial practice, in which service firms are contracted to provide inputs to the central corporation, usually by working in parallel with other, similarly positioned firms as a deadline looms. "Farming out" exists in any number of industries, but in Hollywood it is particularly associated with the allocation of a specified number of shots to particular visual effects houses. Those houses compete for more shots, and that competition—regulated by price but also disciplined by quality standards and specializations (e.g., dust, light, model-building)—allows contracting studios to remain lean. Lucasfilm would find itself on both sides of that negotiation, as both the contracting studio and, increasingly, the contracted house. The second dimension of the farm lies in its connotations of a durable connection to the land and its nonurban location. This dimension will *brand* the studio, and yoke its identity to Lucas's own whims. Unlike the world of contract, which seems both placeless in its flexibility and fictively placed (Hollywood), the farm—or, in this case, the Ranch—allows the studio to partake of a discourse of *real* emplacement. As we will see, Skywalker Ranch brings together the ideas of the American West as a place of unoccupied land, of ranching as a kind of agriculture that allows that land to perdure largely undisturbed, and the particular resonances of Northern California viticulture, including artisanality, long lead times for cultivation, fine discrimination, and consumptive leisure. If we more regularly associate oenophilic cinephilia with Frances Ford Coppola, it is nevertheless true that Coppola gave Lucas the vines that would start his own vineyard. (They died in an "unseasonal frost" and were replaced.)[4] Finally, both dimensions of the farm offer ways of imagining systems in place and across time, less abstract and more socialized than Coase's initial framing.

Yet in the case of Lucasfilm the central explanation for what we might term its spatial career has been cast in individual and ideological terms: because George wanted it this way. That discourse owes a great deal to long-standing histories of New Hollywood cinema, ideas of "independence," and an industrial fascination with biographical detail. The argument can be distilled into an equation: Lucas's commitment to his own independence plus his devotion to technological innovation plus his investment in narratives of nostalgia equals Skywalker Ranch. The Ranch is, as Lucas explained, "that part of the *Star Wars* universe which juts up above the top layer of the myth, into the real world."[5] How that vision of the studio—its discursive shell—took hold requires investigation.

Yet at the same time we should recognize that the terms of Lucasian individualism and technonostalgia float like a cloud city above the gas giant they mine. If the thing was built on the money generated by *Star Wars* (etc.), that money spun off in very particular ways and itself depended on an industrial and cultural configuration that shaped the possibilities of the Ranch throughout. The revolutions at the heart of the Lucasfilm configuration are threefold: (1) temporally, Lucasfilm rides on the radical disarticulation and then scrambling of the phases of motion picture production, particularly in the arenas of sound design and visual effects on which the company would concentrate; (2) conceptually, Lucasfilm benefits from the persistent industrial and cultural prominence of the cinema long after the everyday dominance of television had become a simple fact; and (3) strategically, Lucasfilm successfully pivots from Lucas's idiosyncratic, synthetic nostalgia to a tantalizingly nonpublic exercise in worldbuilding opened to its audience via a delimited, participatory maker-culture typified by reconstruction (e.g., *Star Wars Uncut*) and encyclopedism (e.g., Wookieepedia).

Combined, the discourse of the Ranch and its corporate strategic environment give rise to a particular history. This history offers the organization along with its professional and consumer audiences a rhythm of spatiocontractual crises set against a persistent background utopia of the campus. For as iconic as Skywalker Ranch has become, it represents only one of several instantiations of the Lucasfilm "studio." By correlating the history of those locales with the history of the company's divisions, we see the materialization of a central tension between the centripetal forces of institutionalization and the centrifugal forces of contract labor. Placid institutionalization as a framework for socialized creativity? Campus. Eruptions of contractual contingency among the company's articulated divisions? Crisis.

As a matter of industrial geography, San Francisco's unique promise of cutting-edge independence *outside* Hollywood went hand in hand with a drive for maximal efficiency and a relentless questioning of what businesses Lucasfilm should be *in.* Within that geography, at the corporate scale, Lucas was determined to avoid the boom-and-bust cycles of Francis Ford Coppola's Zoetrope, and to do that, he concentrated his studio-building efforts on what he hoped he could forge into more reliable areas of the revenue stream such as sound, editing, and effects. Thus, at the subcorporate level Lucasian discourses of innovation and micronetworks of collaboration reinforce the campus model of studio. At the same time, the rationalization of moviemaking that was required to farm out chunks of a production allowed for further and further division. As a result, Lucasfilm has become almost as famous for the divisions that have been spun off or shut down (Pixar, THX) as those that remain (Industrial Light and Magic [ILM], Skywalker Sound). The management of that segmentation over time forms part of a larger way of discussing the studio that I call Ranch Discourse.

RANCH DISCOURSE

The first public discussion of Skywalker Ranch in any detail appeared in *Variety* in June of 1980. In what had even then become a standard story, Lucas narrates his career as a series of near-miss catastrophes and slights, vindicated by last-minute megasuccesses. Then he delivers a moral judgment about the powers that be in Hollywood: "They're rather sleazy, unscrupulous people. . . . They don't care about people. . . . I don't want to have anything to do with them. . . . That's why I'm trying to build the ranch." This is news to Jean Vallely, the interviewer:

> *JV:* The ranch?
>
> *GL:* Yeah, I bought 2000 acres in Lucas Valley, California [no relation]—to build a kind of creative-filmmakers' retreat. The idea came out of film school. It was a great environment; a lot of people all very interested in film, exchanging ideas, watching movies, helping each other out. I wondered why we couldn't have a professional environment like that.[6]

The poles are already set: the contract vs. the campus. Only in Lucas's version, instead of moving forward in time from the campus to a world of cutthroat contracting as he did biographically, the Ranch will allow him to wind the clock backward, a move that depends on the ability of a space to become a campus. To make that happen, of course, takes money. *Star Wars* had paid for the land, but to pay for the buildings, Lucas believed he would need to undo the relationship between the company and its environment. He would take the profits from *The Empire Strikes Back* and what was still called *Revenge of the Jedi* and invest them in "outside companies" and then use the profits from those investments to build the Ranch. "It's just the opposite of how studios work. Basically, what we're doing is using the profits of other companies to subsidize a film company, rather than a film organization subsidizing a conglomerate."[7]

The projected constellation of buildings resembles in many ways what the Ranch would become. There is "a big, simple farmhouse" at the center; "shingled outbuildings for the filmmakers and editors"; a version of what would be the Tech Building with a screening room, recording studio, and editing rooms; a special-effects building; and a "little guest house for visiting dignitaries." The farmhouse would be not just big but, as a house, enormous. That scale would then allow the buildings with more specific purposes to appear as mere "outbuildings." Still, such optical legerdemain would not suffice to make the Tech Building seem small. Instead, it would be, as we will see, a tech building in disguise. Unable to hide its bulk, it hides its function. Even this early in the process, Lucas is certain that whatever their individual roles, the buildings' most important aspect will be their relationship to each other: "off to the side, sort of tucked away on a hill," and "way over on the side of the property."[8] The idea of a "filmmakers' retreat" would be programmatic: no major building within sight of another.

All the pieces were still in play that October when Fortune ran "The Empire Pays Off." At the dawn of the Reagan era Fortune was disinclined to tout Lucas's artistry but found a comfortable irony in the relationship between his "distrust of big business" and his own knack for it. Lucas elaborates the same do-si-do of capital, now in a slightly more coherent, sound-bitey form: "I'm trying to turn the system around. The studios use films they don't have the vaguest idea how to make to earn profits for their shareholders. I'm using my profits to make films." In particular, he pledges that he will be making avant-garde "abstract, experimental films that interest *him*"—not more blockbusters.[9]

Yet even this early in the elaboration of Ranch Discourse the organizational inversion can look like a split—a stall in the company's unification. However coherent the vision, the reality is not (yet) as integrated. It is as if the *promise* of spatial unity is an end state that renders the current incarnation essentially *incomplete*. "Until the ranch is completed a few years from now, the business Lucas runs will remain as divided as its boss." This is the material reality of the present. Lucas's personal headquarters are still in Marin County at "a three-house complex" near but not collocated with the "two divisions of the company devoted to making movies."[10] That split, though, is modest compared with the division between the (personal) Bay Area moviemaking operations and the corporate operations in Los Angeles. Lucasfilm in LA is run by CEO Charles Weber. And unlike the genteel home office up north, the southern arm had, in 1980, recently moved from trailers into "a lavishly renovated former egg warehouse"—the kind of upscale adaptive reuse that would be as emblematic of the 1980s as Ralph Lauren's ersatz and eclectic historicism.[11]

The Lucasfilm split pervades the Fortune article, but it is best emblematized by the contrasting in situ photos of Lucas and Weber. Lucas's is the larger, naturally enough. He stands at the center of the image, feet spread, wearing cream jeans, a white shirt, and a navy blazer. His sneakers—perhaps his favored Tretorns—are dirty. A host of massive, unmanned Caterpillar graders line the edges of the frame, receding into the distance. These are the AT-ATs of the impending Ranch. In the distance tan hills splotched with deep green trees rise into sky, frosted with unthreatening clouds. Lucas commands machines and the very land itself; he looks un-awkward and in-process.

In contrast, Weber stands in the corner of an interior balcony bounded by glistening polyurethaned lumber and overlooking constellations of corp-leisure wicker furniture arrayed beneath the Egg Co.'s newly enclosed atrium. Dark green walls and wood so tan it's almost yellow virtually scream 1980s. Large potted trees nudge up against the robust trusses supporting the new roof. Weber wears a tie but no blazer—the opposite of Lucas's corporate casual. His right hand is awkwardly hooked in his pants pocket; his left lies indecisively on the railing, and he seems entirely unsure whether to stand or lean, so he twists oddly. His light-blue shirt and dark-gray pants share nothing with the palette of the place. It is unclear what work he does or commands.

Weber justified the initial split by appealing to Lucas's mistrust of the legacy Hollywood system. By keeping the corporate headquarters in Los Angeles, Weber would be able to monitor the interfirm contractual relationships that were essential to the company's success. As Lucas described Hollywood at the time, "LA is where they make deals, do business in the crass corporate way, which is screw everybody. . . . They're not filmmakers."[12] Yet Lucasfilm's strategy was bound up with the industry both via its contractual relations with Fox for *Star Wars* merchandizing and via its investments in nonentertainment industry companies that were spinning off the capital necessary to build Skywalker Ranch.

Weber would inevitably be the figure at the heart of the company's first spatio-contractual crisis. Whether he actually had the temerity to suggest to Lucas that the Ranch was "a drain" or whether Lucas was offended that overhead had become ostentatious and uncontrolled—"We were one step away from the delivery boy having a company Porsche. We were up here living in poverty row and they had a palatial estate"—the dynamic had shifted.[13] The Egg Co. had morphed from the surveillance outpost that would contain the contamination of Lucasfilm into the portal through which Hollywood "sleaziness" would enter the company. In the most detailed account, Weber had come north to meet with Lucas to discuss the company's course, ostensibly to get the go-ahead to shift its strategy toward more active control of its outside investments—to bring these nonentertainment firms *inside* Lucasfilm. Instead, Lucas hemmed and hawed, ultimately firing Weber. "On May 28, 1981, Lucasfilm Ltd. officially relocated its corporate headquarters from Los Angeles to Marin County, completing what a press release called 'the long-planned consolidation of the company.'"[14] Instead of being located in Los Angeles in order to keep an eye on Fox, Lucasfilm's corporate and licensing operations would now be brought north so that Lucas himself could monitor them. What had initially been cast as a matter of defensive proximity was recast as a matter of hygiene.

The Ranch, then, was a locus of control, a safe distance from Los Angeles, and fundamentally discreet. It was always both on the horizon (it was not a lie to say that the consolidation was *long-planned*) and always *over* the horizon (those plans are put into motion, or not, in response to crises; ILM ultimately never moved there from San Rafael despite having decades to do so). The specific crisis, though, depended on Lucasfilm's unique activation of the possibilities of the Hollywood studio system it was attempting to supplant.

PRODUCTION SERVICES

The crisis over merchandising and investments is only able to emerge within the firm *as* a crisis resulting from the fundamental disarticulation of the components of then-contemporary media production. Indeed, Lucasfilm's efforts concentrated on those "chunks" of the moviemaking process that might reasonably be farmed out *by or to others:* effects, editing, sound work, and merchandising were joined by new media endeavors, including both videogames and digital effects (Pixar). What they were *not* joined by were facilities for principal photography: fabrication and art departments (except as related to effects), soundstages, backlots, or ranches of the classical Hollywood sort. Lucasfilm was thus an integrated studio with a hole at the center where the "studio"—defined in a particular way—would have been. Combined with Lucas's own resistance to Hollywood guild oversight, that donut-hole approach to filmmaking would routinely push the company's physical production to rented facilities in the UK and other locations, creating a shifting constellation of temporary, even more far-flung, outposts to the company.

If there was something novel about the company's commitments to excentric portions of the filmmaking process, the strategy nevertheless spoke to the persistent industrial question of the integration of the service firm. From the early days of classical Hollywood single-purpose effects houses (Williams and Dunning), camera equipment providers (Mitchell, Panavision), film labs, lighting companies, and promotional services would set up shop just outside the studios. David Bordwell, Janet Staiger, and Kristin Thompson were the first to build a history of the Hollywood system that moved the articulation of production services firms and studios to the center.[15] Their effort to balance individual corporate histories against the role of collective organizations such as the Academy's Research Council and the Society of Motion Picture Engineers has been a tremendous spur to further work.[16] Still, the question of the firm persists. The vertically integrated studios of the classical era, the diversified conglomerates of the 1960s and 1970s, and the reintegrated media megaconglomerates that have followed have all asked whether these pan-industrial services be brought into a particular studio or not.

Yet until Lucasfilm, even the most expansive visions of integration had not yet included a one-stop shop for effects work. Julie Turnock's *Plastic Reality* sets the stage for this revolution in capacity. "The independents had been performing the bulk of optical work for decades, while the studios tended to concentrate on rear-projection work in-house. Subcontracting was usually fairly small-scale, a few shots per film."[17] In the wake of *Star Wars'* success, though, Lucas simultaneously formally incorporated Industrial Light and Magic as a separate division and brought it north from Van Nuys to Marin County. As Turnock has elaborated, in this period between 1978 and *The Empire Strikes Back,* ILM honed its particular form of photorealism "that favors closer meshing between the location shooting and the effects material."[18] For my purposes, though, what matters more than the aesthetic that emerged from ILM was the spatial reconfiguration of the industry. As a complete provider, ILM would necessarily be brought into projects early on—at the concept art stage, ideally—and would be on a show until deep into postproduction. That early incorporation gave the firm an advantage in competing for work, but it also meant that it was able to demand a greater degree of organizational autonomy; that is, it could set up in the Bay Area because it did not need to scramble for work as a project reached its crunch time.

Meanwhile, back in Van Nuys, John Dykstra's Apogee effects house moved into the space vacated by ILM. Apogee would be one of many firms attempting to emulate ILM's stem-to-stern approach to special and visual effects work.[19] Up north, ILM occupied a collection of nondescript office buildings, hard against Kerner Blvd. and labeled "Kerner Optical" in a half-hearted attempt to deflect public attention. If the Ranch would be spatially isolated enough to hide itself behind a gate, ILM would go incognito as just another bland tenant of another bland industrial park.

OCCUPATION

In contrast, the Ranch itself would be boldly discreet. When it opened in 1985, Lucasfilm relocated the company's back-office operations right away. Lucas also hired sound editor Tom Kobayashi to oversee much of the construction of the Tech Building, which had yet to be built but would be finished in 1987. Lucas's invitation to Kobayashi was the bold part: "'George's famous comment,' Kobayashi says, 'was, "We're going on a covered wagon West and we're going to be fighting a bunch of Indians." I came up and looked around, and I said, "It's a nice covered wagon."'"[20]

By calling on a movie version of the US's settler colonial history, Lucas tied the effort to build Skywalker Ranch to earlier models of occupation. That historical relation was, again, discursive. Whatever the history of the First Nations on the parcel, Lucas was aligning the Indians with his Marin County neighbors and, per-haps, his competitors in Los Angeles. Still, the invocation of history *as such* was not simply an artifact of 1980s ersatz (as at the Egg Co.) or Lucas's own nostalgia.

Rather, it was a further exercise in worldbuilding, the fantasy of total specification that made the Star Wars films so compelling and that would separate the Ranch from ILM. In place of the banal office park, Skywalker would be *descript*. It would also be fictitious. Lucas imagined an elaborate family melodrama behind the Ranch's construction over time. The whole thing would begin with a sea captain; his children would possess varying degrees of piety and entrepreneurial skill. Together they would leave behind them a tastefully eclectic mix of buildings:

> As a help to the architects, Lucas devised a fanciful quick history for each of the buildings. The main house, a large white mansion with a deep veranda, is in the Victorian style and dates from 1869, with a library wing added in 1910, he explained. The head of the mythical founding family added a gate house in 1870 and expanded it in 1915, when he also built a carriage house. The stable house dates from 1870 and the brook house (indeed built over a brook), which is designed in the Craftsman style Lucas frequently admired in houses in Berkeley, dates from 1913. The great brick winery, which is, in fact, the Tech Building that contains the postproduction facilities and the recording stage, is partly from 1880 but extended and remodeled in the Art Moderne style in 1934.[21]

Fiction and discretion went hand in hand. As Lucas historian J. W. Rinzler put it in a series of lengthy blog posts that have since been taken down: "Hidden technology was one of the themes at the ranch." Nearly every commentator notes the fundamentally hidden nature of its workings. "On Skywalker ranch, in fact, there are fourteen fantasy structures concealing a secret movie factory with all the most up-to-date, computerized film-editing and sound equipment that modern film-making has to offer."[22] "Beneath the shaggy meadows is an elaborate power distribution system, masses of telephone and computer cables, and a self-sufficient irrigation and water distribution system."[23] "The buildings should intrude upon the tranquil landscape as little as possible, should seem to have belonged to the land for a long time, and should be invisible from the highway, the building clusters even out of sight from each other. The majority of the cars would be (and are) stashed out of sight in underground garages. All the utilities are also underground, combined in a huge master conduit."[24] Indeed, the disappearance of technological infrastructure is so pronounced it overwhelms its own absence. That gap actually *announces* the presence of the Ranch. According to Rinzler, you knew you had reached the property's entrance by "the sudden absence of telephone or electrical wires overhead—Lucas had paid to put them underground, to enhance the natural setting."[25]

That emphasis on enforced discretion extends to the Ranch's fire department. Located down the hill near the entrance, the Skywalker Ranch Fire Safety Division resembles a small-town pumper station. As an extensive profile in *9-1-1 Magazine* made clear, the fire company has a mutual aid relation with Nicasio's public volunteer fire department. Just as the main house hides a large subterranean parking garage, so the fire department is the front for Lucasfilm's security operation. "Confrontational situations are infrequent but aggressively handled. 'We have a desire to have a private, non-obstructive company out here and we would like people to respect that,' said [Assistant Fire Chief Matt] Gustafson. 'We don't have a lot of tolerance for people who don't respect that.'"[26]

If the quaint fire department is the happy face on the aggressive security enforcement, that conflict was matched with a percolating battle with the Ranch's neighbors. Lucas's expansion plans were met each step of the way by objections. As Rex Weiner explained in *Variety*, "Though isolated geographically from Hollywood infighting and distractions, Skywalker Ranch is beset by local opposition to expansion of its operations, a factor stalling key components of Lucas's long-range plans."[27] The results of that stall are a continuing spatial dispersion. Rinzler goes on: "Lucas's goal had been to unite all of his moviemaking subsidiaries in one place, but Skywalker Ranch was zoned for only about 300 employees. The 1,000 or so members of ILM therefore stayed put in the industrial zone of San Rafael, about 25 minutes away, where they could also continue to make use of hazardous materials and explosives. The videogame branch, LucasArts, also kept its 350 or so people in a nondescript office building about 15 minutes east, next to the 101 freeway, for lack of space."[28]

In the zoning battles the reality of the Ranch was on full display: rules governed how many employees each facility could host and how many car trips would be added by the construction and later by new jobs. Touring the Ranch, Patricia Lee Brown from *Architectural Digest* attempts to flatter Lucas by comparing the setting to "an idealized turn-of-the-last-century town in which the mayor happens to be a brilliant billionaire movie director." Lucas can't help but disagree, echoing Kobayashi's affect while admitting that what he has built is something else: "It's not exactly a small town," Lucas muses. "If anything, it's an industrial park. But it's a nice industrial park."[29]

SPACES

The dream of the Ranch, however unfulfilled, stood in stark contrast to the long industrial legacy of the studio ranches of the greater Los Angeles area. Those ranches were set up across the San Fernando Valley to provide a range of open landscapes, particularly for westerns, within the "Thirty Mile Zone." By staying within the zone, the studios could shoot "on location" without incurring substantial extra costs. Disney had the old Republic ranch in Golden Oaks in Placerita; Fox in Calabasas; Paramount near Agoura Hills; RKO in Encino; and Warner Bros. in Woodland Hills. These were joined by numerous independent ranches such as the Spahn, the Iverson, and Corriganville. But as Laura Barraclough explains, after World War II a culturewide shift away from westerns and the construction of the freeway network made the studio ranches less viable. That process accelerated as the studio system dis-integrated. The ranches were either developed or purchased by localities to preserve "open space" and made into parkland.[30]

Lucas's extensive real estate investments thus bucked the broader industry trend. Even the core backlots of the legacy major studios were being radically reshaped. The broader economic shift toward "flexible specialization" was decoupling the studio from its spaces.[31] MGM's lot was sold for real estate development as was much of Fox. Columbia left Gower to join Warner Bros. in Burbank. That space itself would now be controlled by "The Burbank Studios," while Columbia's former facilities would become Sunset Gower Studios. The trend was not universal. Paramount had purchased the former RKO lot from Desilu in 1967 as part of a larger real estate strategy, and Universal retained its Burbank lot. Indeed, the multiple options are further evidence that what emerges in the late 1960s and early 1970s is not an absolute *demand* that studios shed their real estate holdings but *the question* of whether they should shed their real estate holdings (exchange value vs. use value in Stephanie Frank's terms). Lucas's position here is thus doubly distinct. Not only is he pursuing the less common strategy of investing in real estate, but he does so precisely *not* with an eye toward the eventual development of the acreage but with the aim of controlling its nondevelopment.

If the RKO ranch really was a place with horses, Skywalker Ranch allowed Lucas to bring his own spin to what Louise Mozingo has called "pastoral capitalism." In her history of the suburbanization of the corporation—particularly its managerial and research functions—Mozingo emphasizes the rhetorical role of the campus: "By 1960 the term *campus* or *campus-like* became shorthand for corporate facilities in the suburbs that included at least some trimming of green around low-rise buildings."[32] That campus model was brought to California in the Ramo-Wooldridge Research Laboratories, but the crucial contemporaneous analogue for Lucas's efforts was IBM's Santa Teresa Laboratory:

> In 1977, as its software market became as essential as computer hardware, IBM consolidated 2,000 programmers into the West Coast Programming Center.... IBM defined the intent of the new center in this way: "A campus-like cluster of identifiable buildings is desired that blends with the natural environment in a pleasing and reserved fashion. The offices should be conducive to productive and creative work." On a property of over 1,000 acres extending from the edge of the Santa Clara Valley floor up into the Santa Cruz Mountains, the flat 90-acre project site nestled at the base of hillsides covered with seasonal grasses. Remnant fruit orchards surrounded the parking lots, and buildings clustered around a precise, central quadrangle—actually a roof deck over a large computer facility and library.[33]

Located a hundred miles south of Skywalker Ranch, IBM's new programming center occupied a similarly tiny portion of a vast landscape. The proportions might have been similar, but the configurations of actually existing corporate campuses high-light the distance between the reality and the rhetoric of Lucas's "campus" model. There is no "central quadrangle" at Skywalker Ranch. Moreover, the design plan, with its diverse styles and its fictional backstories for each building, had little in com-mon with the corporate campuses Mozingo discusses. Given the centrality of the Victorian house, Skywalker Ranch has more in common with the "estate" version of the headquarters: "an imposing building complex arrived at by a coursing entry drive through a scenically designed landscape of 200 acres or more. . . . Corpora-tions used the corporate estates' image as a public relations tool in communicating with employees, local residents, stockholders, competitors, and bankers."[34]

Skywalker Ranch offered a version of Mozingo's "splendid pastoral isolation."[35] Unlike other estates, which might be centered on a lake (Deere Company) or give onto a sculpture garden (PepsiCo), Lucas's Ranch was decisively shaped by its Bay Area surround: among the cluster of high-tech buildings, but not within the vast undeveloped backcountry, Lucas would plant some grapes. It is hard to overstate the importance of viticulture to the cultivated gentility of the greater Bay Area. And while Marin County was not an ideal location for a winery, Lucas attempted to follow in Coppola's Napa County footsteps. Wineries are exceptionally good melders of rhetoric and practice. They combine an apparent harmony with the landscape—an acceptance of its climatic givens—with an experimenter's faith in serendipity—the chance of a good year—to produce a low-pollution, high-margin commodity. In the immediate wake of "The Judgment of Paris" in 1976 that placed California wines at the top of the world rankings, Lucas's tripartite land division was thus even more a configuration of its era.[36]

If the overarching land-use pattern at the Ranch was typical of Marin County and other Bay hinterlands, the commitment to high-tech moving-image cultural production was as well. Years later, Lucas would enter the publishing business directly, launching his imprint with two volumes that are seemingly about the world Lucas made but that seek to ground that world in traditions. *George Lucas's Blockbusting* (2010) takes its readers through the history of the Hollywood block-buster, one profitable story at a time.[37] Lucas's films appear not only among the all-time lists and all-time franchises but also (with *American Graffiti*) in the list of films with the biggest return on the "small" (under $10 million) budget. But if that is the book about how Lucas changed Hollywood to the south, *Cinema by the Bay* puts Lucas in his geographic context.[38] Far from the first filmmaker to set up shop in the region, Lucas is simply the most profitable. Still, the book tells the inter-locked stories of five studios and a dozen directors in an effort to demonstrate the continuing tradition of filmmaking in San Francisco.

Any organization in the midst of understanding its place among other, similar organizations—the usual terms are "ecosystem" when thinking about interde-pendence; "space" when thinking about markets—also establishes relations to its supports, at every scale. In the case of Lucasfilm perhaps the most basic of those supports is the evolving ecoregulatory system of Marin County. The relationship between the firm and its site takes shape as a discourse of relative smoothness. At times, when the aims of Lucasfilm and its regulatory surround are in harmony, the discursive presences of the state and other interest groups will drop out, and Lucasfilm will appear to take up an almost unmediated relation to "the land." The terms become individualist and aesthetic. This is the "because George wants it" form of evolving Ranch Discourse. At other times, though, the aims of Lucasfilm and its regulatory surround are more opposed, and the frictions in the process will give rise to a public petulance. Lucas followed the successful build-out of Sky-walker Ranch with the development of a sister complex at Big Rock Ranch. Though delayed, that process ultimately succeeded.

A third phase of the project, however, at Grady Ranch, ultimately came to naught. At Grady Lucas intended to plug the hole in the studio donut by building a pair of soundstages. Local opposition was vocal, and despite support in the county government, Lucas was unable to build as quickly as he had hoped. Frus-trated, he changed course and announced he would not be building studio facili-ties. Instead, he would pursue an easier course by building new housing. Not con-tent to simply declare defeat and leave with a tidy profit, Lucasfilm issued an elaborately snide statement, pledging to work to build low-income housing. "We love working and living in Marin, but the residents of Lucas Valley have fought this project for 25 years, and enough is enough," they said. "We hope we will be able to find a developer who will be interested in low-income housing since it is scarce in Marin. If everyone feels that housing is less impactful on the land, then we are hoping that people who need it the most will benefit."[39] With the pursuit of new housing construction, Lucas found himself in the position the major studios were in at the beginning of the Ranch project.

LABOR

Lucasfilm's siting and development are constrained by a contest for authority between governments and the corporation, and the discourse surrounding that emplacement oscillates accordingly. In contrast, Lucasfilm's relation to its labor market and attendant technical supports takes the form of a durable network of suppliers and an insistent publicization of its own industrial preeminence. Most emblematic would be the feeder campus structure. As Turnock explains, "A number of Southern California 'farm schools' trained students specifically to enter particular entertainment job markets."[40] As part of his regular recourse to the lost utopia of film school, Lucas would invoke "Room 108, where we had screenings going on all the time, and then we'd go out in the grassy courtyard and talk about films, share our ideas and help each other with our problems."[41] Perhaps nothing could be less essential to the experience of film school than the number of the principal screening room, yet when USC built its new facilities—largely under the aegis of Lucas—the largest screening room was, again, Room 108. As the school's most significant donor, it was no surprise that Lucas had ideas about architecture and design that he wanted to see realized in the new buildings. But the "easter-egging" of the screening room conveys the intensity of Lucas's desire to shape the campus-to-studio pipeline according to the affective legacy of his time at USC. However technologically advanced the facilities, however innovative the work that would go on within them, they would still, ideally, inculcate that desire to dwell in the collective discussion of cinematic arts.

A room number is merely an emblem, but it is an emblem for a broad swath of labor relations that the Lucas companies rely on. These are the innovation hinter-lands of Skywalker Ranch, and while they are far less integrated than, for example, the fire station, they are nevertheless part of the studio's dance of incorporation. Two merit further specification. First is SIGGRAPH, the "Special Interest Group" of the Association of Computing Machinery dedicated to computer graphics. Fol-lowing early work establishing standard graphic language, a journal, and a news-letter, the SIG launched its own freestanding conference in 1974. That conference grew more formalized, and for the 1977 conference in San Jose the group began strictly reviewing papers.[42] Volumes of proceedings followed, and in keeping with the cutting-edge nature of the work being presented, the SIG's publications became electronic early on. The growth of the SIG and the conference were astonishing, quickly reaching thousands, then tens of thousands of attendees. Such events serve as crucial nodes in the evolving labor and technology networks in an industry, a place where representatives of a firm are able to tout the company's competence and recruit new talent.

Such dynamics work in multiple directions. For the 1980 SIGGRAPH in Seattle, Loren Carpenter produced a legendary short film, *Vol Libre*, as a sort of moving-image-resume to encourage Lucasfilm to hire him away from Boeing. Ed Catmull and Alvy Ray Smith, then running Lucasfilm's Computer Division that would become Pixar, "offered him a job on the spot."[43] In contrast, at the 1983 conference the division displayed "The Road to Point Reyes," a "one-frame movie" that included asphalt and rock textures, particle-system generated vegetation, a double rainbow and depth cueing, and a partial reflection in a roadside puddle among its wonders. The image is regularly reproduced as an emblem of the state-of-the-art work at Lucasfilm, but it is also an incarnation of the sitedness of that work. How-ever advanced Lucasfilm might be, the picture seemed to say, it was just around the corner from the Point Reyes National Seashore. The easy linkage between the ray-tracing work rendered in the image, the software program itself (called Reyes, a backronym for "Renders Everything You Ever Saw"), and the space it depicted is more than a mere emblem; it is an advertisement for itself.[44]

Much of the talent that would converge at SIGGRAPH emerged from universities, of course, and in those early days new and perhaps unexpected institutions took the lead. One of those was the New York Institute of Technology in Brooklyn—across the country and about as far removed from the "Hollywood" sphere of influence as one could imagine. Still, the rise of Lucasfilm as a crucial site for innovative work in computer graphics reconfigured the labor market even for university-based researchers. Over time, Lucas and his division heads would lure many of NYIT's key players. "Those who were interested in going to Lucasfilm would take interim jobs elsewhere—'laundering' themselves, as the group called it. Catmull would bring them in when he could. The plan went without a hitch."[45]

In the early days the migration from university campus to corporate campus was more conceptual than literal. Initially the Computer Division was located above an antique store in San Anselmo next to the office where Marcia Lucas was still overseeing design work for the construction of Skywalker Ranch. It then moved to a former laundromat, then to an industrial park in Novato, and in 1982 to Building C in the stretch of Kerner Boulevard in San Rafael where ILM and Sprocket Systems (the sound division) were located. The moves would continue: some of Pixar would move to the Ranch in 1986, just as Lucas was in the process of selling it to Steve Jobs. Pixar remained in San Rafael until 1990, when it was squeezed out of its space by an expanding ILM, whereupon it moved across the bay to Point Richmond and then to Emeryville.[46] Moving from one "nice industrial park" to another does not necessarily amount to a brandable moment or a threat to a corporate or individual identity. But in an industry where labor inputs and evaluations are configured along quasi-educative lines with campuses, conferences, and feeder schools, such moves are as fraught as any collegiate transfer.

CONCLUSION

In the twenty-first century Lucas continued to shift his divisions, but a new dynamic appeared: a gradual reurbanization. In 1999 Lucas won the rights to redevelop fifteen acres in The Presidio in San Francisco as part of the public-private partnership tasked with taking over the facility from the federal government and making it self-funding. The 850,000-square-foot Letterman Digital Arts Center opened in 2005 as the combined home of ILM and LucasArts.[47] (The marketing, online, and licensing divisions moved in 2012.) In 2006 Lucas donated $175 million to USC's School of Cinematic Arts—with $75 million of that earmarked for the construction of a set of buildings that might pass for studio architecture circa 1929. The new facilities opened in 2009.[48] In 2012 Lucas sold Lucasfilm to Disney, but a host of long-planned satellite "campuses" opened shortly thereafter. In 2013 Lucasfilm Singapore opened "The Sandcrawler," a 240,000-square-foot, mixed-use building that looks like the sandcrawler from *A New Hope*.[49] That same year, a small branch of ILM opened in Vancouver; London followed in 2014. In 2017, after a long, multicity search, Lucas (and the Board of Directors) chose Los Angeles for the Lucas Museum of Narrative Art, scheduled to open in 2021.[50]

By the 2010s, then, all three revolutions that had driven Lucasfilm toward the Ranch and its contractual utopia had been recontextualized. Production temporality remained scrambled; cinema remained conceptually preeminent; and, strategically, the pivot to worldbuilding as a mode of durable audience enlistment was unquestioned. But it was no longer necessary to escape the city to forge those revolutions; every corporatizable aspect of Lucas's individual resistance to Hollywood had become constitutive of the contemporary, IP-driven, blockbuster-centric industry as a whole. Urban unions posed almost no threat to radical readjustments to the labor process. Adaptive reuse and citywide upscaling had become baseline assumptions in San Francisco and Los Angeles as those cities competed (and collaborated) with fellow global culture centers to maintain their prominence in the flows of capital. Lucas's organizational flexibility, his indomitable dissatisfaction with the corporate form, has become the emblem of the new culture city, not its enemy.

To be sure, Skywalker Ranch continues to be the home of Skywalker Sound (and vineyards).[51] And, to be sure, the Letterman Digital Arts Center (LDAC), with its vast parking lot hidden underground, abuts the landscaped "Great Lawn."[52] But the Presidio facility is decidedly an urban park, not a pastoral enclave. It and Lucas's other public-facing institutions thrive not on separation but on spatial collision. Such developments emerge from and exemplify a new configuration in which municipalities look for marquee partners to lead redevelopment projects and programmatically incorporate "mixed uses"—not simply industrially adjacent firms or support providers such as restaurants, daycare facilities, and so on, but also similarly high-wage, low-nuisance tenants such as financial firms (Mithril, Maverick, and Thiel Capital), tech developers (Zenreach, Revinate), and nonprofits. At the same time, Lucas's (and Disney's) commitments are always revisable. LDAC and these other "campuses" are flexible, able to respond as a Lucasfilm project staffs up or when a crisis hits. When Disney shut down LucasArts' game development arm and laid off those employees, the freed space could be rented to another tenant. Like Pixar and THX, which were both sold off, the ILM branches might be closed if there is insufficient revenue to support them. Until that happens, branding suffuses everything. The Yoda fountain announces ILM to the public; behind him stands LDAC's Building B, which has been named to evoke ILM's nondescript San Rafael complex. Against this nostalgia for functionalism, the "splendid isolation" of Skywalker Ranch now appears to be a dream of the past.

NOTES

1. Ronald Coase, "The Nature of the Firm," *Economica* (1937) 4, no. 16 (1937): 388; see also Jacobsen, "On Robinson, Coase, and 'The Nature of the Firm.'"

2. For a crucial early registration of the "flexibilization" of the industry see Gustafson, "'What's Happening to Our Pix Biz?'" 574–86. While Gustafson is primarily tracing the forces behind conglomeratization, he is attentive to the shifting constellation of components within the New Hollywood companies, in particular the partial displacement of theatrical exhibition from the center of the firm: "the perennially risky theatrical distribution of films has become secondary to the more stable broadcast television sales of films and the lucrative new technologies of cable television and satellite transmission which also support the film industry. Warner Bros. has therefore found itself to be protected rather than devoured by its new conglomerate structure" (575).

3. Frank, "Why a Studio without a Backlot Isn't like a Ten-Story Building without an Elevator."

4. Champlin, *George Lucas,* 174.

5. Seabrook, "Letter from Skywalker Ranch," 195.

6. Vallely, "*The Empire Strikes Back* and So Does Filmmaker George Lucas with His Sequel to *Star Wars,*" 94.

7. Vallely, 94–95.

8. Vallely, 94.

9. Stratford P. Sherman, "The Empire Pays Off," *Fortune,* Oct. 6, 1980, 52–55, 53.

10. Sherman, 53.

11. This was obvious at the time. See John Morris Dixon, "Decade of Detachment," *Progressive Architecture* 71, no. 1 (Jan. 1990): 7. In addition to the stylistic trends, Dixon highlights the congelation of NIMBYism, particularly in San Francisco. Those forces would eventually provide a major restriction to Lucas's aims.

12. Vallely, 93.

13. Pollock, *Skywalking,* 251.

14. Pollock, 253.

15. See Bordwell, Staiger, and Thompson, *Classical Hollywood Cinema,* esp. parts 4 and 6: "Film Style and Technology to 1930" and "Film Style and Technology 1930–60."

16. The flourishing of media industry studies and science and technology studies paradigms has resulted in a rapid increase in the historical literature on the Hollywood service companies across crafts. Crucial contributions that concentrate on organizational consequences include Turnock, *Plastic Reality;* Marzola, "Engineering Hollywood"; Marzola, "Better Pictures through Chemistry"; and Dootson, "'The Hollywood Powder Puff War.'"

17. Turnock, *Plastic Reality,* 81.

18. Turnock, 213.

19. Turnock, 214–18.

20. Champlin, *George Lucas,* 179.

21. Champlin, 174.

22. Salewicz, *George Lucas Close Up,* 94–95.

23. Pollock, *Skywalking,* 259.

24. Champlin, *George Lucas,* 171.

25. J. W. Rinzler, "The Rise and Fall of Star Wars, Blog 5," June 30, 2017, blog discontinued but archived at the Wayback Machine, web.archive.org/web/20170705074345/http://www.jwrinzler.com:80/blog/the-rise-and-fall-of-star-wars-blog-5.

26. Randall D. Larson, "Safety and Security at Skywalker Ranch," *9-1-1 Magazine,* Sept./Oct. 1996. This model of the studio as minicompany town—one subject to particularly strained relations with its

host city—recalls the studio cities of the 1910s discussed in Jacobson, *Studios Before the System*, especially chapter 5.

27. Weiner, "Lucas the Loner Returns to *Wars*," 186.

28. Rinzler, "The Rise and Fall of Star Wars, Blog 5."

29. Patricia Lee Brown, "Tour George Lucas's Office at Skywalker Ranch," *Architectural Digest*, March 2004, www.architecturaldigest.com/story/george-lucas-skywalker-ranch-tour.

30. Barraclough, *Making the San Fernando Valley*, 147–48.

31. "Flexible Specialization" is a term coined by Susan Christopherson and Michael Storper and deployed in their foundational essay "The City as Studio; the World as Back Lot: The Impact of Vertical Disintegration on the Location of the Motion Picture Industry," *Environment and Planning D: Society and Space* 4, no. 3 (1986): 305–20. They trace a double movement in which the studios in the 1960s increasingly shoot outside Los Angeles while other phases of production "reagglomerate" in the LA area. This pattern is only partially applicable to Lucasfilm.

32. Mozingo, *Pastoral Capitalism*, 90.

33. Mozingo, 93–95.

34. Mozingo, 12.

35. Mozingo, 96.

36. Taber, *Judgment of Paris*.

37. Ben Block and Wilson, *George Lucas's Blockbusting*.

38. Avni, *Cinema by the Bay*.

39. The *Marin Independent Journal* offered the best, sustained coverage of the tussles between Lucas and his neighbors. See Nels Johnson, "Lucasfilm Stuns Marin, Pulls Plug on Grady Ranch Movie Studio Project," *Marin Independent Journal*, April 10, 2012, www.marinij.com/2012/04/10/lucasfilm-stuns-marin-pulls-plug-on-grady-ranch-movie-studio-project. The low-income (and senior) housing plan faced similar resistance and was apparently abandoned without fanfare in 2016. Johnson, "Marin Says Zoning Allows up to 240 Units at Grady Ranch Owned by George Lucas," August 18, 2012, www .marinij.com/2012/08/18/marin-says-zoning-allows-up-to-240-units-at-grady-ranch-owned-by-george-lucas; Valerie Veteto, "George Lucas' Ambitious Affordable Housing Project in Marin County Appears Stalled," *Livabl_*, Nov. 16, 2016, www.livabl.com/2016/11/george-lucas-affordable-housing-marin-county-stalled.html.

40. Turnock, *Plastic Reality*, 292n53.

41. Audie Bock, "George Lucas: An Interview," *Take One*, May 1979, 6.

42. Judy Brown and Steve Cunningham, "A History of ACM SIGGRAPH," *Communications of the ACM* 50, no. 5 (May 2007): 54–61.

43. Price, *Pixar Touch*, 37.

44. Price, 43.

45. Price, 33. For an account of the importance of the University of Utah's department see Gaboury, "Other Places of Invention."

46. Paik, *To Infinity and Beyond!* 164–66.

47. David S. Cohen, "Building a Legacy," *Variety*, Feb. 14, 2005, 58.

48. USC School of Cinematic Arts, Untitled [Giving Presentation Book], n.p. [6].

49. Kirsten Han, "Yoda and His 24 Billion Dots at Lucasfilm's Singapore Headquarters," *ArchiExpo*, no. 10, June 30, 2015, www.archiexpo.com/emag/issue-10/deconstruction-singapore-lucasfilm-sand-crawler-1018.html.

50. John King, "Lucas Museum Timeline: From Presidio to Treasure Island," *San Francisco Chronicle*, Oct. 26, 2016, www.sfchronicle.com/bayarea/article/Lucas-Museum-timeline-From-Presidio-to-Treasure-10415341.php.

51. With the departure of the Lucasfilm corporate offices, Lucas has proposed converting much of the Big Rock Ranch complex to guest rooms. Nels Johnson, "George Lucas's Plan: 57 Overnight Guest Rooms at Big Rock Ranch under Review," *Marin Independent Journal,* April 27, 2016, www.marinij .com/2016/04/27/george-lucas-plan-57-overnight-guest-rooms-at-big-rock-ranch-under-review.

52. Watry Design, "Letterman Digital Center Parking Structure at the Presidio," n.d., https:// watrydesign.com/project/letterman-digital-center-parking-structure-at-the-presidio.

12

"Make It What You Want It to Be"

Logistics, Labor, and Land Financialization via the
Globalized Free Zone Studio

Kay Dickinson

Syriana (Stephen Gaghan, 2005), *The Kingdom* (Peter Berg, 2007), *Wall Street: Money Never Sleeps* (Oliver Stone, 2010), *Dabangg* (Abhinav Kashyap, 2010), *Mission: Impossible—Ghost Protocol* (Brad Bird, 2011), *The Bourne Legacy* (Tony Gilroy, 2012), *Dabangg 2* (Arbaaz Khan, 2012), *Happy New Year* (Farah Khan, 2014), *Star Wars: The Force Awakens* (J. J. Abrams, 2015), *Furious 7* (James Wan, 2015), *Welcome Back* (Anees Bazmee, 2015), *Housefull 3* (Sajid and Farhad Samji, 2016), *Star Trek Beyond* (Justin Lin, 2016), *Airlift* (Raja Krishna Menon, 2016), *Independence Day: Resurgence* (Roland Emmerich, 2016), *Ki & Ka* (R. Balki, 2016), *Gong fu yu jia* (Stanley Tong, 2017), and *Mission: Impossible—Fallout* (Christopher McQuarrie, 2018)—these are some of the most recognized of the now-hundreds of feature films shot in the United Arab Emirates this century. All were made, at least in part, and, as their titles evidence, by largely non-Emirati enterprises.

It would be improvident to dismiss the occasions when big budget cinema stops off at sites like these as merely their producers' quests for a precise plot-determined mise-en-scène. Instead, we urgently need to grasp how such itineraries explicitly mean to exploit a global division of labor through practices of offshoring. Offshoring the world over is eased into place—specific places—through local governments' engineering of legal, financial, and infrastructural systems. It requires a particular architecture that conforms to the circuitry and ideologies of global supply chains. Film offshoring is no exception. Proliferating, yet extremely vulnerable to replacement, offshore centers must maintain a competitive edge. As Michael Curtin and Kevin Sanson note, "studio bosses and producers have made it clear that they intend to keep scouring the globe for lower labor rates and less regulated environs . . . playing off one place against another in a never-ending quest to secure the most favorable conditions for their bottom lines."[1] The interchangeability of these sites therefore renders the study of one of them relevant to the comprehension of not only others but also the abiding capitalist structures that arrange and hierarchize the world's production thus and that bear consequences for us all. This essay seeks to expose the cost of these maneuvers to human life.

As a dry desert state, the UAE tenders the reliable light and weather that first helped inaugurate Los Angeles as a filmmaking heartland. Similarly, the "blank canvas" appeal—as political in its obfuscation of real territories and their people's concerns as it has been in Hollywood history—repeats. While Dubai's trademark Burj Khalifa assumes a leading role in, say, *Mission: Impossible—Ghost Protocol*'s climactic scene, the country just as readily stands in for other locations: Iran in *Syriana*, Saudi Arabia in *The Kingdom*, Kuwait in *Airlift*, the fictional futuristic Yorktown of *Star Trek Beyond*, and even a galaxy far, far away in *Star Wars: The Force Awakens*. Such are the demands for anonymity, disguise, and flexibility within contemporary multi-sited film production, where narrative prerogatives meet practical and budgetary priorities beyond most audiences' recognition of actual locale. As the Dubai Film and TV Commission tagline beseeches, "Make it what you want it to be."

This potential is nowhere more achievable than within the multidimensional blank canvas of the film studio itself. As a controllable, manipulable cocoon primed for transformation into whatever is technically possible, a studio aims to shut out the real world's messy contingencies. Its erasure of not only the means, but also the *sites,* of production stands as a central pillar of fiction film entertainment. In this essay I endeavor to unfurl the outcomes of this double mystification, as well as to reflect on the systems that divide the manageable from the disorderly and logistically regulate the necessary movements between each. After all, the hermetic capabilities of the contemporary studio are only commercially attractive because of how looped they are into a larger worldwide grid, through the international roster of people and objects the studio hosts, through superior access to undersea and satellite connections, through the stories being told, and through the vast distances the finished product will later traverse. Abetted by widespread globalization and deregulation, digital financial and data transfer technologies, and uncomplicated world travel for filmmaking personnel and equipment, a movie can just as simply, and more cheaply, be (partially) shot beyond its historical centers, if the conditions are right.

Nevertheless, while the portion of any film completed in a studio might disaggregate from the geographical hub it is presumed to "come from" (Hollywood, for instance), mainstream cinematic output cannot materialize just anywhere. Unlike certain decentralized, post-Fordist film work, which might be undertaken in home offices, even coffee shops, studio shooting calls for expensive equipment housed in structures purpose-built to industry specifications, ones that hook back, through all these means, to established centers.[2] Standardization crafts requisite corre-

FIGURE 12.1. Dubai Studio City free zone, administered by the Dubai Creative Clusters Authority. Photo by Kay Dickinson.

spondences but also a pecking order that deputizes a circumscribed set of duties to more "peripheral" outfits.

One such space is Dubai Studio City, a recent US$500 million entrant into this lattice of globalized film, television, and digital content creation, replete with some of the world's largest soundstages, a backlot, water tanks, production offices, and operational support structures, including the on-site Dubai Film and TV Commission (fig. 12.1).[3] Although owned by the state, Studio City unusually slants itself less toward manufacturing media for its own country and more toward serving as a cog within a globally dispersed supply chain for an equally transnational cinema. While it once made great economic sense to keep everything in-house, fundamental shifts, such as those brought to a head by the Paramount Decree, helped trigger the decentralization of, for instance, the Hollywood majors, which have increasingly either sold off portions of their studio complexes or rented them out to other companies. A situation has thus arisen whereby independently owned studios— unattached to transnational entertainment corporations and subsisting by renting amenities, rather than generating their own movies from scratch—could assert themselves into nonlocation shooting schedules.[4] With films like *Star Trek Beyond* deciding not just to shoot on location in the UAE but also to avail themselves of Studio City's facilities, the emirate aims to capture a sizable portion of the film industry's offshored activity.

Studio City's primary allure, however, derives from its genesis within an intricate and highly planned matrix of legislative, logistical, service-oriented, and labor capacities that, although unseen in the end result, can recommend Dubai as a destination and nodal point for Hollywood, Bollywood, Chinese, and other international productions. Attention to these architectures (not just the buildings but a more pervasive influence over design) opens us out onto the broader systems that govern offshoring and vice versa. If, for Mark Shiel, "movie studios prioritized utility, efficiency, profit, and methods and materials specific to industrial and commercial construction"[5] or, in the words of Brian Jacobson, sought "accessibility, control, and [again] efficiency,"[6] Dubai Studio City recalibrates these persistent requests to the current norms of split location production, drawing on dispersed capabilities aided by sectors that dominate now even more than they did in the past: logistics, real estate, and finance capital.[7] As a stronghold of all three, the UAE has configured a studio complex that advertises these industries' substantial streamlining of the film production process. While the country cannot claim a long history in moviemaking, it can definitely peddle, and with appreciable reason and purchase, other long-honed skills to the advantage of globalized cinema. It is these predispositions that the Emirates mobilize in order to confer "film friendliness" upon themselves, much of it driven by an autocratic form of governance that controls land, resources, and services to the advantage of external demand. Lodging movie business foreign direct investment in terrains like these begs political analysis of the histories, geographies, and lived outcomes of the policies and activities they encourage.

"LOGISTIFYING" THE GREENFIELD WHILE THE GREENFIELD AMPLIFIES LOGISTICS

Studio City deviates from traditional destinations for offshored production such as Rome's Cinecittà or London's Pinewood in that it has not evolved out of an infrastructure built for and in tandem use by a well-developed national industry. For Ben Goldsmith et al. places like Studio City fall into the category of "greenfields locations," built quickly from scratch, often with the aim of supporting a range of different scales of production, serving anyone from immediate local clients to international ones. Studio City can adaptively accommodate the full range of productions, in reality settling for and catering with ease to lower-budget enterprises, from lucratively long-term television runs (it is home to the *MasterChef* franchise's Arab world iteration) to commercials and digital content.

Staggeringly speculative and entrepreneurial impetuses guide large-scale developments like Studio City, ones that in Dubai are simultaneously centrally planned and administered by the state.[8] Anyone familiar with the mythologies, stereotypes, and substantiated facts about the emirate will recognize this hallmark modus operandi, a strategy of "build it and they will come." To endow a measure of the import given to construction itself, it should be noted that the very first Strategic Objective listed by the Dubai Creative Clusters Authority, which manages Studio City, is "Ensure world-class infrastructure."[9] Studio City's sheer scale and top-of-the-range facilities have emerged briskly from the ground up rather than, as has been the case elsewhere, incrementally, as updates over many years to meet needs. The big splash has ever been Dubai's hook, as its luxury showcase hotels and biggest-ever malls attest.

Uptake of Studio City, however, cannot depend on the mere fact of superlative facilities, particularly when it comes to big budget cinema. Although Dubai is leaping forward within other realms of audiovisual media, it remains an outlier in film production. Studio City needs to convincingly establish the sort of trust from clients that would inspire them to make the journey there rather than anywhere else in the world. Through comprehensive measures, the UAE devotes copious ideological and geopolitical energy to avowing its image as a safe, stable, and welcoming locality within the otherwise turbulent or quarantined region of the Middle East. Targeting the media industries more precisely, the government has stepped in, as is typical the world over, to establish the Dubai Film and TV Commission (DFTC), which is dedicated to swiftly issuing shooting and work permits, providing location services, and assembling incentive packages.[10] Concomitantly, the DFTC spotlights the benefits to filmmaking of the sectors in which it already excels and that, with enough foresight on behalf of producers, should furnish significant reductions in overheads.[11]

The first of these is the most general: expertise in transshipment or reexportation, in essence, the splitting up or coordinating of flows of goods geographically so as to take fullest advantage of cheaper costs, be they labor-, transport-, or tax exemption–related. Very few of the vast array of products that pass through Dubai's port—one of the world's largest—begin or end their lives in the UAE, and plentiful revenues accrue from Dubai's workforce efficiently routing them elsewhere. If further profit can be generated in-country without diminishing this highly saleable synchronization and rapidity of transit, so much the better. Thus inclined, the Emirates are well poised to carry out competent plug-ins to goods— here films—already in motion down the supply chain. Split and partial production, however, require more than a ready mind-set. The ensuing working practices and infrastructure to support it demand our scrutiny, not least in terms of the added burden they place on the humans and environments involved.

In Dubai, much of this is taken on by and funneled through a sector in which the emirate is enormously globally competitive and that, in turn, advertises Studio City as worthy of cinema's attention: its logistics industry. Logistics is the management science of coordinating supply chains so that they run as effectively, promptly, and cheaply as possible. For Jesse LeCavalier, logistics "concerns the entire life of a product and works to flatten, connect, smooth, and lubricate as it organizes material in both space and time."[12] Such attention has begotten the ascendency of some of the world's richest transnational corporations, from Walmart to Amazon. Logistics trades on being fully cognizant of how fast information and data now travel in comparison to people, goods, and equipment—a fact that patently demarcates the transmission of filmed content in relation to the workers and material needed to make it. Films are notoriously slower and costlier to make than other goods; logistics promises to up that pace and axe those outlays. Accordingly, within the promotional literature, videos, and press generated by both the DFTC and Studio City, the term "one-stop shop" recurs persistently. In actuality these services are drawn in from the DFTC's database of hundreds of ever-ready independent companies, including local and international crew.[13] Logistics helps articulate all these disjointed moving parts. Moreover, it offers to animate split location production as a means of saving on salary, securing the speediest routes to bring all the necessary components into alignment and then disperse them in a trouble-free fashion. If the people involved assume a secondary role in an elaboration of logistics, then this should be read as testament to logistics' own suppression and pressurizing of the humans that invisibly and perforce uphold its race to the finish line through a less noticeable, but distinctly more painful, race to the bottom. The accent typically falls instead on spaces of flow rather than those managing, sustaining, or refining them.

From the onset, it must be stressed that, within Dubai in particular, "logisticization" reaches far beyond scouting out the fastest routes and cheapest inputs. An abundance of wide-ranging policies and lawmaking boosts and is inspired by the ambitions of logistics. In 2016 Dubai apportioned a staggering 35 percent of budget spending to infrastructure expansion (from roads and ports to telecommunications), in comparison to 3 percent in the US and Saudi Arabia.[14] At the industry end of the spectrum the government's installation of the DFTC serves as a ready example of logisticization, working not only to service industry needs but also to put in place regulations that rationalize the production process, including pushing for the issuing of multiple location shooting permits within a mere seventy-two hours of application and crew work permits within twenty-four (although political affiliation or history have become an increasingly preclusive sticking point in this equation).[15] The speed on offer most adamantly exacts tremendous toll on those employed to uphold such promises, though they are not justly credited for their assumption of these ever-escalating duties. These workers advise on suitable locations across the emirate and negotiate deals on hotels, personnel transportation, and shipping, squeezing countless others along the way, all adding to the coffers of the government-owned enterprises such as the Emirates airline, the Jebel Ali con-

FIGURE 12.2. Studio City's warehouse-like architecture. Photo by Kay Dickinson.

tainer port, and the Jumeirah luxury hotel chain. The top-down command governance that stewards all this also enacts, as will become apparent, comprehensive
labor legislature that drives costs down considerably further and across the board
rather than purely in relation to the entertainment sector.

A macro attention to logistics concurrently and purposefully crafts Dubai's built
environment, including Studio City. Situating itself as a hub powered by logistics'
managerial priorities is exactly how Studio City intends its ascendency. Throughout
its history the film studio has always been pragmatic in design, form following
function. In the Fordist era its centralization made for exactly these sorts of efficiencies along a production line by force of proximity to the other elements to which it
connected in order to minimize lags in the movement of people, sets, and equipment. With these objectives giving way to cheaper production possibilities elsewhere, the stripped-down functionality of the studio in the Dubai context renders
it flexible and mutable (just as its ever-changing interior sets are) to the needs of a
dispersed supply chain. The studio's affinity is now less with the factory (to which it
has been regularly compared) than with the newer architectures of logistics, such as
the similarly bland, windowless design of the warehouse, the distribution center,
and even the big-box store (fig. 12.2). Unsurprisingly (and as was the case historically in Los Angeles), Studio City dwells right next to a largely warehouse district,
Al Quoz. These days increasingly repurposed by the creative economy for galleries
and art studios, Al Quoz's proximity renders it a pleasing segue into activities in

Studio City, freighting companies cheek by jowl with cultural production in ways that reconcile the two activities, compelling us to acknowledge the shared dimensions of each. All three building types—the warehouse, the distribution center, and the big-box store—grease the machinations of logistics. Barely noticeable, integrated rather than discrete, their configuration favors what LeCavalier categorizes as the principles of "control, predictability, measurement, division, and management."[16] Considering them analogous to the modern studio therefore fruitfully discloses a number of intended, but often concealed, outcomes.

These structures return us to logistics' roots in the same etymology that brings us "lodging," or temporary housing.[17] Their success rests on moving goods in and out at maximum velocity. This premise, it should be noted, shapes the significant yet perhaps less conspicuous topography of the Dubai cityscape, its planning attuned to several centuries of port activity. Distribution centers and warehouses have played a quiet yet central role in Dubai's economy. It is not hard to imagine the emirate, this powerhouse of transshipment, as one large distribution center. This proclivity adheres to what Thomas J. Sigler identifies as a "relational city," a metropolis that accrues prodigious income from the movement, rather than the start-to-finish manufacture, of goods, its real estate acclimated to provide a transitory home, perhaps with minor inputs added, during a much longer journey.[18] However nimble supply chains are, they still require points where additions can be made, new trajectories charted, and flows managed—hence the need to understand contemporary capitalism through the architecture of such spaces, of which the greater film studio complex is just one example. To draw on LeCavalier once more, here describing a Walmart store, but in terms that conform to the studio surprisingly well, especially its infrastructural ambitions, these built environments function "more as valves regulating flow than as reservoirs for capturing it; they are containers, but they are also conduits."[19] To make good on this attribute, Studio City boasts its clients' affordable integration into fiber-optic networks and satellite services, courtesy of government-owned Samacom, itself now an investor in extra-territorial Smart City developments.[20]

All these buildings and infrastructures, it should be underscored, exist in concrete local terms, eased into the landscape by intricate town planning and legislative measures, feeding into and out of the greater world in a just-in-time fashion that belies the seemingly inward facing nature of studio design. To aid in this mission, such buildings are also strategically situated. No more so than in their frequent placement within free zones. While free zones are typically understood as traditional industrial manufacturing precincts, Dubai has made it its duty to found scores dedicated to other activities. The Dubai Creative Clusters Authority, which also encompasses Internet City, Media City, Knowledge Park, Design District, and International Academic City, commands exceptional labor, ownership, taxation, and freedom of expression affordances, divorced from those of the state at large. It would be wrong to understand free zones as fenced off entities purely because they sit at a certain remove from the city proper. It is no accident that we find them close to transport hubs, with Studio City a mere fifteen minutes away from the international passenger and freight airports and near the docks. In this respect and many others free zones acquiesce comprehensively to the global market, which freely courses through all of them.

LABOR COSTS AND THE COST TO HUMAN LABOR

Beyond a focus on the movement of product within and through such terrains, acknowledging a parallel traffic in workers, brought in on nonpermanent contracts, is an even more urgent imperative. As Julie Cidell observes of distribution center employees, but in ways that seem strikingly pertinent to itinerant film personnel too, "the temporary nature of employment means that workers are like the goods they move in more ways than one, as they flow in and out of the building on a time scale that differs only slightly from the freight, their own 'workplaces' distributed over the range . . . [that meets the needs of their ever-changing] clients."[21] Multisited production creates a transnational workforce, not only as the film moves from place to place but also as skilled recruits move in to contribute to it, an updating of patterns in migrations that have marked film history since close to its inception, rendering epicenters like Hollywood enormously demographically diverse. The ebbs and flows of these movements are exemplified in an observation tendered by Jamal Al Sharif, chairman of the DFTC and managing director of Studio City: "during the making of Star Trek I was very impressed with the fact that about 60 percent to 70 percent were local residents, not exactly national Emiratis, but I had Colombians, South Africans, etc. This is compared to five years ago where it was the opposite. 70 percent to 80 percent of the crew was imported, the rest were local crews. Today we have over 400 different types of production companies. I think these companies see the future of this market because of the regional situation and the connectivity."[22] This vaunted connectivity speaks less of the limits of a national workforce than of the facilitated choreography of a global one.

Legislatively, labor in the UAE has already been fine-tuned to the just-in-time, partial, and easily dissolvable precepts of logistics. As I have intimated, the red tape required to bring in foreign labor is streamlined. Labor migration in the UAE subsumes migration in its totality, dependent as it is on company sponsorship; no other quotas, such as those responding to asylum claims, contribute to the inflow of people. With a conservatively estimated 89 percent of Dubai's workforce believed to be nonnationals, the allowances for keeping people around for only the duration of a project are the extent of how work is configured contractually. As almost all employees are visitors or guests—even when they are employed for decades by one or more sponsor—an acutely precarious relationship to work is enshrined. This forecloses the potential to challenge employment conditions, given how tenure in the city depends on such contracts. One is always replaceable, easily sent home, if one becomes "troublesome."[23]

Such dispensations may well function as a clear incentive to film here—more so in the free zone, where unionization is legally prohibited. This state of affairs governs not only those working directly in creative roles on any designated project; it also extends to those who maintain the buildings and those who have erected them and their constantly changing sets. As Human Rights Watch has stressed, sectors such as construction have adopted international recruitment strategies in poorer countries that border on indenture, workers bonded to employers in order to pay back their high recruitment fees; sometimes their passports are even withheld to deter them from absconding. In 2006 the average wage in this line of work was estimated to be around US$175 per month, often before enforced company deductions for food, and this salary rate does not appear to have increased in the interim.[24]

The significant financial incentives on offer for locating film production in the UAE blind those enticed to this real cost of the tightening of wages. At the time of this writing, in neighboring Abu Dhabi, another of the UAE's emirates, international film companies were being offered a 30 percent tax rebate, one of the world's most generous. Dubai itself is tax free but still offers various individually tailored support packages weighted in favor of how prominently the emirate features promotionally onscreen, how comprehensively the company draws on local resources and therefore injects into the economy. Figured as discounts, both these tax exemptions and the low cost of specific wages erase living labor conditions analogously to the way a film—and the convertible studio environment more particularly—diverts our attention from certain troubling elements of real-life circumstances. Insulated within this fantasy, an audience will rarely broach the (distinctive national) conditions under which their films come to life. Even less so if they remain barely conscious of the policies at play in spaces like Dubai, departing as they do from our imagined sense of a profligate and lavish economy: Dubai's, the film industry's, and film's narrative preoccupations alike.

To be sure, employees at the luxury end of all this contribute foundationally to the filmmaking process, too. These people's roles therefore require examination in line with a logistification of the industry, now in terms of how its hierarchies maintain uneven access power and income. Hubs such as Hollywood still retain control and top-down design. The displacement of other worse paid, less prestigious sorts of labor, equipment, and resource provision, plus their coordination, can be handed over to a hungry offshore site that is eager to get in on the action by countenancing more abusive working conditions. Allen J. Scott notes that split location film production remains dependent on the reliable provision of adjunct services.[25] For this reason I find it crucial to retain the nomenclature of offshoring, given that the scattered contributors to any given film are not afforded equal rights, diminished, typically, by distance from any of the centers imprinting the primary stamp on an international production. Dubai's economy runs to large extent on its service provision, as exemplified by the sorts of compliance and subservience that distinguish its shopping and tourism as some of the world's most hyped. The DFTC, we should remember, promotes itself as a time- and effort-saving enterprise, taking on sourcing everyone from local crew and locations to filming and work permits. It shoulders a lot of the thinking for the production company but from within what will be defined as a service rather than a creative capacity, the former garnering indubitably less cachet than the latter. In so doing, the DFTC knits into the broader economy of service that is perhaps more integral to split location production than is typically acknowledged in the study of the studio (or in film studies more generally).

The material realities of competition in these fields figure crucially. For instance, while Eastern Europe was seized on as a comparable offshore filmmaking site after the demise of state communism (what with the sudden availability of previously nationalized studio complexes and well-established filmmaking expertise), the region incited persistent critique because it lacked both an acquiescent can-do culture and suitable high-end hotels for above-the-line employees.[26] Not so Dubai, whose service workers' very residency hinges on them shining in their jobs. They sustain, at undeniable human cost, the country's luxury leisure facilities, its hotels, beaches, and plethora of expensive restaurants, the first-class indulgences of the Emirates airline that eases the journey there and away. As such, this site can market itself as a location for filmmaking where, for some lucky arrivals, the experience will feel "less like work," more like an extravagant holiday.

Here the weave of interconnected local concerns benefiting from international film spending, beyond the state-managed freight and airline giants essential to the sustenance of split location filmmaking, is palpably tighter. The Dubai Creative Clusters Authority, the free zone group in which Studio City is nested, is managed by Tecom, a subsidiary of Dubai Holding, a government-owned holding company with a capacious assortment of assets, including the Jumeirah Group of luxury hotels and resorts. Dubai Holding's sister investment company, Dubai World, is responsible for the famous reclaimed land megaprojects, The World and The Palm, while also managing the Jebel Ali port and DP World, one of the world's largest marine terminal operators. Dubai Holding's interest in mixed yet integrated property investment coordinates with another local giant, Emaar Properties, whose portfolio includes the famous Dubai Mall and the world's tallest building, Burj Khalifa, along with Arabian Ranges, an exclusive gated community, replete with a golf course, that neighbors Studio City. DSC boss Jamal Al Sharif openly lays out how real estate interests drove the free zone's inception:

The whole focus was to build the real estate, build the structure, prepare it as fast as possible because eventually down the road you will have to build the people, build the industry, build the knowledge and this is what's happening. The approach is to change them, to build the future. The Dubai Creative Cluster was built to fund, support and develop the local industry, which is going to drive the real estate. The real estate is done. Now it's time for us to fill up the studios, make more films, more TV, nurture our local filmmakers.[27]

This statement exposes a "real estate first" policy, the bank accounts of construction and contracting firms, it must be emphasized, flourishing on account of migrant labor exploitation in the extreme. Braided into an associated economy of housing, hotels, and transportation, unpredictable fluctuations in rental income for somewhere like Studio City are dampened.

THE STUDIO ASSET LEVERAGED FOR FINANCIALIZATION

By understanding Studio City within this vertical and horizontal web of proprietorship, we can begin to grasp the free zone as not simply a spirited new entrant into global film production but also as part of a much more expansive and designed compulsion to make headway within real estate markets. If there is one thing almost everyone knows about Dubai, it is its unprecedented growth as a built environment, oil and gas wealth pumped into massive commercial developments. These moves have concocted a modern city from almost scratch over a very short period, urbanization functioning as an engine for diversified capital accumulation, transforming oil into property to accelerate further growth. As the UAE official free zones website vaunts, here speaking of private rather than public backers, Dubai Studio City presents (foreign) businesses setting up shop there with the "opportunity to channel the vast amount of untapped wealth from local investors for project finance and long-term investment."[28]

Real estate has proven cheap, quick, and easy to build in the UAE, thanks to a poorly paid, subjugated workforce and a top-down governance structure that can formulate, coordinate, and finance in a planned fashion. Legally, the ruling family (the very people in control of corporations like Dubai Holding) is the default owner of undeveloped land in the emirate. Accordingly, costs are low, and speculative ventures, like the greenfields entry into film studio rental and services, require less effort than they might elsewhere. Such endeavors figure beyond immediate primitive accumulation in the Marxian sense, whereby a local population (alongside an equally resourceless international migrant workforce) is dispossessed of land and reduced to dependence on selling their own labor at whatever its market cost in order to survive. In the Dubai context dispossession actually congeals more as citizen dependence on a benevolent welfare state and a consequent disenfranchisement from the job market because Emiratis expect higher salaries and are often less skilled than migrants.

Saskia Sassen condemns this drive to profit from land and its ramifications. Although she concentrates on foreign acquisition, her insights remain just as pertinent to rental and leasing in the UAE as they do to related Emirati purchasing overseas. Both speak to a long history of the enclosure of the commons as a motor for capitalism:

> Acquisition of foreign land . . . requires, and in turn stimulates, the making of a vast global market for land. It entails the development of an also vast specialized servicing infrastructure to enable sales and acquisitions, secure property or leasing rights, develop appropriate legal instruments, and even push for the making of new law to accommodate such purchases in a sovereign country. This is an infrastructure that goes well beyond supporting the mere act of purchasing. . . . As it develops, this specialized sector, in turn, depends on further acquisitions of foreign land as a source of profits. We see the beginnings of a large-scale commodification of land, which may in turn lead to the financializing of the commodity we still call, simply, land.[29]

In keeping with these patterns, Dubai has increasingly reconfigured the legal and financial systems that sustain it so that capital can be further liquefied and financialized via real estate. To understand how, it is first essential to fathom how Studio City, courtesy of the international currents of people, equipment, and commodities streaming through it, contributes to this distinct set of economic imperatives—less as a factory, more as a specific type of asset.

With real estate developments mushrooming, the emirate logically seeks to populate them on a largely rental- and leasing-for-profit basis. Who are their clients? As workers throughout the world are denuded of what they need to make ends meet in home countries—in part by the forceful transfer of public land in countries from Egypt to India to private ownership and into the hands of foreign companies that include Emaar and Dubai Holding—they routinely try their luck as migrant workers in countries like the UAE, especially as doors slam shut across Europe and the United States. For cinema this tendency has been intensified by the decimation of once-nationalized film industries in the region, such as those of Egypt and Syria, many of whose personnel have since moved to Dubai to work in the privatized media. Another advantage of the majority migrant population surfaces. As has already been determined, these inhabitants are interpellated wholly as temporary, in step not only with an elasticity and flexibility recognized from logistics and neoliberal precarity at large but also with the expendability and replaceability on which a rental economy prospers. Under their conditions it is harder to buy, easier and more sensible to rent or lease. Wealth concurrently spawns from economic instability and primitive accumulation elsewhere.

Yet another border-crossing vector interjects. As I have already pointed out, film workers attracted to the UAE contribute not so much to local productions as to those of transnational corporations. Some of these companies are short-term visitors, while others (cinema-based or media-focused more generally) have regionally headquartered in the Dubai Creative Clusters Authority. Their roster includes Fox International, STAR, NBC International, MTV, Endemol, the Korean Broadcasting System, Sony Music Entertainment, MBC, Dolby, and an incubator space for YouTube, to name but a few of hundreds with offices in these free zones.

Economists Piyush Tiwari and Michael White have observed that global and regional headquartering has, as of late, shifted increasingly and en masse toward what are known as "emerging economies."[30] Their detractors see transnational corporations contributing to dispossession at the same time as amplifying their global reach over ever multiplying spaces of production, thanks, in the Dubai context, to an easy flow of equally transnational cheap labor that can service their (in Dubai tax-free) ascendency. As business school academics Vanessa Strauss-Kahn and Xavier Vives summarize, "Headquarters relocate to metropolitan areas with good airport facilities—with a dramatic impact, low corporate taxes, low average wages, high level of business services, same industry specialization, and agglomeration of headquarters in the same sector of activity."[31] Dubai (and Studio City) offer these advantages in spades, helping position the country at number sixteen out of 148 in terms of ease of doing business according to the World Economic Forum's 2016–17 *Global Competitiveness Report.*[32] The UAE's much-touted stability is enforced through extensive securitization, foreign policy agreements, and a stable currency pegged to the US dollar. And, most particularly, the appeal of headquartering here rests on no less than the globalization of property markets, buttressed by technological innovations and legal and financial systems that make relocation or growth possible. The infrastructure and globalized network potential on which Dubai prides itself finds its match in an assimilation of and into economic and business practices (see fig. 12.3).

Integration into regional trade blocs, such as the Gulf Cooperation Council, reduces or eliminates tariffs for headquartered businesses, easing entry to the vast markets of neighboring oil-rich nations. Dubai profits, too, from its natural proximity to the major markets of Russia, China, and India (who also stand as the United Arab Emirates' major outside investors in real estate). The Free Zone Authority has itself striven to accommodate global capital's imperatives through business-ready legislation. One major instance has been the license for foreign companies to leasehold in spaces like Studio City (an opportunity blocked in most other parts of the emirate). Another allowance that reigns within the media free zones, yet not outside them, is that of freedom of expression, which stands as testament to how flexible and acquiescent the now variegated Dubai legal system is in bending to the needs of transnational media corporations. If such laws and practices seem less conceivable

FIGURE 12.3. "Film strip" bridges architecturally imply creative interlinkage and ease of movement. Photo by Kay Dickinson.

within the traditional mores of the country itself, then the free zones function as realms of exception held at arm's length from the laws governing the emirate at large, while also serving to forcefully globalize it. We might read this as the cultivation within sociopolitical quarters of the standardization recognized from less seemingly intrusive compliances, like those of studio design and technological conformity. The arrival of transnational corporations pushes the local market to further globalize via what the former demand of the latter.

In a sense the "any city" potential that the Dubai cityscape offers the filmmaker (where it can even stand in as "the future" in *Star Trek Beyond*) spills over as an asset to the real estate market. Dubai is now a flexible and almost identikit nodal point in a global economy it helps lubricate, as capable of representing a generic world onscreen as it is in contributing to one in actuality. Everything possible is done to connect Dubai with globalized free trade; a service economy ethos rolls out across politics and economics in a manner bearing consequences for those involved.

If Dubai presents itself and is consumed as a safe, according, and homogeneous environment in which to conduct global business (media or otherwise), there are repercussions down the scale. Smaller film companies, from equipment renters to digital effects companies, feel obligated likewise to set up shop here. A good number of these are run or staffed by people whose options in their homelands have been significantly curtailed by political instability, warfare, or the privatization of their own media systems. Many are refugees, more still economic migrants. The rents that spaces like Studio City command are distinctly higher than those in places of origin, justified largely by the competitive advantages, including the unbending legal framing of migrant worker rights, that Dubai proffers the transnational corporation. All the while, Dubai accrues not only purchasing expenditure but also ground rents and maintenance fees for the free zones' state managers.[33]

This feeds back into how the diversification of oil money into real estate promises a reliable way of generating ongoing income. But it does more than this; it allows for a transmogrification of financial systems that positions concerns like Studio City within a larger series of political and legal shifts. As has been the case across the globe, real estate investment has enabled the rise within traditional banking of mortgages, debt, and securitization, the absorption of practices that are not only often dangerously speculative and dependent on fictitious capital but that also allow, more than ever before, assets that had been considered concrete (bricks and mortar) to be liquefied, rapidly traded, and thus enfolded into diversified investment portfolios. Real estate is generally considered the main benefactor of augmented financialization, absorbing liquidity and allowing for leverage that can outweigh more traditional asset value. For sure, Dubai ballasts itself against some of these volatilities: it has built on government-owned land at low cost, its legislature has reduced red tape and sluggish planning permission processes. Yet the aim, ultimately, as Michelle Buckley and Adam Hanieh argue, has been not simply to use real estate investment to lock into global supply chains, including film's, but also to instigate real estate liberalization itself in order to drive "most fundamentally the formation of markets, regulatory mechanisms and class factions to facilitate novel capital circulation and accumulation activities. . . . The recent integration of real estate and financial markets is not simply a by-product of property-market liberalization or growing access by global finance capital to local real estate assets; rather, marketized urbanization has in part constituted a strategy of geofinancial re-engineering, in which materially tangible real estate mega-projects have provided a key mechanism for Gulf states to fuel growth and diversification in the financial circuit."[34]

In this way Dubai Studio City helps conform to Ben Goldsmith and Tom O'Regan's assertion that greenfields studio complexes perhaps act less to actually make media and more to *enable something else*. For these two authors, enabling involves creating a sector, boosting a media economy, or developing a suitable infrastructure—one that enfranchises and coordinates governmental and private actors.[35] In Dubai, what is being similarly empowered is the diversification of the economy away from an ever-dwindling supply of oil to a present and future in rents and property trade whose profits can then be reinvested globally, in property as well as other sectors. These maneuvers serve as a direct response to the fact that access to financing is deemed the UAE's second most conspicuous barrier to trade.[36] Historically, cash payment has been the norm and direct debt against GDP stands at only 14 percent, as compared to the US's 104 percent.[37] Tellingly, the two largest (and growing) contributors to this overall percentage are personal loans for business, at 21 percent, and construction and real estate, at 17 percent.[38] The deployment of logistical principles in reducing friction finds its equivalents within real estate pathways through financial circuits.

To flesh out Buckley and Hanieh's assertions, the global rise of derivatives markets allows spatially fixed real estate to be invested and traded almost as simply as more fugacious carriers of capital like stocks and shares, thanks to advances in information technology and the deregulation and harmonization of markets across the world. As a consequence, property, including in Dubai, epitomizes a plain relation of ownership, leasing, and renting, while also being parceled off into diversified investment portfolios from anywhere on the planet, largely undertaken and managed by insurance and pensions companies, mutual funds, trusts, and private equity funds.[39] Many of us may have our financial futures invested in Dubai without even knowing it.

As Buckley and Hanieh further elaborate, oil money funneled into real estate that engenders foreign direct investment (FDI) acts as a pivot for these largely state-owned enterprises to distance themselves from regionally specific moral impediments that inhibit the UAE's financial sector. They stress how Islamic banking, with its adherence to Shari'a law, a mainstay for the citizenry of the region, forbids both the accrual of profit from interest and excessive risk (which is considered akin to gambling).[40] As these are the lifeblood of the neoliberal economy— the very same one Dubai aims to link into and profit from—loopholes must be sought. Investing, via direct acquisitions, in concrete projects with lucrative returns has arisen as one advantageous get-out. Another strategy has been to nurture FDI whose provenance need not hang on Islamic code. The globalization of the real estate sector, with its readily available external loans for foreign investors, can then participate prominently in this fix, orbiting as it does at a distance from religious protocols. The encouragement is toward debt, from which such institutions profit and which, after centuries of minimal impact, is rapidly overtaking the UAE.[41] The major contributing factor here is the rise in costs of living, a direct result of inflation confected by overleveraging.

Those benefiting from these ballooning rents, including sovereign concerns like Dubai Holding, Emaar, and DP World, have since reached out into all the corners under global real estate's dominion. From Azerbaijan to Germany these companies have amassed property portfolios embracing everything from housing and shopping complexes to ports and logistics hubs, converting nonrenewable current resources (oil and gas) into mobile capital that territorializes to allow wealth to renew and grow. One net effect, of course, is the influence these built environments have on the lives of those working and living in them. Just as transnational corporations headquartered in Dubai compel a tranche of legislative and economic insistences, so, too, an Emirati presence overseas can coerce local governments into submitting to its own whims. The political and financial structures that care better for owners and landlords than those who rent from them is accordingly also consolidated through the expectations extrapolated by their architectures and infrastructural logics. Although we may only occasionally "see" Dubai onscreen when foreign films are shot there, the capital they help generate flows outward in financialized and concrete forms that invigorate a certain macroeconomy. As the film-focused examples investigated in this essay have only begun to illustrate, their armatures jeopardize the stability of countless people and, by implication, almost all of us.

Refusing to understand something like a film studio as merely a solid, single-sited entity and grappling with how it instrumentalizes the current vicissitudes of both the global supply chain and the international property market is to get closer to the impact of capital's harmfully mercurial character. Marx's M-C-M (money-commodity-money) general formula, which facilitates the primacy of exchange-value schemas, is perpetuated.[42] The abstract quality of capital persists as it travels and mutates, while the exploitation of the workers inputting into its value can be obscured. It must be underscored that offshored enterprises explicitly, and those compliant with the regimes of debt and profit in particular, hold precious little loyalty toward their localized workforce or its rights. As has been evinced, there is little that is "free" or "natural" about the movements into these formations by all concerned: renters, employers, or employees. At a profound political level their principles are buttressed by patent restrictions and abuses endured by those workers who keep commodities—studios and films included—in circulation and here under direct threat of losing their livelihoods, even their right to remain in the country.

The point here has not been to demonize Dubai above and beyond an "anywhere else" that is just as much a confluence of global neoliberal currents, even though a good deal of the site-specific actions this essay has discussed clearly warrant critique. Rather, Dubai's "success" evidences precise motivations, strategies, and agendas that might just as easily work against it. The modular character of contemporary offshore production leaves its workers enormously vulnerable as the industry ceaselessly exchanges and substitutes real locations and employees along its journey into and out of markets. One studio complex's cost efficiency will likely supplant another's, the competitive pricing of labor an ultimate bargaining chip here. Dubai Studio City's adeptness at riding these currents remains to be seen, and entering into speculation about its own potential mirrors too closely the mechanics of the futures market. For the moment, Studio City persists as a telling demonstration of how split-location supply-chain cinema colludes with broader economic, legislative and labor regimes, how its sites leverage the privatization, financialization, and globalization of the actual space in which most of us endeavor to survive through highly precarious means.

NOTES

1. Curtin and Sanson, *Precarious Creativity*, 1–2.

2. Within the literature on studios Goldsmith and O'Regan's *The Film Studio* is one of the few to think about these sites as globally networked and, most particularly, what it means to operate as a satellite studio servicing a more developed film industry.

3. The cost of building Studio City courtesy of Nick Vivarelli, "Dubai Studio City Chief Jamal Al-Sharif Talks New Strategy to Stimulate Local Production," *Variety*, Dec. 9, 2016, http://variety.com/2016/film/global/dubai-studio-city-chief-jamal-al-sharif-on-new-strategy-to-stimulate-local-content-industry-1201938058.

4. Scott, *On Hollywood*, 80.

5. Shiel, *Hollywood Cinema and the Real Los Angeles*, 129–30.

6. Jacobson, *Studios Before the System*, 188.

7. This is not to dismiss how crucial logistics, real estate, and finance capital were to the development of previous studio hubs but more to insist that these three sectors hold a more prominent and consciously recognized position in today's economy.

8. Goldsmith and O'Regan understand this as a recurrent trend: "Perhaps the common characteristic of all of these [greenfields] developments is their risk-taking entrepreneurialism. Each share an *extreme* character that defies common sense, accepted wisdom, and routine film industry risk assessments." Goldsmith and O'Regan, *The Film Studio*, 78.

9. Government of Dubai, "About DCCA," https://dcca.gov.ae/en/about-dcca.

10. Dubai Film and TV Commission, *Limitless Possibilities*, 2.

11. Government of Dubai, "Dubai Film and TV Commission: Services."

12. LeCavalier, *The Rule of Logistics*, 6.

13. Government of Dubai, "Dubai Film and TV Commission: Local Production Companies."

14. Unitas Consultancy, *Dubai*, 15.

15. Speed of processing data from Editor in Chief, "Dubai's Prime for Film Production"; and Official Website for UAE Free Zones, "Dubai Studio City."

16. LeCavalier, *The Rule of Logistics*, 7.

17. LeCavalier, 34.

18. Sigler, "Relational Cities."

19. LeCavalier, *The Rule of Logistics*, 13.

20. Official Website for UAE Free Zones, "Dubai Studio City."

21. Cidell, "Distribution Centers as Distributed Places," 27–28.

22. In Editor in Chief, "Dubai's Prime for Film Production."

23. I discuss the labor conditions of film workers in the Dubai free zones in greater detail in Dickinson, *Arab Cinema Travels*, 153–58.

24. Human Rights Watch, *Building Towers, Cheating Workers*, 7; and Human Rights Watch, *Island of Happiness Revisited*, 51.

25. Scott, *On Hollywood*, 85.

26. Goldsmith, Ward, and O'Regan, *Local Hollywood,* 89; Goldsmith and O'Regan, *The Film Studio,* 6.

27. Quoted in Editor in Chief, "Dubai's Prime for Film Production."

28. Official Website for UAE Free Zones, "Dubai Studio City."

29. Sassen, *Expulsions,* 81.

30. Tiwari and White, *Real Estate Finance and the New Economy,* 115–16, 58.

31. Strauss-Kahn and Vives, "Why and Where Do Headquarters Move?" 1.

32. Schwab, *Global Competitiveness Report, 2016–2017,* 5.

33. Official Website for UAE Free Zones, "Dubai Studio City."

34. Buckley and Hanieh, "Diversification by Urbanization," 168, 171.

35. Goldsmith and O'Regan, *The Film Studio,* 77.

36. So claim the results of the World Economic Forum's Executive Opinion Survey, as cited in Schwab, *Global Competitiveness Report, 2016–2017,* 352. The UAE ranks twenty-eighth globally on financial market development, which, notes Schwab, is low in comparison to its standing for other economic determinants (353).

37. Unitas Consultancy, *Dubai,* 7.

38. Unitas Consultancy, 11.

39. Tiwari and White, *Real Estate Finance and the New Economy,* 156–57.

40. Buckley and Hanieh, "Diversification by Urbanization," 169. It should be noted that most Emirati banks provide only Islamic-compliant windows rather than running entirely according to Shari'a principles. But overt profit from interest or risk imperils the good standing of the state more generally.

41. John Richards, CEO of compareit4me, summarized some of the results of a poll his company undertook in 2014: "There are however 28 percent of respondents who are finding debt repayments difficult and this is a concern. The cost of living in Dubai is rising and unfortunately at a faster rate than salaries. This is forcing some to use debt to cover basic costs like rent which is clearly not sustainable." Quoted in "Rise in UAE Residents Using Credit Cards, Loans to Clear Existing Debts," *Arabian Business,* Oct. 29, 2014, www.arabianbusiness.com/rise-in-uae-residents-using-credit-cards-loans-clear-existing-debts-569814.html.

42. Marx, *Capital,* 247–57.

SELECTED BIBLIOGRAPHY

ARCHIVAL SOURCES

Archivio Centrale dello Stato, Rome
    Allied Control Command
Archivio dell'Ufficio Storico dello Stato Maggiore dell'Esercito, Rome
    Fondo N-1/11; L-10
Archivo General de la Nación, Mexico City
    Fondo Lazaro Cardenas
    Fondo Pascual Ortiz Rubio
Arquivo Geral da Cidade do Rio de Janeiro
    Coleção Pedro Lima
BBC Written Archives Centre
The British Entertainment History Project: Interviews conducted by BECTU
    https://historyproject.org.uk
Bundesarchiv, Berlin
    Politisches Archiv des Auswärtigen Amts
Cinemateca Brasileira
    Arquivo Pedro Lima
Cinémathèque française, Bibliothèque du film
    Fonds Lucien Aguettand
    Fonds Louis Gaumont
Cranbrook Educational Community
    Cranbrook Foundation, Office Records
Gosfil'mofond, Moscow
Imperial War Museum Sound Archive, London
    Lowe, Alfred Charles (Oral History)

Instituto Nacional de Antropología e Historia
 Archivo de la Palabra, Proyecto de cine mexicano, PHO/2/8
Library of Congress, Washington, DC
 Manuscript Division, Charles and Ray Eames Papers
National Archives of the United Kingdom, Kew, Richmond
 Foreign Office Records
 War Office Records
National Archives at College Park, Maryland
 General Records of the Department of State
 Records of the Office of Strategic Services
Russian State Archive of Literature and Art (RGALI)
State Central Museum of Cinema in Moscow (GTsMK)
SUNY Buffalo, University Archives
 Department of Media Study: Records 1959–2009
Watry Design, Inc.
 watrydesign.com
Woody Vasulka Archive
 www.vasulka.org
YIVO Institute for Jewish Research, New York

SELECTED PERIODICAL SOURCES

A Federação
Annals of the American Academy of Political and Social Science
A Noite
Arabian Business
ArchiExpo
Architectural Digest
Architectural Forum
Architectural Record
Artforum
Arts & Architecture
Boletín de informes de la Secretaria de Hacienda y Crédito Publico
Box Office
Broadcasting
Buffalo Courier-Express
Cinearte
Cinema
Cinema Reporter
Communications of the ACM
Correio do Povo
Crimen: Documentario settimanale di criminologia
Diário de Notícias
Diário Trabalhista
Economica

El Día
El Economista
El Informador
El Mundo (Las Vegas, NV)
El Nacional
El Nacional Revolucionario
El Popular
El Porvenir
El Trimestre Económico
El Universal
The Engineer
Environment and Planning D: Society and Space
Estado de São Paulo
Excélsior
Film Culture
Film Daily
Film History
Film Industry
Film-Kurier
Fortune
Galveston Daily News
Gudok
Hollywood Reporter
Intercine
Interiors
Izvestiia
Journal of the Society of Motion Picture Engineers
Jueves de Excélsior
Kinematograph Weekly
Kinematograph Weekly Studio Review
Kinematograph Year Book
Kino-gazeta
Kinovedcheskie zapiski
Mañana
Marin Independent Journal
Motion Picture Daily
Motion Picture Herald
Motion Picture News
Nature
New York Times
9-1-1 Magazine
Novedades
October
O Estado de Minas
O Imparcial

O Jornal
O Libertador
Para Todos
Pencil Points
Photoplay
Popular Wireless and Television Times
Pravda
Progressive Architecture
Proletarskoe kino
Radio Times
Radio World
RCA Broadcast News
Revista de Semana
San Francisco Chronicle
Selecta
Shinario
Showman's Trade Review
South African Outlook
Sovetskoe iskusstvo
Sovetskoe kino
Star
Supplement to Film Industry
Take One
Television: The World's First Television Journal
The Times (London)
USSR in Construction
Variety
Wireless World and Radio Review
Yomiuri shinbun
Za bol'shevistskii fil'm

PRIMARY AND SECONDARY SOURCES

Alexander, Zeynep Çelik. "The Core That Wasn't." *Harvard Design Magazine* 35 (2012): 84–89.

———. *Kinaesthetic Knowing: Aesthetics, Epistemology, Modern Design*. Chicago: University of Chicago Press, 2017.

Almanak Laemmert: Annuario Administrativo, Agricola, Profissional, Mercantil e Industrial dos Estados Unidos do Brasil, 1909.

Alpers, Svetlana. *Rembrandt's Enterprise: The Studio and the Market*. Chicago: University of Chicago Press, 1988.

———. "The Studio, the Laboratory, and the Vexations of Art." In *Picturing Science, Producing Art*, edited by Caroline A. Jones and Peter Galison, 401–17. New York: Routledge, 1998.

Anderson, Benedict. *Imagined Communities: Reflections on the Origins and Spread of Nationalism*. London: Verso, 2006.

Anderson, Christopher. *Hollywood TV: The Studio System in the Fifties*. Austin: University of Texas Press, 1994.

Anderson, Joseph L., and Donald Richie. *The Japanese Film: Art and Industry*. Exp. ed. Princeton, NJ: Princeton University Press, 1982.

Appadurai, Arjun. "Disjuncture and Difference in the Global Cultural Economy." *Public Culture* 2, no. 2 (Spring 1990): 1–24.

Araújo, Vicente de Paula. *A bela época do cinema brasileiro*. São Paulo: Perspectiva, 1976.

Arendt, Hannah. *The Origins of Totalitarianism*. New York: Harcourt, Brace, 1951.

Argentieri, Mino. *L'asse cinematografico Roma-Berlino*. Naples: Sapere, 1986.

Arnheim, Rudolf. "Seeing Afar Off." *Intercine* 7, no. 2 (Feb. 1935): 71–82.

Aso, Noriko. *Public Properties: Museums in Imperial Japan*. Durham, NC: Duke University Press, 2014.

Autran, Arthur. *O pensamento industrial cinematográfico brasileiro*. São Paulo: Hucitec, 2013.

———. "Pedro Lima em *Selecta*." *Cinemais* 7 (1997): 53–65.

Avni, Sheerly. *Cinema by the Bay*. New York: George Lucas Books (Welcome Books), 2006.

Baba Hiroe. "Sugiyama Shigemaru Mukōjima tei: Kodama Jinja to Nikkatsu Mukōjima Satsueijo" (Sugiyama Shigemaru's Mukōjima residence: Kodama Shrine and Nikkatsu Mukōjima studio). In *Tami o oya ni su: Yumeno Kyūsaku to Sugiyama 3-dai kenkyūkai kaihō* (Treat the people as they were your parents: Bulletin of the Society of Research on Yumeno Kyūsaku and three generations of the Sugiyama family), Vol. 3, edited by Yumeno Kyūsaku to Sugiyama 3-Dai Kenkyūkai, 61–73. Fukuoka: Tosho Shuppan Shiranui Shobō, 2015.

Barraclough, Laura R. *Making the San Fernando Valley: Rural Landscapes, Urban Development, and White Privilege*. Athens: University of Georgia Press, 2010.

Barros, Luiz de. *Minhas memórias de cineasta*. Rio de Janeiro: Artenova, 1978.

Barsacq, Léon. *Caligari's Cabinet and Other Grand Illusions: A History of Film Design*. Edited by Elliott Stein. Translated by Michael Bullock. New York: Little, Brown, 1976.

———. *Le Décor de film*. Paris: Seghers, 1970.

Baxter, Peter. "On the History and Ideology of Film Lighting." *Screen* 16, no. 3 (Oct. 1975): 83–106.

Bean, Jennifer M. "Technologies of Early Stardom and the Extraordinary Body." *Camera Obscura* 16, no. 3 (2001): 8–57.

Beatty, Edward. *Technology and the Search for Progress in Modern Mexico*. Berkeley: University of California Press, 2015.

Becker, Ron. "'Hear-and-See Radio' in the World of Tomorrow: RCA and the Presentation of Television at the World's Fair, 1939–1940." *Historical Journal of Film, Radio and Television* 21, no. 4 (2001): 361–78.

Belodubrovskaya, Maria. *Not According to Plan: Filmmaking under Stalin*. Ithaca, NY: Cornell University Press, 2017.

Ben Block, Alex, and Lucy Autrey Wilson. *George Lucas's Blockbusting*. New York: George Lucas Books (HarperCollins), 2010.

Ben-Ghiat, Ruth. *Italian Fascism's Empire Cinema*. Bloomington: Indiana University Press, 2015.

Ben-Ghiat, Ruth, and Stephanie Malia Hom. Introduction to *Italian Mobilities*, edited by Ruth Ben-Ghiat and Stephanie Malia Hom, 1–19. London: Routledge, 2015.

Benjamin, Walter. "Paris, the Capital of the Nineteenth Century." Translated by Howard Eiland. In *Walter Benjamin: Selected Writings, Volume 3, 1935–1938*, edited by Howard Eiland and Michael W. Jennings, translated by Edmund Jephcott, Howard Eiland, and Others, 32–49. Cambridge, MA: Belknap Press of Harvard University Press, 2002.

———. "The Work of Art in the Age of Its Technological Reproducibility (Second Version)." In *Walter Benjamin: Selected Writings, Volume 3, 1935–1938*, edited by Howard Eiland and Michael W. Jennings, translated by Edmund Jephcott, Howard Eiland, and Others, 101–33. Cambridge, MA: Belknap Press of Harvard University Press, 2002.

Bennett, Tony. "The Exhibitionary Complex." *new formations*, no. 4 (Spring 1988): 73–102.

Bentes, Ivana. "The *Sertão* and the *Favela* in Contemporary Brazilian Cinema." In *New Brazilian Cinema*, edited by Lúcia Nagib, 121–38. London: I. B. Tauris, 2003.

Bergfelder, Tim, Sue Harris, and Sarah Street. *Film Architecture and the Transnational Imagination: Set Design in 1930s European Cinema*. Amsterdam: Amsterdam University Press, 2007.

Bernardet, Jean-Claude. *Historiografia clássica do cinema brasileiro: Metodologia e pedagogia*. São Paulo: Annablume, 1995.

Bernardi, Joanne. *Writing in Light: The Silent Scenario and the Japanese Pure Film Movement*. Detroit, MI: Wayne State University Press, 2001.

Bird, Robert. "Medvedkin na voine." In *Perezhit' voinu: Sovetskaia kinoindustriia v SSSR, 1939–1949*, 295–313. Moscow: ROSSPEN, 2018.

Biskind, Peter. *Easy Riders, Raging Bulls: How the Sex, Drugs, and Rock 'n' Roll Generation Saved Hollywood*. New York: Simon and Schuster, 1999.

Boddy, William. *Fifties Television: The Industry and Its Critics*. Urbana: University of Illinois Press, 1992.

Boime, Albert. *The Magisterial Gaze: Manifest Destiny and American Landscape Painting*. Washington, DC: Smithsonian Institution Press, 1991.

Bolter, Jay David, and Richard Grusin. *Remediation: Understanding New Media*. Cambridge, MA: MIT Press, 1999.

Bonfioli, Igino, dir. *Exposição de galinhas e cavalos*. Belo Horizonte, 1920.

Bordwell, David, Janet Staiger, and Kristin Thompson. *The Classical Hollywood Cinema: Film Style and Mode of Production to 1960*. New York: Columbia University Press, 1985.

Botha, Kevin Frank. "Warriors without Weapons: Black Servicemen in the Union Defence Force during the Second World War." Master's thesis, University of Witwatersrand, Johannesburg, 1992. http://hdl.handle.net/10539/20885.

Bozak, Nadia. *The Cinematic Footprint: Lights, Camera, Natural Resources*. New Brunswick, NJ: Rutgers University Press, 2012.

Brown, Simon, Sarah Street, and Liz Watkins. *British Colour Cinema: Practices and Theories*. London: British Film Institute/Palgrave Macmillan, 2013.

Bruno, Giuliana. *Surface: Matters of Aesthetics, Materiality, and Media*. Chicago: University of Chicago Press, 2014.

Buckley, Michelle, and Adam Hanieh. "Diversification by Urbanization: Tracing the Property-Finance Nexus in Dubai and the Gulf." *International Journal of Urban and Regional Research* 38, no. 1 (Jan. 2014): 155–75.

Burns, Russell W. *British Television: The Formative Years*. London: Institution of Electrical Engineers, 1986.

———. *John Logie Baird, Television Pioneer.* London: Institution of Electrical Engineers, 2000.

———. *Television: An International History of the Formative Years.* London: Institution of Electrical Engineers, 1998.

Burns, Sarah. *Inventing the Modern Artist.* New Haven, CT: Yale University Press, 1996.

Canclini, Nestor García, Alejandro Castellanos, and Ana Rosas Mantecón. *La ciudad de los viajeros: Travesías e imaginarios urbanos, México 1940–2000.* México, DF: Universidad Autónoma Metropolitana, Iztapalapa, 1996.

Chaiklin, Martha. "A Miracle of Industry: The Struggle to Produce Sheet Glass in Modernizing Japan." In *Building a Modern Japan: Science, Technology, and Medicine in the Meiji Era and Beyond,* edited by Morris Low, 161–82. New York: Palgrave Macmillan, 2005.

Chambers, Deborah. "Designing Early Television for the Ideal Home: The Roles of Industrial Designers and Exhibitions, 1930s-1950s." *Journal of Popular Television* 7, no. 2 (2019): 145–59.

Champlin, Charles. *George Lucas: The Creative Impulse, Lucasfilm's First Twenty Years.* New York: Abrams, 1992.

Chibnall, Stephen, and Brian McFarlane. *The British 'B' Film.* London: British Film Institute/Palgrave Macmillan, 2009.

Christensen, Jerome. *America's Corporate Art: The Studio Authorship of Hollywood Motion Pictures.* Stanford, CA: Stanford University Press, 2012.

Cidell, Julie. "Distribution Centers as Distributed Places: Mobility, Infrastructure and Truck Traffic." In *Cargomobilities: Moving Materials in a Global Age,* edited by Thomas Birchnell, Satya Savitzky, and John Urry, 17–34. New York: Routledge, 2015.

Cleveland, David, and Brian Pritchard. *How Films Were Made and Shown.* Manningtree, Essex: David Cleveland, 2015.

Cohen, Wesley M., Richard Florida, Lucien Randazzese, and John Walsh. "Industry and the Academy: Uneasy Partners in the Cause of Technological Advance." In *Challenges to Research Universities,* edited by Roger G. Noll, 171–200. Washington, DC: Brookings Institution Press, 1998.

Cohen-Cole, Jamie. *The Open Mind: Cold War Politics and the Sciences of Human Nature.* Chicago: University of Chicago Press, 2014.

Colomina, Beatriz. "Media as Modern Architecture." In *Architecture between Spectacle and Use,* edited by Anthony Vidler, 58–73. New Haven, CT: Yale University Press, 2008.

———. "The Media House." *Assemblage,* no. 27 (August 1995): 55–66.

———. *Privacy and Publicity: Modern Architecture as Mass Media.* Cambridge, MA: MIT Press, 1996.

Cooper, Marg Garrett. *Universal Women: Filmmaking and Institutional Change in Early Hollywood.* Urbana: University of Illinois Press, 2010.

Corrêa de Araújo, Luciana. "O cinema silencioso pernambucano segundo as revistas cariocas." *Estudos SOCINE de Cinema IV,* 236–42. São Paulo: Nojesa Edições, 2005.

Crafton, Donald. *The Talkies: American Cinema's Transition to Sound, 1926–1931.* Berkeley: University of California Press, 1999.

Curtin, Michael, and Kevin Sanson, eds. *Precarious Creativity: Global Media, Local Labor.* Oakland: University of California Press, 2016.

Davenport, Charles. "Chairs, Fairs, and Films." In *An Eames Anthology*, edited by Daniel Ostroff, 228–29. New Haven, CT: Yale University Press, 2015.

Delavaud, Gilles. *L'art de la télévision: Histoire et esthétique de la dramatique télévisée (1950–1965)*. Bruxelles: De Boeck, 2005.

Deriabin, A. S. "Ves' Medvedkin." *Kinovedcheskie zapiski* 49 (2000): 88–89.

Doordan, Dennis P. "Design at CBS." *Design Issues* 6, no. 2 (Spring 1990): 4–17.

del Buono, Oreste, and Lietta Tornabuoni, eds. *Era Cinecittà: Vita, morte e miracoli di una fabbrica di film*. Milano: Bompiani, 1979.

Dickinson, Kay. *Arab Cinema Travels: Transnational Syria, Palestine, Dubai and Beyond*. London: BFI/Palgrave Macmillan, 2016.

Dickinson, Margaret, and Sarah Street. *Cinema and State: The Film Industry and the British Government, 1927–84*. London: British Film Institute, 1985.

Dimendberg, Edward. *Diller Scofidio + Renfro: Architecture after Images*. Chicago: University of Chicago Press, 2013.

Dixon, Wheeler Winston. "The Doubled Image: Montgomery Tully's *Boys in Brown* and the Independent Frame Process." In *Re-viewing British Cinema: Essays and Interviews*, edited by Wheeler Winston Dixon, 41–52. New York: SUNY, 1994.

Dollmann, Eugen. *Nazi Fugitive: The True Story of a German on the Run*. Translated by Edward Fitzgerald. Originally titled *Call Me Coward*. London: William Kimber, 1956; New York: Skyhorse, 2017.

Dootson, Kirsty. "'The Hollywood Powder Puff War': Technicolor Cosmetics in the 1930s." *Film History* 28, no. 1 (Jan. 2016): 107–31.

dos Santos, Sales Augusto. "Historical Roots of the 'Whitening' of Brazil." Translated by Laurence Hallewell. *Latin American Perspectives* 29, no. 1 (Jan. 2002): 61–82.

Dubai Film and TV Commission. *Limitless Possibilities*. Dubai: Government of Dubai, n.d.

"Dubai Studio City." www.fbsemirates.com/docs_dub/dsc-corporate-presentation.pdf.

Durgnat, Raymond. *A Mirror for England: British Movies from Austerity to Affluence*. London: Faber and Faber, 1970; 3rd edition, BFI/Palgrave Macmillan, 2011.

Dyer, Richard. *White*. New York: Routledge, 1997.

Eames, Charles. "Design, Designer, Industry." In *An Eames Anthology*, edited by Daniel Ostroff, 97–99. New Haven, CT: Yale University Press, 2015.

Ede, Laurie. *British Film Design*. London: I. B. Tauris, 2010.

Editor in Chief. "Dubai's Prime for Film Production." *Leaders Middle East*, Feb. 11, 2016. www.leadersme.com/dubais-prime-for-film-production.

Eiland, Howard, and Michael W. Jennings. *Walter Benjamin: A Critical Life*. Cambridge, MA: Belknap Press of Harvard University Press, 2014.

Eizenshtein, S. M. *Izbrannye proizvedeniia*. Vol. 5. Moscow: Iskusstvo, 1968.

Enko kōgyōshi (A history of Asakusa Rokku entertainment). Tokyo: Daitō Kyōiku Iinkai, 1983.

Ericson, Staffan, Kristina Riegert, and Patrik Åker. Introduction to *Media Houses: Architecture, Media and the Production of Centrality*, edited by Staffan Ericson and Kristina Riegert, 1–18. New York: Peter Lang, 2010.

Ericson, Staffen, and Kristina Riegert, eds. *Media Houses: Architecture, Media, and the Production of Centrality*. New York: Peter Lang, 2010.

Everson, William K. "Review of *Poet's Pub* in Program Notes for the New School for Social Research, 1979," reprinted in *Film History* 15, no. 3 (2003): 347.

Eyles, Allen. *Odeon Cinemas 2: From J. Arthur Rank to the Multiplex.* London: British Film Institute, 2005.

Fay, Jennifer. "Buster Keaton's Climate Change." *Modernism/Modernity* 21, no. 1 (Jan. 2014): 25–49.

———. *Inhospitable World: Cinema in the Time of the Anthropocene.* New York: Oxford University Press, 2018.

Fein, Seth. "From Collaboration to Containment: Hollywood and the International Political-Economy of Mexican Cinema after the Second World War." In *Mexico's Cinema: A Century of Films and Filmmakers,* edited by Joanne Hershfield and David R. Maciel, 123–64. Wilmington, DE: SR Books, 1999.

Ferriss, Hugh. *The Metropolis of Tomorrow.* New York: Ives Washburn, 1929.

Fickers, Andreas. "Presenting the 'Window on the World' to the World: Competing Narratives of the Presentation of Television at the World's Fairs in Paris (1937) and New York (1939)." *Historical Journal of Film, Radio and Television* 28, no. 3 (2008): 291–310.

Field, Allyson Nadia, Jan-Christopher Horak, and Jacqueline Najuma Stewart, eds. *L.A. Rebellion: Creating a New Black Cinema.* Oakland: University of California Press, 2015.

Fischer, Greg. "Don Lee and the Transformation of Los Angeles." *Southern California Quarterly* 96, no. 1 (Spring 2014): 87–115.

Fischer, Lucy. "Frampton and the Magellan Metaphor." *American Film* 4, no. 7 (May 1979): 58–63.

Fore, Devin. "The Operative Word in Soviet Factography." *October* 118 (Fall 2006): 95–131.

Frampton, Hollis. "For a Metahistory of Film." In Jenkins, *On the Camera Arts,* 131–39.

———. "Hollis Frampton in His Own Words." In Vasulka and Weibel, *Buffalo Heads,* 150–54.

———. "The Invention without a Future." In Jenkins, *On the Camera Arts,* 171–79.

———. "Letter to Donald Richie." In Jenkins, *On the Camera Arts,* 159–62.

———. "Proposal: Hardware and Software for Computer-Processed and -Generated Video." In Jenkins, *On the Camera Arts,* 269–71.

———. "VITA." In Vasulka and Weibel, *Buffalo Heads,* 146–49.

Frank, Roberta. "Interdisciplinarity: The First 50 Years." In *Words: For Robert Burchfield's Sixty-Fifth Birthday,* edited by E.G. Stanley and T.F. Hoad, 91–101. Cambridge: D.S. Brewer, 1998.

Frank, Stephanie. "Why a Studio without a Backlot Isn't like a Ten-Story Building without an Elevator: Land Planning in the Postfordist Film Industry." *Journal of Planning History* 15, no. 2 (2016): 129–48.

Freddi, Luigi. *Il cinema.* Vol. 2. Rome: L'arnia, 1949.

Fuss, Diana. *The Sense of an Interior: Four Rooms and the Writers That Shaped Them.* New York: Routledge, 2004.

Gaboury, Jacob. "Other Places of Invention: Computer Graphics at the University of Utah." In *Communities of Computing: Computer Science and Society at the ACM,* edited by Thomas J. Misa, 259–85. Minneapolis: University of Minnesota Press, 2017.

Galili, Doron. *Seeing by Electricity: The Emergence of Television, 1878–1939.* Durham, NC: Duke University Press, 2020.

Galison, Peter, and Caroline A. Jones. "Factory, Laboratory, Studio: Dispersing Sites of Production." In *The Architecture of Science,* edited by Peter Galison and Emily Thompson, 497–540. Cambridge, MA: MIT Press, 1999.

Galvão, Maria Rita. *Crônica do cinema paulistano.* São Paulo: Ática, 1975.

———. *Burguesia e cinema: O caso Vera Cruz.* Rio de Janeiro: Civilização Brasileira, 1981.

———. "Vera Cruz: A Brazilian Hollywood." In *Brazilian Cinema,* edited by Randal Johnson and Robert Stam, rev. ed., 270–80. New York: Columbia University Press, 1995.

Gary, Bret. *The Nervous Liberals: Propaganda Anxieties from World War I to the Cold War.* New York: Columbia University Press, 1999.

Gerow, Aaron. *Visions of Japanese Modernity: Articulations of Cinema, Nation, and Spectatorship, 1895–1925.* Berkeley: University of California Press, 2010.

Gillett, Philip. *The British Working Class in Postwar Film.* Manchester: Manchester University Press, 2003.

Gleich, Joshua. "The Lost Studio of Atlantis: Norman Bel Geddes's Failed Revolution in Television Form." *Velvet Light Trap* 70 (Fall 2012): 3–17.

Goby, Valerie Priscilla. "Financialization and Outsourcing in a Different Guise: The Ethical Chaos of Workforce Localization in the United Arab Emirates." *Journal of Business Ethics* 131, no. 1 (Oct. 2015): 415–21.

Goldsmith, Ben, and Tom O'Regan. *The Film Studio: Film Production in the Global Economy.* Oxford: Rowman and Littlefield, 2005.

Goldsmith, Ben, Susan Ward, and Tom O'Regan. *Local Hollywood: Global Film Production and the Gold Coast.* St Lucia, Queensland: University of Queensland Press, 2010.

Goldstein, Barbara, ed. *Arts & Architecture: The Entenza Years.* Cambridge, MA: MIT Press, 1990.

Gomes, Paulo Augusto. *Pioneiros do cinema em Minas Gerais.* Belo Horizonte: Crisálida, 2008.

Gonzaga, Alice. *Palácios e poeiras: 100 anos de cinemas no Rio de Janeiro.* Rio de Janeiro: Fundação Nacional de Artes, 1996.

Gordon, Eric. *The Urban Spectator: American Concept-Cities from Kodak to Google.* Hanover, NH: Dartmouth College Press, 2010.

Government of Dubai. "About DCCA." https://dcca.gov.ae/en/about-dcca.

———. "Dubai Film and TV Commission: Local Production Companies." www.filmdubai.gov.ae/filming-in-dubai/local-production-companies.

———. "Dubai Film and TV Commission: Services." www.dubaifilmcommission.ae/why-dubai/services.

Grady College of Journalism. *Eyes of a Generation: Television's Living History.* Athens: University of Georgia, n.d. https://eyesofageneration.com.

Grieveson, Lee. *Cinema and the Wealth of Nations: Media, Capital, and the Liberal World System.* Berkeley: University of California Press, 2018.

Gross, Benjamin. "Living Test Patterns: The Models Who Calibrated Color TV." *The Atlantic,* June 28, 2015. www.theatlantic.com/technology/archive/2015/06/miss-color-tv/396266.

Grundy, Kenneth W. *Soldiers without Politics: Blacks in the South African Armed Forces.* Berkeley: University of California Press, 1983.

Guilbaut, Serge. *How New York Stole the Idea of Modern Art.* Translated by Arthur Goldhammer. Chicago: University of Chicago Press, 1983.

Gunning, Tom. "'The Whole World within Reach': Travel Images without Borders." In Ruoff, *Virtual Voyages*, 25–41.

Gustafson, Robert. "'What's Happening to Our Pix Biz?' From Warner Bros. to Warner Communications Inc." In *The American Film Industry*, edited by Tino Balio, 574–86. Madison: University of Wisconsin Press, 1985.

Hake, Sabine. "Mapping the Native Body: On Africa and the Colonial Film in the Third Reich." In *The Imperialist Imagination: German Colonialism and Its Legacy*, edited by Sara Friedrichsmeyer, Sara Lennox, and Susanne Zantop, 163–87. Ann Arbor: University of Michigan Press, 1998.

Hansen, Miriam. "Fallen Women, Rising Stars, New Horizons: Shanghai Silent Film as Vernacular Modernism." *Film Quarterly* 54, no. 1 (2000): 10–22.

Harper, Sue, and Vincent Porter. *British Cinema of the 1950s: The Decline of Deference.* Oxford: Oxford University Press, 2003.

Harwood, John. *The Interface: IBM and the Transformation of Corporate Design, 1945–1976.* Minneapolis: University of Minnesota Press, 2011.

———. "R and D: The Eames Office at Work." In *Explorations in Architecture: Teaching, Design, Research*, edited by Reto Geiser, 200–201. Basel: Birkhäuser, 2008.

———. "TV University ca. 1964." *Art Papers*, Jan./Feb. 2015, 24–31.

———. "Wires, Walls, and Wireless: Notes toward an Investigation of Radio Architecture." *NMC: Media N*, n.d. http://median.newmediacaucus.org/art-infrastructures-hardware /wires-walls-and-wireless-notes-toward-an-investigation-of-radio-architecture.

Herb, Michael. *The Wages of Oil: Parliaments and Economic Development in Kuwait and the UAE.* Ithaca, NY: Cornell University Press, 2014.

High, Peter. "The Dawn of Cinema in Japan." *Journal of Contemporary History* 19, no. 1 (Jan. 1984): 23–57.

Hill, Erin. *Never Done: A History of Women's Work in Media Production.* New Brunswick, NJ: Rutgers University Press, 2016.

Hobsbawn, E. J. *The Age of Empire, 1875-1914.* New York: Pantheon, 1987.

Hood, Raymond. "The National Broadcasting Studios New York." *Architectural Record* 64, no. 1 (July 1928): 1–6.

Human Rights Watch. *Building Towers, Cheating Workers: Exploitation of Migrant Construction Workers in the United Arab Emirates.* New York: Human Rights Watch, 2006. www.hrw.org/report/2006/11/11/building-towers-cheating-workers/exploitation-migrant-construction-workers-united.

———. *The Island of Happiness Revisited: A Progress Report on Institutional Commitments to Address Abuses of Migrant Workers on Abu Dhabi's Saadiyat Island.* New York: Human Rights Watch, 2012. www.hrw.org/sites/default/files/reports/uae0312webwcover _0.pdf.

Hur, Namlin. *Prayer and Play in Late Tokugawa Japan: Asakusa Sensōji and Edo Society.* Cambridge, MA: Harvard University Asia Center, 2000.

Ince, Catherine. "Something about the World of Charles and Ray Eames." In *The World of Charles and Ray Eames*, edited by Catherine Ince with Lotte Johnson, 12–19. New York: Rizzoli, 2016.

Irie Yoshirō. "Yoshizawa Shōten shū Kawaura Ken'ichi no sokuseki (1): Yoshizawa Shōten no tanjō." Published English title: "Trajectories of Kawaura Ken'ichi, the Owner of

Yoshizawa & Co. (1)—Origins of the Oldest Film Company." *Kenkyū kiyō / Bulletin of the National Museum of Modern Art, Tokyo,* no. 18 (2014): 32–63.

Jacobs, Jason. *The Intimate Screen: Early British Television Drama.* Oxford: Clarendon, 2000.

Jacobsen, Lowell R. "On Robinson, Coase, And 'The Nature of the Firm.'" *Journal of the History of Economic Thought* 30, no. 1 (2008): 65–80.

Jacobson, Brian R. "Fantastic Functionality: Studio Architecture and the Visual Rhetoric of Early Hollywood." In "Early Hollywood and the Archive," ed. Rob King. Special issue, *Film History* 26, no. 2 (2014): 52–81.

———. "Fire and Failure: Studio Technology, Environmental Control, and the Politics of Progress." *Cinema Journal* 57, no. 2 (Winter 2018): 22–43.

———. *Studios Before the System: Architecture, Technology, and the Emergence of Cinematic Space.* New York: Columbia University Press, 2015.

———. "The 'Imponderable Fluidity' of Modernity: Georges Méliès and the Architectural Origins of Cinema." *Early Popular Visual Culture* 8, no. 2 (2010): 189–207.

James, David. *Allegories of Cinema: American Film in the 1960s.* Princeton, NJ: Princeton University Press, 1989.

Jameson, Fredric. *Archaeologies of the Future: The Desire Called Utopia and Other Science Fictions.* London: Verso, 2007.

Jarvinen, Lisa. *The Rise of Spanish-Language Filmmaking: Out from Hollywood's Shadow, 1929–1939.* New Brunswick, NJ: Rutgers University Press, 2012.

Jenkins, Bruce, ed. *On the Camera Arts and Consecutive Matters: The Writings of Hollis Frampton.* Cambridge, MA: MIT Press, 2009.

Jewell, Richard B. *Slow Fade to Black: The Decline of RKO Radio Pictures.* Berkeley: University of California Press, 2016.

Jinnai Hidenobu. *Tokyo: A Spatial Anthropology.* Translated by Kimiko Nishimura. Berkeley: University of California Press, 1995.

Johnson, Martin L. "The Places You'll Know: From Self-Recognition to Place Recognition in the Local Film." *Moving Image* 10, no. 1 (Spring 2010): 24–50.

Johnson, Randal. *The Film Industry in Brazil: Culture and the State.* Pittsburgh, PA: University of Pittsburgh Press, 1987.

Jones, Caroline A. *Eyesight Alone: Clement Greenberg's Modernism and the Bureaucratization of the Senses.* Chicago: University of Chicago Press, 2005.

———. *Machine in the Studio: Constructing the Postwar American Artist.* Chicago: University of Chicago Press, 1996.

Jung, Uli. "Local Views: A Blind Spot in the Historiography of Early German Cinema." *Historical Journal of Film, Radio and Television* 22, no. 3 (June 2002): 253–73.

Kakushinseru Mukōjima satsueijo (Reforming Mukōjima studio). Tokyo: Nippon Katsudō Kabushiki Kaisha, 1923.

Kamo Reidō. *Nikkatsu shashi to gensei* (Nikkatsu company history and current state of affairs). Tokyo: Nikkatsu No Shashi To Gensei Kankōkai, 1930.

Kant, Immanuel. *The Conflict of the Faculties.* Translated by Mary J. Gregor. New York: Abaris, 1979.

Kerr, Clark. *The Uses of the University.* Cambridge, MA: Harvard University Press, 2001.

Killingray, David. *Fighting for Britain: African Soldiers in the Second World War.* Woodbridge, UK: James Currey, 2010.

Kirn, Gal. "Past Activism: Between Socialist Modernization and Cinematic Modernism: The Revolutionary Politics of Aesthetics of Medvedkin's Cinema-Train." In *Marxism and Film Activism: Screening Alternative Worlds,* edited by Ewa Mazierska and Lars Kristensen, 29–57. New York: Berghahn, 2015.

Kline, Sally, ed. *George Lucas Interviews.* Jackson: University Press of Mississippi, 1999.

Klose, Alexander. *The Container Principle: How a Box Changes the Way We Think.* Translated by Charles Marcrum II. Cambridge, MA: MIT Press, 2015.

König, Gudrun M. *Konsumkultur: Inszenierte Warenwelt um 1900.* Wien: Böhlau, 2009.

Koolhaas, Rem. *Delirious New York: A Retroactive Manifesto of Manhattan.* New York: Monacelli Press, 2014.

———. "Junkspace." In Koolhaas and Foster, *Junkspace with Running Room.*

Koolhaas, Rem, and Hal Foster. *Junkspace with Running Room.* London: Notting Hill, 2013.

Kracauer, Siegfried. "Calico World: The Ufa City in Neubabelsberg." In *Film Architecture: Set Designs from "Metropolis" to "Blade Runner,"* edited by Dietrich Neumann, 191–93. Munich: Prestel, 1996.

Krivosheev, Iu. B., and R. A. Sokolov. *Aleksandr Nevskii: Sozdanie kinoshedevra. Istoricheskoe issledovanie.* St. Petersburg: Liki Rossii, 2012.

Kruse, Michael. "The Lost City of Trump." *Politico,* June 19, 2018, www.politico.com/magazine/story/2018/06/29/trump-robert-moses-new-york-television-city-urban-development-1980s-218836.

Kusahara, Machiko. "The Panorama Craze in Meiji Japan: The Beginning." In *The Panorama Phenomenon: The World Round,* edited by Tom Rombout, 81–88. Rijswijk: P/F Kunstbeeld, 2006.

Larkin, Brian. *Signal and Noise: Media, Infrastructure, and Urban Culture in Nigeria.* Durham, NC: Duke University Press, 2008.

Lary, Nikita, and Jay Leyda, eds. and trans. *The Alexander Medvedkin Reader.* Chicago: University of Chicago Press, 2016.

LeCavalier, Jesse. *The Rule of Logistics: Walmart and the Architecture of Fulfillment.* Minneapolis: University of Minnesota Press, 2016.

Le Corbusier. *The City of To-morrow and Its Planning.* Translated by Frederick Etchells. New York: Dover, 1987.

———. *The Radiant City: Elements of a Doctrine of Urbanism to Be Used as the Basis of Our Machine-Age Civilization.* Translated by Pamela Knight, Eleanor Levieux, and Derek Coltman. New York: Orion, 1964.

———. *Towards a New Architecture.* Translated by Frederick Etchells. New York: Dover, 1986.

Lenzi, Umberto. *Terrore ad Harlem.* Rome: Coniglio, 2009.

Levine Packer, Renee. *This Life of Sounds: Evening for New Music in Buffalo.* Oxford: Oxford University Press, 2010.

Lewis, Diane Wei. "*Blood and Soul* (1923) and the Cultural Politics of Japanese Film Reform." *positions: asia critique* 26, no. 3 (August 2018): 450–82.

———. *Powers of the Real: Cinema, Gender, and Emotion in Interwar Japan.* Cambridge, MA: Harvard University Asia Center, 2019.

Liotta, Salvator-John A., and Masaru Miyawaki. "A Study on the History of 'Cinema-City' in Asakusa, Tokyo: Analysis of Land Use and Landscape Transformations Based on Cadastral Maps and Photos." *Nihon Kenchiku Gakkai Keikakukei Ronbunshū / Journal of Architecture and Planning* 74, no. 637 (March 2009): 617–25.

López, Ana M. "The São Paulo Connection: The Companhia Cinematográfica Vera Cruz and *O Cangaceiro*." *Nuevo Texto Crítico* 11, no. 21/22 (Jan.–Dec. 1998): 127–54.

Lugon, Olivier. "Entre l'affiche et le monument, le photomural dans les années 1930." In *Exposition et médias: Photographie, cinéma, télévision,* edited by Olivier Lugon, 79–123. Lausanne: L'Âge d'Homme, 2012.

Luna Freire, Rafael de. "Carnaval, mistério e gangsters: O filme policial no Brasil (1915–1950)." PhD diss., Universidade Federal Fluminense, 2011.

———. "O Cinema no Rio de Janeiro (1914 a 1929)." In *Nova história do cinema brasileiro vol. I,* edited by Fernão Pessoa Ramos and Sheila Schvarzman, 252–93. São Paulo: Serviço Social do Comércio, 2018.

Macnab, Geoffrey. *J. Arthur Rank and the British Film Industry.* London: Routledge, 1993.

Maeda Ai. "Asakusa as Theater: Kawabata Yasunari's *The Crimson Gang of Asakusa*." Translated by Edward Fowler. In *Text and the City: Essays on Japanese Modernity,* edited by James A. Fujii, 145–62. Durham, NC: Duke University Press, 2004.

Majanlahti, Anthony, and Amedeo Osti Guerrazzi, eds. *Roma occupata, 1943–1944: Itinerari, storie, immagini.* Milan: il Saggiatore, 2010.

Martin, Reinhold. "Atrocities; or Curtain Wall as Mass Medium." *Perspecta* 32 (2001): 66–75.

Martin, Sara. *Gino Peressutti, l'architetto di Cinecittà.* Udine: Forum, 2013.

Marx, Karl. *Capital.* Vol. 1. Translated by Ben Fowkes. London: Penguin, 1990.

Marzola, Luci. "Better Pictures through Chemistry: DuPont and the Fight for the Hollywood Film Stock Market." *Velvet Light Trap* 76 (Fall 2015): 3–18.

———. "Engineering Hollywood: Technology, Technicians, and the Science of Building the Studio System." PhD diss., University of Southern California, 2016.

Matchlup, Fritz. *The Production and Distribution of Knowledge in the United States.* Princeton, NJ: Princeton University Press, 1962.

Mattern, Shannon. *Code and Clay, Data and Dirt: Five Thousand Years of Urban Media.* Minneapolis: University of Minnesota Press, 2017. Kindle.

Mayer, Vicki, Miranda J. Banks, and John T. Caldwell. "Introduction: Production Studies: Roots and Routes." In *Production Studies: Cultural Studies of Media Industries,* edited by Vicki Mayer, Miranda J. Banks, and John T. Caldwell, 1–12. New York: Routledge, 2009.

McQuire, Scott. *The Media City: Media, Architecture, and Urban Space.* London: Sage, 2008. Kindle.

Medhurst, Jamie. "What a Hullabaloo! Launching BBC Television in 1936 and BBC2 in 1964." *Journal of British Cinema and Television* 14, no. 3 (2017): 264–82.

Medvedkin, Alexander. "The Kino-Train: 294 Days on Wheels." In Lary and Leyda, *The Alexander Medvedkin Reader,* 27–95.

———. "Satire: An Assailant's Weapon." In Lary and Leyda, *The Alexander Medvedkin Reader,* 246–56.

Medvedkin, Aleksandr. "Razdum'ia." *Dokumental'noe kino segodnia.* Moscow: Iskusstvo, 1963.

Melo Souza, José Inácio de. "As imperfeições do crime da mala: Cine-gêneros e re-encenações no cinema dos primórdios." *Revista Universidade de São Paulo* 45 (2000): 106–12.

———. *Imagens do passado: São Paulo e Rio de Janeiro nos primórdios do cinema.* São Paulo: Serviço Nacional de Aprendizagem Comercial, 2004.

Mierau, Fritz. *Erfindung und Korrektur: Tretjakows Ästhetik der Operativität.* Berlin: Akademie, 1976.

Miller, Ian Jared. *The Nature of the Beasts: Empire and Exhibition at the Tokyo Imperial Zoo.* Berkeley: University of California Press, 2013.

Morales, Doris. "La Importancia de llamarse Bolling y Harry Wright." Morelia Film Festival website, Oct. 23, 2010. https://moreliafilmfest.com/la-importancia-de-llamarse-bolling-y-harry-wright.

Morettin, Eduardo. "Cinema e Estado no Brasil: A Exposição Internacional do Centenário da Independência em 1922 e 1923." *Novos Estudos* 89 (March 2011): 137–48.

Mozingo, Louise. *Pastoral Capitalism: A History of Suburban Corporate Landscapes.* Cambridge, MA: MIT Press, 2011.

Mukōjima satsueijo to shinpa eiga no jidai ten (Exhibition: Mukōjima studio and the age of shinpa film). Tokyo: Waseda Daigaku Tsubouchi Hakushi Kinen Engeki Hakubutsukan, 2011.

Murray, Susan. *Bright Signals: A History of Color Television.* Durham, NC: Duke University Press, 2018.

Musser, Charles. *The Emergence of Cinema: The American Screen to 1907.* New York: Scribner, 1990.

Nagl, Tobias. "Louis Brody and the Black Presence in German Film before 1945." In *Not So Plain as Black and White: Afro-German Culture and History, 1890–2000,* edited by Patricia Mazón and Reinhild Steingröver, 109–35. Rochester, NY: University of Rochester Press, 2005.

Nakanodō, Kazunobu. "Modern Japanese Glass." In *Kindai Nihon no garasu kōgei: Meiji shoki kara gendai made.* Published English title: *Modern Japanese Glass: Early Meiji to Present.* Tokyo: Tokyo Kokuritsu Kindai Bijutsukan, 1982.

Navitski, Rielle. *Public Spectacles of Violence: Sensational Cinema and Journalism in Early Twentieth-Century Mexico and Brazil.* Durham, NC: Duke University Press, 2017.

Nelson, George. "The New Subscape" (1950). In *Problems of Design.* New York: Whitney, 1957.

Neuhart, John, and Marilyn Neuhart, with Ray Eames. *Eames Design: The Work of the Office of Charles and Ray Eames.* New York: Harry N. Abrams, 1989.

Neuhart, Marilyn, with John Neuhart. *The Story of Eames Furniture, Book 1.* Gestalten: Berlin, 2010.

Niblo, Stephen R. *Mexico in the 1940s: Modernity, Politics, and Corruption.* Wilmington, DE: Scholarly Resources, 1999.

Nieland, Justus. *Happiness by Design: Modernism and Media in the Eames Era.* Minneapolis: University of Minnesota Press, 2020.

Nikkatsu shijūnenshi (Nikkatsu's forty-year history). Tokyo: Nikkatsu Kabushiki Kaisha, 1952.

Noronha, Jurandyr. *No tempo da manivela.* Rio de Janeiro: Embrafilme, 1987.

Nye, David. *Electrifying America: Social Meanings of a New Technology, 1880–1940.* Cambridge, MA: MIT Press, 1990.

O'Doherty, Brian. *Studio and Cube: On the Relationship between Where Art Is Made and Where Art Is Displayed.* New York: Temple Hoyne Buell Center for the Study of American Architecture, 2007.

Official Guide to the Louisiana Purchase Exposition. St. Louis, MO: Louisiana Purchase Exposition, 1904.

Official Website for UAE Free Zones. "Dubai Studio City." www.uaefreezones.com/fz_dubai_studiocity.html.

O'Grady, Gerald. "Sound-Track for a Tele-vision." In Vasulka and Weibel, *Buffalo Heads,* 81–84.

Oka Yasumasa. "Bīdoro kara garasu e: Katoki garasu no shomondai" (From *bīdoro* to glass: Various issues pertaining to glass during the transitional period). In *Meiji no garasu ten: Bīdoro kara garasu e: Kobe kaiko 120-nen kinen tokubetsuten.* Published English title: *Glasses in the Meiji Period: The Years When Glass Was Called "Biidoro" through to Those When Called "Garasu": Special Exhibition,* 75–83. Kobe: Kobe Shiritsu Hakubutsukan, 1987.

Okrent, Daniel. *Great Fortune: The Epic of Rockefeller Center.* New York: Penguin, 2004.

Oshima, Ken Tadashi. "Denenchōfu: Building the Garden City in Japan." *Journal of the Society of Architectural Historians* 55, no. 2 (June 1996): 140–51.

Packer, Jeremy, and Stephen B. Crofts, eds. *Communication Matters: Materialist Approaches to Media, Mobility and Networks.* New York: Routledge, 2012.

Paik, Karen. *To Infinity and Beyond! The Story of Pixar Animation Studios.* San Francisco: Disney Enterprises, 2007.

Parezo, Nancy J., and Don D. Fowler. *Anthropology Goes to the Fair.* Lincoln: University of Nebraska Press, 2007.

Parks, Lisa, and Nicole Starosielski, eds. *Signal Traffic: Critical Studies of Media Infrastructures.* Urbana: University of Illinois Press, 2015.

Paxman, Andrew. *Jenkins of Mexico: How a Southern Farm Boy Became a Mexican Magnate.* New York: Oxford University Press, 2017.

———. "Who Killed the Mexican Film Industry? The Decline of the Golden Age, 1946–1960." *Estudios Interdisciplinarios de América Latina* 29, no. 1 (2018): 9–33.

Peredo Castro, Francisco. "La batalla por los Estudios Churubusco: El cine mexicano y Hollywood en las contiendas por el control de la producción fílmica para latinoamérica (1942–1953)." *Archivos de la Filmoteca* (Oct. 2004): 134–52.

Pérez Turrent, Tomás. *La fábrica de sueños: Estudios Churubusco, 1945–1985.* México: Instituto Mexicano de Cinematografía, 1985.

———. "The Studios." In *Mexican Cinema,* edited by Paulo Antonio Paranaguá, translated by Ana M. López, 133–44. London: BFI; Mexico City: Instituto Mexicano de Cinematografía, 1995.

Perry, George. *Movies from the Mansion: A History of Pinewood Studios.* London: Pavilion, 1986.

Peters, John Durham. *The Marvelous Clouds: Toward an Elemental Philosophy of Media.* Chicago: University of Chicago Press, 2015.

Pollock, Dale. *Skywalking: The Life and Films of George Lucas.* Updated edition. New York: Da Capo, 1999.

Powell, Michael. *Million-Dollar Movie.* London: Heinemann, 1992.

Price, David. *The Pixar Touch: The Making of a Company.* New York: Knopf, 2008.

Radiolympia: National Radio Exhibition Official Catalogue. London: Radio Manufacturers' Association, 1937.

Radiolympia: National Radio Exhibition Official Catalogue. London: Radio Manufacturers' Association, 1938.

Reyes, Aurelio de los. *Cine y sociedad en México: 1896–1930.* Vol. 2, *Bajo el cielo de México.* México: Universidad Nacional Autónoma de México, Instituto de Investigaciones Estéticas, 1993.

Riesman, David. "Abundance for What?" In *Abundance for What? and Other Essays,* 300–308. New York: Doubleday, 1964.

———. "Leisure and Work in Postindustrial Society." In *Abundance for What? and Other Essays,* 162–83. New York: Doubleday, 1964.

Robinson, Julia. "Before Attitudes Became Forms—New Realisms, 1957–1962." In *New Realisms, 1957–1962: Object Strategies between Readymade and Spectacle,* edited by Julia Robinson, 23–39. Cambridge, MA: MIT Press, 2010.

Rocha, Glauber. "An Esthetic of Hunger." Translated by Randal Johnson and Burnes Hollyman. In *New Latin American Cinema.* Vol. 1, *Theory, Practices and Transcontinental Articulations,* edited by Michael Martin, 59–61. Detroit: Wayne State University Press, 1997.

———. *Revisão crítica do cinema brasileiro.* São Paulo: Cosaic and Naify, 2003.

Ruoff, Jeffrey, ed. *Virtual Voyages: Cinema and Travel.* Durham, NC: Duke University Press, 2006.

Ryan, Deborah S. *The Ideal Home through the 20th Century: The Daily Mail Ideal Home Exhibition.* London: Hazar, 1997.

Salewicz, Chris. *George Lucas Close Up.* New York: Thunder's Mouth, 1999.

Salles Gomes, Paulo Emílio. "Cinema: A Trajectory within Underdevelopment." Translated by Randal Johnson and Robert Stam. In *Brazilian Cinema,* edited by Randal Johnson and Robert Stam, rev. ed., 245–55. New York: Columbia University Press, 1995.

———. *Humberto Mauro, Cataguases, Cinearte.* São Paulo: Perspectiva, 1974.

Salt, Barry. *Film Style and Technology: History & Analysis.* London: Starwood, 1983.

Salys, Rimgaila. *The Musical Comedy Films of Grigorii Aleksandrov: Laughing Matters.* Bristol, UK: Intellect, 2009.

Sassen, Saskia. *Expulsions: Brutality and Complexity in the Global Economy.* Cambridge, MA: Harvard University Press, 2014.

Scannell, Paddy. *Television, Radio, and Modern Life.* London: Wiley Blackwell, 1996.

Schivelbusch, Wolfgang. *The Railway Journey: The Industrialization of Time and Space in the 19th Century.* Berkeley: University of California Press, 1986.

Schmalisch, Romana. *Mobile Cinema.* Berlin: Archive Books, 2017.

Schuldenfrei, Eric. *The Films of Charles and Ray Eames: A Universal Sense of Expectation.* London: Routledge, 2015.

Schvarzman, Sheila. *Humberto Mauro e as imagens do Brasil.* Universidade Estadual de São Paulo, 2003.

Schwab, Klaus. *The Global Competitiveness Report, 2016–2017.* Geneva: World Economic Forum, 2016.

Sconce, Jeffrey. *Haunted Media: Electronic Presence from Radio to Television.* Durham, NC: Duke University Press, 2000.

Scott, Allen John. *On Hollywood: The Place, the Industry.* Princeton, NJ: Princeton University Press, 2005.

Seabrook, John. "Letter from Skywalker Ranch: Why Is the Force Still with Us?" In Kline, *George Lucas Interviews,* 190–215. Originally published in the *New Yorker,* Jan. 6, 1997, 40–53.

Sei, Keiko. "Malcolm X, McLuhan, Media Study." In Vasulka and Weibel, *Buffalo Heads,* 135–39.

Serna, Laura Isabel. *Making Cinelandia: American Films and Mexican Film Culture before the Golden Age.* Durham, NC: Duke University Press, 2014.

Sewell, Philip W. *Television in the Age of Radio: Modernity, Imagination, and the Making of a Medium.* New Brunswick, NJ: Rutgers University Press, 2014.

Shaw, Deborah, and Stephanie Dennison. *Brazilian National Cinema.* New York: Routledge, 2007.

Shiel, Mark. *Hollywood Cinema and the Real Los Angeles.* London: Reaktion, 2012.

Sigler, Thomas J. "Relational Cities: Doha, Panama City, and Dubai as 21st Century Entrepôts." *Urban Geography* 35, no. 5 (2013): 612–33.

Sitney, P. Adams. *Visionary Film.* Oxford: Oxford University Press, 2002.

Slight, Frederick W. Exhibition Catalog for Exhibition of Leonard Goldenson's Paintings, Palm Springs Desert Museum. Palm Springs, CA: Palm Springs Desert Museum, 1978.

Snow, Michael. "On Hollis Frampton, 1984." In *The Collected Writings of Michael Snow,* 241–50. Waterloo, Ontario: Wilfred Laurier University Press, 1994.

Souza, Carlos Roberto de. "O Cinema em Campinas nos Anos 20, ou Uma Hollywood Brasileira." Master's thesis, Universidade de São Paulo, 1979.

Spigel, Lynn. *TV by Design: Modern Art and the Rise of Network Television.* Chicago: University of Chicago Press, 2008.

Steimatsky, Noa. "Cinecittà campo profughi, 1944–1950." Translated by Barbara Garbin and Alberto Zambenedetti. Part 1 in *Bianco e nero,* no. 560 (Nov. 2008): 164–81. Part 2 in *Bianco e nero* 561/562 (May 2009): 171–94.

———. "The Cinecittà Refugee Camp (1944–1950)." *October,* no. 128 (Spring 2009): 22–50.

Steele, James, ed. *William Pereira.* Los Angeles: USC Architectural Guild Press, 2002.

Sterne, Jonathan. *The Audible Past: Cultural Origins of Sound Reproduction.* Durham, NC: Duke University Press, 2003.

Sterne, Jonathan, and Dylan Mulvin. "The Low Acuity for Blue: Perceptual Technics and American Color Television." *Journal of Visual Culture* 13 (2014): 118–38.

Stigger, Helena. "*Amor que redime:* Reconstituição do pioneirismo do cinema gaúcho." In *Cinema gaúcho: Diversidades e inovações,* edited by Cristiane Freitas Gutfreind and Carlos Gerbase, 39–64. Porto Alegre: Sulina, 2009.

Strauss-Kahn, Vanessa, and Xavier Vives. "Why and Where Do Headquarters Move?" Working Paper. IESE Business School—University of Navarra, July 17, 2006. www.iese .edu/research/pdfs/DI-0650-E.pdf.

Street, Sarah. *Transatlantic Crossings: British Feature Films in the USA.* New York: Continuum, 2002.

Susman, Warren I. "The People's Fair: Cultural Contradictions of a Consumer Society." In *Culture as History: The Transformation of American Society in the Twentieth Century,* 211–29. Washington, DC: Smithsonian Press, 2003.

Swayze, Harold. *Political Control of Literature in the USSR, 1946–1959*. Cambridge, MA: Harvard University Press, 1962.

Taber, George. *Judgment of Paris: California vs. France and the Historic 1976 Paris Tasting That Revolutionized Wine*. New York: Scribner, 2010.

Thompson, Emily. "Machines, Music, and the Quest for Fidelity: Marketing the Edison Phonograph in America, 1877–1925." *Musical Quarterly* 79, no. 1 (1995): 131–71.

———. *The Soundscape of Modernity: Architectural Acoustics and the Culture of Listening in America, 1900–1933*. Cambridge, MA: MIT Press, 2002.

Thompson, Kristin. *Exporting Entertainment: America in the World Film Market, 1907–1934*. London: British Film Institute, 1985.

Thorburn, David, and Henry Jenkins. "Introduction: Towards an Aesthetics of Transition." In *Rethinking Media Change: The Aesthetics of Transition*, edited by David Thorburn, Henry Jenkins, and Brad Seawell, 1–16. Cambridge, MA: MIT Press, 2004.

Threadgall, Derek. *Shepperton Studios: An Independent View*. London: British Film Institute, 1994.

Tiwari, Piyush, and Michael White. *Real Estate Finance and the New Economy*. Chichester, UK: John Wiley and Sons, 2014.

Tode, Thomas, and Barbara Wurm, eds. *Dziga Vertov: Die Vertov-Sammlung im Österreichischen Filmmuseum*. Vienna: Österreichisches Filmmuseum, 2006.

Tomita Mika. "Eiga toshi Kyōto ni okeru eiga bunka no seisei to jyuyō ni tsuite" (Regarding the formation and reception of film culture in film city Kyoto). *Kyōto āto entateinmento sōsei hōkoku sho* (Innovative research into Kyoto art and entertainment newsletter), 2003 report (2004): 41–44.

Toulmin, Vanessa, and Martin Loiperdinger. "Is It You? Recognition, Representation and Response in Relation to the Local Film." *Film History* 17, no. 1 (Spring 2005): 7–18.

Trenker, Luis. *Alles gut gegangen: Geschichten aus meinem Leben*. 2nd rev. ed. Munich: Bertelsmann, 1979.

Tret'iakov, Sergei. "The Writer and the Socialist Village." Translated by Devin Fore. *October* 118 (Fall 2006): 63–70.

Tsutsui, William M. "The Pelagic Empire: Reconsidering Japanese Expansionism." In *Japan at Nature's Edge: The Environmental Context of a Global Power*, edited by Ian Jared Miller, Julia Adeney Thomas, and Brett L. Walker, 21–38. Honolulu: University of Hawai'i Press, 2013.

Turnock, Julie. *Plastic Reality: Special Effects, Technology, and the Emergence of 1970s Blockbuster Aesthetics*. New York: Columbia University Press, 2015.

Udelson, Joseph H. *The Great Television Race: A History of the American Television Industry, 1925–1941*. Tuscaloosa: University of Alabama Press, 1982.

Uhrich, Andy. "Pressed into the Service of Cinema: Issues in Preserving the Software of Hollis Frampton and the Digital Arts Lab." *Moving Image* 12, no. 1 (Spring 2012): 20–21.

Unitas Consultancy. *Dubai: Financialization and Its Discontents*. Dubai: GCP and Reidin Real Estate Information, 2016. http://blog.reidin.com/PublicReports/UAE160624.pdf.

Urabe Kumeko. "Eiga koso waga inochi" (Film is my life). In Urabe, Sugai, and Kawazu, *Eiga wazurai* (Film struck), 7–90.

Urabe Kumeko, Sugai Ichirō, and Kawazu Seizaburō. *Eiga wazurai* (Film struck). Tokyo: Rokugei Shobō, 1966.

Uricchio, William. "A 'Proper Point of View': The Panorama and Some of Its Early Media Iterations." *Early Popular Visual Culture* 9, no. 3 (August 2011): 225–38.

———. "Television, Film and the Struggle for Media Identity." *Film History* 10, no. 2 (1998): 118–27.

USC School of Cinematic Arts. Untitled [Giving Presentation Book]. Los Angeles: USC School of Cinematic Arts, 2012. https://cinema.usc.edu/giving/presentationbook.pdf.

Vallely, Jean. "*The Empire Strikes Back* and So Does Filmmaker George Lucas with His Sequel to *Star Wars*." In Kline, *George Lucas Interviews*, 87–97. Originally published in *Rolling Stone*, June 12, 1980, 31–33.

Vallye, Anna. "Design and the Politics of Knowledge in America, 1937–1967: Walter Gropius, György Kepes." PhD diss., Columbia University, 2011.

Vasulka, Woody, and Peter Weibel, eds. *Buffalo Heads: Media Study, Media Practice, Media Pioneers, 1973–1990*. Cambridge, MA: MIT Press, 2008.

Vatulescu, Cristina. *Police Aesthetics: Literature, Film, and the Secret Police in Soviet Times*. Stanford, CA: Stanford University Press, 2010.

Vaughan, Hunter. *Hollywood's Dirtiest Secret: The Hidden Environmental Costs of the Movies*. New York: Columbia University Press, 2019.

Vega Alfaro, Eduardo de la. "The Decline of the Golden Age and the Making of the Crisis." In *Mexico's Cinema: A Century of Film and Filmmakers*, edited by Joanne Hershfield and David R. Maciel, 165–91. Wilmington, DE: SR Books, 1999.

Vignal, Leïla, ed. *The Transnational Middle East: People, Places, Borders*. Abingdon, Oxon: Routledge, 2017.

Virilio, Paul. *Speed and Politics*. Translated by Mark Polizzotti. New York: Semio(texte), 1986.

Wade, Robert J. *Designing for TV: The Arts and Crafts of Television Production*. New York: Pellegrini and Cudahy, 1953.

Ward, Janet. *Weimar Surfaces: Urban Visual Culture in 1920s Germany*. Berkeley: University of California Press, 2001.

Weber, Anne-Katrin. "L'exposition de la télévision dans l'entre-deux-guerres: Entre appropriations nationales et échanges transnationaux." *Relations internationales* 4, no. 164 (2016): 75–92.

———. *Interwar Television on Display. New Media and Exhibition Culture in Europe and the United States, 1928–1939*. Amsterdam: Amsterdam University Press, forthcoming.

Weiner, Rex. "Lucas the Loner Returns to *Wars*." In Kline, *George Lucas Interviews*, 184–89. Originally published in *Variety*, June 5, 1995, 1, 59.

Westinghouse Electric & Manufacturing Co. *The Middleton Family at the World's Fair*. New York: Audio Productions, 1939, 55 min. https://archive.org/details/middleton_family_worlds_fair_1939.

Wheatley, Helen. *Spectacular Television: Exploring Televisual Pleasure*. London: I. B. Tauris, 2016.

———. "Television in the Ideal Home." In *Television for Women: New Directions*, edited by Rachel Moseley, Helen Wheatley, and Helen Wood, 205–22. London: Routledge, 2016.

Widdis, Emma. *Alexander Medvedkin*. London: I. B. Tauris, 2005.

Wigley, Mark. *White Walls, Designer Dresses: The Fashioning of Modern Architecture*. Cambridge, MA: MIT Press, 2001.

Williams, Raymond. *Television: Technology and Cultural Form.* New York: Schocken, 1975.

Wionczek, Miguel S. "The State and the Electric Power Industry in Mexico, 1895–1965." *Business History Review* 39, no. 4 (Winter 1965): 527–56.

Wolfe, Tom. *The Painted Word.* New York: Farrar, Straus and Giroux, 1975.

Wood, Alan. *Mr. Rank: A Study of J. Arthur Rank and British Films.* London: Hodden and Stoughton, 1952.

Xavier, Ismail. *Sétima arte: Um culto moderno—O idealismo estético e o cinema.* São Paulo: Perspectiva, 1978.

Yonemura Atsuko. "Meiji kōki kara Taishō shoki no jūtaku no saikō ni tsuite: Kazoku shitsu no nanmenka to mado garasu no fukyū." Published English title: "Daylighting of Housing from the Latter Years of the Meiji Era to the Early Years of the Taisho Era: Application in the South Part of the Family Room and Spreading Use of Window Glass." *Kaseigaku kenkyū* (Home economics research) 29, no. 2 (1983): 121–28.

Yoshimi Shun'ya. *Media jidai no bunka shakaigaku* (Cultural sociology of the media age). Tokyo: Shin'yōsha, 1994.

———. *Toshi no doramaturgī: Tōkyō sakariba no shakaishi* (Dramaturgy of the city: A social history of Tokyo's entertainment centers). Tokyo: Kawabe Shobō Shinsha, 1987.

Zambenedetti, Alberto. "Italians on the Move: Toward a History of Migration Cinema." PhD diss., New York University, 2012.

Zryd, Mike. "History and Ambivalence in Hollis Frampton's Magellan." *October* 109 (Summer, 2004): 119–42.

CONTRIBUTORS

ROBERT BIRD'S primary area of interest is the aesthetic practice and theory of Russian/Soviet modernism. He has published books on Andrei Tarkovsky, among others, and essays on a variety of topics in Russian literature, intellectual history, film and video art, including the filmmakers Aleksandr Medvedkin, Aleksandr Sokurov, and Olga Chernysheva. Most recently, he coedited (with Christina Kiaer and Zachary Cahill) *Revolution Every Day: A Calendar* (Milan: Mousse, 2017), the catalogue to the eponymous exhibition at the Smart Museum of Art at the University of Chicago. He is currently completing a book, "Soul Machine: Soviet Film Models Socialism," which analyzes the rise of socialist realism as a modeling aesthetic, and he is beginning a new book, "The Underground: A History of a Cultural Resistance." Bird teaches in the Departments of Slavic Languages and Literatures and Cinema and Media Studies at the University of Chicago.

J. D. CONNOR is an associate professor of cinema and media studies at USC's School of Cinematic Arts. He is the author of *The Studios after the Studios* (2015) and *Hollywood Math and Aftermath* (2018). He continues to plug away at a history of tape recording, *Archives of the Ambient,* but is regularly distracted by other things. He writes occasionally for the *Los Angeles Review of Books,* tweets more frequently @jdconnor, and collects his work at www.johnconnorliketheterminator.com.

KAY DICKINSON is a professor of film studies at Concordia University, Montreal. She is the author of *Arab Cinema Travels: Transnational Syria, Palestine, Dubai and Beyond* (London: BFI, 2016) and the compiler of *Arab Film and Video Manifestos: Forty-Five Years of the Moving Image amid Revolution* (New York: Palgrave, 2018). She is currently working on a manuscript entitled "Supply Chain Cinema, Supply Chain Education."

BRIAN R. JACOBSON is a professor of visual culture at the California Institute of Technology and the author of *Studios Before the System: Architecture, Technology, and the Emergence of Cinematic Space* (New York: Columbia University Press, 2015).

DIANE WEI LEWIS is an assistant professor of film and media studies at Washington University in St. Louis. She specializes in Japanese media, early cinema, mass culture, and modernity, with a focus on gender and emotion. Her essays have appeared in *Cinema Journal, positions: asia critique, Feminist Media Histories,* and *Screen.* She is the author of *Powers of the Real: Cinema, Gender, and Emotion in Interwar Japan* (Cambridge, MA: Harvard University Asia Center, 2019).

JEFF MENNE is associate professor of screen studies at Oklahoma State University. He is the author of *Post-Fordist Cinema: Hollywood Auteurs and the Corporate Counterculture* (New York: Columbia University Press, 2019) and *Francis Ford Coppola* (Urbana: University of Illinois Press, 2015).

RIELLE NAVITSKI is an associate professor in the Department of Theatre and Film Studies at the University of Georgia. She is the author of *Public Spectacles of Violence: Sensational Cinema and Journalism in Early Twentieth-Century Mexico and Brazil* (Durham, NC: Duke University Press, 2017) and coeditor of *Cosmopolitan Film Cultures in Latin America, 1896–1960* (Bloomington: Indiana University Press, 2017). Her research takes a comparative approach to Latin American cinema with an emphasis on silent and early sound film, links between the moving image and the illustrated press, and institutions of film culture. Currently, she is at work on a book-length project entitled "Transatlantic Cinephilia: Film Culture between Latin America and France, 1945–1965."

JUSTUS NIELAND is a professor of English and teaches in the Film Studies Program at Michigan State University. His most recent book is *Happiness by Design: Modernism and Media in the Eames Era* (Minneapolis: University of Minnesota Press, 2020). He is also the author of *Feeling Modern: The Eccentricities of Public Life* (Urbana: University of Illinois Press, 2008), *David Lynch* (Urbana: University of Illinois Press, 2012), and coauthor of *Film Noir: Hard-Boiled Modernity and the Cultures of Globalization* (New York: Routledge, 2010). With Jennifer Fay he is coeditor of the Contemporary Film Directors book series at the University of Illinois Press.

LAURA ISABEL SERNA is an associate professor of cinema and media studies at the University of Southern California. She is the author of *Making Cinelandia: American Films and Mexican Film Culture before the Golden Age* (Durham, NC: Duke University Press, 2014). She has published essays on film culture on the US-Mexico border, government-sponsored film in the early 1970s, and the media culture of ethnic Mexican communities in early twentieth-century Los Angeles.

LYNN SPIGEL is the Frances Willard Professor of Screen Cultures at Northwestern University. Her books include *Make Room for TV: Television and the Family Ideal in Postwar America* (Chicago: University of Chicago Press, 1992), *TV by Design: Modern Art and the Rise of Network TV* (Chicago: University of Chicago Press, 2008), and *TV Snapshots: An Archive of Everyday Life* (Durham: Duke University Press, forthcoming).

NOA STEIMATSKY is the author of *Italian Locations: Reinhabiting the Past in Postwar Cinema* (Minneapolis: University of Minnesota Press, 2008) and the award-winning *The Face on Film* (New York: Oxford University Press, 2017). She was a recipient of the Fulbright Award, the Getty Research Grant, the NEH Rome Prize, and the ACLS Fellowship. Steimatsky was faculty member at Yale University, tenured at the University of Chicago, and visiting faculty at Stanford, UC-Berkeley, and Sarah Lawrence College. Her work on 1940s Cinecittà inspired a documentary film and is currently being expanded into a book with the support of an NEH Grant and the Guggenheim Fellowship.

SARAH STREET is a professor of film at the University of Bristol, UK. She has published widely, including *British National Cinema* (New York: Routledge, 1997; 2nd ed. 2009), *Transatlantic Crossings: British Feature Films in the USA* (New York: Continuum, 2002), *Black Narcissus* (London: I. B. Tauris, 2005), and (with Tim Bergfelder and Sue Harris) *Film Architecture and the Transnational Imagination: Set Design in 1930s European Cinema* (Amsterdam: Amsterdam University Press, 2007). Her latest publications are on color film, including *Colour Films in Britain: The Negotiation of Innovation, 1900–55* (London: BFI/ Palgrave Macmillan, 2012), winner of the British Association of Film, Television and Screen Studies prize for Best Monograph, and two coedited collections (with Simon Brown and Liz Watkins), *Color and the Moving Image: History, Theory, Aesthetics, Archive* (London: Routledge, 2012) and *British Colour Cinema: Practices and Theories* (London: BFI/Palgrave Macmillan, 2013). Her latest books are *Deborah Kerr* (in the BFI/Palgrave Macmillan 'Stars' series, 2018), and *Chromatic Modernity: Color, Cinema, and Media of the 1920s,* coauthored with Joshua Yumibe (New York: Columbia University Press, 2019). She is the principal investigator on the European Research Council Advanced Grant "STUDIOTEC: Film Studios: Infrastructure, Culture, Innovation in Britain, France, Germany and Italy, 1930–60," a research project that runs from 2019 to 2024.

ANNE-KATRIN WEBER is a lecturer at the Section d'histoire et esthétique du cinéma at the University of Lausanne. Her research examines the history of television outside broadcasting institutions. She is currently preparing her first monograph on interwar television and exhibition culture. She is the editor of *La télévision du téléphonoscope à YouTube: Pour une archéologie de l'audiovision* (with Mireille Berton; Lausanne: Antipodes, 2009) and an issue of *View: Journal of European Television History and Culture* ("Archaeologies of Tele-Visions and -Realities," with Andreas Fickers, 2015).

INDEX

Founded in 1893,
UNIVERSITY OF CALIFORNIA PRESS
publishes bold, progressive books and journals
on topics in the arts, humanities, social sciences,
and natural sciences—with a focus on social
justice issues—that inspire thought and action
among readers worldwide.

The UC PRESS FOUNDATION
raises funds to uphold the press's vital role
as an independent, nonprofit publisher, and
receives philanthropic support from a wide
range of individuals and institutions—and from
committed readers like you. To learn more, visit
ucpress.edu/supportus.